RIVER OF YEARS

JOSEPH FORT NEWTON

River of Years

AN AUTOBIOGRAPHY

····· ✿ ·····

BY

JOSEPH FORT NEWTON

"LET US MOVE FORWARD WITH
STRONG AND ACTIVE FAITH."
—*F. D. Roosevelt*

"A MAN IS JUST ABOUT AS HAPPY
AS HE MAKES UP HIS MIND TO BE."
—*Lincoln*

"WE ARE ALL NEEDED, BUT NONE
OF US VERY MUCH." —*Emerson*

····· ✿ ·····

J. B. LIPPINCOTT COMPANY
PHILADELPHIA   NEW YORK

COPYRIGHT, 1946, BY
JOSEPH FORT NEWTON

PRINTED IN THE
UNITED STATES OF AMERICA

FIRST EDITION

To My
Little Grand-Daughters,
Virginia, Sarah Ann, and Elizabeth,
Three Stars in My Crown
Of Love and Hope and Joy.

FOREWORD

Dr. Guy Emery Shipler, editor of *The Churchman*—the oldest religious journal in the English-speaking world—is really responsible for this record. He it was, I understand, who suggested to the publishers that they ask me to write it. Otherwise, it would probably not have been written. He will have much to answer for at the last great day, but there is one comfort: he cannot be held to account for anything said in this life-story.

In 1934, I believe it was, while preaching for the summer in London, I wrote a spicy letter to Dr. Shipler, saying, among other outrageous things, that "the Anglican Church is dead and knows it, and the Free Church is dead and does not know it." Also, I added the famous remark of W. E. Orchard, that "preaching in the Anglican Church is really worse than necessary." Having a sense of fun, as well as an eye for the picturesque, Dr. Shipler lifted these lines from my letter, and printed them. But, unfortunately, even he could not print a smile, and I was severely pounded for my joke. It has long since been forgiven, if not forgotten—but humor, we may remember, has its penalty, no less than sin.

For the rest, years ago an old friend sent me a wish, a word of wisdom, for the New Year, which I beg to expand a bit, and pass on to my readers: Hope much; fear not at all; if you have danger, dare it; if you find a little fun, share it; do your best, and seek the best in others; and trust the veiled Father of men, whose mercy and magnanimity endure forever.

—J. F. N.

Church of St. Luke and Epiphany
Philadelphia

Grateful acknowledgment is made to Harper and
Brothers for permission to reprint passages from—

Living Every Day

The Stuff of Life

Living Up to Life

Live, Love and Learn

His Cross and Ours

CONTENTS

RIVER OF YEARS

••••• ◉ •••••

Backgrounds

AN OLD CHINESE proverb tells us that there are five points of the compass: North, East, South, West, and the point where we are. Obviously, the point where we are is very important. Not only does it decide our point of view, and hence our view, of the pageant of events; but if we do not know our location, we can hardly find our direction. Also, if we grow in soul as life unfolds, our point of view will be changed—both by depth of insight and breadth of outlook; yet certain traits of nature and trends of mind will remain, and may be traced through the years, as this record will reveal. While this is not merely a personal history, it is necessary to tell enough about myself to show the angle from which life has been seen betimes, the changes wrought by experience of the vicissitudes of the years, and what living has taught me.

The writing of this story has been made extremely difficult by a defect—a tragic defect to me—which has tormented all my days. It is an inveterate shyness in respect to my inner life, which has never been entirely overcome; it is still a handicap. To be sure, it has stood me in good stead at times, keeping me from speaking blazing words when I was boiling inside. But, alas! it has also left me hesitant and half articulate even when sympathy wrung my heart, making me appear aloof and cold, which was as far as possible from the truth. By the same fact, the pulpit has been my place of release from inner solitude and silence. The pulpit is a public place, but its message has to do with the most intimate and inward affairs of the human heart—things we seldom say to anyone or allow anyone to say to us, save in the most confidential friendship, or in hours of crisis and disaster when the soul is near the surface. Yet the awful public-privacy of the pulpit not only permits, but invites, the opening of heart to heart, and one may speak to a thousand people words which one would hardly speak to a friend. Such is the wonder of preaching; it is unlike any other speech known among men.

Of course, few of us really remember anything as it actually happened. Unconsciously we read back into yesterday the ideas and feelings of today—not, as cynics say, merely to escape the disillusionment of discovering that we did not always know as much as we imagine we know now. Nor is it an unwillingness to face ourselves as we really were. Years ago in London I met the late W. H. Hudson, shortly after his *Far Away and Long Ago* appeared. He was a tall, slender, angular man, shy unspeakably, gentle-hearted and gracious to know. He remembered his childhood in astonishing detail, and wrote about it in a style simple, vivid, warm. But he had no illusions—he knew he was seeing his early days with other and later eyes, erasing here, retouching there, recoloring the whole. "In going back we take our present selves with us; the mind has taken a different hue and this is thrown back upon our past," he explained. Then he recalled a Swedish writer who told how, returning to his native land after many years, he saw on the dock, awaiting him, the slight figure of the boy he used to be. "But he did not see with the eyes of that boy; he saw the boy with the eyes of an old man," Hudson added. Indeed it could not be otherwise. "I remember when I was a boy," we often hear a man say. But does he? No, the scene is blurred, the perspective is different—it is always an idealized picture painted by the imagination; and for that reason truer.

Genius does seem to remember the past in detail, as Hudson did—genius may be largely memory, for aught we know; no one has fathomed that "time-binding" quality of the mind, without which life would be chaos and confusion. Men of genius seem able to keep a gate open into the past, or else they have a profounder memory, going far back and deep down until it taps the great world-memory: like a fluted, pink sea shell which brings murmured echoes of distant seas that drift and sing. Just as we take the present with us when we go back in memory to the past, so we carry the past with us into the present. Each influences, and helps to interpret, the other, and together they bring us as near to the truth as we may hope to arrive. Still, if a man writes the story of his heart—as is here attempted—he must face the plain fact that he cannot tell the truth about himself, even if he honestly tries to do so; because he does not know the truth—that belongs to God. All he can do is to look into his own heart, searching for the meaning of his days, aided by a light, dim or clear, which "flashes across the soul from within."

After all, how little we remember of "the time past of our life"; wholly hidden are a thousand things amid which we walked lightly or sadly. We see the hilltops, but the valleys between are lost to view, except some "glen of gloom," as the Scotch say, where we lost our way and groped in the dark. Some successes we remember, some bad mistakes, some bitter sorrows, some goals achieved, some dreams come true, some faces that never fade, some stupid things said or done in a cruel, careless hour, which we wish we could forget; but the road has become invisible, like a thin thread flung over the hills. Then, suddenly, a little thing, a whiff of perfume, a snatch of a song sung long ago, a face in the street, a chance happening, a voice—I have always been sensitive to voices—an old familiar place, brings back troops of memories of people and things we thought we had forgotten: memories that break our heart—and mend it. Always, as we look back to the days that come not back, we can see a figure on the road, ourselves in different stages of the journey, the child, the boy, the youth, in comparison with what we are today. The mystic continuity of identity, the transmigration of the soul through the years—here is the miracle of memory, the mystery of which gathers and grows. The longer one lives the more one feels that the best part of our education is some golden memory—tender, holy, happy—given us in childhood; even one such saving memory to look back upon and cherish, can redeem a life from defeat and despair; and in these treasures my life has been fabulously rich. Given good memories, and nothing—not even death—can take from us the blessed and lovely things we have had. "Poetry is emotion remembered in tranquillity," said a great poet. When we read the past aright, in due perspective, with the aid of the Interpreter, Memory, we see that we have been led in a way we knew not by One who knew the way.

THOSE GONE BEFORE

Few of us take much thought of our ancestors until late in life. Often it is too late, because those who could have told us many interesting and intimate things have passed away. What was experience to them is history to us, had we been alert enough to make a record of it. Fortunately, my cousin, Miriam Fort, explored the hinterlands of the Battle, Fort and Ligon families, three of the four families whose blood, with minor tributaries, mingles in my veins. It was like her to lay emphasis upon their aristocratic backgrounds and traditions; she had an honorable pride—not a vanity—in blood and extraction. She was not interested in the Newtons, she said, implying, with roguish fun, that they were hardly acceptable socially. When she proved that Henry Clay was our kinsman, it was necessary, by way of reprisal, to remind her not only of Sir Isaac Newton, but also of Sir Richard, Sir John, Sir Thomas, Sir Henry, and many Lord Newtons, as well as the crest and coat of arms. She professed to be properly impressed, and struck an attitude of mock modesty—across the years her gay laughter echoes in my heart. In her counterattack she brought forward facts—unknown to me then, but since confirmed by records—showing that through the Ligon family we were both related to the Washington and Lee families; so the argument ended with the honors even.

The Newtons are in fact a large tribe, spread over England and America. Of Anglo-Norman origin, we find them in England soon after the advent of William the Conqueror; in Lincolnshire, Yorkshire, Gloucestershire, Herefordshire, and elsewhere, in Scotland and in Wales. A location name, it was spelled in various ways—Neweton, Nuten, Niuton, Newtten, to name no others—before it took its final form. They appeared in New England as early as 1632, in Boston and along the Atlantic Coast line; then in Maryland in 1660, where John Newton paused, before going on into Virginia in 1670, in Westmoreland County—only to discover that Richard and Francis Newton had settled in the same colony in 1635, in James City County, and others in Isle of Wight County in 1643. They took a leading part in the affairs of the Colony—one an Episcopal Bishop, a number of judges—and were influential in political and civic life.

Dr. Richard Newton—a latecomer—born in Liverpool, England, in 1813, was for many years rector of the Church of the Epiphany in Philadelphia, which, in 1898, was united with the Church of St. Luke, to make my present parish. He was the first clergyman in this country to preach and publish sermons for children; and then for the first time, it was said, their parents understood him. His son, Heber Newton, was rector of Old St. Paul's Church in Philadelphia; then followed a brilliant ministry in New York, during which he was branded as a "heretic," and even a "socialist," which were awful names in those days. He died as chaplain of the Leland Stanford University, in California.

Like all the early families, the Newtons pushed on westward into Tennessee and beyond, my grandfather, Isaac Newton, making his home in the Republic of Texas. He had four sons, three of whom were preachers—my being a preacher was clearly a matter of predestination—called by the angels of ancestry to that office. Always a sturdy folk, the Newtons were both public-minded and spiritually minded; they sought a new life in a new land.

Of the Battle family, to which my mother belonged, we have a chronicle, well-nigh complete, in *The Battle Book,* by H. B. Battle—an amazing family record. Yet the origin of the family remains obscure, in spite of all research. Were they Huguenots who were ill at ease on the Continent even before the edict of Nantes was revoked? Or were they dissenters of

some other kind—Baptists, perhaps? Nobody knows. A place-
name, it was spelled in a dozen different ways. A town in
Sussex bears their name, derived from the Battle of Senlac or
Hastings, fought close by. At any rate they seem to have been
unhappy in England, owing to an "old ecclesiastic edict," and
made their way to Ireland—"fled" is the word employed. They
could hardly have been fleeing from the Church of England,
not in the days of Cromwell, when the church was under ban,
its Prayer Book outlawed, its worship disrupted. Not all of the
Battles went to Ireland. Charles Lamb speaks of old Sarah
Battle who, next to religion, loved a good game of whist, and
Thomas Hood sings of Ben Battle, a soldier bold. As late as
1881 a Battle was Lord Mayor of London, and during my ministry in London three Battles were listed in the city directory.
But the bulk of the family, after a brief stay in Ireland, went
to Virginia in 1653. Why? They wanted to get away from the
old lumber-room of Europe—the same ecclesiastical edict was
in force in Ireland—and, like all the early settlers of the New
World, they were land-hungry; they wanted freedom and more
space.

From Virginia they went in large numbers into North Carolina, and had a notable part in shaping that commonwealth;
many of them still live in the land of the "tar-heel." Almost
from the first the name Battle has been associated with the State
University at Chapel Hill, as well as with all enterprises having
to do with the cultural and spiritual life of the state. Inevitably
they joined the great trek west and southwest—a few going
north—some going to the Pacific Coast. My grandfather, R. J.
Battle—he had twelve names, too many for me to learn—was
born in Jackson, Mississippi, and was carried as a child to
Texas, then a Mexican territory, the Mexican authorities having offered large grants of land to attract settlers. His father
made his home in what afterward became Bowie County, and
carved out a huge plantation, surrounded by swarms of servants—they were not called "slaves," nor were they treated as
such. He it was who named Texarkana, and in that country, as
it afterwards became, he and his family lived under four flags—

the Mexican, Texas, United States and Confederate flags, and again under the Stars and Stripes. They were pioneers, and in the early days knew the hardship and loneliness of pioneer life; my great-grandmother had no guest for three years.

MINGLING STREAMS

My great-grandmother, on the maternal side, was Diana Coleman Ligon—a cousin of Henry Clay—born in Halifax County, Virginia, in 1797. In 1816 she was married to Dr. Josiah W. Fort, Robertson County, Tennessee. Thus two other families mingled in my bloodstream: two families very different, but each notable in its distinction and tradition. Full records of the Ligon family are available, or soon will be, thanks to the patient and diligent researches of Colonel William D. Ligon, Jr., whose book, *The Ligon Family,* is the result of years of labor. The Ligons are a very old family, both in England and in America—in fact they go back beyond William the Conqueror to Charlemagne, and even to the year 400 A.D. Their ancestral home in England is Madresfield Court, near Malvern, in Worcestershire. As is the custom among noble families in England, the oldest son inherits the title, and the younger sons go to the ends of the earth to make their homes. Colonel Thomas Ligon became the founder of the family in the New World, settling in Jamestown, Virginia, in 1641, accompanied by his cousin, Sir William Berkeley, Royal Governor of the Colony. Diana was a direct descendant from Sir Thomas, along with many others, including two presidents, senators, judges, ministers of religion, teachers, lawyers, merchants, railroad builders, and various bigwigs. Many military men were also members of the family—indeed all of the four families in my line furnished both soldiers and officers for the War of the Revolution.

The Fort family, whose record is in preparation, were of different antecedents. No doubt they came from the Continent originally—the name is familiar in France—but, brushing aside the three-brother legend, they were English of long standing.

When we first meet them in the record, they were Quaker folk, who settled in New Jersey, but were unhappy there because their neighbors did not approve of their quaint bonnets and quiet worship; and they went to Virginia, where the name of Elias Fort, Sr.—a favorite family name—appears in jury files, deeds and wills, as early as 1667. They settled in the Isle of Wight County, where, later, one of the family was arrested for not going to church—meaning the Episcopal Church, no doubt, which was practically the State Church before Jefferson won the Statute of Religious Liberty, of which he was so justly proud. Up until that time, one had to be an Episcopalian in the Old Dominion, or one suffered many disabilities. (Just as in New England one had to be a Congregationalist for the same reason. If a Quaker, he might be hanged on Boston Common. If a Baptist, he might be turned out into a New England winter in the hope that he would freeze to death, as had happened to Roger Williams.) We Americans have always been bigoted in religion, and so narrow that we could see through a keyhole with both eyes at the same time. In Virginia there was even a statute permitting the burning of heretics, but, fortunately, it was never enforced, not because of liberality, but because my ancestors were more interested in fox-hunting than in theology. Only the Quakers, although often persecuted, never persecuted others. My Fort forebears, however, evidently did not keep their Quaker faith at full strength, for we hear of another Elias Fort, of Halifax County, North Carolina, who was an officer in the War of Independence. Indeed, none of my immediate Fort ancestors were members of the Society of Friends; and yet something of that noble tradition must have slept warm in my blood, as will appear in certain spiritual experiences to be related later, which closely resemble the Quaker pattern. Always I have had an affinity, if not a kinship, with the Society of Friends, and William Penn has been to me not only one of the greatest of men, but the First American.

When, in 1838, Susan Green Fort was married to R. J. Battle, of Texas, three families were braided together; they lived in Red River County, Bowie County being as yet unknown—it was

shortly after the Battle of San Jacinto; and it ought to be added
that one of the signers of the Resolution of Independence of
Texas, drawn up in 1836, was a Ligon. Life was primitive in
those days, but hardy; houses were built of logs, with stick and
dirt chimneys. Cotton and woolen yarns, colored with dyes
made from berries, roots and bark, were woven into cloth on
a homemade loom. Food would have been a problem, at first,
had not game been so plentiful. There was much sickness, due
to malaria, and infant mortality was high. A "house raising"
was a kind of picnic in which the whole community joined,
doubly so if a church or schoolhouse was to be built. For years
there was no coffee, no sugar, no flour, but there were stout
hearts, fine manners, tallow candles and good books. Serious,
but never solemn, piety was not long-faced; there was much fun
and frolic. My grandfather made himself a fiddle which he
played at the family and neighborhood parties, while he called
the changes in the old Virginia reel. He could himself "trip the
light fantastic" betimes, and did not disdain "Turkey in the
Straw." He wanted his family to have fun without filth, lightness without levity, always observing the decorum as befitted
folk of refinement and religion. In his old age I knew my
grandfather Battle, and held him in warm affection when he
visited us—he was the only one of my grandparents whom I had
the honor of seeing and knowing. Tall, finely formed, with
sideburns and lovely eyes, he nearly always wore his Prince
Albert coat; a gentleman of the old school—his knowledge of
Latin poetry was astonishing. Having too much illness on the
first plantation, the family bought a large body of land in the
pine forests near old Myrtle Springs. There they built an imposing house of hewn logs, back from the bottoms in the pine
hills, which became the homestead for many years.

Five daughters and one son "sirvived" in the home of Grandfather Battle. The oldest daughter, Sally, married very early—
the wife of William Burton; my mother was second—the three
younger daughters, Molly, Hattie, Ida, being much younger;
the son, Uncle "Dock" we called him, came between. When
Grandmother died, my mother became both sister and mother

to her younger sisters, as, in her old age, Ida, her youngest sister, became both sister and mother to her, taking care of her with a patient tenderness and loyal lovingkindness which only a good woman can know. Just how old Mother was I never knew exactly; she kept her secret. According to scant information and no little calculation, she must have been born just before Texas was annexed to the United States—or, as Texans prefer to say, when the United States was annexed to Texas! As a girl she must have been very beautiful, with her dark hair, her great dark eyes, her vivid and expressive face and her brilliant mind. She was the only daughter who enjoyed a college education—except Hattie, who much later went to the University of Chicago, making her own way. Mother was sent to Mary Sharpe College in Tennessee—one of the best colleges for women in the South—where she was superbly trained in those branches of learning which it was deemed "proper," in those days, for a young woman to receive: Latin, Greek, literature, music, the fine arts—she found mathematics difficult, having "no head for figures." She was graduated and made the journey back, most of it by boat, down the Ohio, down the Mississippi, and up Red River to the plantation home, just as the guns of Civil War were sounding.

TEXAS PIONEERS

All of my ancestors were pioneers, both in America and in Texas. Robust folk, wholesome, free from the major maladies, they united the spirit of adventure and independence with religion, culture and self-reliance. Nothing daunted them— neither the harshness of nature nor wild human nature. In the early days the Texas Rangers—men of steel and yet gentle— enforced the law, and, if law did not exist, they made it, justly and fairly. If my forebears got stuck in the mud, they pulled themselves out. They did not expect someone else to do it. They pulled through spells of ague, bad crops—even in my time one dry year followed another—and every kind of disappointment and hardship. They put their shoulders to the wheel, tightened their belts, knuckled down, made over clothes, replanted and rebuilt. Of course, in times of disaster, everybody was incredibly kind, helpful, practical. Yet, through it all, they kept up their standards and had the stamina to stand by them. Their faith in education was a passion; their religion—if somber in its theology—was real, and furnished inward sustaining and unfailing hope. If they liked some things in life better than others, they did not question the value of life itself—as became the sickly habit of aftertimes. They were quick in sympathy, but not "softies" either in body or in spirit; they could be stern, uncompromising in faith, and therefore unconquerable of soul.

For the sake of the record, Dr. Joseph Fort—whose name I bear—brother of my grandmother Battle, went from Texas to Philadelphia to study medicine in Jefferson Medical College. He rode horseback to Memphis, sold his horse, went by boat to Wheeling, West Virginia, thence by stage over the Alleghenies to Cumberland, Maryland, where he saw his first railroad, and rode in the cars to Philadelphia. Being from Texas, he was regarded as a "curiosity," and played up to the role, telling tales about Texas, all of them exaggerated, some of them manufactured, to shock his Quaker friends. He graduated in 1852, and returned to practice in Texas. He was the first physician in his region to accept the germ-theory of disease, and at the meetings of the Texas Medical Society he was greeted, "Ah, here is Dr. Fort with his bugs." In later life he went on a long journey to the Near East, recording his experiences in a book, *The Texas Doctor and the Arab Donkey*. Because of certain observations about the caliber of missionaries, he brought down upon himself an avalanche of wrath from the leaders of the Baptist Church, in which he was a leading layman. No matter; he said his say, stood his ground, and took it all with great gusto. He became increasingly heretical, and for that reason— aside from kinship—took a great interest in my ministry, trying to get me started "right."

Always, in the background of my mind—like a distant drumbeat in my very blood—was the romantic and electrifying story of Texas, its epic struggle for liberty and its right to rule itself. Houston, Austin, Crockett, Bowie, all that "glorious company," were names to conjure with in my heart—a rosary of heroic memory. "Thermopylæ had its messenger of defeat, the Alamo had none," was a cry at once gallant and ghastly. The massacre of Fannin and his garrison, after they surrendered at Goliad, fired the hearts of Texans to a fury. Little quarter was asked or given after that atrocity. Then followed a swift and brilliant campaign, led by Sam Houston, ending in the Battle of San Jacinto, where the Mexican armies were routed, and the President of Mexico was captured and made a prisoner of war. Texas was free and became a Republic, with Sam Houston its first President. To this day, in the capital city of Austin, stands the home built for the Ambassador of the Republic of France to the Republic of Texas. Many of the finest people of the South poured into Texas; the commonwealth grew by leaps and bounds. The proposal that Texas be annexed to the Union—a voluntary annexion, it ought to be added—was opposed by many, due, in part, to the suggestion that Texas be cut up into three or four states. Once, on a train going from St. Louis to Texas, I fell in with a typical, old-time Texan, as fine a specimen of human being as ever lived. When I mentioned that my family were original Texans, he said very earnestly, "It was a mistake, pardner; a big mistake. Texas was an empire in itself, and still is. In variety of soil, climate and the quality of our people, we had everything. Why, sir, when I was a lad and we went to the house of a neighbor to borrow something, and the neighbor was not at home, we took what we wanted, and left a note. No doors were locked. But the d—— Yankees ruined everything!"

Yet fourteen years later Texas withdrew from the Union. The American Civil War—the War between the States, as Southern people prefer to call it—was the saddest and most stupid of all wars, if one war can be more stupid than another. It is incredible to our generation that folk of one race, one religion, and one ideal of life could find no better way to settle any dispute than to draw their swords and throw the scabbards away. If the Union could be divided North and South, it could be divided East, West and every other way—what would a divided America be worth in a divided world? Yet for four years long lines of Blue and Gray swayed to and fro, amid blood, fire and tears. Toward the end it became "total" war, so far as property was concerned—albeit not in the savage sense of "total war" as we learned it later, with mass murders, cruelties subhuman in their horror, the extermination of races and populations, the while a thick stench of death floated on all the winds of the world. But the South was devastated; the wealth of my grandfather vanished; the fortunes of the family were altered radically. But, being pioneers, they met an untoward situation with courage and resourcefulness. On top of it all came the infamous Carpet-Bag regime, with its unspeakable corruptions and indignities; such things would not have happened if Lincoln had lived and could have had his way. But perhaps he was fortunate in his death; even he might have been torn to pieces by the wild and bitter passions released by the war.

2 ......

Childhood and Education

My EARLIEST MEMORY is omitted here, because nobody would believe it; even Mother had her doubts about it, although it did clear up a matter which had puzzled her. Of Lee Newton, my father, my memories are few and dim, only one of them happy. It was not his fault; he died when I was six and a half years old. Busy in law, politics and other affairs, I remember him chiefly in hours of crisis and distress. As when, on an awful day, I saw him stretched on a bed sobbing as if his heart would break. A child often sees his mother cry, but when his father breaks down, his sobs half a groan, it is different—as if the bottom had fallen out. Mother was desperately ill and not expected to live. My aunt led me into the room where she lay, but she did not know me. She looked at me with unseeing eyes, talking softly and happily in her delirium, using the sheet as dough of which she was making biscuits, as I had often seen her do. To this day the forlornness of that moment haunts me. I felt appallingly alone, insecure, baffled. Kipling was right: "Thank God, we can never again suffer as we did when we were young!"

A happy memory of my father was hearing him deliver an address. The meeting was held in a church, but was not a worship-service, as I remember it. It was held, apparently, to discuss some subject or project of importance, more like a debate than a discussion. My father was not preaching—by that time he had left the ministry for the law—but while the topic of the hour was beyond my grasp I can see my father as he spoke, his slender figure, his fine face, his gestures, and I can almost hear the sound of his voice. He seems to have won his point, to judge

24

from the satisfied attitude of my mother. Many years later one of his old friends said to me when I spoke at Fort Worth: "Your father was a dangerous antagonist on the other side of a lawsuit, as I learned to my sorrow, We thought we had an iron-clad case, but he ripped it to pieces, and licked us to a frazzle. Anyway, I learned a lesson, and thereafter, in self-protection, I retained him as my attorney."

Some time later—just how long is not clear—a hush fell over our home. Father was very ill. Once, slyly, I got a glimpse of him—his head turning to and fro in agony. The next time I saw him he was white and still and untroubled; he was among the silent people we call the dead. On a snowy day when a keen wind was blowing—a "norther," we called it—my father was buried; a wood fire was burning nearby. Clinging to the hand of my little mother, I looked for the first time into an open grave—to a sensitive child a strange, terrifying experience.

The old country minister adjusted his glasses and read the words of Jesus, "I am the resurrection and the life—Let not your hearts be troubled." Never shall I forget the power of those words. It was as if a great, gentle Hand, stronger than the hand of man and more tender than the hand of any woman, had been put forth from the Unseen to caress and heal my spirit—from that day to this I have loved Jesus beyond the power of words to tell! The Masonic Lodge, of which Father had been Master, read, or recited, their simple ritual; the Master in his high hat, the men standing in a square, wearing white aprons; each dropping a sprig of evergreen into the grave—a symbol, as I was to learn later, of their faith in the immortal life. Again and again, in afterdays, men from that Lodge came to ask Mother if they could help her in any way. Forty-six years later I stood on the same spot, when my little mother was laid away; and again the words of Jesus—calm, unhurried, confident —spoke to me out of the depths of death—nay, out of the heart of God—and there was sunrise in the west!

FATHER AND MOTHER

My father had been a soldier in the Southern army, hardly more than a boy, afraid the war would be over before he got into it. Afterward he was afraid it would never be over. He was made a Mason in a military Lodge, and wore a red string in the lapel of his coat. Taken prisoner at Arkansas Post, he was carried up the Mississippi River to Rock Island, Illinois. The Northern climate was severe on Southern men, as the records of the War Department reveal. My father became ill, desperately ill, and made himself known as a Mason to an officer of the prison. The officer took him to his own home and nursed him back to life. When the war ended, he loaned Father money to pay his way back to his Texas home, and gave him a pearl-handled pistol to protect himself. They remained close friends, and my father tried, later, to induce his officer-friend to come to Texas and be his partner at law. This experience of my father, when I learned about it, had a very great influence upon my life, as will appear later; the fact that such a fraternity of men could exist, mitigating the harshness of war, and remain unbroken when states and churches were torn in two, became a wonder; and it is not strange that I tried for years to repay my debt to it.

After the war, Father became a teacher and a preacher, but whether he ever held a pastorate or not I do not know. As head of a school in Denton County he employed Miss Sue Green Battle as his associate; their friendship ripened into romance, and they were married in 1868. Mother was a born teacher, the best teacher—for me—that ever lived, having more patience, resource and strategy than anyone I have known; I owe my education largely to her. Latin and Greek she read easily, and her knowledge of English literature was amazing, especially of the older writers from Shakespeare to Scott—whom she greatly admired—and the poets; Dickens she knew as few have known him, even his minor characters. Later English writers, like Hardy and Meredith, she did not so much enjoy because they had no victorious faith. Of Hardy she said, "Fatalism is not faith, it is faith without freedom—a black faith." Later Father and Mother edited a temperance paper, *The Texas Sentinel,* published at Weatherford. In files of the paper, preserved by Mother, I read editorials by my father, and poems and stories written by my mother—more poems than stories. (Before her marriage she wrote a rather long narrative poem and entrusted the manuscript to a young minister-friend, who thought he could find a publisher. Nothing was ever heard of the man or the manuscript; she suspected that he had been a victim of some kind of foul play. She could not reproduce it.)

For some reason, unknown to me, Father gave up the Baptist ministry and entered the practice of law. Naturally, such a move has puzzled me much. Something happened in him spiritually—it may have been an eclipse of faith, or a revolt against the theology of his church and time. Mother was utterly loyal to Father, but in regard to these matters she was reticent—she could keep silent in seven languages. Whether she regretted his leaving the ministry or not I was never able to make out. Indeed, she was in some ways too loyal to my father, as when she, a brilliant musician, declined to teach me music because Father thought music a feminine accomplishment. "I do not want my son to be a cotton-headed dude sitting up playing a piano!"—shades of the master musicians!

Music I love profoundly, and it would have been at once a relaxation and an inspiration—what havoc a silly idea in the mind of a parent can work in the life of a child. Often I have wished that I might have known my father; if he had lived my life might have been very different—he would almost certainly have been a Member of Congress. Life is strange; much of it is shaped for us before we are born, our race, color, sex, our physical outfit and our spiritual tendency—many influences play upon our spirits of which we are unaware. Often, in the chemistry of heredity, the trait of some remote ancestor is passed on to one child, making him like a little stranger in the home. What a grab-bag it all is, beyond our understanding.

By the time my father had entered the practice of law, he

made his home in Decatur, Wise County, and about that "city set upon a hill" my childhood memories are clustered. To my childish mind it was a very great city, with its towering Court House; and the home of Dan Wagner on the hill to the east looked like a fairy castle to my eyes. (Many years later, when I revisited Decatur on a speaking tour during the first World War, it had shriveled to a village, although it had actually grown, the Baptist Church having built a college there, and brick churches having replaced the old wooden structures.) Six children were born to Father and Mother, only two of whom survived to maturity. Robert, the oldest, died at the age of six, before I was born. Of Minnie I seem to have a faint memory— I always wanted a sister—but she went away. Two were born nameless, due, I have been told, to epidemics. Thus I was the oldest child surviving, born July 21st, 1876—my mother said I prevented her from attending the Centennial Exposition in Philadelphia—and my brother, five years my junior, Dr. William Burton Newton, an Ear, Eye, Nose and Throat physician, living in Alpena, Michigan.

There may be better men upon this earth than my brother, but I have never met one, nor can any words tell how much I love him. His brilliant mind, his tender heart, his skill in his profession, his fun and philosophy, all the qualities which make his personality, make him lovable and charming to live with. In appearance he is a Battle; I a mixture of Fort and Newton. Three younger sisters of my mother lived with us. Molly died before my time. Hattie, dazzlingly beautiful and gifted, became a teacher, and married Prof. W. J. J. Terrell. Ida, the youngest, later became an assistant in the teaching of music, by which Mother made her way and maintained her home. Mother was my teacher too, with regular hours and clear-cut courses; she was good at discipline—and she never nagged.

Some time later Mother sold her home in Decatur and went to live with my uncle, William Burton—husband of her oldest sister—at Slidell, who had a large family and a ranch of several thousand acres. My uncle promptly built a schoolhouse, adjoining his home, and again Mother was a teacher, his children and myself and my brother making the school. Life was simple in those days, wholesome, and happy. We had none of the gadgets we have now. All the world did not pour in upon us over the radio, nor did all the family go out in the auto. Even our toys, if we had any, had to be invented—leaving much to the imagination. Lithe, sinewy greyhound dogs chasing jack-rabbits, was a sport. There were spelling-bees and various kinds of parties. Movies did not exist and fiction was not filthy. Divorce was unknown. The word "sex" was seldom, if ever, used. The church—a Baptist Church—was the center of the community. In spite of its theology of threats and thunders, it was a place of fellowship and prayer—a plain white meeting house, innocent of adornment, not even an organ. Our pastor, Grand Crystal—one of a large family of that name—was a man whose life was sweet with certainties, and rich in wisdom—he had as fine a face, at once strong and gentle, as I have ever seen. Only some of his doctrinal sermons made my soul writhe, even as a child. How strange, after a sermon on a blazing, eternal hell, to hear the neighbors talk and tell stories, or bring each other up to date on gossip. To me it was horrible—either they did not believe what the preacher said, or they lacked the imagination to realize what it meant. The idea of God back of it all was intolerable—not one of those good people would do what the preacher said God would do!

Yet, at other times, our pastor had flashes of real insight, and some of his sermons remain in my memory to this day. One day he talked of Jesus feeding the five thousand, saying that when the boy, John Mark, stepped forward and offered Jesus all the food he had, then everybody shelled out the food they had hidden, and there was enough for all and to spare. The change from selfish hoarding to happy sharing, he said, was the real miracle. Some of the brethren were a bit dubious about the explanation, but they had to admit that it had its point. Of course our pastor did not question any miracle. Again, taking as his text the words of Jesus when Lazarus had been awakened from the sleep of death, "Loose him, and let him go," he said that we should not think of our dead as bound in grave clothes, but loose them, think of them as living and growing. So long as we think of them as dead, they are dead to us—as when a great Frenchman said, whose words I read years later, "I regret that in my heart I let the dead die." This sermon, I need hardly add, made a profound impression, and it is not strange that it has been a benediction to me through all the years.

At the time of my next vivid memory, Mother and Aunt Ida were living at Chico, in the western part of the county, where they had a large number of pupils studying music. Chico was nestled amid hills and streams bordered by woodland, in contrast with Slidell, which was on a wide prairie, stretching away, a black, waxy, gumbo, fertile land, so sticky in wet weather that travel was difficult. But the prairie had a beauty of its own, besides its far-sweeping distances; there were wild chickens aplenty, in the spring and summer wildflowers made it a carpet of color—queen blue bonnet holding court; and in the winter when the north wind tumbled out of bed and went racing over the prairie, it swept the broomweed into huge, tumbling rows against the wire fences. Every kind of country is beautiful, in its own style, if we have eyes to see—I have often wished that I had acquired a more detailed knowledge of nature, of birds, of flowers, of all her ancient ways, as some of my friends did later. The ritual of the seasons—seed-time, summer splendor, and autumn harvest, followed by the white death of winter—has been a perpetual wonder to me.

LIFE'S CHANGES

By this time I had begun to grow up and wear long trousers, which made me feel very important. Working at various jobs, chopping cotton, picking cotton, in which I became an adept, or helping some farmer, I bought my own clothing, every suit I have ever worn, except one which, years later, my late friend Arthur Nash, a clothing manufacturer, gave me; outfitting me from head to foot—just for fun and friendship. There was only one weekly newspaper in the county, reporting local affairs, chiefly; the big world was remote and unknown—foreign affairs might have transpired on some other planet, Russia was a Big Bear, England a Lion whose tail was made to be twisted, China a land to which we sent missionaries. In my desire to know something of the world, I subscribed for the weekly edition of the Louisville *Courier-Journal,* and read the editorials of Henry Watterson—always picturesque—the last voice of the old South, but forward-looking; and the Atlanta *Constitution,* to read the editorials of Henry Grady, the thrilling voice of the new South; also the humorous skits of M. Quad, Sarge Pluckett, and the Uncle Remus stories by Joel Chandler Harris. After this manner I kept in touch, somewhat, with the strange ways of the world, and some of its gifted minds; the church papers were deadly dull—the religious mind, then, as now, being pre-occupied with issues which did not greatly interest me; debates about dogmas, or petty feuds within the church.

Also, whereas in Slidell there had been only one church—Baptist—in Chico there were several churches, too many for the town; including two Methodist churches, one North, one South —relics of the schism which rent that communion at the time of the Civil War. It was my first contact with Protestant sectarian-ism, and even as a lad I saw its absurdity; it magnified little dif-ferences and overlooked great agreements. Our people worked together, played together, friends and neighbors; but when they went to worship, each went his own way, not knowing, not caring, apparently, about the faith of others.

In other words, religion, which ought to have united the com-munity, divided it. It was almost unanimous politically; in Chico for the first time I saw a Republican, knowing him to be such, but very few belonged to that party. Even then sectarian-ism seemed to me absurd; today it is akin to sacrilege. Our Baptist church was a plain rather weather-beaten structure, bare as a barn, where we had preaching twice a month, but the Sunday School flourished. My mother taught a class and con-ducted the music. She conceived the idea of getting an organ, and we had parties and saved pennies until we had enough to buy a small Esty organ. When it arrived, we made the back of the box into a door, put on hinges, so when Sunday School was ended, it could be slipped back into the box and pushed to the back of the church—there was no separate room for the Church School. Some of the brethren look askance at that box. Finally, at a business meeting of the church, held on a Saturday, one brother made a tearful speech, saying that he could not pray with that "contraption" in the church. He made a motion that it be removed and that a committee be appointed to remove it. The motion was carried, and the committee solemnly picked up the little organ and set it down under a tree outside. The expression on the face of my mother was a study, a blend of amusement, indignation and bewilderment; but I was furious. We took the organ to the home of one of the church families and had many a sing-song.

Just the same, for some time after this atrocity, I felt hurt at the church of my fathers—as if music were an evil menace, as if beauty were a blight in the worship of God. One Sunday, when there was no service at our church, I left after Sunday School and went to the Methodist Church North, where I heard a sermon which I remember to this day. Our own minister made no impression upon me whatsoever; I do not even remember his name. The Methodist minister, who had a benign face, a sweet voice and a reverent manner, preached from the text, "Ye are God's husbandry,"—God's farm, he translated it. The trouble, he said, is that we want to be the farmer, want to dictate to God how the work should be done. It was an attack—if that is the right word—on our self-seeking, complacent piety.

Prayer, he explained, is not intended to tell God what we want Him to do—He knows what we want, as well as what we need, which may be two very different things. No, prayer is asking Him to do something with us, asking Him to make us ready and willing and worthy to do what He wants done. Religion, he said, is response. We may believe in God, in Jesus, in the future life—I noted that he named only basic truths—but if we do not respond to them religiously, we are not really religious. He was a visiting minister, as I learned later, but he gave me something to think about, something to live by. When I told Mother what I had done she was uncertain, but when I gave her a report of the sermon she was interested and happy, saying that I had been wise in leaving "the holy Baptist church," which betrayed a hurt in her own heart about the organ. The Methodist church had an organ, and the music was good, considering that the choir was a voluntary group; I enjoyed it, the while I wondered, indignantly, why our church had shut music out of the House of God. It implied that my mother, by teaching music, was engaged in an evil trade.

The Protestant churches of our town did not attack each other, although I later heard a Methodist and a Baptist debate for ten days issues which seemed to me of little importance, except, perhaps, the question whether we could "fall from grace," or whether "once in grace we are always in grace"; St. Paul had fears lest he who had preached the gospel might become a "castaway." But our pastor had a grudge against the Catholic Church, a phobia. In season and out of season he denounced it as the Scarlet Woman of the Book of Revelation and everything he could lay his tongue to. Whether other pastors in the town joined in his anger, I did not know. As there was only one Catholic family in the town, it did not seem fair—in fact I did not think that our pastor knew what he was talking about. Nor did I, but one day I read a reference in the *Courier-Journal*, which said that Cardinal Gibbons lived in Baltimore. Greatly daring, and keeping my act a dead secret, I wrote him a letter, telling him the awful things I had heard my pastor say about his church, and that I wanted to know the truth. In due time a letter came in return, not dictated to a secretary, but written with his own hand, commending my attitude as wise. One should not condemn any church or any man without knowing the facts. One may not accept the teachings of the Roman Church, he said, but one ought to try to understand it at its best, rather than accept a garbled and distorted version of it. To that end, he added, he was sending me a copy of his book *The Faith of Our Fathers*, which arrived in due time. I read the book and kept it for many years. Mother was not quite happy about what I had done. To my amazement she shared, to some degree, the prejudice of our pastor against the Roman Church; but she read the book and it cleared matters up somewhat. Half a life later, when Cardinal Gibbons died, a Mass was sung for him in the Cathedral in New York, and I attended the service—just because a great man had taken time out of his busy life to answer with his own hand the scrawled letter of a boy in Texas.

BEING A BOY

But my life as a boy was not all concerned with church affairs; far from it. There was fun and frolic aplenty—baseball, for example. In some way I was the first boy in town to learn how to throw a ball that curved to the left, which made a right-handed batter look foolish fanning the air. I can still see the old men, with their long beards, lined up behind the home plate, to see with their own eyes whether a curved ball could be thrown. Then groups of us would go into the woodlands at night, catch an opossum, roast him, along with sweet potatoes and eggs, and have a feast; going early enough to have a swim in the creek. Hunting wildcats was also a sport, and some fishing. There were also parties in which the girls took part, but no dancing—I have always wished that I knew how to dance; it has been a part of the rituals of many religions. Not even the old-time "square dances," as they were called, were allowed—so strict were the rules of our time. Quietly, but vigilantly, our elders watched us, keeping us in the straight and narrow way. Even Diamond Dick Dead-Shot stories had to be read on the sly—they did us no good, and no harm—at least they were stories of action. Just living was a joy, just the ecstasy of being young was enough for hardy, growing boys; we played, we did not pay to see others play. We tried to chew tobacco, but it made us sick enough to die—seasick on land. One of our group told dirty stories, but he did not get very far; it takes a lot of wit to disinfect smut, and he did not have the wit. Dirt for the sake of dirt is disgusting. Our training was severe; profanity was banned—the rule was seldom broken—in our home at least we had to watch both our diction and our deportment.

Outside my window, "in that dim hour 'twixt dreams and

dawn, lone in the hush of sleeping things," a mockingbird used to sing his morning hymn. Swaying to and fro on a twig, he sang for very joy till he could bear it no longer, and then he would bound into the air in sheer glee. Alighting upon the twig once more, he took up the next stanza, which ended, as before, in an outburst of joy which swept him away. What sweet madness of joy! What prodigal outpouring of variegated melody! Long years later, in England, I tried to hear a nightingale sing, and failed; but I doubt if any bird on earth can surpass the mockingbird. He is accused of plagiarism, but no one can deny that he is an artist, as the blue jay is a beautiful rascal. An English officer once told me how, amid one of the great battles in Flanders, he heard a little bird singing with all his might, as if trying to drown the din of war with his song. Remembering the bird which sang to me years before, joined with the Le Gallienne poem, "To a Bird at Dawn," suggested a sermon entitled "Why Do the Birds Sing?" which was published. Thomas Hardy puzzled over that question, wondering why and by what right the birds have to sing—he who saw the world as a worm-eaten apple on a dying tree! He finally concluded that the birds may know a secret which we have failed to find.

And there is something the song saith
That makes me unafraid of death.

Hear now a tribute, written in gratitude and affection, to the dog-friends of my boyhood. The cats are cut out; they are lovely as kittens, but when they grow up they become haughty and condescending, loving as much as they think we deserve; whereas a dog loves us with all his might. His loyalty never falters, his forgiveness never fails. Even as a small child, when we lived at Decatur, I used to run away and go up the hill to the courthouse square, to my father's office, to visit David Sparkman, his young partner—a reddish-haired, blue-eyed, jolly-hearted man, "Spark" we called him, who was my friend. Mother was uneasy about these runaway escapades, fearing for my safety. But she need not have been alarmed. With me went a glorious Newfoundland dog, Shay by name, as black as ink, alert, graceful, who made me his responsibility every step of the way. He allowed people to speak to me, but if anyone approached me he had to show credentials satisfactory to Shay. Later Shay was stolen or killed, and shortly thereafter an attempt was made on the life of my father. We put two and two together: nobody could have come near the house if Shay had been at home. Then there was a beautiful Shepherd dog on my uncle's ranch—intelligent enough to go to school— who, when told to bring the milch-cows to the barn, bounded off with glee, singled them out, rounded them up and brought them home; if they walked too slowly, he snapped at their heels and quickened their pace. Even the cows came to understand, and started home as soon as they saw him coming. Bruno was a dog of a different breed, all aglow with life, full of fun and ready for any game. One dog, dearly beloved, I had to shoot, because it was diseased—it was a hard thing to do. Anyway, I maneuvered so that he never knew who or what hit him—but it left an ache in my heart. When I think of all those dog-friends I am sometimes tempted, as Wesley was, to believe in the immortality of animals; each had a distinct individuality, hard to know from personality—they still bark and romp in my memory.

About this time—one cannot date inner events accurately by the calendar—somehow I got hold of a copy of *War and Peace,* by Tolstoi—Howells was then introducing the American mind to Russian literature. It would be impossible for me to describe the impression made upon me by that stupendous story, perhaps the greatest novel ever written. Mother, of course, got more out of the story than I did—its vast canvas, its throng of characters, with jaw-breaking Russian names, confused me somewhat. But one scene stuck in my mind and stayed, the talk of the old Freemason with Pierre when the nobleman said he did not believe in God: "You do not know Him, Sir, and that is why you are unhappy. Of Whom were we speaking? Whom dost thou deny? Who invented Him, if He were not? How came there within thee the conception that there is such an incomprehensible Being? . . . Yes, God exists, but to know Him is hard. It is not attained by reason, but by life."

Thus to Tolstoi I owe an insight which has guided me through the years—that religion would not exist if the Object of religion did not exist; its Object which is also its origin. There would be nothing to suggest it, nothing to sustain it. For that reason, I have never tried to prove God—what kind of a God could my little mind prove? How would I go about it?

DAWNING MANHOOD

In the meantime—all the time—my studies went on regularly, directed by my mother; except in mathematics, in which she was no adept. Algebra was an agony to both of us. For a time she had me tutored by a queer, chubby little man named Rogers, whose history I never knew. He never talked about himself, and I asked no questions. Bald as a billiard ball, with keen blue eyes, a bachelor apparently, he was a born teacher, and delightful to know. He knew mathematics, but the great passion of his life—his idolatry—was Shakespeare, and he knew the plays from end to end. He even went so far as to argue that our planet ought to be named for its greatest poet. As he recited great passages from the dramas, his eyes glowed with an admiration akin to worship. Hamlet, he insisted, is the most elaborately painted character in literature, a soul laid bare, like a beehive made of glass; Hamlet was Shakespeare, and we know him more intimately than we know our closest friend. In him the sea which washes between soul and soul, is rolled away. Each of us ought to study Hamlet thoroughly once every five years, and the new glories discovered in it would show how much we had grown—like the notch I had cut on the kitchen door to measure how tall I was getting to be. It was a wise hint, and I followed it for years, to my joy and benefit. In the *Courier-Journal* I had read how Watterson, strangely enough, had argued that Bacon was the author of the plays ascribed to Shakespeare. When I mentioned that idea, my tutor almost had apoplexy—he blasted the theory to bits. Also, he taught me how much one can do by saving and filling the little gaps of time, which too often we fritter away; his suggestion became a habit with me, one of the best habits I ever formed, and the most rewarding.

To my mother, chiefly, I owe my love of great literature, which has been such an inspiration and comfort. She knew Shakespeare too—the enthusiasm of my tutor made her happy —but Scott and Dickens were her cronies; Scott gave her a sense of the solidity of things, the rich variety of character and personality, while for Dickens the streets of London were "a pantomime and a masquerade." In afteryears, when I lived in London, I often wished she could have been with me, but, alas, she never saw that old gray city. In her teaching of literature she never made it a grinding at grammar, as so often happens, never a preoccupation with the verse structure of a poet, or the story-architecture of a novelist; but always the wonder of genius, the growth of character, the artistry—not merely the artifice—in the style of a writer. Yet she found delight in certain stories, much in vogue at the time, such as *St. Elmo,* by Augusta Evans, which did not appeal to me at all; feminine preoccupations have always puzzled me. But Mother knew her Bible, as she knew no other book; she lived with it, loved its idiom and its inspiration, and the artlessness of its art. Literature? Yes, if by literature we mean "the lasting expression in words of the meaning of life"; but something more than literature. She loved it devotionally, and her use of it was both a culture and a consecration. When W. R. Harper began to talk of the "higher criticism" of the Bible, she was frightened, if not furious. She actually thought he was a servant of Satan, with horns, a harpoon tail, and a wicked glitter in his eye. If she had known Dr. Harper, as I came to know him later, she would have been won by his simple faith and his sincere piety. Of course it was the word "criticism" that did it, implying that the new scholars were finding fault with the Bible, tearing it to tatters; whereas the word was used as Matthew Arnold used it when he said that "poetry is a criticism of life." Poetry, as a process of picking life to pieces,

would hardly be poetry. No, "criticism" meant estimate, understanding, interpretation; studying the books of the Bible as
we study any other ancient documents—discovering, when possible, when a book was written, by whom, and to whom it was
addressed, and so learning its message. But Mother, like all
the people of her time, held a theory about the Bible as a
whole, unknown to the Bible itself, which put the whole book
on the same level, and did not take account of the unfolding
of its vision—a plane, not a mountain range, with shadowy
valleys and peaks of amazing height. Anyway, it was bread,
meat and medicine to her spirit, as it has seldom been to anyone since.

Then, suddenly, unaccountably, to my deep dismay, Mother
married a Baptist minister named W. B. Long, a man of some
ability, but hard to live with at times, as we were to find out.
As Mrs. Gamp would say, "We are born into a Wale and we
must take the consekences of sich a sitivation." What grieved
me was the fact that she had made me, her oldest son, her con-
fidant in so many matters, but this important move she kept
to herself. Aunt Ida told me about it but swore me to silence.
Brother and I tried to make the best of the business, and not
let it make the worst of us—sometimes the going was difficult.

To add to our adversities, Aunt Ida married Dr. John
Turner, who had just finished his medical studies in Nash-
ville, and went away to make her own home. A more devoted
couple I have never known in my life, because both were so
utterly unselfish. Their one great sorrow was the death of their
only daughter, which well-nigh broke their hearts. My uncle
carried that deep hurt with him when he went away. He was as
true a man as I have ever known, sound in judgment, infinitely
patient, unfailingly kind. Owing to a defect of eyesight he had
to give up the practice of medicine, but he was an expert phar-
macist, and his son Battle Turner became his assistant. I can
still see him holding a prescription or a bottle close to his eyes,
in order to read it. The goodness of my Uncle John and Aunt
Ida to my mother in her declining years can never be forgotten,
even if I had the honor of paying them for their kindness; some

things are priceless and can neither be bought nor sold. It meant everything to me, when I was far away in London and New York, to know that Mother was being cared for with the utmost loving-kindness. In those days one never heard of a home for old people; it was a point of honor to care for the aged, as for the young.

Anyway, our home was broken up and we went with our step-father to live in Hardy, a town in Montague County, where a home was built. My step-father had a circuit of country and villages churches, to which he ministered; I heard many of his sermons but do not remember a single one—his preaching was chiefly doctrinal, and I detested the doctrines he preached. My brother and I rented land and raised a cotton crop, at a time when the price of cotton was ridiculously low. The cotton seed, except what we needed to replant or to feed the milch-cows, was a dead loss in those days. The land was more sandy, and less sticky, than the black belt in which we had formerly lived. The town was nestled amid hills and streams, but not far away the prairie stretched away toward the east. Almost for the first time I went to a school, first under Professor Otis, and later under two charming young men, Ben Gafford and Charles Wrenn. My mother still had some music pupils, but on most weekends she went with her husband to his preaching engagements. For a brief time I went and stayed with two of my uncles, in Greenville, Hunt County, where they edited a daily paper. There I learned to set type, and there I got printer's ink in my blood—like yeast in dough, once there, always there; nothing can take it out.

There must have been some kind of a church in the town of Hardy, but I do not seem to remember it, since most religious services were held in the schoolhouse. It was there that I attended my first Episcopal service, a rector from Gainesville conducted the service and preached the sermon which, if not memorable, was at least thoughtful and winsome. He wore a black gown, no surplice or stole. It was the first time I had ever seen a gown worn in a pulpit. As there were no Prayer Books, he read the office of Evening Prayer, explaining it as he went along, announcing the titles of the prayers. The service was largely attended, not due entirely to curiosity. The rector no doubt had it in mind to start a mission, but as he never came again he must have given up the idea. After the service a number of people objected to "praying out of a book"; but I could not see the point, since the prayers were so stately and noble in style and thought, in contrast to the meandering, extemporaneous prayers, full of stereotyped phrases, to which we were accustomed. Besides, since we read the lessons out of a book, and sang praises out of a hymnbook, why not read great prayers which have been used by millions of people—like the steps of a church trodden by generations, worn by many feet, seeking solace from a source Unseen. Just the same, I sent and got a Prayer Book, which Emerson later described for me as "an anthology of the piety of ages and nations"; and it became a friend and aider of my spirit.

VISION MOMENTS

Around this time, when I was about fourteen years of age, something happened to me—happened in me—which no words can ever really tell. Whether I can tell it now, or ought to try to tell it, save for the record, is doubtful. The shadow of a great sorrow lay dark over our home. The news that my grandfather Battle had died had reached us. I loved him very much, and his going left me lonely of heart. To youth sorrow is new, strange, terrifying, all the more because it does not understand; it does not yet know the quiet joy of an outlived sorrow. Mother was prostrated, and I felt like a lost soul, baffled. It was a summer day, still, lucid, gentle. Not knowing what to do, I went for a walk, climbed a hill near our home, and sat down— before me lay the valley of Willa Walla creek, and beyond a woodland, and in the distance the prairie. Not far away a lone cottonwood tree stood stately against a violet sky. Suddenly all my trouble, all my fear, left me. Life itself seemed to speak to my spirit. God became very near, very real, not awful but gentle as a Friend; Jesus infinitely enlarged in every way—but something more. My whole being was aware of Him, with an intense stillness. There was no voice, no vision, but old Bible words came into my mind, almost as if someone had spoken them into my ear: "Fear not; underneath are the everlasting arms." At last—how long I do not know—sunset touched the scene with glory. It was not merely an idea of God needed to explain life—I was not thinking of Him. No, it was God Himself, He without whom we cannot live, He upon whom we rely, unconsciously, when all else fails: "We cannot go where God is not." Since that hour I have never been lonely, never afraid of death—my body may be dreading the process of dying, but not my spirit. Here is the one certainty of my life, in the midst of many uncertainties—the center of all my habits, memories, purposes, hopes and efforts. Since then I have doubted the doubts of men, not their faiths.

As this experience, unsought, in nowise self-induced, and often repeated—a sense of God lighted by vision-moments—is really the thread on which my days are strung, something more may be said about it, even at the risk of anticipating my story. No mature man—no saint, even—could have been as happy as I was when I fell in love with God and knew that He loved me. Again and again, through the years, a sense of the near neighborliness and far friendliness of God, ineffable and satisfying, has returned to me. In quiet places, in the rush of great cities, in work and in worship, and once on a rain-swept battlefield in Flanders, I have known God as real and near. Not always the same text—sometimes no text at all—came with it. Other words of the Bible have been written in letters of light in my heart. Once it was the great saying of St. Paul: "If God be for us, who can be against us?" Those words have been a fortress to my spirit, making me doubt all the scepticisms, pessimisms and cynicisms of my race. Once, in the vivid dimness of Cologne Cathedral, the words that came with new light and wonder—as of a silver lamp always burning in a window—were the words of Jesus: "Him that cometh to Me I will in no wise cast out." There it is, unforgettable, a door always open, a hand extended in welcome, and no one turned away. On another day, dark and confused, the 23rd Psalm became a thing of unutterable joy: "The Lord is my Shepherd; I shall not want." Since that day the little Psalm has been the last prayer in my heart when the day darkens into the tiny death called sleep, and the first words to greet the wonder of morning.

Some may say that it is all illusion, if not delusion. It does not matter; it is the one thing I know as I know nothing else, with far more assurance than anything can be known by science or law or philosophy. Since that day, its joy repeated and renewed, I have never doubted God, nor have I ever tried to "prove" Him. Why should I try, when He proves Himself by the warmth and astonishment of my heart. Nor have I ever had that gnawing anxiety about spiritual reality which has tortured so many men far better and wiser than I can ever be: Pascal and Newman, for example. The peril of dealing with the idea of God is that it is apt to become just an idea. Yes, I know —I was later to learn—all the great arguments for God, but all they can do is to prove that there ought to be a God—not that there is a God, much less what God is. In religion, which is life at its highest, it is God Himself that we need, He in Whom "we live and move and have our being"; not argument but discernment, not speculation but experience. Since that summer day my thought of God has changed radically, and if it is less than true today, as it surely is, something inconceivably better is true. But my experience of God has not changed— save to deepen with the years—giving me serenity in tumult, quietness and confidence in confusion; turning my mind from outer events to inner values. Nothing is too good to be true, because God is. Of course I have my quota of human vanity, but I have never been vain enough to imagine that I could think thoughts, or dream dreams, too beautiful or too good for God to fulfill. The truth, when we are true enough to know it, will rise above, not fall below, what faith will show. When I am most alive—in hours of clear vision and firm decision— God is most real and revealing. If He seems unreal, it is due to fatigue, to the chaos of hurry, or the drag of inertia. Pray

God it may be so until the falling daylight, and death hangs his sickle at my garden gate.

WHITE MOUND

But, back to my story. The home at Hardy was sold and we moved to White Mound, in Grayson County, little more than a wide place in the road, but a charming community withal. There were a post office, two stores, two churches—Baptist and Methodist—a blacksmith shop, a schoolhouse, and a number of cottages. There were some good families in the town, and others not so good, as is true of every town. Indeed, a feud, or something like it, seemed to exist between two rather large families. Soon after we arrived, on a Saturday, both families were in town—all except one, an Elder in the Methodist Church, who turned up later—well filled with liquor, and there followed such a free-for-all, knock-down-drag-out fight, as I had never seen in my life. When it was over the scene looked like a battlefield —Mother was frightened, I was amazed; there were black eyes, smashed noses, and some broken ribs. I can still see that Methodist Elder, who had taken no part in the fracas, standing, with an infinite sadness in his face. The whole performance, while it did not make me a prohibitionist—an idea not yet on the horizon—did fill me with deep dismay at the stupidity of men who drank "hell-fire water," as the Indians called it, which turned them into maniacs and made them beat one another into a pulp. Such a thing never happened again; the indignation of the community made itself felt in no uncertain terms.

My step-father was becoming increasingly difficult. Always moody, his moods became sullen and sulky, and he often carried a thundercloud in the face. So long as he vented his spleen on Brother and me it did not matter, we could handle him. But when he began to threaten Mother it was different—something had to be done. The duty devolved upon me, the oldest son, and I told him plainly, in words of one syllable, what had to be stopped, and what he must do—or else! My mother, with her incredibly tenacious loyalty, quoted Scripture to me, "Touch not the Lord's anointed." Happily I did not have to touch him, because at heart a bully is always a coward, and he mended his ways. He became actually amiable, almost charming, as he could be when he wanted to be. As I was talking of entering the ministry, he gave me many points of value about the making of sermons and how to conduct myself, especially as regards women. What training for the ministry he had had I never knew. I never saw him read any book except a book of theology, and seldom even that much. He told me, what I did not know, that Beecher always wrote his prayers with care and memorized them, not wishing to come into the presence of God with wandering, improvised thoughts. This hint, together with my love of the Book of Common Prayer, may have been the germ of a little book which appeared many years later, *Altar Stairs,* which went far and wide over the English-speaking world; and still goes on its way—a little book that softly talks with God.

A queer little man came to our town, named Jenkin Roberts, as head of the village school, diffident but wise. One ear stuck out farther than the other, as if it had leaned out to hear something interesting, and had forgotten to go back to its proper place. His face was a maze of criss-cross wrinkles, where smiles fell asleep when they were weary—he saw so many funny things in life. His hat was an ancient institution, which could be wadded up and tucked into his pocket. I did not attend his school because I was still continuing my studies with Mother, who was by this time teaching me Greek, but he organized a debating society, which I was allowed to join. At each meeting we selected the subject to be discussed at the next session, but we did not know on which side we were to speak until the time came. We had to think out a speech on both sides of the subject, ready to present and answer our own arguments. No one was permitted to use notes, except when statistics were employed, and even that was discouraged. When the time came we had to "choose up," as when we played ball, and speak on the side on which we were chosen. At first our speeches were

clumsy, awkward, and half articulate, but finally we found our
tongues, learned to think on our feet, using all our wits in re-
buttal; which was what our leader had in mind. It was one of
the best bits of training I ever had, helping me to overcome
my shyness and to order my thought, as well as to speak to
the point. Woman suffrage, whether Grant or Lee was the
greater commander, were some of the subjects we debated.
Judges listened to our arguments and decided who had won
—sometimes one side lost, sometimes the other. Knowing that
I had thoughts of entering the ministry, Jenkin Roberts made
an epigram which stuck in my memory: "If a preacher cannot
remember his own sermon long enough to preach it, nobody
will remember it long after he does preach it." The epigram
appeared, many years later, in a series of lectures given to the
College of Preachers in Washington, entitled *The New Preaching*. It got under the skin of some of the brethren, who, with
fear and trembling, laid aside their manuscripts and learned to
speak to their people eye to eye, soul to soul.

Still I was in a quandary about entering the Baptist ministry,
feeling that I had no right to accept service in a church whose
theology I did not believe. At one time I thought of becoming
a Methodist minister, but put it aside, not only because it
would wound Mother deeply, but it would have outraged my
family, who had been Baptists for generations. It was not the
religion of my fathers which I rejected, far from it, but a
theology which was intolerable, not only particular doctrines,
but its basic idea of God, implied or assumed. The idea that
we need a good Jesus to save us from a mad, if not a bad, God
was unthinkable, as was the intimation that Jesus did something which made it possible for God to forgive man. He did
something for man which man could not do for himself, but
He did not reconcile God to man; He reconciled man to God.
Vicarious suffering? Yes, because we are all bound together in
one bundle of life, and the wrongdoing of one may bring suffering to others, even the innocent, as I had seen it do. But
substitutionary suffering? No, since guilt is not transferable,
except upon the theory that, inasmuch as there has been a

murder there must be a hanging; and even a civilized man, much less a just and merciful God, would never do such a thing. Surely it is not too much to believe that God is as good as a good man: "If ye being evil know how to give good gifts to your children, how much more your Father," said Jesus.

To me the dogma of eternal hell was abhorrent; it meant the worship of a defeated God. The idea that the tiny will of man —stubborn as it often is—can forever resist the wise strategy and persuasion of the loving will of God, was absurd. Punishment in the eternal world? Yes, but in the eternal world there is neither time nor distance; "a thousand years are as a day." There is a gleam of hope in the Catholic dogma of Purgatory, but the Protestant hell surging on in omnipotent fury forever is the most frightful dogma ever promulgated in times not actually barbaric. Yet my church believed it, just as they believed that the world would go from bad to worse until, at last, God, in the desperation of despair, would burn it up and make a new start, as in the days of Noah He scoured it and began anew. Good men were black pessimists.

CRISIS AND COUNSEL

Ages ago Dante said that theology is "God's poetry." Some of it is, certainly; but, except in the Methodist Church, where the emphasis was laid on the inner experience of religion— which, God be thanked, I had never lost—the theology I heard preached in my boyhood sounded like ragged prose; some of it downright doggerel. Clearly things were shaping up for me toward a bitter inward crisis; I began to understand why my father left the ministry for the law. My revolt against the teaching of my church was complete, basic, tragic, and it might have been violent but for the wise counsel of my mother. She felt the tension of my spirit, she was my only confidante, and we talked together:

"But, Mother, if Jesus was right about God, the Baptist Church is wrong; it gets God and the devil mixed. If we are wrong about God we cannot be right about anything else, or very little."

"My son," she said, looking at me with her great dark eyes, "listen only to Jesus. Accept what He says about God, what He shows God to be in His life, nothing else, nothing less; test everything by Him—forget the rest."

The tension of my spirit relaxed, only to tighten again, not in revolt but in awestruck wonder at the terrific demands He made, and still makes, upon me; giving all, and asking all in clean and complete commitment: "Follow Me." Here is the greatest adventure of the human soul, the most daring, the most exacting—we are not asked to understand Jesus, we are only asked to obey Him, following "where no path is made—save by His feet," as I wrote years later, in a little poem interpreting the walk to Emmaus. Always I have followed the counsel of my mother; it has made my ministry positive, never negative. Dogmas which my heart denied I have never discussed; they have been quietly ignored. As Edmond Gosse put it later, "Let sleeping dogmas lie." It was as if a heavy load had fallen off my spirit; I had found a faith to satisfy my mind and sanctify my heart—a faith asking for all that I had of fortitude and faithfulness.

"The rest does not matter," Mother added; hence my indifference to the little differences which divide the churches—they do not signify. Whether one is baptized in much water or by a little is of no importance, so long as one honestly intends to obey the Master. It was amazing how little people missed what was left out of my preaching. When, at last, I entered the ministry, they were unaware of what was omitted.

Early in my life I learned the difference between the clerical and the lay minds, long before John Galsworthy pointed out the difference in his story, *Freelands,* where he spoke of a woman of religious temperament as "ever trimming her course down the exact channel marked out with buoys by the Port Authorities, and really incapable of imagining spiritual wants in others that could not be satisfied by what satisfied herself." Which describes what perpetuates our divisions about little realities, and even unrealities—old habits and customs of creed and worship, which we are accustomed to. People so easily find reasons for what they want to believe, or do. Of course the clerical mind is not limited to the clergy; many a layman has a clerical mentality, as some clergy are essentially laymen in outlook. The clerical mind consists, if we may believe John Morley, in that "treacherous playing with words which underlies even the most vigorous efforts to make phrases of the old creed hold the reality of a new faith." In short, it is tortuous, pedantic, rigid, timid, lacking in sympathy and imagination; if that is the clerical mind, and I have not found it so, may the good Lord deliver us from it!

My mother had regular periods of devotion, and a definite method. She would go to her room, read a passage from the Bible, sing a stanza from a hymn, and offer her prayer audibly. Sometimes I listened in on her worship, when she did not know it. Once, about this time, I heard my name mentioned in her prayer. She was lifting my life before God, detaining it there, invoking His guidance and blessing upon me. It moved me beyond the power of words to tell. Anyway, I made my decision, the die was cast—I entered the ministry; really I had never desired, never dreamed of doing anything else. The ordination service was held in the Methodist Church, the largest in town, and the place was crowded. The sermon was preached by J. K. P. Williams, noted as a debater, who took for his text the words of St. Paul—the Apostle Paul, the word Saint was not used in our church—"But we have this treasure in earthen vessels, that the excellency of the power may be of God, and not of us." He talked of the "treasure," which to him was a body of doctrine to be kept from alteration and pollution; I was thinking of the "vessel," wondering whether anyone was worthy of so high a calling as the ministry. After a few routine questions, I knelt, and the brethren laid their hands upon me, setting me apart to preach the Gospel; if anyone had used the word "priest," it would have broken up the meeting. Then a "charge" was given me, urging me to be diligent as a student of the Word and faithful in my service of

Christ and His Church. My step-father pronounced the benediction, and the service was ended.

AMATEUR PREACHER

My first sermon, as an ordained minister, was preached the following Sunday in the Baptist Church, a building badly in need of paint, whose seats, or pews, creaked as if in complaint. A goodly company assembled to hear my sermon, even some Methodists, and I remember still how frightened I was; making a speech was one thing, but preaching was something else. My text was taken from the great anthem with which the 8th Chapter of Romans closes: I am persuaded . . . that nothing in all creation, shall be able to separate us from the love of God, which is in Christ Jesus our Lord. The details of the sermon I do not recall—it must have been pretty poor stuff— but the theme has been the keynote of all my ministry—the Love of God, His "loving-kindness," as the prophets called it, being both the origin and end of our life; its tenderness, its tenacity, its final triumph. Long years later, when asked to contribute to a symposium, *If I Had But One Sermon to Preach,* I took the same text, pointing out that every preacher has only one sermon to preach, no matter how many texts or topics he may employ, the truth nearest to his own heart, "his truth," the truth central in his faith; albeit he may use many variations and improvisations of emphasis and appeal. If one takes a great text, or a truth which fills the earth and the sky— like "the love which moves the sun and all the stars," as Dante said—the people get something, even if the sermon is poor. By the same fact, if the Love of God is the first reality and the final revelation of life, many other things are not true—one need not point them out.

My first pastorate was in a little church at Rose Hill, in Whiteside County, only a few miles away. There was no church building, and the services were held in the Schoolhouse, twice a month, alternating with the Methodists. But "the Jews had no dealings with the Samaritans"; the two groups might have lived on different planets. In those days the members of one Baptist church were not allowed to commune with another Baptist church, on the theory, logical enough, that one ought to commune with the church under whose discipline he lived; but even then church discipline was largely a legend. Just the same, I began to build bridges and break down barriers. Many of the Methodist young people attended my services, and I was happy to have them. Somehow I got a gig and a beautiful brown pony, Selim, and went to and fro to my appointments, looking, Jenkins Roberts said, like a jockey. Usually I went down on a Friday, the guest of one of the church families, and so in time made the rounds. They were dear people, friendly, hospitable, infinitely kind to a boy-preacher—the Fletchers, the Hollingsworths, the Parvins, the Joneses, and one who stands out like a star, Robert Peterson, who had a rare gift of prayer, which is as much a distinct gift as the writing of poetry. Often I used to call upon him to pray at the service; he seemed actually to climb upon the knees of God and talk to Him as a little child. His prayers did me more good than my sermons ever did anyone. They were never the same; he employed the idiom of the Bible, in which not only his style but his very soul was saturated.

Oddly enough, I do not remember what salary, if any, the Rose Hill Church paid me for my services. They must have paid me something, but I have never had much interest in money. Brother and I raised crops of cotton, and for a time I worked in a cotton-gin—hard work, but great fun—watching the cotton pour out of the gin in white waves, which we gathered up, pressed into the baler, and made into bales. Carlyle was right; physical labor cleanses our minds and eyes and souls; it gives us insights and understandings of truth not to be achieved by leisure or enjoyment. However, there was one slight rift in the lute:

"So far, I have never heard you refer to the wrath and indignation of God," said one of my deacons one day, the last man from whom I would have expected it.

"Really, do you think that God ever gets mad?" I replied;

"He ought to be able to control His temper." He believed in
the Love of God—yes, certainly, he hastened to say—but apparently it was somehow conditioned by His indignation, as has
been true in many books of theology I have read since that
day. How strange that Christian people have found it so hard
to believe in the God of Jesus; anyway I was not a damnationist,
and did not propose to be.

Again and again my step-father warned me in regard to my
relations with women, on the ground that the good name of a
preacher ought to be above reproach. Of course he was right,
but there was no reason for fear, although I nearly got caught
in a mess, when a girl asked to ride with me as far as Tom
Bean, the nearest railroad station, on my way home. Two of my
church boys tipped me off, telling me that her reputation was
none too good, and so I did not take her for a ride. The famil-
iarities in which young people indulge today—petting and the
like—were unknown in my boyhood; such things were simply
not done, not even thought of. Among the girl friends of my
youth two stand out vividly: Lizzie McCracken, with her crown
of golden hair, her big blue eyes, her pretty ways, and Birdie
Lackey, with her raven black hair and dark eyes, slim, trim,
and lovely. There was a woman, Miss Emma Payne, much
older than myself—I was ordained at the ripe age of nineteen
—a kind of goddess whom I worshiped afar off. The same thing
is true of nearly every boy; if the women do not know it, here
is information for them. Many years later on a London street
I saw a woman the living image of Miss Emma, as we called
her. No doubt I stared at her, astonished that two people could
be so much alike. She began to talk with me; whereupon I
made signs resembling the deaf and dumb alphabet. "A d——
deafy," she said, in a rich Cockney accent, and went her way.
She was disgusted, and so was I—angry that one of her ilk should
look like the woman I adored in days gone by.

My ministry at Rose Hill was a success; we had revival services—a "protracted meeting," it was called—and many young
people came into the church. In a clear pool of water I baptized twenty-five in one day, one almost old enough to be my

grandfather. Since those days I have had a deep sympathy for the congregations of rural and village churches who serve as punching-bags, so to speak, on which young men learn to preach. Yet there is no other way to learn to preach but by preaching, and I still marvel at the patient kindness of the people. Those kindly folk—except, perhaps, some of the boys and girls—have long since fallen into dust, but I remember them with gratitude and affection. At last I went away to the Southern Baptist Theological Seminary, at Louisville, Kentucky, and never returned to the first church of which it was my honor to be pastor.

..... 3 .....

Seminary and Heresy

MY WELCOME to the Baptist Seminary in Louisville, Kentucky, in 1894 was an earthquake! It happened early in the morning, soon after I arrived, and I escaped injury by getting up early. I was shaving the fuzz off my face. There was a brief shock and rumble, and a huge block of plaster from the ceiling of the room fell on the bed where I had been sleeping; it would have smashed me badly. It gave one a creepy feeling. At first we did not know what it was, thinking it some kind of explosion, but the excitement was intense. Across the street, diagonally, from New York Hall, our dormitory, stood a huge colored church. In an incredibly short time frantic crowds of colored people were shouting, praying, trying to get into the church— they thought the end of the world had come. But policemen stood guard, refusing to allow them to enter. It was the first earthquake shock I had ever experienced, and the last.

In those days the Seminary stood in the center of the city, at the corner of Broadway and Fifth Streets, New York Hall fronting on Fifth Street, Norton Hall, containing the class-rooms and offices of the faculty, on Broadway. The Library was a detached building across Fifth Street. The Seminary buildings covered almost an entire city block, except the eastern end where two famous Presbyterian Churches stood, Warren Memorial and the Fourth Church. Since my day the entire Seminary, I understand, has been moved from the center of the city, and a new plant has been built in the suburbs; I have never seen it. Time and again, I have been told, the question has come up whether I should be invited back to my old seminary, but I have never been forgiven, apparently, for leaving the Baptist Church. It was, and is, the greatest Theological Seminary in the world, as regards numbers, except for the Mohammedan Seminary in Cairo, Egypt, where young men memorize the Koran. When we had 325 students we celebrated the event.

John A. Broadus, so long President, at once an orator and a scholar, had just passed to his crowning; I never saw him. But his book, *Preparation and Delivery of Sermons,* a classic in that field—three times revised since his day—was a textbook. He was followed in the presidency by William H. Whitsitt, a gracious gentleman, who had taught Greek in Richmond College, and now taught church history and the graduate course in philosophy, to which courses in mysticism and psychology were attached. Why mysticism—the word does not matter, but the reality does—without which the head of religion is cold and its hands limp—was shunted off into a sideshow, I was never able to understand. In after years I studied deeply the masters of the inner life, seeking their method of the "inward doing of good," their technique of being "in Christ," which was a key-phrase with St. Paul; but in this adventure my seminary gave me no aid at all. One may have the skeleton of scholarship, exact and accurate, but if he does not know how to apply spiritual energy in daily life, he may fail of those achievements of spiritual culture most worth while.

In the same way, psychology was crowded into a corner. Yet Freud, Jung, Adler and others were beginning their work, exploring "the abysmal depths of personality"; but news of their findings did not reach our seminary—if it did it was kept as a "military secret," to be shared only with the elect. Freud, to be sure, overemphasized "sex," and was essentially materialistic and pessimistic, with his "id, ego, and superego." Jung stressed too much the sense of "inferiority"—soul-shyness; but Adler was optimistic, if not idealistic. There were also James, Ames, Pratt, and many others, helping us to understand the various types of spiritual experience and social psychology as well; helping us toward the fulfillment of the ancient maxim, "Know thyself." These studies affected profoundly the interpretation of religion in its inner meanings; they freed me from the "sin obsession," which has afflicted so many theologians, to which Jesus was a stranger. There is sin enough in the world and in ourselves—God knows—but not as much as some people seem to think. Indeed, in my short lifetime, I have seen the growth of all the psyche-sciences, not only psychology, but psychiatry, psychotherapy, and psychoanalysis, all coming in response to a deep need. The first book on *The Psychology of Religion* was written by Edwin Starbuck, later my colleague in the University of Iowa; he used the questionnaire method largely, because no other device was then available. Today we know that religious experience is not for one type of temperament capable of an emotional explosion, as was held, quite unconsciously, in my boyhood; but that a man may pass from "death unto life," and not be able to fix the date, as was true of Phillips Brooks.

Dr. Sampey taught the Old Testament. Slender and graceful of figure, with raven black hair and dark blue eyes, he was at once incisive and impassioned in his exposition of the prophets, the greatest dynasty of moral genius in the history of religion. It was understood that he was writing a Commentary on Isaiah, for which I waited and watched for years, but in vain. The New Testament was taught by Dr. A. T. Robertson, who looked like a member of the Battle family, with a slight hint of a stammer in his voice. He was an amazing scholar, whose monumental *Grammar of the Greek New Testament* was a prodigious feat of research; he gave us many popular books besides, including the *Life of Broadus,* his father-in-law, and *Luke the Historian.* Many years later, after my return from the City Temple, I was called to the King's Weigh House Church in London, whose minister, W. E. Orchard, had entered the Roman Church. The fact was duly noted in the Baptist press, and the prediction was made that I might be headed in the same direction. Dr. Robertson happened to be preaching in Philadelphia, and spent an afternoon with me, just to assure himself that one of his "boys" had no intention of entering the Church of Rome. He need not have had any fear; such a thought had never entered my mind. Dr. E. C. Dargan was Professor of Preaching, and he was a master of the art. A tiny man, he seemed to catch fire when he preached, and if he quoted poetry, one could not tell where the poetry ended and his prose began. A sermon, he insisted, is a work of art, or should be, as truly as a lyric or an epic. Its purpose is to convince the mind—less by argument than by insight—to fire the heart, and to move the will; it must have an object as well as a subject. One of the best loved men on our campus was Henry Herbert Harris, Professor of Apologetics; "Old Soc," we called him, because of his ability to reduce a student to a heap of white ashes by slyly asking a few questions, after the manner of Socrates, and then healing the hurt with a smile.

LINES OF LIFE

In theology our teacher was Dr. F. H. Kerfort, "Old Tige," we nicknamed him, because of his sideburns and his piercing blue-gray eyes. He was a bit more aloof than his colleagues, but a kindly, gentle-hearted man when one penetrated the barrier of shyness behind which he lived. I do not remember that he ever invited a group of students to his home, as the other professors did. Diligently I mastered the definitions and distinctions of historic theology, in the familiar pattern of Calvinism, as set forth on the *Theology* of Boyce, our textbook; Boyce was to our seminary what Hodge was to Princeton. To me that theology was as dead as the dodo and as dull as ditch water. Robert Browning, with his insight as swift as zigzag lightning, meant more to me than Jonathan Edwards, with his "Sinners in the Hands of an Angry God." Indeed, the poets have always taught me more and better theology than the theologians. Once a year, instead of a lecture, Dr. Kerfort preached to us, always from the same text, "Sir, we would see Jesus"—I know the sermon by heart. It was deeply moving, showing the simple religion of our teacher and the focus of his faith. In the class one day Dr. Kerfort casually remarked, "Brethren, do not read the sermons of Fred Robertson until your theology is fixed." It was bad psychology; I for one did not want my theology fixed, petrified, and hermetically sealed. When the class closed, I hot-footed it to the library to get the sermons of Robertson, some of which, like "The Loneliness of Jesus," are among the greatest in the language. Here was a master of simple lucid English, a vital mind, a soul alive to the deepest issues of life and faith, who had known the agony of doubt and the triumph of faith. It was impossible for Robertson to be commonplace, and his sermon-structure was perfect. Then I read his *Life, Letters and Addresses,* edited by Stopford Brooke, and learned that he was a frail man of many moods, a member of an old Army family in England, but, disappointed that his commission did not come soon enough, entered the Church. He held a private service in the chapel and solemnly buried the soldier in him, all except his courage, vowing never to allow his pulpit to become "a coward's castle." How anyone could regard Frederick Robertson as dangerous to the theology of anyone, remains a mystery to me. Later I preached in Holy Trinity Church, in Brighton, where he exercised his brief ministry and left a tradition of haunting goodness. Also, reading his popular lectures on great poets, given to workingmen, put an idea into my mind, which became a policy of my ministry, using the mid-week service of the church to interpret great literature. Thus, in a left-handed way, my teacher rendered me a very great service.

A few blocks down Broadway stood a great Jewish Synagogue, and, greatly daring, I attended a Sunday morning service. Some of my fellow students regarded it as nothing short of a scandal. It was the first time I had ever entered a synagogue, and the service was most impressive to me, especially when the Cantor sang a Psalm in Hebrew, which stirred me strangely, like a voice from the far past; and the reading from the Torah —the Law—from a scroll in Hebrew. Rabbi Adolphus Moses was a stately, grave and noble preacher, with a slight brogue in his voice which I was unable to identify. Later, after the service, I spoke to him and asked if it would be proper for me to attend a Friday evening service, since the Jewish Sabbath begins on Friday evening. "Certainly, my son, worship with us whenever you like, and know that you are always welcome." The service on Friday evening was different in one particular —the names of those who had died were called and their loved-ones stood up; prayers were then offered for the living and the dead. The dead, I understood, were remembered in the prayers of the congregation for a year after they had passed away. My fellow students, when I related these things, were horrified; they agreed that my heresy was going from bad to worse, and there was no telling where it would end. To me prayer, if it is valid at all, must be valid always, everywhere and for everybody. "Out of sight, out of mind," may be true of an animal, but not of a human being. The human heart, in its love and loss and longing, was more to be trusted than any theory of theology—it is older and deeper. For me the Love and Grace of God were absolute, and to try to limit either by a creed or a coffin lid was not only unbelief, but sheer vanity, making our petty minds the limit of what is limitless. It is larger than any diagram of dogma. Here was my quarrel with the church of my fathers—its inability to believe that "life is ever lord of death, and love can never lose its own." Yet I do not remember ever to have offered prayers for the departed, until, years later, I entered the Episcopal Church, where such prayers are a part not only of the Office of the Dead, but of the Holy Communion. Even there, by implication at least, prayers are limited to "those who have finished their course in faith," whereas it is blind souls who have lost their way in the dark who stand in need of prayer. Death does not end the love of God or the hope of man. Rabbi Moses and I became good friends; I often talked with him in his study about problems of Old Testament interpretation, and after his death exchanged letters with his wife.

About this time, in 1894, I read an article by Andrew Carnegie entitled "Look Ahead," in the *North American Review,* as I remember it. He boldly proposed an all-out federal union of Great Britain and the United States, and a common citizenship; or, failing that, a defensive alliance, or at least a pooling of naval forces. The suggestion was seconded by Sir George Clarke of England, in a later issue. Finally Captain Mahan, of our Navy, an authority on sea power in history, reviewed the subject. From the point of view of sea strategy, as well as the kinship of the two peoples, he was in favor of the proposal; but not at that time. For one thing, America was not then interested in sea power, but he said the time would come when it would be. Nor were the people of Britain ready to entertain such a suggestion seriously. The proposal was premature, he said, and would remain so "antecedent to the great teacher, Experience"; because neither nation as yet realized the common interest. "The ground is not yet prepared," he concluded. Those articles impressed me profoundly, and it became a conviction with me that some such project would have to be adopted, sooner or later. The two bases of our one civilization, as I interpreted it, were, and are, the Holy Scriptures and the Common Law, the Bible and Blackstone. Having so much in common, it was my belief that "the lands of the Common Law," as Dicey put it, had a common obligation to keep the peace and security of the world. Joseph Chamberlain and John Hay talked about such things, but they talked in whispers. For thirty years I went to and fro between America and England, advocating closer fellowship, understanding and co-operation. In America my plea was received with a polite silence, in England with an amused tolerance. It takes a major operation to get an idea into the human mind. If the suggestion of Andrew Carnegie and Captain Mahan had been adopted in 1894, two world wars might have been averted. Yet I have lived to hear a British Prime Minister propose a common citizenship for Americans and Britons in an address at Harvard University; my dream has come true in part, albeit not without "blood, sweat and tears."

Dwight L. Moody passed through Louisville and preached at the Fourth Presbyterian Church. Always I had wanted to see and hear him, and by going early I got a seat in the gallery. The church was packed, there was hardly room for Moody to stand. A short, stockily built man, with brown beard touched with gray, wearing a Prince Albert coat, he talked directly, as if a business man were laying down a proposition—he was so wise that he was simple, and so simple that he was wise. He told his religious experience as artlessly as a little child; men wept. I have seldom been more stirred in my life. Men rarely talk of such intimate, inward things today, even in the pulpit; the Oxford Group tried to bring this "heavenly gossip" back into vogue, but did not get very far. In his address he used two famous sentences, which had meant much to hundreds of thousands of men, as they did to Wilfred Grenfell, a young medical student in London, who went to a Moody meeting to see what the Yankee evangelist looked like, and came away a new man, God-dedicated: "Let God have your life, He can do more with it than you can"; and a little later, "No one can estimate what God can do with one completely consecrated life." Moody himself was an example of the meaning of his words. Later I was to know his brother-in-law, Fleming H. Revell, one of my first publishers, a man of the same type. The words of Bossuet were in my mind as I listened to Moody: "Speak to me only of necessary truths." Moody ignored debated issues, as when, during the controversy about Evolution, he took Henry Drummond into his team, regardless of his views on the subject.

For more than a year, during my seminary days, I served as associate chaplain of a great gray prison across the river, in Indiana. It gave me a permanent interest in the problems of crime and its literature, crime which weaves a dark fringe on the border of society and sometimes strikes at its heart. As all prisoners were required to attend chapel services, I was always assured of a congregation. Looking into their faces was a study—hard faces, weak faces, and now and then an attractive face. In talking with the men in their cells, I never found a single "guilty" man; all had been "framed," or the judge was "unjust," or someone had a grudge against them—yet they had committed the most atrocious crimes. What struck me was that they had the mentality of boys of ten, or less, and no moral sense at all. They talked of how a man was "rubbed out" or "bumped off," as one might talk of a fly pulped on a windowpane. They were devoid of emotion; not immoral but amoral. No one has learned how to step up the emotional development of a human being. Reading case histories was a heartbreaking task. One learned of the homes in which the men had grown up, their social environment, the hard-scrabble poverty, and often of the cruelty of their parents. "It is sad to see no good in goodness," wrote Gogol; but here were men for whom truth, beauty and goodness did not exist.

Later, in London, I came to know H. B. Irving, the actor, son of Sir Henry Irving, who, from playing criminal parts on the stage, was led into the study of the psychology of crime, and wrote books about it. He spoke for me at the Thursday noon service in the City Temple, on "Religion and the Drama." He held that the people in prison are much like the people outside, only they yielded to the wild, mad moods and passions which visit all of us betimes, from which we are mercifully restrained obeying. But that does not explain the mystery and horror of congenital crime, some "defect of will and taint of blood," some twist which cannot be untied, as in the story of the Jukes family which left a dark trail in our history. An execution is not a pretty thing to witness; some men crumpled up at the end, others, hard as nails, went laughing or cursing to their fate. The cost of crime is fabulous; its cause remains a mystery. Anyway I am sure that my preaching to prisoners did little good, if any.

MUD THROWING

Years earlier, it appeared, Dr. Whitsitt, our Professor of Church History, before he became President, had written an article on "The Baptists," for *Johnson's Encyclopedia,* signing it with his initials, "W. H." In his article he remarked that it is impossible to trace an unbroken line of Baptist Churches from the days of the Apostles down to our own time; the evidence does not justify it—the Baptists did not practice immersion until 1640. Someone discovered the article and launched a vicious attack upon our President, intending to drive him out of office. No issue of orthodoxy was involved; it was purely a matter of historical research, a bit of church mythology having no basis in fact. The attack was ruthless, with petty heel-snapping criticism, but Dr. Whitsitt made no reply in kind; indeed he made no reply at all. Some of us felt that the President knew more about the subject than all of his sandlot enemies, and we came to his defense, writing articles for the church press in his behalf. Then we, in turn, were attacked in a different way—we were accused of being light-headed, if not actually immoral. How odd that one should be deemed immoral on the ground of a difference of opinion on a matter of history—if you differ from me you are rotten. One paper, published in the western part of Kentucky, reported that our group defending "Uncle Billy," as our President was affectionately called, had been seen attending the Buckingham Theater on a Sunday afternoon, a dive theater.

The editor knew the facts, or he could have easily found them out. He told the truth, but not the whole truth, and a half truth was equal to a lie. B. Fay Mills, an evangelist, was holding a series of meetings in the city, and a group from our seminary, and from the Presbyterian Seminary, served as a board of ushers. It was in our capacity as ushers that we attended the Buckingham Theater, not otherwise. The editor knew that fact, but he deliberately tried to besmear a group of young ministers, brand them for life as heretics, and make their future more difficult, all because of a difference of historical interpretation. In short, here was a man trying to prove himself a loyal Baptist by failing to be a gentleman, much less a Christian. He accused us, by inference, of being immoral—if it is immoral to go to a theater, which it is not—while he himself was downright dishonest and defamatory. At the time, the whole affair made me smoke with indignation; but time passes and one forgets—we must forgive in order to live. One thing I learned from "the Whitsitt controversy," as it came to be known, which John Galsworthy pointed out later: people are more tenacious of, more bigoted about, inherited traditional beliefs than they are about ideas they may have arrived at in their own thinking. No doubt it is because inherited beliefs are habitual and steeped in emotion, and it is how we are "emotionally conditioned" in youth, to use the modern jargon, that decides the set of our minds. Hence our fear and dread of change in matters in which our emotions are involved; it is easier to change a way of thinking than a way of feeling. William James went so far as to say that few people ever have fresh ideas after they are twenty-five, which explains the awful load of inertia every leader of the race must drag in the slow advance.

EXTRA-CURRICULAR

It is astonishing how much one can accomplish by the diligent use of those heel-taps and fag-ends of time which we too often throw into the wastebasket. One of our professors was almost invariably a few minutes late for his lecture, and by going a little early to class and keeping a book in my desk, I read many books not included in our courses of study. If I should make a complete list, it would be almost unbelievable. Looking back upon my seminary days, I gratefully admit an unpayable debt to my teachers, great scholars and great gentlemen—more, perhaps, to the men themselves than to what they taught me—and I can never do more than make a payment "on account." Yet the fact remains that the things which did most for my development, and lived longest in my heart, were the books I read outside the field of theology—except the Bampton Lectures of Canon W. H. Fremantle, on *The World as the Subject of Redemption,* which impressed me indelibly and influenced all my thinking for years, because it talked in terms of salvation, not salvage. Few sermons were read except those of Newman, Robertson, and David Swing, who was a new kind of preacher, whose *Truths For Today* were among my guideposts.

About this time my uncle, Dr. J. M. Fort, sent me two books, which I read with deep interest: *The History of the Warfare Between Science and Theology,* by Andrew D. White, President of Cornell University, and a one volume edition of the works of Channing. The first book, carefully documented, told the sad story of the opposition of theology to all the advances of science—always an unseeing, often an unscrupulous, opposition. The second book, noble in thought and style, opened many windows; some of its great passages haunt me to this day.

Poetry, fiction, drama, essays, biography fed my soul; here were free spirits who had insight and art—serenity, vision, beauty. As John Morley said, "The purpose of wise reading is to bring sunshine into our hearts and to drive moonshine out of our heads."

For example, the reading of *Adam Bede,* by George Eliot, was an unforgettable experience, in the light of her own life, written, as she said of Savonarola, "in virtue of yesterday's faith, hoping it will return tomorrow." How such a mind could have fallen under the spell of Strauss, who turned everything into myth, legend, symbol—"Strauss-sick; it makes me ill," she said—remains a mystery to me, as does her captivity to the wooden philosophy of Herbert Spencer. It is hard to realize that Spencer was at one time a little tin deity, especially to young college folk, who swallowed his ponderous phrase, "an infinite and eternal energy from which all things proceed," as if it had been a divine revelation. No doubt he expressed a mood, and when the mood passed, he passed with it; nothing of Spencer remains except his prophecy of "the coming tyranny of the masses," which we have seen fulfilled in the statism of our day. It was lucky that George Eliot did not marry Spencer; he was a porcupine and would have ruined her life—she who had the mind of a man and the sensitive, clinging needs of a woman. The prayer of Dinah Morris in *Adam Bede,* offered for poor Hetty crumpled up in her cell, frozen with fear, her heart hard with hatred, is one of the loveliest in the language, but for George Eliot it was but the memory of a faded faith. After her maturity, Christianity was a thing ineffable and haunting, but only a tale of beauty and pity, heart-spun not brain-woven. This vacuum in her heart deepened her native melancholy, if it did not mar her art. Yet her sense of the moral law and its relentless nemesis remained vivid and valid; there is a smoking Mt. Sinai in every one of her stories, but no Mt. Olivet. Her idealists fall not in combat with dragons; they break their necks by the stumbling of a horse. With the loss of faith in the immortal life, only a congregation of echoes was left—

> Of those immortal dead who live again
> In minds made better by their presence.

At first Walt Whitman repelled me, both by the formlessness of his poetry, and by what sounded like a vague, dreamy, self-celebration. That is, until I learned that "Song of Myself" is a song of all souls, rich, poor, high, low, and that his poetry is really a celebration of the worth and wonder of life. He is the one universalist in our history; he excludes all exclusiveness— in no one else do we find such all-embracing comradeship. The greatest poetic personality our land has known, he is a mystic whose vision is turned not upon another world, but upon our prodigal and abundant America. The very names of its cities are to him as a rosary. There is no sediment of cynicism in his heart, no fear, no sense of futility; he is very sure of God, and his lyric love of life is joyous and contagious. Nor has anyone else heard such "Whispers of Heavenly Death"—the death, that is, of all that is unheavenly within us. Toward the end Lincoln, taught by Mary Harlan, learned to love his long, silvery lines affirming the immortal life. Lincoln did not doubt the immortal life, he only doubted his worthiness of it. All through the years Whitman has been a source of strength and inward sustaining; he has helped me to believe in America as I believe in God, helped me to keep its great Dream alive in my heart. "Faith is the antiseptic of the soul," he said; it disinfects us of doubt and dull dismay, of the cynicism that seeps into the soul; it finds meaning in life, and arms us to withstand the siege of battering days.

It was thrilling to read the poems of Emily Dickinson, as they appeared first in 1890, and in 1894. "Bolts of melody," they were later described, and not inaptly, but better still in her own words, they are—

> Like signal esoteric sips
> Of sacramental wine.

How such an ethereal being, half elf and half angel, a radiant rebel, was allowed to live in the solemn air of the valley of the Connecticut, is hard to know. She was stardust, lightning and fragrance all mixed up with a smile, "the confederate of every contraband desire." Elusive, aloof, alone but never lonely, she was incredibly happy, playing hide-and-seek with God. To live, she said, is so startling that it leaves little time for other occupations. She looked upon "this curious earth" with deep-seeing eyes, jotting her thoughts down on bits of paper, with now and then a line that flashed like a silver arrow shot in the twilight; a seer of piercing insight. She learned the "other loneliness," as few have ever done. In spite of her incurable happiness she was never able to disengage herself from "that eternal preoccupation with death." She had no fear of death, but only wonder at the "overtakelessness" of those who have accomplished it. As these words are written, more than half a thousand of her poems, hitherto unknown, have leaped to light, with the same blend of levity and profundity, and with lines that sting the mind and stir the heart.

No words can ever tell my debt to Emerson, whose serene and luminous spirit touched me when it was most needed. He helped me to see life and believe in it, to fear God and not be afraid of Him; the world seemed to move in a new orbit. Years have come and gone, but that day I became acquainted with him is fresh and vivid in my memory, and his spell has lost none of its power. "The foregoing generations beheld God and nature face to face; we, through their eyes. Why should not we enjoy an original relation to the universe? Why should we not have a religion of revelation to us?" God is not dead. There is more truth in the written, and the unwritten, word of God. If we are brave enough to trust our vision and obey it, we can know God as did the men of old. Emerson did not argue;

he let in the light. He was a seer, a sayer, a servant of the truth, telling what he saw with the dignity of a golden voice. Fortunately we have his diaries from the age of fifteen almost to the end; his life was as stainless as a mortal life can be. All men felt that life was larger, more exalted and ennobled because the great soul of Emerson passed through it. What a legacy of light to leave to his race!

Such readings—and others too many to name, ranging far and wide—saved me from the dull dronings of theology, its dogmas mere echoes of older echoes. Theology, by rights, ought to be the most entrancing of subjects; it has to do with God, who alone is permanently interesting, God who is the meaning of life and its mystery; God first, God last; God, infinitesimally vast; God whose love is without limit, the Creator and Redeemer of man. It deals with the piteous, passionate, pathetic life of man, his groping after unity within, his effort to feel at home in a universe, now lucid and lovely, now dark and terrible; his loneliness, his fellowship; his hurrying days and his strange exodus; his questions Whence? Why? Whither?—his heroic faith; his death-defying hope; his heavenly Brother, Jesus. What stupendous themes for thought, as far and as fast as the mind can fly. Art, whether in music, poetry, drama, architecture, liturgy, symbol, sacrament, is the language of religion; but theology speaks in drab prose, its style as heavy-footed as a procession of elephants, with seldom a flash of insight and beauty. Never have I read a book of theology which was also a work of art; not one!

HENRY WATTERSON

In order to eke out an income, always slender—a situation not unfamiliar to theological students—I sought service on the Louisville *Courier-Journal* as a reporter of religious news in the city. This meant that I had the honor of meeting the editor, Henry Watterson—"Marse Henry," he was called—an extraordinary personality; a man of authentic genius, who had that spurt of spirit which makes a champion. His ambition was to be a musician, but an accident which injured an eye and a hand turned him into journalism. He did his writing in the morning, in bed, came to his office at noon, and stayed until the paper was "put to bed." He received me most cordially, and I told him how many years I had taken his paper just to read his editorials. He asked me if I intended to enter journalism. No, I told him, having put my hand to the plow as a minister, I intended to plow a straight furrow to the end. He said that a training in journalism would stand me in good stead. It would show me how to state things simply and directly; a minister, he added, is often content to get ideas out of his own mind, but a journalist must get them into other minds. He talked, brilliantly, of "the nose for news," of how an incident or an idea has news value only as it is related to public interest of the moment.

Then he took a book from the top of his desk and gave it to me, saying, "There, Laddie, read that and learn how to write." It was a copy of his favorite book, *Pendennis,* by W. M. Thackeray, whom he regarded as the greatest master of narrative style in our language. All the while I was wondering by what magic the chubby man before me, with his tousled hair and stubby mustache, his keen gray eyes, and his arms shorter than they had a right to be, could take ordinary, everyday words and make them gleam and dance and sing, as if he had some rhythm and cadence of his own. Style is the man, the accent of his mind, the gesture of his soul. It is more than a mastery of the weight, worth, color and music of words, it is a blending of words which turns sounds into song. Some men are able to communicate personality in print, others cannot do it. Others can do it in the spoken word, but when what they say is printed it is as colorless as a cash-register. No one knows the secret, and if he does he cannot impart it to anyone else. It remains a mystery past finding out, alike for the man who writes and the man who reads.

On another day, in a mood of reminiscence, the Colonel told me how, in 1866, he went to London, with a young wife and a roll of ambitious manuscript, found work to do and a publisher, but he never would tell what the manuscript was about. Armed with a letter of introduction from the sister of Professor Huxley, all doors were open, and he lived in the clouds of two worlds, that of Bohemia, of which the Savage Club was the center, and that of the new apocalypse of science which eddied about the *Fortnightly Review*. He met and knew Huxley, Tyndall, Spencer and George Eliot, and, through Artemus Ward, then in London, he came to know the Keenes and Kembles, still upon the stage. His beloved Thackeray was gone, but Dickens still lived and wrote. There was a look of far-away and long-ago in his eyes as he told of those gay days and of old London town which he loved so much. Also, he confided to me that he was preparing to write a Life of Lincoln, and had made some researches, clearing up disputed points, among other things, the story that Lincoln was born out of wedlock, which had been hawked about in the "black market" of gossip for years. He had gone to Hardin County, Kentucky, and, finding no record of the marriage there, it occurred to him that the young couple might have gone to the next county for their wedding. His surmise was correct; in Washington County he found the record intact, and, learning that the minister who married them was still living, he secured his affidavit that he had officiated at the ceremony. Lincoln himself died without knowing the truth.

Watterson went to Switzerland to write his Life of Lincoln, but no sooner had he arrived and settled down to his task than W. J. Bryan was nominated on the Democratic ticket for the Presidency, on a "free silver" platform, following his famous "Cross of Gold" speech. Watterson sent his answer to the challenge, "No compromise with dishonor!" dropped everything and came home to fight the new "heresy." His Life of Lincoln was never written, to our great regret—it would have been a gem. Needless to say he fought with glittering weapons, supporting the Palmer-Buckner ticket, intended to draw off enough conservative Democrats to defeat the "boy-orator." It was a wild and whirling campaign, the first national election I had ever witnessed, and it was great fun to attend all kinds of meetings, listening to excited oratory, mostly sound and fury, signifying little. The "sound-money" parade was a big show, with bands and banners, thousands brought in from Indiana and Ohio to swell the ranks, superbly organized by Mark Hanna and carried through with fervor and flub-dub. The Democratic counterattacks were equally enthusiastic, but not so well set up. The finest speech that I heard was delivered by former President Benjamin Harrison, across the river at New Albany, in Indiana. His forthright thought, his stripped and clipped simplicity of style were most attractive; if I had been old enough to vote I would have voted his ticket. The funniest speech was by Job Hedges of New York, whom I came to know in later years. Everything he did or said was funny, and he paid the penalty for it. When he tried to be serious no one took him seriously. Contemplated from afar, objectively, the campaign was an orgy of oratory, a jamboree, an emotional debauch. When it was over many felt that the country had been "saved," as we always do when our side wins. At this distance, when all the world is off "the gold standard" and may have to go through proceedings of bankruptcy, the issues of that campaign seem remote and unreal; a big pow-wow about money and nothing else. Our world today is so unlike the world of that day that it might well be another planet.

LADY BROWN-EYES

My room-mate, S. R. Williams, was studying to be a medical missionary in China. To add to his income he was pastor of a church at Sanders, Kentucky, midway between Louisville and Cincinnati. He had a rather prostrating illness and asked me to take his pulpit for a month, which was a turning point in my life. It was all accidental, as we say, knowing not what we say—perhaps there is no such thing as an accident. There I met the Dream Girl; she played the organ, and that was where the music started—a beautiful, long-lasting romance. My room-mate was interested in the same girl too, as I learned to my dismay, and that posed a problem for me. However, her father

did not relish the idea of his daughter going to China as the
wife of a missionary. In fact he was not enthusiastic about foreign missions, an attitude with which, at the moment and for
purposes of strategy, I fully agreed. Of course, I did not wish
my room-mate to have a long illness, but I thought that an
indefinite period of rest would do him good. His sickness did
last for quite a while, and that gave me an opportunity to fix
matters up. By the time he returned to his pulpit he did not
have a ghost of a chance. The brethren looked at me askance
for having defended our President when he was attacked, but
Lady Brown-eyes stood by me through thick and thin and
fought my battles, as she has done through all the years.

In regard to the missionary enterprise, about which my
father-in-law-to-be was indifferent, if not sceptical, I was deeply
puzzled. In our seminary we were told about Carey and his
work in India, and Judson and his adventure in Burma, but
the idea of exporting Baptist dogmas to far-off lands did not
excite my zeal. The reply of Gandhi to Stanley Jones, who
asked him how he could bring the religion of Jesus to India,
seemed apt: "Leave your dogmas at home. The trouble is that
your people have been inoculated with a mild form of Christianity, which renders them immune to the real thing." In our
seminary we were taught little about other Christian churches,
much less about the whole sweep and romance of the Christian
advance to the ends of the earth. Nor were we taught anything
about the great religions of the world, to which thousands and
millions of human beings owe their allegiance and in which
they find solace for today and hope for the morrow. They were,
in fact, regarded—by implication at least—as so many devices
of the devil invented to deceive mankind. One would have
thought that in a Divinity School one would have been taught
the story of religion; but no.

By chance I found in the library two books by James Freeman Clarke, *Ten Great Religions* and *Events and Epochs in
Religious History,* which opened a fascinating field of study.
Later I read books no end, trying to grasp the central idea in
each great religion, its world-view, and its method of spiritual

culture. The result of these studies was a sense—a vision—of
the Spirit of God moving within all the multi-colored forms
of religion, making my life an adventure in discovering the
unity of the spiritual life of the race; just as John Woolman,
the Quaker, rejoiced in finding Thomas à Kempis a brother,
albeit wearing a different ecclesiastical habit and living in a far-
off time. Religions are many, Religion is one, perhaps one thing
—the life of God in the soul of man, which, because it is life,
takes many forms, differing in degree of development, depth
of insight and method of appeal, but one in the profound human experience of fellowship with the Father of spirits. Instead of weakening my faith in Christianity, it greatly increased
it, making me at home in every place where men foregather to
pray, knowing that the Church of Christ includes St. Peter's at
Rome, St. Paul's in London, the plain chapel of Martineau,
and a Quaker Meeting House.

All teachers in aid of faith became my friends and helpers,
whether Augustine or Emerson, Wesley or Fénelon—mystic,
rationalist, sacramentalist—since the devout life is the same,
however its outlook of intellect may differ. Thereafter, I was
ready and eager to sit at the feet of any saint or sage who had
any truth to tell, although I found it difficult to follow the
Eastern mind in its devotion to abstract, impersonal law, in
contrast with the vivid, glowing Personality of Jesus, whose
teachings are dipped and dyed in all the colors of human life,
in the book of white samite where the sweet Voice sounds and
the Vision dwells. Such studies, if they made me impatient
with religion as then organized, if not actually unfit for it,
at least made me a member of the Church of the Spirit—a fellow
pilgrim with all the seekers and finders of God.

GREAT PREACHING

To me Louisville is a city of many memories, not only of
noble scholars and dear teachers, but of fellowships which time
cannot destroy. "Who is the greatest preacher in the city?" I
asked Mr. Watterson one day. "Edward Powell, of course," he

replied, as if I should have known without asking. Next Sunday
I went to the old church at Fourth and Walnut, its stone steps
and huge pillars looking more like a Greek temple than the
First Christian Church. The church was crowded to the doors,
but a kindly usher found a chair for me tucked away in a far
corner, just as the preacher entered the pulpit. He was a man
of slight figure, thin light hair, and keen gray eyes—not a
graceful man, his gestures rather awkward at times, but he
seemed instantly to unite people who had walked many scattered ways into one, lifting us out of our loneliness into a fellowship of need and longing. It was all so reverent, so impressive, so real. He conducted the service less as a leader of
worship than as a leading worshiper; he read the Bible as one
who was himself a listener at the portals of the Book of the
Will of God for the Life of Man. His prayer was direct, tender,
far-ranging in its sympathies, as if he remembered the object
of his office—to lift men out of the mire of materialism into
the higher air of God and detain them there. It besought the
grace of God in that moral self-legislation which each must
enact and execute, if he is to verify truth in character. When
an hour of worship is remembered in detail—the tones of the
preacher, the insight of his sermon, the atmosphere of the
service—for forty-six years, it argues something unusual.

The sermon began quietly, but he had not spoken two para-
graphs before the spark caught, and the man, his theme, and his
audience were alike transfigured. It had to do with the holiness
of God, taking its text from the vision of the boy Isaiah in the
Temple, when he was anointed a prophet. Not a hackneyed
phrase was used; the preacher had poured the old wine into
new bottles and thrown away the lees. He did not argue, did
not make his sermons a solo-forum to debate some problem
of life or a proposition of theology. It was a pure flame, a
white light subduing, searching, exalting human souls. No one
ever forgot the terrifying vision of a universe ruled by an unholy God, where men sit by the poisoned springs of life, looking
at polluted flowers, and lifting up hands to abominable hills.
It made the very soul shudder, and often a shudder is an argu-

ment. Man can endure an indifferent world. He does not lose heart when told that the flowers are heartless and would as soon adorn a grave as a bridal altar, or when he hears the carefree song of birds in the midst of his grief. But a malignant universe is intolerable. Not only the value but the very existence of his soul is in jeopardy, and all our dear human world is cast into shadow, pent up in the kingdom of pity and death. Then followed, by contrast, a picture of a lucid and wise order where righteousness reigns, where every mountain is an altar, and all the laws of life are God's ten thousand commandments. It shook the poison out of all our wild-flowers; the vision of a man who saw the holiness of beauty, no less than the beauty of holiness. His slight figure seemed to tower to the proportions of a giant; his whole being vibrated with moral electricity; yet all was held in bounds by a firm directing hand. It was the burning speech of a man to his fellow-souls whereby they knew that in his innermost heart he was a believer.

No art of oratory could have invoked such a wonder. We were not listening to an echo of our own voices, but to a Voice other than our own, without which we are no more capable of making a better world today than we were capable of creating it in the first place. It was the haunting, thrilling voice heard in all ages of the Church; it came from beyond differences of theology and forms of worship, more vivid than music and more eloquent than architecture, its spell more mysterious than the wind in the trees; a sacrament, an incarnation and then an art. Whether spoken on bare hillsides beneath a crucifix or in a plain country meetinghouse, such words will never lose their power while human nature is the same. This quality of spirituality, so rare in men of great powers, inspires a kind of awe; men bow to it, as a field of grain bows at the breath of the winds, and are touched, if only for a moment, with that old homesickness of the soul which is the root of all religion—the sense that they are pilgrims and strangers in the earth, seeking a City that hath foundations. No wonder that radiant hour, with its glow-point of vision, still shines as a star in my heart.

TWO LITTLE BOOKS

On my way back to Texas—my seminary days ended—in a second-hand bookshop in St. Louis I picked up two tiny volumes which had an enduring influence upon my inner life. One was *Some Fruits of Solitude,* to which were added *More Fruits of Solitude,* by William Penn: epigrams jotted down in old age, summing up his spiritual insight and practical wisdom. At once a man of the spirit and a man of affairs, serene, intelligent, wise, a certain stillness brooded over his words. There was somewhat of the Eternal in the man; he was not bound by the times in which he lived, but still moves among men, turning their hearts to the wisdom of love. He founded a Christian Commonwealth in our New World; he wrote down the principles and laws which afterwards took form in our Constitution—his little books gave me a life-long interest in him as one of the greatest of the sons of men. Some of his words remain to this day as maxims of spiritual wisdom:

> The humble, merciful, just, and devout souls are everywhere of one religion; and when death hath taken off the mask, they will know one another.
> Neither despise, nor oppose, what thou dost not understand. We must not be concerned above the value of the thing that engages us; nor raised above reason, in maintaining what we think is reasonable.
> A devout man is one thing, a stickler is quite another. To be furious in religion, is to be irreligiously religious. It were better to be of no Church, than to be bitter for any.
> They that love beyond the world, cannot be separated by it. Death cannot kill, what never dies. Nor can spirits ever be divided that love and live in the same Divine principle. If absence be not death, neither is theirs.
> Death is but crossing the world, as friends do the seas; they live in one another still. They needs must be present, that love and live in that which is omnipresent.

The other little book, *The Practice of the Presence of God,* by Nicholas Herman of Lorraine, was written more than two hundred and fifty years ago. Herman was of humble life and

untrained; he had been a footman, a soldier, and was admitted
as a lay member in a community of the Carmelites in Paris, in
1666. He became known as "Brother Lawrence," because he
attained to a high degree of spiritual culture, albeit he was
only a cook and a dish-washer. He died at eighty, and his
friends brought together four conversations and fifteen of his
letters and made what proved to be a spiritual classic. Devoted
to lowly service, he hated the work he had to do. Yet he learned
a secret, almost too simple to be found out—how to think of
himself, his work, his friends as always in the presence of God.
He practiced that secret, day and night, until it became the
habit of his life. At last it freed him from drudgery, from hurry,
worry, weariness and fear; work and prayer became alike. He
could not grasp the theology of the Order to which he belonged;
he was too busy to use its elaborate spiritual exercises. His
brethren were sons of Mary; he was a son of Martha. But he
learned to live with God and do his menial work for God.
Such an art is within the reach of everyone, no matter how
humble his lot; it turns tedium into *Te Deum,* if we make it
a habit of the heart.

Here lay my deepest need, and that was why the little book
did so much for me, helping me to form new habits of the heart.
It is not enough to go to church on Sunday, or to pray each
day, just as it is not enough to eat one meal a week. One must
have some method, some day-by-day habit of making spiritual
truth true within us, and a definite spiritual objective—else
one lives at random. The older spiritual "exercises" are too
elaborate, too long, and take too much time—they were suited
to an older, slower time. One must avoid all gadgetry, and yet
one must work out a strategy of the inner life, a habit of meditation, an art for the practice of salvation, and diligently use
it, whereby to escape aimless drifting or the drag of inertia.
Most people want religion, that is, they want its consolations
without its commitments, its delights without its disciplines;
but they cannot have one without the other. They have a
capacity for religion, but not religion itself. In short, they are
only haunted by religion, unwilling to make the extra effort to

realize religion in their lives. At least "Brother Lawrence" taught me how to be a victor over life, not a victim of it.

A STAR WITNESS

How badly I needed every possible spiritual resource, I was soon to discover. After a short stay at home, I became pastor of the First Baptist Church of Paris, Texas, a town of some ten thousand people. My uncle, Dr. Joseph Fort, was a leading layman in the church, which had recently built a beautiful new church. But, alas! the congregation had been divided—split wide open, in fact—by the theology of its minister, Dr. George M. Fortune, an able man, but too iconoclastic; the feud had gone beyond all hope of reconciliation. As usual, many factors entered into the situation, both sides had become adepts in the black art of gossip—the whole town was stirred by an ugly spirit. Dr. Fortune had been accused of immorality, on no grounds whatsoever, except the dictum: "We have all the truth; if you disagree with us it is because your life is rotten." It was spiritually ridiculous to me, there was nothing resembling the spirit of Jesus in it. A cocoanut in a village of peanuts, Dr. Fortune left the pulpit for the law. Aside from the personal equation, the point of theology was the hair-splitting distinction whether Christ died "for us" or "instead of us," like a Divine scapegoat. The minority had withdrawn and set itself up to be the First Church, and suit had been filed against the majority on the plea that, having departed from the true Baptist faith, the majority had forfeited their property rights.

The case came up for trial soon after I arrived, and I served as star witness for the defense. All we had to prove was that no one theory of the Atonement had been adopted by the Baptist Church, and that eminent leaders of the Church, "in full fellowship and good standing," held various interpretations—an easy enough task. However, the old judge was up for re-election, and he decided against us. The case was duly appealed to the Supreme Court of Texas, and his decision was reversed on every count—we had our beautiful new church. Some of the minority group returned to the church, others drifted away. Later they pulled themselves together and called a pastor, but did not get far. With this unhappy spirit, with a town torn by bigotry and bitterness, I had to deal, and it asked for all that I had of tact, patience and skill. About the same time the First Christian Church was without a pastor. As I had friends and relatives in both congregations, the suggestion was made that I be called to the vacant pulpit and that the two churches be put together, using our new church and selling the wooden structure of the other church. At first the proposal was received with enthusiasm, but they could not agree on what the name of the united church should be! At a meeting called to confer on the matter, at which dinner was served, one brother spoke tearfully, "If this merger goes through, we'll never see those ladies carrying buns through that door any more!"

The project fell through; here were folk of sincere intentions, friends, neighbors, some of them kinsmen, who could not worship together. It was my first contact with the concrete fact of sectarianism, and it left me profoundly depressed—I was butting against a stone wall.

Yet, in spite of angry debate and blind bigotry, there were lovely things. Calling one day on a church family, I found the mother at home, and her baby girl crawling on the carpet. She suggested that I write a letter to the baby, telling her the kind of woman I hoped she would become. I did so, and forgot all about it. Seventeen years later, on her eighteenth birthday, the mother delivered my letter to her daughter. The girl answered it, sending me a picture of herself, looking very like her mother. The letter reached me in London, where I was then living. She told me that she was just a wholesome, happy American girl, but had not sprouted the wings I had hoped she would grow. Later, while on a speaking-tour in America, telling our people what the World War was like, I spoke in Dallas. After the meeting, she introduced herself, Miss Ruth Dewitt, and the young man she was engaged to marry. The story ought to end by saying that I officiated at her wedding, but we could not arrange the dates. Few have written a letter and received an answer to it—seventeen years later!

Indeed, for a time I was in dire plight in respect to the Church as I knew it, wondering whether I could go on in its service. The Church called me with many voices, and every voice a memory and a command; but it looked as if the church —spelled with a small "c"—broken and in disarray, were standing in the way of the real Church, the fellowship of the seekers and finders of God. It was hard to think of leaving the Church, and equally hard to remain in it, though I was at home in every sect and able to speak the dialect of each, because my solitary concern was with what they held in common. Unhappy, ill at ease, I was looking and longing for the Church of Christ, who never laid stress on a petty, picayunish issue in His life. My case was much like that of the old New England deacon who was excommunicated by his church, but refused to go out. For twenty-five years he came to every communion service, bringing a bit of bread and a sip of wine of his own. There, in the privacy of his high pew, he communed with the Church when the Church would not commune with him. When a man brings his own communion, who can say nay? In the same forlorn way, I still clung to the Church as the family of God, albeit a house divided against itself, while it majored in minor issues of no importance, when its methods were archaic and ineffective, and its theology was a museum of faded antiques, because there was nowhere else to go.

My dilemma may be taken as a profile of the period. Each church emphasized, even magnified, its little differences; no one seemed to see the great agreements, which were like the sky above and the earth beneath the stream of human years. The tragedy was that little realities, often unrealities, were made tests of fellowship, and the golden circle was broken: it was "the sin of making a Christ of our opinions and worshiping it." Even the Church of the Disciples, to whose pulpit I had been so warmly welcomed, originally born of an authentic impulse in behalf of Christian unity, had become just another

sect, following the familiar pattern—one more factor in a bewildering agglomeration of factional feud. Its founders and
early leaders—Campbell, Stone, Scott—were men of clear vision,
seeking the fellowship of a beloved community in Christ, but
their dream had bogged down in a too literal reading of the
Bible, amid dogmas and rites which looked like the "mint,
anise, and cummin" in the days of Jesus. Their famous maxim,
"In essentials, unity; in non-essentials, liberty; in all things,
charity," failed to function, since the question as to what are
the "essentials" was left unsettled. Thus a sincere and prophetic
hope ended in the development of another denomination, to be
added to a list already too long.

Such limited co-operation of churches as we know in our
time was unknown in those days; each sect might have been
built on a separate planet. No wonder half the people in town
were outside of the churches, kept out by dogmas and rites
they did not understand, and which had nothing to do with
life as they knew it. My effort to build bridges between churches
failed, and to be shut up as the servant of one sect, running on
in the same old ruts, became increasingly difficult, an agony
in my mind, an anguish in my heart. To me the Church of
Christ included all our churches, and more than we had dared
to dream—not a huddle of sects, but a gulf-stream of the Love
of God flowing in the life of man. When I spoke of these things
people only stared, nobody was stirred or took heed. Instead,
I was deemed a heretic, yet never for a day did I lose that deep,
divine orthodoxy of the heart underlying all our differences.
Yet something had to be done, if only to save my ministry
from frustration and futility.

At Christmas time, 1899, I went to Kentucky to see Lady
Brown-eyes. On my way I stopped off at St. Louis to see Dr.
R. C. Cave, the founder and minister of the Non-Sectarian
Church of that city, an uncle of Dr. Edward Powell of Louis-
ville. An old Virginian gentleman, he received me with great
kindness, and for hours we talked man to man, heart to heart,
he telling me why he had broken away from the Church of the
Disciples, I pouring out my heart to one who knew and under-

stood. On my way back I saw Dr. Cave again, and he asked
me to become associated with him in the work of the Church,
which invitation I accepted. Soon after the first of the year, to
the bewilderment of my mother, I left my native state and the
Church of the people of my fathers, seeking a wider, freer fellowship, as well as a more untrammeled ministry; and a new
phase of my life began.

4

An Independent

IN SPITE of the negative attitude implied in its name, the Non-Sectarian Church of St. Louis was more than a mere protest. The church stood at the corner of Lindell Boulevard and Van Deventer Avenue, simple in architecture, with a porch, making it homey and inviting, rather than imposing. It was a friendly church, a shrine of simple faith and good fellowship. It was positive both in its message and its methods, an appeal to the Church outside of the church, not a revolt against faith but an affirmation of the things really essential to religion as it stands in the service of life. No creed, no rite was made a test of fellowship, but the desire to know God and to follow Jesus. Its congregation was made up, about half and half, of people who had been alienated from the churches or only nominally attached to them, because their churches made little things big and big things little, and of people who had never belonged to a church. All my life I had heard the churches arguing about how Jesus came into the world and how He went out of it, while overlooking what He did and what He taught us to do in the world. No words can tell my relief—release!—from minor issues of faith to explore its great ideas and employ its great adventures.

Dr. Cave was a new species of preacher. A man of rare personal and intellectual charm, he had that absorbent magnetism which made one want to watch everything he did and hear every word he uttered. He was never sensational, he never dealt with topics of the day. In nowise pietistic, he was a man with Christ in his very blood, whose sole aim was to make the Master and His laws and principles real and vivid to his fellow souls.

There was no fluffy oratory, no flowery emptiness, but deep feeling held in restraint. His sermons were carefully and closely woven, by a process of "mental composition," as he called it, while he paced his study floor. Not memorized, but so fixed in his mind that he spoke directly, without a note, in clear, concise, simple style, as soul to soul. He never debated issues of theology, never lashed out at other churches, but set forth the life of Jesus, His spirit, His teaching for everyday living, His office as Savior of man from himself, from brute fact and dark fatality. Such preaching attracted thoughtful, soul-hungry men, influenced influential folk, and built a strong church, free in its faith, fraternal in its fellowship, fruitful in its work.

Indeed, the Non-Sectarian Church was one of many such churches in the Mid-West and far Western states, followed, later, by the Community Church movement, each organized about some able and attractive leader; all efforts to escape from sectarianism into a gospel of freedom and service. So far there has been no adequate record and interpretation of this phase of the religious life of America; at one time I intended to write a book called *The Independents,* but too many tasks prevented me. First came "The Church of the Christian Unity," at Rockford, Illinois, founded by Dr. Thomas Kerr, in 1870. The pastor was a native of Aberdeen, Scotland, and came to this country in 1845, a practicing physician. He entered the Baptist ministry, but left that church to establish an absolutely unsectarian church, having neither a creedal nor a ceremonial test of fellowship. Later, in 1875, David Swing, after his trial for heresy in the Presbyterian Church, founded "Central Church," in Chicago, its bond of union being allegiance to Jesus as "the Savior that man in his ignorance and sinfulness needs; and that all accepting and obeying Christ as their Way, Truth and Life are fully entitled to the name and hope of the Christian."

A little later came "The People's Church of Chicago," whose minister was H. W. Thomas, formerly a Methodist, which held its services in McVicker's Theater. Still later we find Jenkin Lloyd Jones—"the inspired buffalo," he was called, with his bushy beard, looking very like Walt Whitman—turning a Unitarian Church into "Abraham Lincoln Center," where, to a most winsome kind of preaching, was added a wide-ranging social and cultural ministry. Other churches of a sort similar were led by Smith in Indianapolis, Martin in Tacoma, Myron Reed of Denver, and J. E. Roberts and his "Church of this World," in Kansas City. All these churches, and others too many to name here, were various in their emphasis and appeal —Roberts being a forerunner of the Humanist groups—but they had one thing in common: all were unsectarian, they were built on a different basis of fellowship. The tragedy of sectarianism lies not only in what it shuts in but in what it shuts out. Here were vast congregations of people following leaders of ability and vision, public-spirited people of active and high moral excellence who felt themselves debarred from Christian fellowship by tiny matters of rite and rote, which meant nothing to them and were in no way related to the religion of Jesus! In this tradition our church stood, a token of spiritual need, a sign of the times.

THREE RICH MEN

Three very rich men belonged to our church. They were able men, good men, who made their money honestly and used it generously—how generously I knew better than anyone else. All three had been born in North Carolina, where the oldest had been a young country doctor; the other two were members of the Battle family—kinsmen of mine. They arrived in St. Louis with fifteen dollars between them and had made their fortunes as manufacturing chemists. Of the three, one was radiantly happy. He would have been happy in any case; it was his temperament—his wealth did not do it. One was very unhappy; he would not have been happy under any conditions. To him life was a blight; he saw all its shadows and lived in fear of dying in a flop-house—that was his temperament. The third was made unhappy by his wealth. He himself was able to own his wealth and not be owned by it, having had a stern upbringing, but his money ruined his two children. Both went to their graves before he did. His wife soon followed, leaving him a

broken man with nothing but money. They loved the church
devotedly. They did not try to dictate its policy, they merely
wanted to pay all its expenses, and that would have been fatal
to the church. Instead, I asked them to let me use their money
in the doing of good, to which they gladly agreed, provided
that I kept it an absolute secret. After these many years it can
be told—how I helped families in dire need, or a struggling
student over a hard place, or an old minister turned out to grass
before churches provided pensions.

About that time St. Louis had a city-wide streetcar strike,
lasting through a ghastly winter, a bitter fight to the finish, with
no end of suffering among the families of the strikers. Violence
flamed now here, now there; it was the first hoarse, raucous cry
of industrial strife that I had heard. Having grown up in the
country and in small towns, such a situation was unknown to
me—it made me shudder. The details of the struggle are dark
to me even to this day, but not its hardship and horror, least
of all its bitter hatred. Anyway, using the money of my three
rich friends, I helped many a family in sore need, and tried to
get on the inside of the conflict and understand it.

"Hey, there, why are you running away from me?" said one
of my rich friends, who caught me after church.

"Because I have spent so much of your money I am afraid to
meet you," I replied.

"Shucks, son; we have not even felt it; full speed ahead."

After that they had no complaint; but I had the feeling that
I was serving as a kind of Good Samaritan, helping people who
were hurt, but doing nothing to clear the streets of bandits!
The attitude of the church toward battle confounded me—it
did not lift a hand, it had no word to say!

At an intersection of streets, near the Union Station, where
many streetcars diverged, I saw a mob—the first I had ever seen,
and I hope it will be the last. A mob is an ugly thing, a mass
of organized anger and unreason. As individuals we may be
decent and restrained, but a mob is ruled by the lowest type
of mind. Our group-life is our great tragedy, as a convoy takes
its pace from the slowest ship. Years have come and gone, but

I can still feel the awfulness of that scene. "The d—— scabs!
Kill the dirty rats!" was the cry that swept through the mob.
Three streetcars had been wrecked and their crews beaten to a
pulp. The police were helpless, or they may have been sympathetic with the strikers. Then, suddenly, a wagon of some kind
made its way into the center of the mob, and in it stood Father
Coffey, of the nearby Catholic parish. He was clad in his priestly
robes. Angry voices ceased, a hush fell over the mob, as if they
had seen an apparition.

"Go home, I tell you; go home now," he said.

He waited quietly, and in a few minutes the mob had melted
away. It was an amazing example of the power of the Church,
the influence of a man who was known for his simple, unforced
goodness. Such a man was worth knowing, and I followed him
to his church and told him how profoundly his act had impressed me. There I met Father McErlane, who became my
friend and has been one of my saints ever since—the most self-
spending human being I have ever known.

"A SLEUTH OF SOULS"

Father Mac, as he was called, was a frail man, living with
only one lung; his life was dedicated to the forlorn and the
forsaken. No dive was too dark for him to invade, no man too
desperate for him to help. To him there were no lost souls,
however far wandering, however far fallen. He was the friend
of the jailbird and the last support of the wretch going to the
gallows. He sought out the ruffian brought low by drink and
the diseases that follow the fast, foul life. He made real to them
the God who had been only an oath to them. "Shall I send for
a priest?" said a doctor to a dying down-and-outer. "What, a
priest for me?" said the man. "It's no use. He wouldn't come.
When I go, there goes nothing."

No one knew how Father Mac found it out—he seemed to
have a sixth sense—but when the doctor returned the man said:

"Yes, he got me. Did you tell him? He must have climbed in
the window like a second story artist. When I dozed off and

woke up there he was, smiling, and saying, 'Well, I found you. My motto is: Let no guilty man escape.' We had a talk, and I guess it's all right."

All kinds of people, blacks as well as whites, made their peace through Father Mac—he knew no race, no color. If he found a man raving in blasphemy, he left him murmuring half-forgotten prayers, dim memories of a day when life was new and clean. He not only led men to salvation hereafter, he saved them here; he picked up pieces of men out of the waste basket of the city and set them on their feet. He seemed almost to create souls where none had been before. On his "beat"—maybe while visiting her lover in jail—he met the wayward girl, who closed her eyes in weariness and opened them without hope. Or dragging herself to the home where her name had not been heard for years to die, Father Mac was on her trail to comfort and cheer. Never can I forget the strange congregation which assembled at his funeral. It filled the church and trickled into all the streets, upper-world folk, under-world folk, preachers and pug-uglies jostled one another in an assortment of human beings never seen before. Such was the power of God-fire and human love in the heart of a good man—he wrought in miracles. The very thought of him is a consecration, and the memory of him is like music.

It was William Marion Reedy who called Father Mac "a sleuth of souls," God's detective seeking those lost in the dark and bringing them back to the light. Reedy was one of the best friends of my St. Louis days; he it was who urged me to write and encouraged me to try it, more by example than by precept. The man could paint and pray and sob and sing with his pen. At times he could almost convey the color of an idea and the form of a taste. To him words seemed to have values and affinities which dictated their union with other words in such wise as to produce the effects of music and painting. Reedy was a man made to be loved, brave, true-hearted, generous, his humor a gentle ridicule of his own pathos. Remembering his huge figure and his dazzling mind, what times we talked the hours away, somehow he seems to have lived on with me through the years. If he squandered life, he did it lavishly, laughingly, and with a wide-sweeping sympathy which is another name for religion. As a bookman I have never known his like. He seemed to have read everything and to have forgotten nothing. His ability to recall a scene, a character, an epigram in a story or play years gone by was astonishing. His criticisms were not only appreciative, but creative, and a volume of them would be a treasure; he was not a fault-finder but a star-finder. Some of my earliest writings appeared anonymously in his social and literary weekly, *The Mirror—Reedy's Mirror,* it was called, because it projected his personality and reflected his spirit. The journal was the man; it revealed a vital mind, keen, beauty-loving, far-ranging, watching, now with indignation, now with amusement, and always with pity, the often strange medley of human events. Long afterward I edited a little book of his essays entitled *The Literature of Childhood*—dainty, wistful, elfin in spirit—showing that he had kept the child-heart despite the tramp of heavy years.

One evening Reedy invited me to be his guest at a meeting of the St. Louis Press Club, not telling me what the program was to be. It turned out to be a dinner in honor of Mark Twain, whom the Club had waylaid on his last visit to the country of Tom Sawyer and Huckleberry Finn. It was the first time I had seen Mark Twain, and, sitting not far from him, I studied his face, with its shock of white hair—a face with a thousand wrinkles, but never a smile, even when he told a funny story; the face of a man whose mood was one of settled sadness. In a little speech at the end he said that he wanted to preach a sermon, since he was as reverend as anybody. He took for his text a story of St. Francis, how he asked one of the Brothers to go with him into the village to preach. Arm in arm they walked down the hill, rejoicing in the soft spring sunlight, talking of the love of God, happy in their fellowship. On through the village they went, up the hill on the other side, then back again to the monastery gate, without stopping. "But are we not going to preach today?" asked the Brother. "We have preached," said Francis. "We have been happy in the love of

God and the glory of His sunlight—that is our sermon for the day." It was plain that Mark Twain was thinking of what kind of a sermon he had preached as he had walked down the years. All of us agreed, as we went home, that he had preached a good sermon, adding to the joy of the world, despite his many sorrows. Reedy did not think so well of his *Joan of Arc* as others did, albeit admitting its superb style, but he argued that *Huckleberry Finn* is a great historical novel, in that it captured a now vanished phase of American life and fixed it in the eternal repose of art. All the while I was thinking of how Mark Twain idolized Joan of Arc, wondering what deep, hidden need in his nature that worship satisfied.

Reedy and I remained close friends until his death in 1920, while attending a convention in San Francisco. "I am tired," he wrote me two days before his death; then, suddenly, on weary eyes there softly lay the stillest of all slumbers. The Roycrofters published a book of his essays, entitled *The Law of Love*, in 1905. It contained his famous essay on "Ginx's Baby," his pean on Sappho, and his eulogy of one of his best-loved books, *Marius, the Epicurean*. Some friends bless us by what they do, others by what they are—Reedy was an influence, an inspiration, without which my life might have journeyed a different path. A more gracious man I have never known or hope to know.

"ETERNAL MARRIAGE"

On June 14th, 1900, Virginia Mai Deatherage—Lady Browneyes—and I were married in the old Fifth Avenue Hotel in Louisville, Kentucky. Her brother and sister formed the party, and Dr. Whitsitt, the President of the Seminary where I had studied, officiated. We went at once to St. Louis, making our home in a family hotel just off Grand Avenue, then a chief street of the city, and one of the longest streets in the world; we did not "keep house" until some time later. As neither of us, except for my days as student and reporter in Louisville, had lived in a city, there were all sorts of places to go, many interesting people to meet. The two ladies who presided over the residential hotel where we lived were sisters, one of whom was the wife of the Reverend Louis G. Landenberger, of the Swedenborgian Church; and we attended some of his classes. As young married folk, naturally we were fascinated by the doctrine of "eternal marriage," as taught by the famous seer; since we wished our marriage to be of that kind. Here, again, I met a new spiritual influence, which greatly enriched my life.

Up until that time I knew nothing of Emanuel Swedenborg except the essay by Emerson, who called him "a colossal soul" —almost a universal genius. As Beecher said, no one can understand the religious thought of the last century who does not know Swedenborg, whose serene and emancipating vision influenced faith more than can be measured. He was a man who, after his illumination, lived in the spiritual world while walking among men upon earth. In his *Divine Love and Wisdom* I found a new approach, a clearer insight, in my thinking about God, very unlike what I had ever known before. It made the Trinity more than a mathematical riddle and a metaphysical puzzle, and the Atonement an act of God reconciling man to Himself, not Jesus reconciling God to man. In short, man is saved by what he is, not by virtue of what he believes and does; "man is not in heaven until heaven is in man." There was still a conflict between my heart and my mind, due to the dark theology taught me in my boyhood—my heart was at peace, but my mind was agitated; Swedenborg helped to harmonize the two. Few realize what schism an unworthy theology brings into a human heart, and what agony it is to get free of it.

A book which did much to shape my thinking henceforth was *Heaven and Hell,* by Swedenborg—one of the great books of the race. He taught the continuity of life and carried the idea of law over into the spiritual world long before Drummond lived; indeed he lived two hundred years too soon. Caprice vanished, along with arbitrary almightiness, and the Unseen World became a realm of law and order and growth, not another life but life further on, unbroken and unfolding. It was like the discovery of a new star out on the edge of the sky. For many, for most people today the old scenery of faith—a city in the sky, with gates of pearl and streets of gold—has faded, and there is nothing to take its place; just a blank, silent void. It is not a failure of faith, but a breakdown of the imagination—people not realizing, as Bushnell said, that the gospel is a gift of God to the imagination. Such scenery of faith does not fit into the new universe, as science describes it. Swedenborg, thinking with moral clarity and spiritual clairvoyance, portrays life further on in a way to satisfy and exalt, showing that no soul grows worse than it is after its deliverance from the flesh. Indeed, he painted the only heaven into which one would care to enter and the only hell of which anyone need be afraid. Withal, a calm certitude is felt in all his writings, as of one whose penetrating insight had unveiled what lies beyond for all souls, in which justice and love are united. It lifted a pall from my heart and opened lengthening vistas and lifting skies. No one can touch the mind of a great seer and not be changed by it.

NEW ENGLAND

More and more it became clear that I needed to take further courses of study. Much as I admired Dr. Cave and loved to work with him, I wanted to make new contacts and explore new fields. Besides, I wanted a church of my own, as every young man does. As Lady Brown-eyes was called to her old Kentucky home by illness in the family, I went to Boston—through the roar of Chicago, stopping off to see the wonder of Niagara Falls, and on over the Berkshire Hills, "as the flying gold of ruined woodlands drove through the air." It was a gorgeous picture of multi-colored, magnificent autumn, the trees now pale yellow, now dusky red, against a background of evergreens, and every so often one wearing a robe of flame, like the burning bush. Stone fences and walls broke into blushes with their trailing vines, with here and there a tall, blasted tree, covered with creepers, glowing like a torch, as if the lightning flash which withered it had become tangled forever in its spectral branches. And so to Boston, with its crooked crazy streets—cow paths become thoroughfares—where, if one keeps going he will come back to where he started. Yet a lovely city withal, saturated with history and legend, but with a different air from any I had breathed before, while the curious twang of Yankee talk made me feel, at first, like an alien.

Along those narrow streets Cotton Mather saw Satan walking at twilight, dragging a chain. So did I, only the chain was disguised as a rope of roses to trip the light feet of the wayward. For a brief time I was on the staff of the Everyday Church, on Shawmut Avenue, whose pastor, George L. Perrin, had visited me in St. Louis. One of his activities was a rescue home in the gaunt slums of the North End, whither I went with a good woman dedicated to the work. What sights I saw in the dingy streets near the old North Church, where every path seemed to lead to hell! Then there was the other Boston, intellectually so stimulating, with so many persons and groups to meet; its treasures of art, especially the Abbey and Sargent paintings in the Public Library, the one portraying the quest of the Holy Grail and the other the story of religion and the pageant of the prophets. The personality of Abbey did not appeal to me as peculiarly winning, but once at least the glory of things eternal, which is God shining through our tears, so blinded him that he saw.

On a lovely day I went to Concord and stood by the pink boulder which marks the grave of Emerson, whereon is carved his name, the dates of his birth and death, and these lines from his pen:

> The passive master lent his hand
> To the vast soul that o'er him planned.

Of course the great names of New England literature were only names, lofty and revered, but at Concord I went to see Frank B. Sanborn, who had known all of them and later wrote the best brief biography of Emerson we have. (Later we were to meet again and become friends; he it was who started me on my long study of Lincoln.) Phillips Brooks was gone, and it has always been a regret that I did not hear him preach, and that

I never saw Edwin Booth on the stage. But Edward Everett Hale
was living, his face a benediction, and he was infinitely kind
to a young man who sought his counsel. John Fiske, too, received me graciously, and talked brilliantly, and then played
the piano for me for an hour—we talked of an all-out alliance
between Britain and America, which he partly favored. Park
Street Church—"Brimstone Corner"—was too hot for me, but
King's Chapel was a haven. In the morning I often went to
Tremont Temple to hear Lorimer, and "roosted" in the gallery
of the New Old South Church in the evening, where George
Gordon attracted so many young students by his interpretations
of the grandeur and tenderness of the Christian faith. He was a
man made for a great painter, rugged but gentle; he became
my friend until his death, and my debt to him is great.

In my talks with New England folk, as well as from the "feel"
of the atmosphere, I learned one thing: Whereas in matters of
religion New England is liberal, in political and economic
thinking it is rigid and frigid. By contrast, the people of the
Mid-West are liberal in political thinking, but in religion they
are, or were, in the grip of a narrow orthodoxy. Hence, no
doubt, the reason for the non-sectarian movements I have
named, in protest and revolt.

On a Sunday afternoon, chill, bleak, drizzly, overhung with
frazzled tatters of gray clouds, I crossed the Common to old
Arlington Church to attend vespers. Life seemed drab and
forlorn, and I was a bit homesick. In that dismal mood I entered
the historic church just as the chimes began to play the tune
which takes its name from the church. At the left of the pulpit
was a marble slab bearing the names of Channing and Her-
ford, two poets who had been preachers there. The service
moved with the accent and rhythm of a poem. The preacher,
Paul Revere Frothingham, seemed to know all about me. At
any rate, he spoke right into my heart, taking something warm
out of his own soul and breathing it into mine, though at that
time he did not know my name. The service ended and the
doors were opened. A soft snow had fallen over the gray city,
hiding its ugliness and lending an air of mysticism to the scene.

The sunset touched the picture with magic, turning the dome of the State House into a huge jewel set against the sky. For one swift, timeless moment, dross-drained and luminous, life dropped its veil and revealed its meaning. It was an open window of divine surprise, as if the eternal life had become the only reality, making my human shape but a symbol and vesture. The sunset was transfigured with a far-beyondness, aglow with a light not of earth, falling from some higher sky. Life was no longer drab, but boundless, utterly blessed, free from fear and foreboding. It was the glow of spiritual enchantment, sorely needed, for which to thank God.

PRACTICING PREACHER

On Lincoln Day I heard Senator Hoar deliver a noble address in the State House. Next day, going to a preaching engagement, I saw him on the train with a pile of Wild West stories in his seat, one of which he was reading. It amazed me so much that I ventured to speak to him, telling him that I had heard his address the day before, and that I was astonished at the kind of books he was reading.

"That is just to rest my mind," he said, shyly, but I suspected that there was something of the boy still in his heart despite his age.

"Do you not find it easier to speak as you grow older—you spoke with such inevitable ease yesterday?" I inquired.

"No, it is much harder, perhaps because the thoughts of the years have gone so deep down in my mind that it is difficult to bring them to the surface. It frightens me more to speak now than when I was a young man."

His remark interested me greatly, and I have lived long enough to understand, in part at least, what he meant.

During the autumn and winter I preached in many kinds of churches, feeling at home in each. One happy Sunday I remember spending with the old Second Church, where Emerson had been pastor when a young man and where he left the ministry because the Lord's Supper no longer meant anything to him. Some people, like the Society of Friends, are not symbol-minded; they do not need sacraments. Nor did Emerson, to whom all life was a sacrament, as in his essay on "Nature" he taught us. For five Sundays I went to Provincetown, out on the tip of Cape Cod. At the Allen House, where the lounge was full of old seamen when I arrived, I registered from Texas, just for fun. While I was being shown to my room, the gang found out where I was from, and they were ready for me. They had found a new audience for their old stories, and for hours they told stories, some of them rather tall, about the sea and ships and storms. It was a new atmosphere for me, a new language, and I enjoyed it. The next day the whole gang came to church, each in his best "bib and tucker," a thing never known in town before. They hardly knew how to act in church. It was so each Sunday of my engagement—they were a rare group, loyal to the end, making me acquainted with the ways and wonders of the sea.

It is we ourselves who develop and educate ourselves; "so build we up the being that we are." Many ideas, insights, persons, influences play upon our spirit, blending with our nature and need. An inventory of them is impossible. The men I met in New England and talked with—or rather listened to—united the two most precious things in life, the spiritual quality and the vital mind. No one who met William James can ever forget him—he did not look like a philosopher, but more like a surgeon or a country squire; his eyes seemed to change color with his moods. His style, vivid, thrusting, picturesque, was as unpredictable as the man himself. Both spirited and spiritual, he opened windows and let in fresh air. To Josiah Royce I owe a new dimension of my vision of "the Beloved Community," to which was added his Gospel of Loyalty. Palmer, Peabody, Gordon, enriched my mind with great ideas and my heart with clearer insight. Nothing in life is quite like the touch upon us of great minds when they are needed; they unlock doors hitherto closed, and release within us thoughts and dreams of which we were hardly aware; they help us to find the rest of ourselves.

A PEOPLE'S CHURCH

In March, 1903, I left New England—not without regret—and went to Illinois, my destination Dixon, a community sitting astride Rock River. The spring thaw was busy melting the ice, the streets were streams; it looked its ugliest—drab, unkempt, forlorn, like a station on the way to somewhere else. Neither a town nor a city, it was in the awkward gosling stage, which made it an interesting but difficult setting in which to live, as we discovered; Lady Brown-eyes joined me soon after I arrived. There had been a Dixon College, but it was defunct. A shoe factory and a plant for condensing milk were the chief industries. One Catholic Church served a large parish, and there was a full set of Protestant sects, running in deep ruts, each going its separate way—half the people in town were outside of the churches. In short, a scene of spiritual dearth and intellectual desolation, and that was the challenge of it. Chicago was not far away, fortunately, and there one found kindred spirits; thither I often went, like a fish coming up for a breath of air.

One man, seeing the situation, had agreed to back me in an effort to form a People's Church, to be made up of unchurched folk. We had the use of a stone church building where the Universalists had tried to maintain a society and had failed. It had been closed for a long time and had to be reopened, the carpet patched, cleaned up and put in order—a dreary undertaking, but at last it was done. Frank W. Gunsaulus—my friend, almost like a father in those days—came out from Chicago and opened the church, as only he could do. Two young men, owners and editors of the Dixon *Daily Sun,* also stood behind my enterprise and opened their pages to me, publishing an ample synopsis of my sermon each Monday. Soon after the opening of the church I began a series of Sunday evening talks on "Great Men and Great Books," which attracted large crowds; this feature continued throughout my ministry in Dixon, and for years later. The church was free in its fellow-

ship, requiring no rite, no confession of dogma; its creed, in
fact, being the Lord's Prayer—a prayer become a creed, a creed
become a prayer, each praying for all, and all for each one.
People who had not been in a church for years joined and
became good workers, devoted if not devout; kindly people,
public-spirited, with a passion for real service.

It was an experiment which I had wanted for years to make,
and the initial results were most encouraging, but there was
opposition. A rotten political gang had a stranglehold on the
county and the town; almost all the members of the City Council were saloon-keepers or their henchmen. Such a state of affairs was a disgrace; it made the very word "politics" stink to
high heaven. Of course it was made possible by the connivance
of prominent people in the town, most of whom were church
folk, one of whom was the head of a Sunday School, who
thought himself very clever in serving both God and the devil
at the same time. Anyway, it effectively muffled the churches,
who avoided the issue by laying all emphasis on personal decision in religion, ignoring any social obligation and action; all
churches, that is, except mine.

The liquor traffic—always hoggish, always lawless—was having a bad time, owing to the "local option law," whereby each
community could vote itself "wet" or "dry" as it liked. Liquor
men had the jitters, not knowing when or where they would be
hit. The law worked curiously in that if one county went
"dry" the adjoining county would go "wet," and this see-saw
went on for years. Being neither a radical nor a political re-
former, my interest was in bringing the situation out into the
light, which made the political machine nervous and my church
suspect. A small town is a human laboratory in which one can
study things close-up and in the raw better than in a great city.

In a sermon I discussed the question, "What is the matter
with Dixon?" giving my diagnosis and asking the people to
write me their version. The results were most revealing; no
end of letters came, one saying that Dixon was "a city without
a soul." But others were more specific, going into details, which
showed how well the people knew what was going on. One let-

ter, written by a prominent citizen, told vividly, in photographic clarity, how the "nice people" were hooked up with the saloon gang, while the politicians played both ends against the middle, and how the "middle class," as he called it, were neutral, merchants in particular, lest they lose a nickel in trade. It was plain that the people were becoming restless under the yoke of such an infamous political game, and no one could tell what kind of an explosion might follow, or when. In a sermon I summed up the findings of the letters written me, laying stress on the absurdity of the idea of bringing national party politics into our community affairs. The sermon did not add to the comfort of the gang in power, and they vowed to discredit me and, if possible, destroy my church. It was feared that I was building a political machine, whereas the only machine I had was an Oliver typewriter, and I knew how to use it to turn on the light.

BILLY SUNDAY

Who did it I never knew for certain, but it was arranged to invite Billy Sunday, the evangelist, to conduct one of his campaigns in Dixon. It was odd to see a putrid political gang so anxious for the people to get a dose of "old-time religion"; but it would divert attention from the game they were playing, which included a house of ill-fame which they allowed to flourish near the end of the bridge. A temporary tabernacle was erected, with its "sawdust trail," and after a hippodrome publicity and build-up, Sunday came, amid much excitement. Almost all the churches—except mine and St. Luke's Episcopal Church—were in the campaign, co-operating for once at least.

The first evening Sunday prayed for every pastor in town, then he stopped suddenly and explained to the Lord that there was one man he could not pray for—meaning me. It seemed that I was outside the pale and beyond praying for, whereas one would have thought that such a person should have been a special object of prayer; but no. The sermon which followed, amid acrobatic oratory, was amazing. It pictured God as a gigantic snake, coiled, its head weaving, ready to strike the peo-

ple—a deliberate appeal to the most primitive of fears. As a
snake-dance it was a success; but it was the most ghastly caricature of religion—to say nothing of the Gospel of Jesus—
which it has ever been my sadness to hear. "The doctrine of the
universal Fatherhood of God and the brotherhood of man is an
infernal lie," it concluded.

The editor of the Dixon *Daily Sun* was so outraged by such
an exhibition that he asked me to "cover" the meetings as a
reporter, giving me a free hand; and I did so. Writing with the
lucidity of a laundry list, I described the snake-dance and other
similar atrocities, giving credit for good points the while—
especially the famous sermon on "Booze," which shook old soaks
in their shoes and made the "gang" wonder whether they had
not, after all, made a bad mistake, since the liquor issue was a
sore spot in the town. Day after day I took first one bit of
skin, then another, off the evangelist, politely but pointedly.
At last my articles began to make themselves felt, and thinking
people began to come down off the fence on my side. My net
conclusion was that if someone could take the vanity and
bigotry out of Sunday, no one could identify the remains. He
eased up in his attacks on me, sensing the changing mood; my
church grew and gathered power. Such campaigns do no end of
injury to a community, leaving it a burnt-over forest. After a
furnace of fanaticism only clinkered religion remains. The
"follow-up" was disappointing, and things were left as they had
been—only worse.

LAW AND ORDER

Some time after the Sunday orgy, since there was no im-
provement in the state of the community, we organized a Law
and Order League, and it fell to my lot to serve as chairman of
the steering committee. Quietly we got a detective to spend
two weeks in town, gathering evidence. He was a slim, soft-
spoken lad from Peoria. I never quite trusted him, fearing
that he might double-cross us. About the same time a new
minister came to the First Methodist Church, Dr. C. C. Maclain,

who, swiftly surveying the scene, joined our Law and Order League, bringing the Baptist minister with him. By chance Maclain learned from the mother of one of his church families that her sons—minors—had been sold liquor in one of the saloons. We presented the case to the City Council, and it was my duty to act as prosecutor. The boys gave their testimony; their mother was there to see that they did. Some of the members of the Council yelled at the boys, as though they were the offenders, which gave me a chance to say some things in words of one syllable, in phrases that cut like whips of fire of how the city had been sold down the river to the brewing companies. The gang was stunned, baffled, confounded; they got some of their thugs to "beat up" Dr. Maclain, but he was not hurt badly—in fact it made him more intent on doing the job.

In the meantime, the detective had made his report, with evidence aplenty. Of course we knew that it would be futile to present the evidence to the prosecuting attorney—he was a bell-wether of the "gang." Still, as a formality, we called on him and told him what had happened. He almost threw us out of his office. But he spread the news that we had employed a detective. It swept all over town like wildfire. The result was astonishing; it well-nigh depopulated the town of its men. Many men, never suspected of doing anything illegal, had business elsewhere for an indefinite time. The house of ill-fame went out of business quickly. Having occasion to go to Chicago, at every station along the road I saw Dixon men asking frantically how things were going. It was a revelation of the fear and frailty of my fellow men which I did not enjoy. But it worked; at the next election the whole "gang" was swept away like cobwebs. The mayor tried to "beat me to pulp," but he was too angry to know what he was doing—I caught him by the arms and held him. Thus ended my first and last adventure of the kind, but when things are rotten something has to be done; and we had a better ordered town.

In the midst of these happenings, our first baby came, a boy born on the centennial of the birth of Emerson, May 26th; and we named him Joseph Emerson. He graduated from Harvard University in due time, took his degree as Master of Arts, and was instructor in English in the University of Pittsburgh. Then he spent twelve years in the American Foreign Service; growing tired of living outside his own country, he is now engaged in realizing his honorable literary ambition. Of beautiful personality and brilliant mind, he will make his mark, having been around the world in the service, at Nagoya, Japan, Singapore, Nassau, Havana, and doing special work in the State Department. My great regret is that he did not enter the ministry.

FIRST CHRISTENING

One day a man came to see me in formal attire, morning coat, spats, even the old top-hat, which looked rather odd. He was a handsome man, his manner elaborately graceful and expressive —I could not quite make him out. Our talk ran along many lines, as talk will, as if each were trying to feel out the other. Finally, after much hesitation, he told me that he was an actor, playing in a drama appearing in the city at the time. Whereupon I began telling him how much I enjoyed the stage and its artists as a young minister, when I lived in St. Louis. Those best remembered were Olga Nethersole, Robert Mantell in "Hamlet," and especially Richard Mansfield, whom I had the honor of meeting. Indeed, Mansfield invited me to attend one of his rehearsals, where he was very exacting—almost harsh—with his company, making them repeat scenes, or pieces of scenes, until they were tired and sick of their lines—so meticulous was he that everything should be as near perfection as possible. To see him play "Peer Gynt," that engaging scapegrace, or starve to death as "Beau Brummell," or die of old age as "Ivan the Terrible," was unforgettable. When Mansfield died I thought of that scene, wondering whether he had met death in so magnificent a manner—he had rehearsed the part so often.

"Then you do believe in and enjoy the theater?" my visitor asked, in surprise.

"Certainly," I told him; "why should the great art of the drama be outlawed? If we study Shakespeare in school, why

can it be an evil thing to witness one of his plays on the stage?
I saw Sothern and Marlowe play 'Romeo and Juliet,' but I did
not think Sothern intellectually big enough to play 'Hamlet.'"

Then my guest told me that he had once played with Mansfield and found him a great man but a hard master. At last, the
ice having been broken, he asked me if I would christen his
baby girl. He had asked five ministers, and all had refused;
hence his shyness in making the request.

"Why should ministers refuse to do a natural, human and
Christian thing?" I asked in amazement.

Then he explained, "They declined evasively, apologetically,
but I could see that it was because my wife is an actress."

It astounded me beyond words.

"One of them said that if anybody would do it, you would,"
he added.

"You are right; it will be both an honor and a joy to christen
your baby." It was so arranged for the next day in their room
at the hotel.

"My wife," he explained, "was formerly an Episcopalian, but
she has a curious fear that if anything should happen to the
baby, its fate might be in doubt. Anyway, she wants the security of the sacrament. Her fear is due, I think, to her grievance
against the Church for its attitude toward her profession as an
actress, and perhaps to a suppressed sense of guilt for having
abandoned her Church."

This too amazed me, for what must she think of a God who
would hold a grudge against her baby on that account. This
feeling I expressed emphatically, saying that if Jesus was right
the whole attitude was wrong. "God, as Jesus showed Him to
us, is not like that at all. He took little children in His arms
and blessed them, and rebuked His disciples for trying to keep
them away from Him, as if they were annoying to Him."

All the while I was remembering that I had been brought
up in a Church which did not christen children—in fact, did
not allow children to belong to it, even by proxy. No doubt the
attitude was logical, but neither life nor love is logical. The
whole thing seemed queer to me. What a mess we have made

of the Gospel of the Love of God with our logic "linked and strong."

As a fact I had never christened a little child, and I was not sure that I knew how to do it. Naturally, since the mother had been an Episcopalian, I turned to the book of Common Prayer; but the service there was unsatisfactory—parts of it were good, the words of Jesus and some of the prayers, parts were atrocious —dull old dogma dished out where it ought not to be. To this day I think the whole baptismal service in the Prayer Book ought to be revised, rewritten, and made human if not more Christian. Then I looked into other books of worship, but was unable to find any service really worthy of the occasion. At last I wrote a ritual of my own, or compiled it, which I memorized and used in the service next day—although I took the Prayer Book along with me. It was a simple rite, tender, dignified, sin-cere—not a thing said by rote. Never have I seen a mother more happy and appreciative. She was radiant. After it was over we sat down and talked, and I said to the mother some of the things I had said to her husband, as he had asked me to do, about God, His unfailing love, and what Jesus said about little children. "You have too much fear," I said to her; "we must not be afraid of God—He loves us more than you love your baby. We are all born out of the depths of His love. Think of God as Jesus taught us to think of Him." And I left her happy.

ACTOR'S CHAPLAIN

To my distress, the story got into the papers—the news serv-ices carried it from end to end of the land—as if I were the only minister who would christen the baby of an actress. No doubt the father was responsible for the report. Soon letters began to come in shoals, commending and condemning me—most of them, at first, condemning me sharply. Then, later, I began to get letters from actors and men associated with the stage, thanking me for being "brave" enough to do such a thing, in the teeth of prejudice. As if it took any special kind of courage to christen a baby, and as for prejudice I was used to it. The upshot of it was that I was soon appointed a chaplain of the Actor's Church Alliance, and served in that capacity for many years. It brought me in contact with stage folk wherever I went, and I found them much like other people, only more expressive and very charming; it added a whole chapter of interest to my life. In England, later, I met Irving, Benson, Lena Ashwell, and others, who lectured for me in my Literary Society in the City Temple. In New York it made me eligible to the privileges of The Players Club, in front of which stands a statue of Edwin Booth. There I came to know many famous men of the theater, or in some way associated with it, including Don Marquis— an evening with him was a "mirthquake." George Cohan and his wife were my good friends; I enjoyed him in "Ah, Wilderness," he having won lasting fame for his songs in the first World War. Whether the Actor's Church Alliance still exists I do not know, but I do know that much of the old brutal prejudice against stage folk is still with us, as it has been, strangely enough, since the most ancient times. One act of simple Christian ministry to a mother in her fear, and what a long-lasting dividend of kindness, compounded many times!

STUDENT YEARS

In spite of these exciting events, the advent of a new baby, the building of a new kind of church, and the fight to the finish with a dirty political gang, my life had other interests and activities. My years at Dixon—during which I preached at Morrison, in the next county, where I had many blessed friends —were student years. Reading widely in English and American literature, I also carried my studies in philosophy further, the while I reviewed all religious books as they appeared for my friend Edwin L. Shuman, literary editor of the Chicago *Record-Herald*. Editing the *Middle-West Magazine* was a work I greatly enjoyed, the more because it brought me in touch with writers in the Middle-West, and it gave me an opportunity to publish some of the stories of my friend Reedy of St. Louis. But the mind that fascinated me most deeply in those days was David

Swing, whose sermons I had discovered in my Seminary years. At last I decided to write a biography of Swing—somewhat late, since he died in 1894—but Central Church in Chicago, which he founded, was a great power still, and, besides, the spirit of the man enchanted me. The art of a great preacher, like the art of an actor, and unlike that of a poet, a painter, or a statesman, dies with him. His monument is a hiatus, a vacancy that is vacated by the passing of the generation to whom he ministered. The more reason, then, that we should remember him, that as little as possible may be lost of the precious treasure of mankind.

No doubt any human life, if written from the inside, would be a romance, but to study a great life makes us, for a brief time, great in our own right. To get the background of the life of Swing, I went to Clermont County, Ohio, where he had been born—the same county in which General Grant had been born—to talk with any who might be living who had known him as a boy. From thence to Miami University, Oxford, Ohio, where he had been a student, and later Professor of Greek. To go into the hinterlands of the life of a man is endlessly interesting; one sees the influences and events which shaped him. My study required me to go through the Chicago papers from 1866 to 1894, and that experience I can never forget. It injured my eyes, for a time, reading the oldest papers, with their dim, yellow pages; but I saw how events, big and sensational at the time, dwindle as time flies. My study brought me in touch with many of the friends of Professor Swing—he never lost that title—especially his two daughters, Mrs. Mary Ricker and Mrs. Helen Starring, who were kindness itself to me, giving me access to all letters and manuscripts in their possession. Swing had left a request that all his papers be burned at his death, but happily the request was not carried out. In any case, the material was abundant. An old farmer, learning that I was writing about Swing, brought me a series of huge scrapbooks in which he had carefully preserved all of the sermons as they had appeared in the Chicago *Inter-Ocean,* the weekly edition of which covered northern Illinois like the dew. Out on his lonely farm the sermons had been as bread and meat to him. Such was the ministry of Swing. Reading those sermons was the experience of a lifetime; it helped me to understand the extraordinary influence of Swing on young and old alike— human souls seem to be set free and bloom at the touch of his spirit.

DAVID SWING

In 1866 Swing came to Chicago as minister of a Presbyterian Church on the North Side. Nine years later he was tried for heresy, prosecuted by Dr. Patton, afterward President of Princeton University. Instead of fighting the case through, Swing left the church, having no interest in the issues involved. His sole concern was with those truths which are "holier in usefulness," as he put it. He intended to go into the law. But the men of Chicago would not have it so. They gathered about him, asking him to found a church of the kind he had dreamed, and backed him up financially; hence Central Church, where for twenty years his voice was heard and his vision shown. The one mighty preacher of beauty, he built his altar near the Board of Trade in Central Music Hall, read his essay-sermons, and vanished, but he wrought in wonders. In some respects he was the most unique preacher America has known and the greatest. It was as if an old Greek who had seen Jesus had wandered out of the world of ancient dream, and out of the ugliness of slaughter-houses and the materialism of business there arose an inspiration and a prophecy. He had genius, poise, culture, sympathy, insight, humor, common sense, and above all religion "as lofty as the love of God, as ample as the needs of man." To radicals he was too conservative—"the soothsayer of a transition," they called him—having kept the old pieties of the heart; to conservatives he was too liberal, because he dealt only in the most universal of truths.

Such a preacher was naturally a magnet for men, especially young and strong men, who were weary of the old speculative theology and yet needed a faith to live by. They were proud to be called "Swing's boys": such men as Lyman Gage and W. E. Curtis, to name no others. As time passed the bitterness of debate subsided, and Swing enjoyed such influence as few

men have ever known over all kinds and conditions of people.
He was more than a personality; he was an institution. When
it was proposed that the Westminster Confession of Faith be
revised, Dr. John Hall of New York suggested that the Confession only needed a footnote expressing the Mercy of God.
"The Mercy of God in a footnote!" exclaimed Swing. "The
Sermon on the Mount might also be added as an appendix!
Logic will follow that church until it has nothing left but
Christ, and then for the first time in its life it will be rich!"
It was reported that Dr. Patton—he of the heresy trial—had
said in a talk to his students that the fate of the pagans might
not be so dark as formerly pictured, which called out a spicy
essay from Swing: "At last Socrates, Plato and dear Penelope
have permission to assemble at the gates of heaven and listen
to some good music! Happy the man who revised his creed
years ago!" It was this quality of his spirit and teaching, making
the gates of heaven a little wider, with hope for all, as well as
his faith in our race and his optimism for its future, which
made a bird-song in my heart. The study of his life put something into me, something beyond the power of words to tell.

No sooner had I finished the biography of David Swing
than I received a call from a church in Cedar Rapids, Iowa,
which I accepted, reluctantly and with regret, remembering our
friends in Dixon. In the summer of 1908 we went to Iowa,
but, alas! we left a little grave behind us. A beautiful boy had
come to us, perfectly formed, with a nobly wrought head and
great dark eyes. He was to be named for David Swing, and we
hoped that he would be the great preacher of the family. But
he died at birth. When I went to the door to meet the doctor,
a wild storm was raging and a huge ball of fire was coming
toward our home. It struck the steeple of St. Luke's Episcopal
Church across the street and shattered it. Our beautiful boy
was gone. Speechless he came, speechless he went; he had no
language, not even a cry. No one now living, perhaps, knows
that he ever visited this earth, but his father and mother have
not forgotten.

5

Cedar Rapids

MY FRIEND Cyrenus Cole, in his *History of Iowa*, remarks that
I was "born in Texas and born again in Iowa"; it was an actual
fact. For me life began anew in Cedar Rapids, which had grown
beyond the awkwardness of a town cut up into cliques, into
the unity of a city with a community consciousness; beyond
antagonism or even tolerance into co-operation and fellowship.
For one who had fought alone against heavy opposition, or dull
unseeing indifference, this was a new atmosphere in which to
work. Such response was inspiring, if not creative. The people
of Cedar Rapids wanted every institution in their city—a college, a church, a business—to be the best in the state; and they
were ready and eager to help make it so. Even to this day,
though I have wandered afar to London, and great cities in
our own land, Cedar Rapids still seems more like home to me
than any place on earth. There I made such friends as one
makes only once in a lifetime; there I found myself and struck
my stride—as preacher, as writer, and in various and sundry
activities for the common good and the culture of the best life.

The church to which I went in Cedar Rapids had been a
Universalist society originally, but it had not been a success—
if not dead, it was living at a dying rate. Accordingly I changed
it from top to bottom, put it upon a new basis, and named it
the Liberal Christian Church—it was better known, later, in
the city and the state, as "The Little Brick Church." If it was
called "liberal" it was not because I liked defining my Christianity by an adjective, for I did not: since those days all such
labels have been rubbed off or grown dim. But, emphatically,
to me the word "liberal" meant that a man was free to be a

Christian, or to try for that goal, not that he held his Christianity loosely or lightly, still less as a denial of the faith of other men. To me a "liberal" was one who had the same charity toward the past as toward the present and was as willing to listen to St. Bernard as to Bernard Shaw. In short, it meant that if the "liberal pulpit" ignored certain dogmas about Christ, it was because it wanted Christ Himself brought nearer to us—with a demand which I knew would plague me with an unsatisfiable passion to be more like Him and do more for Him; or let Him do more with me. If I was discontented with old dogmas of the Atonement, it was because I wanted the Reality, which is too great and deep for any dogma: that we are to be crucified with Christ that He may rise in us. It meant that each soul must dare to stand naked before an All-Loving Holiness, seeking purity rather than repose; any other kind of "liberalism" is, and must be, arid, futile and empty.

It seems necessary thus to emphasize the spirit and nature of our enterprise, if only to show that it was a Liberal *Christian* Church, not a mere protest, but a positive adventure with a definite objective and program. The basis of its fellowship was extremely simple: *"In the spirit of Jesus we unite for the worship of God and the service of man."* That was all; and that was enough. No creed, no rite was made a test of fellowship; the Lord's Prayer was its central focus of faith, comprehensive in its consecration. No sacraments? Worship, fellowship, and preaching are sacraments, or should be—preaching which seeks to make God eloquent to men, to show to what fine issues human life ascends when lived in the love and will of God, and which keeps the gates of the immortal life always open for all; never a sermon without that far-look and eternal hope. Folk from other churches were discouraged from joining "The Little Brick Church," unless they had been inactive in church life or wanted to face a wider and more challenging fellowship. Again, it was an appeal to the unchurched—people unchurched by dogmas they did not understand—human souls, devoted but unpietistic, seeking to learn together what none may know alone. As our undertaking did not conflict with any other

church, it was not antagonized, but was welcomed in behalf
of spiritual faith, freedom and fellowship. What filled me with
deep dismay about our Christianity in those days, whether
liberal or orthodox, was that it was so harmless, so tame, so
timid, so tepid, for many little more than a family tradition,
or a hobby, or a glorified lollipop, even as it is today.

Strong men gathered about me, men strategic in the city
and the state, and the church grew in power; it became one
of the most influential congregations in the Commonwealth,
out of all proportion to its numbers. Young folk came too,
many of them with dreams in their hearts—like William L.
Shirer, who "played hooky" to attend a church where, he tells
me, he got the inspiration to be a writer. His *Berlin Diary* was
to make him famous years later.

My study of *David Swing, Poet-Preacher*, which I had finished in Dixon, ran as a serial in *Unity*, the journal of Abraham Lincoln Center, Chicago. It appeared in a book—my first
book—soon after I settled in Cedar Rapids, and the reviews
were most encouraging. One in particular was notable, by
William E. Curtis, the globe-trotting reporter of the Chicago
Record-Herald; first page, first column—an honor accorded to
very few books. He had been one of "Swing's boys" who never
missed the "open house" kept by the professor on Sunday
evenings in his Lakeshore Drive home, along with George
Carpenter, Eli Sheldon, Frank O. Lowden, and others who
afterwards became distinguished in various walks of life; Lowden later became Governor of Illinois. Curtis closed his tribute
to his gentle and wise mentor by saying, "He thought well of
everybody; he found good in everything. He kept my thoughts
clean; he set a pace and a standard. Whatever I have done that
is a credit to my race, is largely due to David Swing."

OPENING DOORS

To my amazement, about the same time, my friend Luther
Brewer—a good Lutheran, but interested in "The Little Brick
Church"—asked me to allow him to publish my sermons in

the Cedar Rapids *Republican,* of which he was owner. It was so agreed, and the sermon preached one Sunday appeared in the next Sunday edition of the *Republican,* which covered the whole eastern end of the state. He kept the type until the end of the month, then put the sermons into pamphlets, which he sent to any and all who asked for them, "off his own bat," as he admitted; at the end of the year he bound them into books. Also, shortly afterward I began again my literary talks, giving them each Tuesday evening, which proved to be quite a feature in the city. "Christ in Modern Literature" was the general title, which was later expanded, but the Christ-*motif* was never forgotten. The literary talks were also published and included in the monthly pamphlets. Somebody, I never learned who it was precisely, sent copies of the pamphlets to *The Christian World Pulpit,* in London, and my sermons began to appear first monthly, then more often, in that old and widely read journal. The University of Iowa, located at Iowa City, only a few miles away, took note of what was going on, and asked me to give the literary talks, now dignified as "lectures," as a popular Lectureship in English; and this service, which I greatly enjoyed, brought me in touch not only with members of the faculty—great teachers, who became great friends—but also with hundreds of the students. Actually I served as a kind of unofficial chaplain of the University, talking with students over their problems of faith and life, officiating at no end of weddings, making friends some of whom still keep in touch with me, despite the passing of many years. Days—years—went by, crowded with happy labors, surrounded by such friends as few men have ever had.

For the first time since my student days in Louisville and Boston, I had real fellowship with my brethren in the ministry —up until that time, in Dixon as in St. Louis, they had been offish, deeming me an outsider. This new goodwill was due to Dr. Edward Burkhalter, pastor of the First Presbyterian Church, dean of the clergy of the city. Born and brought up in New York City, his dream was to be teacher of Hebrew in Union Seminary. Failing to obtain that post, after a brief pastorate at New Rochelle, he came to Cedar Rapids, where he spent the rest of his life. No man was ever more beloved in any community; no man ever more richly deserved such devotion. The ritual for joining the Minister's Association of the city was to read the *Confessions of St. Augustine* with Dr. Burkhalter, no small part of whose labors, in his later years, was in teaching the clergy. A superb scholar, he was more a born teacher than preacher. Reading Augustine together was a joy, but we did not stop with that book—we went through all the writings of the early Church Fathers, the formative period of Christian theology. His knowledge of that period was complete; his enthusiasm for its great personalities was infectious. Athanasius, Chrysostom—oddly enough, he did not care for Origen—Theodore of Mopsuestia, Clement of Alexandria, and the rest became familiar friends, and their creative thought a storehouse of inspiration. All through the years I have looked back to those readings and studies with Dr. Burkhalter with gratitude, for the deepening of thought and still more for the delight of my fellowship with one who was like a father as well as a friend. Nor can I make any reader of mine realize how gracious he was, with his gentle ways, his little elaborate courtesy, his infinite kindness—he still stands before me, as if refusing to say farewell. Those studies did more for me than my whole Seminary course had done—far more.

A man is only half himself; his friends are the other half—in my case by far the better half. One of the best friends of those years, and all the years since—happily he is still with me, though many have fallen asleep—was W. R. Boyd, at first editorial writer on the Cedar Rapids *Republican,* and later chairman of the finance committee of the State Board of Education. In that office he has served for more than forty years, and has left an indelible imprint upon the educational life of the state. He it was, I have always suspected, who arranged for my literary talks to be given at the University of Iowa—he was always doing the best things for his friends, on the sly. It was love at first sight between us; our understanding was complete, never for an instant marred. It is friendship at its highest, no familiar, back-slapping fellowship; intimacy of thought and love without familiarity. His fine mind, his firmly wrought character, his high integrity of spirit, "the little nameless, unremembered acts of kindness and of love"—unremembered by him, unforgotten by me—all these ineffable things, and more than my words can tell, made him like an older brother. Just to know that he is there, wise in counsel, at once deeply spiritual and practically capable, resourceful in suggestion and the best of companions, has been a source of inward sustaining and strength, far more than he will ever know. No wonder Charles Kingsley, when asked the hidden secret of his life, replied, "I had a friend."

HAPPY ACCIDENT

In 1908 Frank B. Sanborn came to the University of Iowa to deliver some lectures on American history, on which he was an authority. He was a charming man to know, tall, slender, with the stoop of a scholar, and the keenest, kindest blue eyes anyone ever saw, his head crowned with snow-white hair. He was in his late seventies, I was a bit over thirty, and we were strangely drawn to each other—the tie between a very old man and a very young man is unique and beautiful. Of course, having read his *Autobiography,* I knew that he had been the headmaster of the School for Boys in Concord, Massachusetts, in the days when Emerson, Thoreau, Hawthorne, Alcott, Holmes, and that glorious company, were in flower; not only their contemporary but their friend. He had written the best brief biography of Emerson that we have. However, his interests were more political than literary. He was deeply involved in the raid of John Brown at Harper's Ferry, so much so that his arrest was ordered by the Senate, and he had found it profitable to have business in Canada for some time until the storm blew over. To me he was not only a gentle friend but a link uniting me with the great men of a great period of our history: his talk was rich, adding the personal touch to a time gone by.

In the thick of the anti-slavery movement, he was brought

into close touch with Theodore Parker, who was in some respects the greatest preacher America has known; they became
great friends. It was the wish of Parker that Sanborn write
his biography, if any should be written. But man proposes and
woman disposes, and the wife of Parker did not like Sanborn.
Why? Well, just because—woman is not always ruled by reason—and she did not allow him to write the biography, but
allotted that honor and labor to John Wiess, who did a very
good piece of work. But, remembering a great friendship, in
her will she left to Sanborn all the manuscripts and papers of
her husband, making him literary executor. In going through
that mountain of papers Sanborn came upon a correspondence
between William H. Herndon, the law-partner of Lincoln, and
Theodore Parker, which began with the repeal of the Missouri
Compromise, in 1854, and continued until the death of Parker
in Italy, in 1860. He saw at once the value of the letters, only
two or three of which had been used in the Parker biography,
and by some chance he brought the letters with him on his
visit to the University, using a few excerpts from them in one
of his lectures. He must have had in mind some plan, some
hope, regarding them—the hope, perhaps, that he might find
someone to make use of them.

Try to imagine my utter astonishment when, one day, un-
expectedly—I suspect Luther Brewer had something to do with
it—Mr. Sanborn turned the Herndon-Parker letters over to me,
saying, "There, Laddie, see what you can do with this material;
I am too old to handle it properly." Thus my intensive study
of the life of Lincoln began, accidentally as we say, and the
opportunity to make one of the source-books of his life, made
so by the letters on which it was to be based. Here were letters,
never before published—important, vivid, often thrilling—
which passed to and fro from the office of Lincoln & Herndon,
in Springfield, to the study of Theodore Parker, in Boston,
telling what went on behind the scenes, politically, in a critical
period—the period, that is, between 1854 and 1860, including
the repeal of the Compromise achieved by Henry Clay, which
injected the slavery issue anew into the politics of the nation;

the return of Lincoln to public life; the organization of the Republican party; the Frémont campaign; the Lincoln and Douglas debates; the secret pact between Horace Greeley and Stephen A. Douglas working toward the defeat of Lincoln for the Senate in 1858; the maneuvers and counter-maneuvers for the nomination and election of Lincoln to the Presidency. The letters of Herndon, as every biographer of Lincoln has since discovered, are indispensable to an understanding of those years, to which I was able to add other new items, including letters from Horace White, and a speech made by Lincoln at Troy, Kansas, on the day that John Brown was executed, which, if known at all, had been strangely neglected or forgotten. It was a stern speech, almost out of key with his character, not justifying John Brown in his attack upon slavery, "contrary to law," but warning any who might be thinking of attacking the Union in the same reckless manner, adding that as Brown was hanged, "We shall try to do our duty."

LINCOLN'S HERNDON

My book, on which I worked through 1909, amid the Lincoln centennial celebration, and on into 1910, was to be named *Lincoln & Herndon,* taking its title from the old law-shingle which hung at the foot of the stairway on the south side of the Square in Springfield which was later destroyed by fire. It was not intended to be a detailed biography of either Lincoln or Herndon, but a story of their personal and political friendship in thinking through and working out a great national problem, and, in particular, a check-up on the accuracy of Herndon as historian and interpreter of Lincoln. To Herndon we owe an unpayable debt for our knowledge of the early years of Lincoln. He knew more about the early Lincoln than anyone else. He began collecting material for a biography long before anybody else even thought of a biography, and he continued his research as long as he lived. He knew that Lincoln detested eulogy, and he wanted to paint him as he was, "warts and all," believing that he was so great that no fact about him could lower his stature by one inch. In this respect he stood so straight that he seemed to lean backward, and he was cruelly attacked. He was accused of deliberately trying to belittle, if not besmirch, his partner, who was his best friend, his political idol, and to whom he was one of the most self-effacing friends of whom we have record. Of course, no man ever entirely understood another man, even his closest friend. There were doors in Lincoln for which Herndon had no keys—depths he could not fathom—and he made mistakes both of fact and interpretation; and naturally so. He had certain pet theories about Lincoln which he pushed too far, and in his garrulous age he jotted down things absurd and irrelevant, gossip of no importance. None the less, the Herndonian portrait and interpretation of Lincoln, with corrections and modifications, will stand as the final picture of the man in his formative period. At any rate, I wanted to do justice to Herndon, and I hope I made it impossible for anyone else to be unfair to his memory and service—that is, anyone who cares for facts and fair-dealing.

Such a study took me over the Lincoln country, from Springfield to Indiana, and into the heart of Kentcky. It required that I read all that had been written about Lincoln up to that time—books, papers, pamphlets and manuscripts; all material known to exist, except the papers in the hands of Robert Lincoln, which no one was allowed to see, and which in his will he interdicted until 1947. Not that they reflect upon the President, but because they involve others, it is said. Anyway, Robert Lincoln would give me no help, because, like his mother, he hated Herndon, and was not interested in my attempt to vindicate his veracity, but he did inherit from his father the art of telling stories. What those unknown papers may contain remains to be revealed—as to that I make no guess—but I am sure they have to do with the war years, and in no way concern the Lincoln of whom Herndon wrote, not always wisely but honestly. My study could not be repeated today, because the men who taught me most about Lincoln have long since passed away. Even Dr. William Jayne, who had been the Lincoln family physician in the Springfield days, was still living when

I visited the city. He was ninety years old, or nearly so, his faculties intact, his memory clear. In answer to my questions he cleared up certain matters which I wanted to get straight. Other friends of Lincoln talked to me freely, but their talk usually ended in a blur of eulogy. Suddenly they became silent, a light came into their eyes, and one realized what a great reverence really is, and how deeply Lincoln had touched their hearts.

HENRY B. RANKIN

By the kindness of Mrs. Annie Fluery, the daughter of Herndon, I had the honor of meeting Henry B. Rankin, to whom I owe a great debt and whom I can never forget. In his late seventies, retired from business, he did his work on a huge couch in his home—very tall, frail, almost ethereal, with glorious dark eyes, a descendant of the Batcheller family of New England, to which both Webster and Whittier were related, and all were famous for their bright eyes. He received me cordially, but when I stated my mission his attitude was "on the north side of friendly," as the Scotch say, adding that he was not interested in Lincoln students because, he said, "They are unjust to Billy Herndon, who was my friend." Assuring him of my desire to deal fairly with Herndon, I left the Herndon-Parker letters for him to read, asking him to let me know if he would see me after reading them. The result was astonishing; reading the letters was like a resurrection day in his mind, bringing back the past in living vividness. For three days, except the evenings, I listened to him talk of Lincoln, Herndon and the stirring days of old. Often he seemed to forget my presence as he poured out his memories and reflections. It was like looking at the soul of Lincoln reflected in a sensitive mirror—he gave me a vision of Lincoln no book has ever been able to give me.

The mother of Rankin was one of the many women who mothered Lincoln. He was often a guest in her home when Rankin was a lad. She was the confidante of both sides of the courtship of Lincoln and Anne Rutledge, the sweet country girl whom he worshiped as a young man, and whose death cast so long a shadow over his life. It was she who tried to induce Lincoln to make a statement about his religious attitude when he was accused of being an "infidel" by Peter Cartwright in their race for Congress. Lincoln declined, saying that he would not discuss religion on a political platform, but he confided his faith to her and the group gathered in the home, the boy Rankin listening in. So, naturally, when he graduated from Illinois College and decided to study law, he entered the Lincoln-Herndon office in 1856 and remained until 1860, when he stood beside the Wabash train and looked up into the face of Lincoln as he took off his hat and made his brief, beautiful farewell speech to Springfield—a city he was never to see again. Here was a man who had studied for four years in the office of Lincoln—a single large room, on the second floor back, overlooking the litter of a back alley, simply furnished with desks for the two partners, and an old cot; an ideal place to listen to the discussion of cases at law and problems of politics, and to study two very different personalities. He studied Lincoln—the books he read, the books he did not like, his habits of mind—with insight and discrimination, and he had the literary gift to describe his personality, his methods and moods. To Rankin, as to so many young men, the friendship of Lincoln was a spiritual experience; and as he talked it was almost as if Lincoln had entered the room.

When Lincoln was away on the Eight Circuit, trying cases, Rankin stayed with Mary Lincoln, did the chores and helped to take care of the boys. They read French together; he came to know her as no one else knew her. To me that three-day interview was a profound experience—no one can touch the spirit of Lincoln, even indirectly, and not be exalted and enriched, made taller of soul. After much persuasion I induced Rankin to write down what he had told me, telling him that what was memory to him was history to a man of my generation, and that he owed it to both Lincoln and his wife to make such a record. At last, reluctantly, he agreed to do so, despite the difficulties of his age and infirmity, and the result was a book, for which I wrote an introduction, entitled: *Personal Recollections of Abraham Lincoln,* by Henry B. Rankin, published by my friend Major Putnam. It had a wide reading, especially in England, because it gave an understanding of Lincoln no other writer had given; for example, his religious attitude, in regard to which Herndon had erred, by unconsciously reading too much of his own thinking into the mind of Lincoln. Take the story that Lincoln wrote an essay attacking the Christian religion, which one of his friends snatched out of his hands and stuffed into the stove, lest it imperil his political hopes. The document burned was not an essay on theology; it was a love letter. Lincoln did write a religious essay, but it was a scriptural argument about the Love of God. Also, Rankin included a chapter on Mary Lincoln—the first gallant and chivalrous thing ever written about her. No woman in our history has been treated more cruelly, more brutally, more unkindly. One remembers with shame how, in her broken later years—when her mind, always unstable, was confused, erratic, if not irresponsible—she was hounded by a viperous gossip, until she was driven out of her own country and had to live in Europe. For years Charles Sumner fought to get her a pension—how tragic that such a fate should have been visited upon the wife of Abraham Lincoln!

LINCOLN & HERNDON

From Springfield I went to Newcastle, Indiana, and spent a week with Jesse W. Weik, who had collaborated with Herndon in writing the biography of Lincoln, so long delayed. He had nearly all of the original material collected by Herndon, and was most gracious in allowing me to go through it, including all the notes and letters of Herndon. It gave me a curious feeling of nearness to Lincoln to hold in my hand the arithmetic which the boy had made for himself by copying problems on large sheets of paper, then punching holes in the paper and tying the sheets together into a "book," on which he wrote:

Abe Lincoln, his book and pen,
He will be good, but God knows when.

The notes made by Herndon in his old age were mostly trivial, repetitious, and of little value. A big bookful of this gossip was published a few years ago, under the title, *The Real Lincoln,* and played up sensationally, to the deep regret of all Lincoln students. Weik and I remained firm friends until his death. He had intended, he told me, to leave his unique and priceless collection to the Library of Congress, but the Great Depression wrecked him financially, and his treasures had to be sold and, I fear, scattered. My work was done—an enormous piece of research—and my book appeared in 1910. It was accorded a most cordial reception, and is still sought after as a source-book of the period which it covers.

If only by some art I could put into words a tithe of what my fellowship with Lincoln—begun intensively in 1908 and continued quietly ever after—did for me far back and deep down in my being; but it cannot be done. My long, intimate contact with his spirit—following his lonely, sometimes shadowy, God-directed path adown the years, leading him often in a way he knew not, until he became one of the sublime sacrificial spirits of the race, ascending in a chariot of tragedy —has been the profoundest experience of my life, second only to my study and brooding over the life of Jesus. By a strange paradox it made me at once more radical in my sympathies and more conservative in my thinking. No one felt more keenly the wrong of slavery than Lincoln did, yet he would not do wrong to abolish wrong—he believed that the means must justify the end, that righteousness must be done righteously. He had, as Burke would say, "the disposition to conserve and the ability to improve." If we do not conserve what we have, we cannot improve it; nor can we really conserve it without constantly improving it. But, unless we keep our balance, we shall lose what we have in blunderingly, impatiently, trying to get what we want. His one supreme aim and endeavor was to save the Union—without slavery if possible, with slavery if neces-

sary, as he wrote to Greeley, but to save the Union—and that
aim rose in his mind to something like the sublimity and authority of a religious mysticism—nothing could deflect him from
his objective. Today we see how right and far-seeing he was
—what would a divided America be worth in the world?
What a life to study, what noble integrity, what high courage,
what delicate justice and melting pity! What loyalty to the
ideal, what common sense and practical capacity touched by
poetry, what heights of vision and valleys of melancholy, what
tear-freighted humor! Knowing Lincoln has given me a sense
of the majesty of noble human living, a glimpse of the meaning
of life itself, of what lies hidden in the souls of the high and
humble alike; a great faith in my race and in my country.

SPIRITUAL ADVENTURE

When Dr. Burkhalter and I finished reading the Church
Fathers, he stopped, but I went on, exploring the lives of the
saints and mystics, those in the calendar and others outside
—the lives of those who had won spiritual victory, seeking to
know their discipline, their technique, and their vision. It was
indeed a spiritual adventure, becoming acquainted with those
who had triumphed where the rest of us are defeated; made
victors by their stronger faith and clearer vision. In these
studies I found wise mentors in Dean Inge, Evelyn Underhill,
Baron von Hügel, Rufus Jones, sage and seer of the Society of
Friends, and Arthur Edward Waite, all of whom became my
friends of afteryears. My quest was for immediate religion, not
mediated religion—in symbol or sacrament—for direct "contact" with spiritual reality, not an echo of echoes. My mentors
opened the gate and pointed to the paths in a garden per-
fumed by the winds and flowers of heaven, where I found such
truth as I had never known before and an "eternal unanimity"
of testimony of insight and experience in contrast to the arid
speculations of theology, which so often seemed but the jug-
gling of concepts to no avail. Therefore, I went to the saints
and mystics themselves, greatly daring, humbly seeking—saints

are of many sorts, I learned; they belong to all sects and to none. They include Peter, John, Paul, Augustine, Francis, Bernard, but also Tauler, Boehme, Eckhart, Philip Neri, John of the Cross, Bunyan, Wesley, Molinos, Ruysbroeck, Spinoza, Emerson, Lincoln, and not least John Woolman, and others too many to name, some indeed who preferred to remain anonymous.

My catalogue is unorthodox, I know; but that does not matter—it is true—a goodly, glorious company, gracious and appealing, and I remember them with gratitude and joy. Yes, and with wonder too, because they have "words of Eternal Life," their pages sparkle with the dew of morning, as vivid as light, though some of them lived ages ago. Nowhere are the words of the old poem of Finland more true: "We must learn to let go of the old that ages, in order to lay hold of the old that ages not." The All Saints' Day sermon of Thomas Aquinas is as fresh today as when it was preached in 1260; it is untarnished by time.

One of my favorites among that shining company was—and is—Teresa the Carmelite, sanest of mystics and most sensible of saints. She was witty as well as pious, merry as well as devout, and her radiant faith blended perfectly with her rippling humor. She practiced stern self-discipline, but she detested melancholy and the religion of the long face. "Mirth is from God," she taught, "and dullness is from the devil. You can never be too sprightly, you can never be too good-tempered." She was all for health and cleanliness, in an age when disease and dirt were still believed to indicate holiness. She was a great executive, but she knew how to use a scrubbing brush. "God dwells in the scullery, as well as in the chapel," she said. She wanted her sisters to worship with alert minds as well as wakeful hearts. At night—especially at midnight—she said the voice of prayer should not be hushed, for then evil prowls abroad, stealthily, to conquer and stain the world. It may have been a fancy of hers, but it was a sublime fancy—nay, a faith—that a knot of praying women could defeat the regiments of hell, make them waver, falter, and flee.

Ah, the saints were masters of the art of prayer and of those inner techniques which bring spiritual energy into day-by-day life; and how victoriously they employed the art of intercession. Later I tried, stammeringly, to set forth my findings in this radiant field of research in a tiny book called *What Have the Saints To Teach Us?* which, next to my Life of Swing— since a writer loves his first book as a mother loves her first child—I love best of my earlier writings. With which ought to be joined another tiny book, *Wesley and Woolman,* which, studying first Wesley, then Woolman, and then the two together, shows how practical the mystics were, and how their lives gave birth to social movements of great import, long before the "social gospel" was preached and debated among us.

Of course I know how modern psychologists study the saints as specimens of pathology, making catalogues of their ecstasies and excesses, especially the latter, in much the same way that men study insects. How easy to follow the path of some God-entranced soul, looking on from the outside, jotting down here an odd act, there a wild word, and piecing together a pattern of eccentricity. Yet so it is that men of our time, opaque themselves, treat those great souls whose vision, dark with excess of light, flashes with celestial fire, and whose words, as simple as the prayer of a child, bear the wisdom of those who might have returned from the dead. No matter; a book on psychologists written in like vein would be interesting, too—they are such lions in diagnosing others and such lambs in dealing with their own souls. (A psychologist to whom I read this sentence, said, "It is God's truth; only it ought to be underlined, for sake of emphasis.") Yet there is a reason for their attitude—they do not distinguish between the psychic and the mystical; two things totally different, but often confused.

Psychic phenomena and spiritual truths are not the same things. They are often found together, and one is used to prove the other; but that is an error. Spiritual truth stands on its own feet; psychic facts do not prove it, not even the truth of immortality. Often the great saints were psychics too; often, but not always. St. Paul was both. When he tells us that he knew a man—meaning himself—who was caught up into the third heaven and heard "things for which there is no law of utterance," he was speaking as a psychic. When he wrote the 13th Chapter of First Corinthians he was speaking as a mystic —or, if one does not like the word, as a man of the spirit, lifted up, transfigured, his eyes cleansed, whose words haunt us like great music. Failing to make this distinction, men lose their way in confusion; it is both vital and important, and clears up the whole subject.

THE ETERNAL CHRIST

These studies and explorations of the Land of the Spirit, of which the mystics and saints were citizens, continued through the years and formed the background of my first book of religious essays. It was called *The Eternal Christ*, the essays having been read, in synopsis, to the Pastors' Union of the city, in answers to questions propounded by Dr. Burkhalter. A statement of the questions will reveal the spirit and scope of the book. First question: "Is what the poet, the seer, the prophet sees there? If so, why do not all see it? If not, what does he make it out of?" The first question was answered in the affirmative, else the loftiest souls of the race were mad, with an incredible coincidence and collaboration of delusion. If such an affirmation is valid, the other questions do not come up, except to say that some people are God-blind as others are color-blind. Second question: "Is the difference of phraseology, in the expression of teaching, the principal difference between the Christian ages"—and the various Christian communions? This question was also answered affirmatively, meaning that different ages and churches are all trying to say the same thing, albeit with varying dialects. Third question: "What is personality? How is it constituted? What power have we to modify, enlarge, elevate and expand it?" The answer had to do with the very nature of the soul, and the power which religion has, or ought to have, in reshaping its structure, as well as its inner attitude, direction, and development—a daring investigation. Fourth question: "In what sense is Christ eternal? Is He a living, abiding Presence among men? If so, how can He become real to us?" It was, in fact, a walk to Emmaus, showing that Christ is not only a Fact in time, a Force in history, but a Friend of human souls, who will let Him live with them; "a life within our life than self more near, a veiled Presence infinitely clear," with whom life loses its appalling loneliness and becomes a joyous journey. "We are all strings in the concert of His joy; Amen," as Jacob Boehme put it.

In due time the book appeared, enlarged from the essays read to the ministers, its notes showing what Dr. Burkhalter called "a frightful lot of reading," published by my friend Fleming H. Revell, who loved it and found joy in making it known far and wide. My friend Edwin L. Shuman, of the Chicago *Record-Herald,* said that it was "written in pellucid, unobstructive beauty of style, uniting the skyey quality of Emerson with the mellow humanism and magnetism of Brooks, with a radiant faith in the things of the spirit that should give it many friends both inside and outside the churches." Which was more the generous tribute of a friend than the calm judgment of a critic—what I had dreamed rather than what I had actually done. God be thanked for friends who judge us by what we aspire to rather than by what we imperfectly achieve. Dr. Gunsaulus gave a copy of the book to Booker Washington, who carried it in his bag on his endless journeys in behalf of his race, read it, re-read it, and marked it. Later he showed the book as marked to Gunsaulus, who said to me, "Nearly every sentence was underscored, and many doubly underlined." It gave me a vision which haunted me—Booker Washington, one of the greatest men of his race and his generation, riding a Jim-Crow car, reading *The Eternal Christ!* Merciful heaven, how we do get things muddled! Still stands that stubborn prejudice, and others of like kind in grim array—unseeing, undiscriminating—mocking our religion, and blocking the road toward a better world. God forgive us, if He can!

GUNSAULUS

More than once in this record I have spoken of Dr. Frank Gunsaulus, a friend of all the early years of my ministry after my student days in Boston; and what a friend! A man of many moods and manifestations, it was once my plan and dream to write his biography, as I had done for David Swing, but, alas! I was unable to obtain the co-operation of his family, none of whom, except his daughter Helen, had any real estimate of the man and the work he was doing. He was as lonely as the dead. The founder of Armour Institute for the technical education of young people—the result of what was known as "the two million dollar sermon"—he became the minister of Central Church, Chicago, in succession to Dr. Hillis, and for years had a place of command in the life of the city such as few men have ever had in any city. A giant in strength, of fabulous mental and spiritual resource, he did the work of many men and, at last, paid the price for it.

The first time I heard him preach was on the Sunday following the death of Joseph Parker, Minister of the City Temple in London. They had been friends, and some allowance had to be made for the beautiful bias of friendship in his estimate of Parker. It was a vision of the Christian ministry, an extraordinary portrayal, as touch was added to touch, until at last Joseph Parker seemed to live again in the pulpit of Central Church. As I had never seen Parker, it was a revelation to me, albeit I could not follow him when at times he seemed to place Parker above Beecher—no, Parker was a trumpet, Beecher was an orchestra. Today the tones of his voice come back to me from behind the hills, now soft as a flute, now melodious as an organ, as variable as his moods, as just as his character, as sweet as his spirit; such a voice cannot be made in one generation; there has never been another of like range and melody.

No printed sermon by Dr. Gunsaulus shows us more than a third of the man. He was the greatest dramatic preacher America has known, but his art, at its best, was incommunicable

in the printed word. Six times I heard his sermon—I should
like to hear it six times again—which might have been entitled,
"Christ at the Feet of His Disciples," portraying the evening
in the Upper Room when the Master washed the feet of the
Apostles. "And He took a towel," was the text. "He might
have taken a star," said the preacher, the better to show the
august humility of the Servant in the House. Then he became
an artist, reproducing not only the scene but the atmosphere
of the farewell meal. He re-enacted the scene from the point of
view of each disciple as the Master approached him with basin
and towel. Only a man of painter-like sympathy and insight,
joined with extraordinary gifts of characterization, could have
done it. A single false note would have ruined the scene, but
there was no false note. Each disciple stood out distinctly—his
character, his personality, his very soul—as if, by some magic,
the man had been there in the pulpit. The preacher forgot
himself—the congregation forgot the preacher—all were present in the Upper Room long ago. One could have taken a
photograph of Peter, it was all so real, so vivid. It was a solemn,
almost terrifying moment when he came to Judas; strong men
sobbed like children, torn equally between the horror of evil
obsession and the awful mercy of the Master. The sermon,
when reported, lost eighty percent of its power, color, and
vividness. Never again on this earth do I expect to hear such a
sermon now that the great artist-preacher has vanished. Nor
can I make anyone who did not see or hear him realize the
fascination of his personality, majestic, commanding, enchanting, incredibly winsome. When I think of him the words of the
old Hebrew centuries flash into my mind: "My father! My
father! The chariots of Israel and the horseman thereof!"

CITY OF FRIENDS

It was about this time, 1912, as best I remember, that I was
called to the People's Church in St. Paul, Minnesota. Naturally
I went to spend a Sunday with the church, out of respect for
the invitation. Then I learned that Gunsaulus had suggested

it, as, later, he wanted me to follow him in Central Church, Chicago. A day or so after my return, a voice over the telephone told me that there was to be a very important meeting in "The Little Brick Church." To my question asking what it was about I received no answer, except the time of the meeting, and the hope that I would be good enough to attend. It was all very puzzling. When I arrived at the church I found it packed and jammed with all sorts and conditions of people, a distinguished layman of the Methodist Church was presiding. They gave me a chair against the back wall of the church. It was a community meeting called, apparently, to protest against my accepting the invitation to go to St. Paul, and urging me not even to consider it. There were a number of speeches, some by Bohemian people, who made up perhaps a fourth of the population of the city—folk of high type, artistic, lovers of music, the best of good citizens, many of whom belonged to my church, and were my good friends. I do not recall the order of the speeches or the names of most of the speakers. In fact, I was too astonished at what was said, I did not recognize the man they described or the work they said he had done, and was doing; it was like a package delivered to the wrong address, or a premature obituary. When I was called upon at last, I could hardly speak at all—my voice was tear-laden and uncertain; but I did stammer out both my gratitude and my humility, as best I could. I wanted to go far away, somewhere, and have a good cry. The headline in the paper next day, "The Genius of Joseph Fort Newton," was not a statement of fact, unfortunately; far from it. But it was an amazing expression of the loyalty, confidence and responsiveness of a city of friends; it lingers like a perfume in my heart. After such a meeting, of course it was impossible for me to consider going to St. Paul.

One of the speakers, I remember, was Fred J. Lazell, city-editor of the Cedar Rapids *Republican,* an able, modest, retiring man, genuinely gentle-hearted. A fine journalist—later he taught in the School of Journalism at the University of Iowa—he was by vocation a naturalist. He and his wife—two of the most devoted people I have ever known—taught a whole town, or all who would listen and learn, to know the birds and their songs, flowers and their charm, and the wonders of nature in detail. If he had gone to sleep, like Rip van Winkle, when awakened he would have known the time of year by the flowers in bloom, the trees and birds which he read like a book. He was not content to read what John Burroughs called "the fine print of Nature," but interpreted here a line and there a verse of its God-illumined text, as in his essay on "Isaiah as a Nature Lover," which appeared in a series of little books which it was my honor to edit. Written with insight and enthusiasm, it had to do with the nature scenery in the pages of a great prophet— how the out-of-doors was a manuscript which the seer read. While the Bible has no such word as "nature" in its vocabulary, yet it reflects the arch of the sky, the curve of the earth, rising and setting suns, mountains, seas, birds, and flowers.

In the meantime—only it was not a mean time at all—a little girl had come to our home, "out of the nowhere into the here," bringing big brown eyes and dainty baby ways. The date of her birth is "a military secret," and who am I, her father, to be telling tales out of school—women have their rights, after all. All through the years her childish grace, her maiden magic, her womanly charm have been among my joys. In due time she became a beautiful and brilliant woman, a Phi Beta Kappa graduate of Vassar College, but not satisfied with her training, since it taught her what had been done and said in the past, but left her unfitted to do things for herself in the present. Hence an article which she wrote, entitled, "Should Education Have its Face Lifted?" She argued that it should, which made educators squirm and writhe. Also, while I was abroad she wrote an essay for *Scribner's Magazine,* entitled "Youth Challenges the Church," which set everybody agog, and brought much discussion. The editor wanted me to reply to it, but I agreed with nine-tenths of what she had said, and, besides, how can a man argue with his baby? Also, she wrote a college story, which was syndicated, but which she thought not worth putting into a book. She took an intensive training in journalism, taught by my friends of the United Press, and became an adept in advertising for the Macmillan Company, until her marriage. At this writing she is with us "for the duration," with her little daughter, Sarah Ann, "golden-glow," whose loveliness helps her grandfather to recall the days that come not back, when her mother was a little girl.

FREEMASONRY

Earlier in this record I related how my father was made a Freemason in one of the Military Lodges in the Southern Army, and how, as a prisoner of war, taken desperately ill, his life was saved by making himself known as a Mason to a Union officer who nursed him back to life. Thus to Masonry I owe the life of my father, and my feeling toward the Fraternity is much like that of Dr. Oliver Holmes, when he wrote a poem to a painting of his grandmother, wondering who and what he would be if that gracious lady had said "No" to an interesting proposal. In the same way, if Masonry had failed in its benign labor, I would be part myself and part someone else, if I existed at all. No wonder, then, knowing this bit of family history, I joined the Fraternity as soon as I was old enough to be received, in Friendship Lodge, No. 7, Dixon, Illinois. There, to my amazement, I saw men of all churches—except one, and there was no reason in Masonry why that one church should not be represented—gathered about an open Bible. In their churches they could not agree about the teachings of the Bible; in the Lodge they could not disagree, because each one was allowed to interpret it in the way his heart loved best, and asked to allow others the same right; a secret almost too simple to be found out.

Masonry is not a secret order, else the names of its members and the places and times of its meetings would not be known. It is a private fraternity, seeking to select and train men, making them brothers and builders in the service of the best life. Its only secrets are certain signs, grips and passwords whereby its members make themselves known to their fellows in time

of need or danger, and so are able to help one another, unknown to the world. Its work of charity, especially to the aged,
is munificent and never-tiring. Its principles are as public as
the sunlight. What struck me was that Masons, including myself, needed to know more about Masonry, in order to do more
with it and for it. To me it was—and is—one of the great
poetries of the world, religious but not a religion, based upon
the Bible, rich in its labors of doing good. To my surprise the
Grand Master, Louis Block—a man big of body, big of mind,
with a heart as big as all-out-of-doors—made me his Grand
Chaplain, and asked me to write a book telling Masons the
story and meaning of Masonry. Cedar Rapids was the one city
in which to write such a book; one of its treasured institutions
was the greatest Masonic Library in America, if not in the
world. After prodigious labor, studying not only Masonry, but
the symbolism of the race, the result was a book entitled, *The
Builders, A Story and Study of Masonry,* which proved to be—
and still is—far and away the most widely read book on Masonry
in our generation.

Besides many editions in this country and England, *The
Builders* was translated into Dutch by H. J. Ginkel, and published in Amsterdam; into Swedish, and published in Stockholm; two large editions by a group of Brethren of the University of Barcelona, Spain; and a Sanskrit version, published
in Damascus, due to the influence of the late Brother Dr.
Adams, of Beirut College, Syria. It was translated into German
and ready to be published in that country when Hitler and the
brutalitarians came into power and closed all Lodges; as also
happened in Italy, where the "sawdust Caesar" had murdered
the Grand Master of Masons, along with other prominent
Brethren whom he put out of the way—"liquidated," in the
hideous dialect of the Devil, which came into vogue. The book
was revised in England where I was living, in 1918, corrected
by two Research Lodges, and enjoyed the benefit of all the
books, bringing out many new and important facts, in connec-
tion with the two hundredth anniversary celebration of the
Grand Lodge of England in 1919, the celebration having been

put forward until after the first World War had ended. Written to meet a deeply felt need, the book has stood the test of time, and I hope to make another revision, adding a section telling what happened to the gentle Craft of Freemasonry during the ecumenical disaster of the second World War—a melancholy story of ravage and ruin, of Masons killed or starved, of Lodges scattered, their properties confiscated or destroyed in the orgy of horror and fiendish cruelty which made the earth a province of hell, ruled by Satan and his imps. But a new day is at hand, and Masonry will be born anew for new adventures and new blessings.

This was the first of eight other books written at various times, later, for the instruction of Masons in Masonry, its history and its art. It was not an easy book to write; Masonry had not been studied, by the craft in general, in a strict historical manner. One had to go behind legends to find fact, behind fiction to discover truth—it was bewildering, but at last one found the key. In particular, I found that a group of scholars had done what I was trying to do, Gould, Hughan, Speth, Crawley, Thorp, to name no others, filing their findings in the Transactions of the Quatuor Coronati Lodge, No. 2076, in London; twenty four volumes and more. Of course, hundreds of other books were read and digested, as the notes to my book show, but the reports of the Research Lodges of England made it possible for me to do my work in a shorter time. Naturally this fact suggested to me the idea of having a Research Lodge in Iowa to make a better use of the great library and to set our findings in a more popular form for all Masons to read. My suggestion was received with enthusiasm, but it was wisely modified and enlarged, and the result was the National Masonic Research Society, with headquarters in Iowa. Also, it was proposed to publish a journal, monthly, to be called *The Builder*, which I had the honor to edit until I left America. This was delightful work; it brought me in touch with Masonic students all over the land, as well as in Canada, and, of course, in England and Scotland. The contacts formed, the friendships made, became a source of inspiration and joy. My book *The Builders* appeared in December, 1914; the Research Society journal began the following year, as I remember it.

THE BLACK YEAR

1914! It was the black year, dividing modern history into before and after—Europe exploded in a World War, as if all hell were on a holiday. The human world cracked, and the cleavage continued to widen, and, after an interval of Armistice, came economic collapse, world-wide and devastating; then the second edition of the same war, total war, led by megalomaniacs, seeking to establish the foulest and most obscene tyranny which ever crawled across the earth, monsters trying to drag the race down to a sub-human level; disaster following fast and following faster. It has been the most ghastly period in history. Never has our race seen terror and misery, cruelty and ruthless horror and death on so vast a scale, stolid brutality and stark starvation over whole nations since the Black Death swept Europe in the Fourteenth Century. Lewis Mumford is right when he says that a thousand years separate 1930 and 1940, and if we extend the date to 1914, we discover that the crack in human history has become a chasm so wide and deep, that the days before 1914 seem like some "previous state of existence," of which theosophists claim to have dim memories. Those years cannot come to us again, we cannot go back to them, even in imagination. Think of publishing a book on Brotherhood when the brotherhood of the race was broken, of preaching the Gospel of Jesus to the rhythm of great guns and falling bombs—the agony of it, the crucifixion of faith and ideals; the profound discrepancy between the ideal of Christ and the ghastly realities of the world at war, which well-nigh tore the Christian mind in two. Again and again, as this record proceeds, I shall be trying to tell what that awful ordeal did to my soul, and to my fellow souls, with little hope of being able to do so.

In these despites my work went on in the church, in the university, and as editor of *The Builder,* albeit with heavy and aching heart.

Issues which had been abstract and academic suddenly became concrete and acute; some questions had to be asked and answered in my own mind. For one thing, I was unable to take the pacifist position that all war is always wrong, and that war never settles anything. The first would mean that Washington was wicked in fighting for the liberty of his people, and that Lincoln was sinful in fighting to save the Union—did anyone ever hate war more than he? Some wars are right, some are wrong, and others are mixed. To say that all wars are wrong shows a lack of moral insight—for a people to defend their homes when attacked cannot be wrong. War is horrible—later I was to see it close up—but some things are worse: slavery, the degradation of the human spirit, the obliteration of the moral and spiritual life. Wars do settle some things. Our War of the Revolution did settle an issue and made possible our Republic; the Civil War did preserve the Union, the Battle of Tours decided what the religion of Europe was to be. Force, as such, is neither moral nor immoral; it is how we use force, and for what purpose, that counts. For me to accept the liberty and security given by my country, created by the courage and sacrifices of brave men—many of them giving their lives—and not be willing to defend it when attacked, would be immoral. A pacifist, if he does not help his country, helps the enemy—he cannot keep out of war. If he wishes to take insult and injustice without resentment, in obedience to the words of Jesus, it is his right, and he is wise. I have done that too; for example, when the mayor of Dixon tried to kill me for upsetting his game of rotten politics. Jesus said nothing about war or politics; His mission had to do with the kingdom within us. But when the hard-won inheritance of the past, even the existence of civilization, is at stake, to say nothing of our homes and the graves of our fathers, we cannot stand aloof and refuse to defend our country. In my own mind I was convinced that

America would be drawn into the war, soon or late; at any
rate I was not neutral, not for an instant, as the President
asked us to be.

LONDON CALLING

In 1915 R. J. Campbell resigned as Minister of the City
Temple in London. A short while afterward I received a letter
from the editor of *The Christian Commonwealth,* the City
Temple paper, asking permission to publish my sermons, taken
from the pamphlets issued by Luther Brewer. Of course I
agreed, thinking that he meant to use them as a kind of stop-
gap until a new minister of the City Temple had been chosen.
Then, a little later, I had intimations from many sources, from
Dr. Gunsaulus, from Dr. Burkhalter, from Dr. Marquis, President of Coe College in Cedar Rapids, that the City Temple
Church was thinking of calling me to be its minister. Frankly,
I was not only astonished, but frightened—such a possibility
had never entered my mind. Furthermore, I was against it,
since it would mean giving up "The Little Brick Church," my
lectureship in the university, as well as *The Builder,* which I
was editing—in short, pulling up the very roots of my life and
moving four thousand miles away to another country in the
midst of a world war. The suggestion was preposterous; I did
not think that I was able to undertake such a ministry, and I
did not want to cut my life in two. In due time my fears were
fulfilled, and a cablegram from the Board of Deacons asked me
to spend a month preaching in the City Temple. Since it was
only for a month I accepted, and some lines from my Diary tell
of my first journey on the sea:

—If I were a rich pagan instead of a poor Christian, I would
build a temple to the sea. It is so patient and strong to ship or
soul that bravely casts loose upon its mighty promises; so stern
to the unpiloted and unseaworthy. It is a great burden bearer.
It cannot be overloaded. It never grows weary. It never breaks
down. It never needs repairs. It rests the eye with its infinite
variety; it calms the heart with its never-ending music. It has
many moods, now sad, now troubled, now bright with what the
Greeks called its "inextinguishable laughter." A poet speaks of

the "unplumbed, salt, estranging sea," but today we sail a sea whose ways and winds are known. Its tidal rhythms, its measured waves and measureless horizons are symbols of the deep, mysterious thoughts of God; as the stars round off the three divisions of the *Divine Comedy*. Shakespeare caught the very cadence of that eternal sea whose waves are years and whose depth is eternity. How can a man be irreligious on the sea? He may feel secure enough, but when he looks over the side of the boat, up starts that primitive fear which only faith can allay. Religion is a thing of the depths for the depths. There will be companies of believing souls as long as there are deep, unplumbed places in life. In a calm, clear night of stars I sat on the deck of the ship near the prow, the great sea spread out beneath, and the ship's bell rang out; in my heart such a profound and still sense of the reality and nearness of God that when I went to my couch, I knew that if I sank it would not be into the sea—but beyond it!

England was like a picture in a storybook to me, beautiful in her sea-girt island glory; a Blessed Island, for a thousand years the home and the fortress of a wise and ordered liberty. How lovely it was in its vivid green garb, and so dainty withal, like a well-kept park; its people so kindly, soft-spoken and courteous. It seemed more than half like home to me; its spirit in my blood, its great souls among my heroes, its singers my teachers. And London was like a dream come true. As I rambled through it I was haunted by the curious feeling of something half-forgotten, but still dimly remembered. New York is young, spacious, graceful; London, with its monotonous and melancholy houses, seemed like an inharmonious patchwork. Yet it was lovable in its sprawling confusion, pieced together without design, and as I stepped out of Euston Station I saw a procession of women workers, with gay uniforms, jaunty hats, and plumes a-nodding. What would their grandmothers have thought of it if they had seen it! Soldiers, sailors, nurses, ambulances were everywhere; one came out of a time-stained church into an air athrill with the sense of a vast tragedy only a few miles away. London in wartimes, subdued, suffering, heroic, a museum and history and a hive of industry; its people cemented by one spirit of service, all ranks vowed to one motto, "Every man do his bit, stick it, and smile." How unlike America where the war was a far-off echo, as if raging on another planet, where opinion and sympathy were so tragically divided!

At the City Temple I found a queer situation. Founded in 1640, its first Minister Thomas Goodwin, chaplain to Oliver Cromwell, its present building and name were the work of Joseph Parker, in 1874. As I climbed its long, winding pulpit stairs, I thought of all who had knelt in that Place of Hearing, and they seemed to have left something of themselves in return for the blessing they received. In panels near the roof great names were to be read, Cromwell, Bunyan, Wesley, Whitefield, and Spurgeon. Parker was an autocrat who ruled the church with a rod of iron. The Board of Deacons, good men, were his friends—yes-men. Parker had selected Campbell to follow him, the Deacons accepting him as a lovely, ethereal figure, "the little gray angel," as the London papers called him, and treated him as a child; his prematurely white hair, his youthful face, his great dark blue eyes, his gentle ways made his entrance into the pulpit arresting, like an apparition from the Middle Ages. When he announced *The New Theology*—which was neither new nor a theology, but for purposes of publicity well named—the dear old Deacons stood by him loyally, albeit not knowing what it was all about. They were a bit nervous when he adventured into socialism and appeared on Labor platforms and seemed to be leading a radical movement, but they still stood by him. However, when he resigned the City Temple to join the Anglican Church, they were bowled over, as so many others were—we have nothing in our religious life to help us to understand the shock of a Free-Churchman becoming an Anglican, a Non-conformist joining the State Church, for which let us be grateful.

A BAD MUDDLE

Such was the situation when I arrived to be guest preacher at the City Temple. The newspapers of London seemed to think that I was out to capture the City Temple pulpit; *The Westminster Gazette* had an editorial entitled "Preaching 'With a View.'" The guttersnipe press, led by *John Bull*, barked at me as an American, which seemed to be the lowest form of life, while *The Morning Post*, the Tory bible, had a chance for some of its polished satire against our country. The United States had not yet entered the war, and England was in an ugly mood in regard to us, as if, when London took snuff, Washington ought to sneeze. It was most unpleasant, and took some of the edge off my romantic faith in Anglo-American friendship. The Deacons of the City Temple were determined that Dr. John Henry Jowett, an Englishman, at that time pastor of the Fifth Avenue Presbyterian Church in New York City, should be the new minister of the Temple. It was perfectly right for an English preacher to go to an American church, but absurd for an American preacher to go to an English church—it was a one-way street! But the City Temple Church asserted its rights and demanded a voice in the choice of a new minister, to the astonishment of the Deacons, which was apparently a closed, self-perpetuating corporation, in practice at least, up until that time. But the church insisted, and, being a Congregational Church, the Deacons had to hear and heed.

All during the month of my ministry the City Temple had been packed and jammed—clean back to "the Rocky Mountains," as the top gallery was called. Some came out of curiosity, of course, but more for better motives, and there was no anti-American poison in the church or congregation. During the last week of my stay there was a church meeting, and the Deacons put forward the name of Dr. Jowett, but the church would not have it so. There was no chance of Dr. Jowett getting the pulpit which he coveted, and which his friends coveted for him. Years before—as the story was told to me—when "the New Theology controversy" was at its peak, Dr. Jowett had snubbed Mr. Campbell at a luncheon, and the City Temple people never forgave him. "No gentleman would do such a thing," they said; it was their phrase, I only report it to explain what happened at the church meeting, and why. The Deacons nominated Dr. Jowett, an amendment was offered substituting my name instead, and the amendment was carried overwhelmingly—to my utter amazement, when I heard the news a few minutes later.

The Deacons did not take their defeat gracefully. Instead, they called a meeting of the Board which they asked me to attend, with only one item on the agenda. Mr. Chapman, the senior Deacon—a dear, good man he was—told me that if I accepted the invitation of the church to be Minister, the Board of Deacons would resign in a body. While he was speaking two or three of the Deacons smiled at me kindly and gave me a big wink of friendliness. In reply, I asked the Board to do nothing until I had made my decision, after I returned home. The whole setup, I added, was confusing, not to say ridiculous; Christian people should not act in that manner—the majority should rule.

The sermons of the month were published under the title, *An Ambassador*. One of them had to do with "The Religion of Shakespeare," in celebration of the opening of the Memorial Theatre at Stratford-on-Avon. One reviewer remarked, "America used to send to Scotland and England for great preachers, but the tide seems to have turned."

RAMBLINGS

During the month, I had seen much of London and other parts of England and met people I had wanted to meet. A debate in the House of Commons was interesting, the more because the Irish members were still in the House. Soldiers explained to me the strange mixture of humor, prayer and blasphemy among the men at the front. They did not mean to be profane, but something was twisting their insides. One day I went down Dorking Way, stopping at Burford Inn, to Box Hill, where Meredith "learned to live much in the spirit and to see the brightness on the other side of life." Also, I spoke to the Press Club on the Street of Ink—Fleet Street—giving my impressions of the differences between English and American journalism, Lord Northcliffe presiding. Of course I went to St. Paul's, massive and magnificent, and to the Abbey, stately and beautiful in the sunlight, the home of that Eternal Loveliness which breaks the heart—and heals it. What a joy to lunch with Donald Hankey, whose *A Student in Arms* I had read—he was so modest, with his hesitating courtesy of address, his haunting personality. The second series of *A Student in Arms* appeared in the autumn, but, alas! with the tragic line, "Killed in action on the Somme, October 12th, 1916." The memory of him is like a footstep, always light, of one untimely gone away.

It was an honor to take tea with Dr. Thomas Masaryk, of Bohemia, and his daughter, Miss Olga. He had been a member of the Austrian Parliament, and was in London as an exile with a price on his head. At the suggestion of mutual friends in America—his wife was an American—he was a worshiper at the City Temple, albeit a Unitarian in faith. Never in my life have I had a more vivid intuition of the greatness of any man, his moral character, his spiritual idealism, his intellectual realism. One of the few good things that came out of the great war and the little peace was that he became the first President of the Czech-Slovak Republic. He was worthy of every honor.

One invitation which caused no agony of indecision fluttered down upon my desk from Scotland, on the wings of poetry:

> O come awa', O come awa',
> Strang brither o' the West-lan',
> Altho' we hinna meikle gear,
> Yer welcome to our best, man.
>
> O come awa', syne come awa',
> An' be our luckie guest, man.

How could one resist it? Up through the flat fields and dingy cities of the Midlands I went; I do not wonder that Ruskin railed at them—Rugby, Lichfield, Tamworth, Crewe. Then over "the peak country" into Yorkshire, and finally into the Burns country. Never has there been a hospitality more generous or more genuine; never a courtesy more complete in

detail. No anti-American feeling in Scotland, no snippy, snip-
ing criticism. When I rose to speak in Glasgow—the guest of
Lodge Progess—a great American flag was unfurled, and the
audience sang our national anthem. It was too brief a stay, but
there was time for a glimpse of Loch Lomond and the Clyde,
and it was like an enchantment to see Edinburgh at night.

Above, giant searchlights scanned the sky, darting like shining swords through the clouds as if stabbing at airy enemies,
while the moonlight shimmered over the bald-headed hills and
filled the valleys with silver. From whatever side one approaches
Edinburgh it is singularly picturesque, with its happy blend of
hill and sea, of rocky peaks and lofty spires. Having explored
the Castle, St. Giles, and Holyrood, I hurried away down the
East Coast to catch my steamer for America.

At home I found my friends exquisitely kind and strangely
silent. I could hear what they were thinking, but they did not
speak it. Two letters reached me in one envelope: one by
Hugh Black, arguing, point by point, that I should not go to
London; the other from G. Johnston Ross, making a plea,
equally pointed, for me to go. This made my dilemma more
difficult. Dr. Burkhalter was noncommittal—all he gave me
was a quick little hug of sympathy. Even W. R. Boyd—for
years neither of us had made a major decision without talking
it over with the other—was smitten mute; one could not pull a
word out of him with forceps. In Chicago, while in the office of
a banker-friend, he said to me, "Yes, I know what you have
come to talk about; I have no word to say on the subject—it
is your funeral"; a rather cold comfort.

Dr. Gunsaulus was no better. "Cheer up, my boy; whatever
you do you will wish that you had done the other thing. But
cut the knot, decide it, or it will break you." Then he told me
that the illness which left him a cripple was due, partly, to a
call to Broadway Tabernacle, New York, and his ordeal of indecision. My friends in Cedar Rapids offered to build a City
Temple for me. At last, after thinking the matter over, remembering the mess at the City Temple, and the divided

Church in London, I wrote declining the invitation, arguing that the Minister of the Temple ought to be a Britisher. Alas and alack, the invitation was repeated with emphasis, the whole church voting for me, except the Board of Deacons. In response I wrote a letter so qualified that it seemed that it could not be interpreted as an acceptance. Yet, something made me add a postscript—the fact that all signs indicated that our country would be drawn into the war, in which case an American in the City Temple pulpit, standing at the crossroads of the centuries, could do an important work. My postscript was that if they could not find anyone else to do what was needed at the City Temple, I would try to do my best. Only the postscript, I learned later, was read to the church, and I picked up my paper one morning and discovered that I had accepted—the die was cast.

No sooner had my acceptance been announced than a four-paged letter came from a famous Catholic Cardinal of Irish origin, asking, "Why go and preach to those English swine? My dear sir, you will be wasting your time." Then he poured out all his pent-up venom against the English, denouncing them for everything he could lay his pen to. It was a masterpiece of vitriolic writing, scorn, and contempt. He urged me to stay in my own country where God still lives.

Anyway I learned that indecision is an awful thing, a lonely thing; it can tear one in two. Even when we decide an issue, there are those who misunderstand and misinterpret our motives. Often things fall in line when one has made a decision, but things at the City Temple were awry. The Board of Deacons resigned—or rather they were abolished—and a Church Council was formed to guide the church, made up of members of various organizations, and from the congregation. So far as I am aware, there have been no Deacons at the City Temple since. In some ways it made things simpler, in others more complicated. Owing to the war, the transfer to London was difficult—we could take no furniture; we had to sell our beautiful home.

WAS IT A DREAM?

My last service as Minister of "The Little Brick Church" was very trying, both for preacher and people. Eight years before I had come to the city, unknown; I had worked quietly, without sensationalism and without sectarianism. In my sermons I had told the story of my heart—my faith, my hope; in my lectures I had shared my findings as a student of literature; I had touched all kinds of groups, toiling in behalf of the common good. The response was extraordinary; the church, if loosely organized, was a real fellowship—if I tried to name my friends in the church, in other churches, and outside of all churches, it would look like the City Directory. They had forgiven my mistakes and given me encouragement.

There is something infinite in all partings, and I knew that I was looking into faces many of which I would never see again on earth. The older people regarded the pastor and his wife as son and daughter; others, nearer our own age, a great company, had been chums and pals. All my people were my personal friends—I loved each one, I had walked with many through deep, dark places. It was impossible for me to speak personally, my sermon would have been punctuated with sobs. My subject was "The Angel of a New Day," an attempt to forecast the changing vision of religious ideals in tangled, turbulent, stupendous days. It found its way into print, and still has something to say: "Manifestly we stand at the end of an era, condemned to something great!" My heart was aching, my voice was almost breaking. At the end two lines from an old hymn flashed into my mind—nay, they were sent of God to meet my need—and became the benediction to a ministry to which I look back with gladness and gratitude:

> O spread Thy sheltering wings around,
> Till all our wanderings cease. Amen.

And that night I had a dream, if it was a dream, which has visited me twice since, in London and in New York; each time more vivid than before. In my dream, or vision, I stood

at the door of a vast cathedral, dim rather than dark, mellow
with age, as if it remembered all the prayers it had heard. It
was beautiful, but I felt its beauty rather than saw it, felt the
lift of its pillars, the leap of its arches, and the lofty spaces
where the shadow of God seemed to hover and wait. It was
quiet with an intense stillness. Near the door, where I was
standing, the high altar was hidden. A Presence was there, no
Face, but "the sight of a sweepy garment vast and white, with
a hem that I could recognise." No voice was heard, yet, somehow, I knew Who was speaking. Hardly less remarkable was
the congregation gathered there, such as no one ever saw save
in a dream. Not only "the glorious company" of apostles,
prophets and martyrs, but seers and sages and saints from many
lands and ages. Some faces I saw in profile—Moses, Isaiah,
Buddha, Socrates, Confucius, Plato, Plutarch, and the "shining
ones" of the church. But others outside the church were there,
Plotinus, Spinoza, Emerson, Lincoln, whose names may not be
in the calendar but are in the Book of Life. Yet all listened
reverently, and silently gave assent, in an unspoken Amen, to
the words of the Speaker—such words as He uttered in the Sermon on the Mount long ago. Maybe it was only a picture-
projection of what was—and is—deepest in my faith, but I pray
God that the vision may grow and abide; abide because it does
grow in clarity and power until, if I am worthy, I may hear
an echo of that Voice in a heart bowed down!

6

The City Temple

AGAIN LONDON! If I had been set down from anywhere, or from nowhere, I would have known that it was "ye olde London town," where, if you drive on the right side of the street you are wrong; if on the left you are right—as in the *Inferno* of Dante, as I reminded my English friends in fun.

And how quiet! Compared with the din of New York and the nightmare of the Chicago loop, London is like a gentle country village. There were no skyscrapers, but the picture spread out like a panorama from Primrose Hill can never be forgotten. Slowly London worked its ancient spell; everywhere were the hauntings of history. It is a very old city, weary of much experience of war and peace, willing to forgive much because it understands much. From a low dim sky a gentle rain was falling when I arrived, and a soft wind, burdened with damp fragrance, came as a promise of purity at the heart of things. Along the aloof avenues of the rich, and drab streets of the poor, that little wind wandered, like a breath of God, bringing a sudden tenderness and sad beauty to an imaginative soul. At such times the essential spirit of London is revealed; half-hidden things become palpable.

But the question in my mind was, Which London was it? For there are many Londons—the London of the Tower and the Abbey, of Soho and the Strand, of Downing Street and Whitechapel, of Piccadilly Circus and Leicester Square. There is also the London of Whittington and his Cat, of Goody Two-shoes and the Canterbury Shades, of Shakespeare and Chatterton, of Nell Gwynne and Dick Steel—aye, the London of all that is bizarre in history and strange in romance. They are all there, in a gigantic medley of past and present, of misery and magnificence. Sometimes it was hard for me to know which held the closest, the London of fact or the London of fiction, or the London of literature, which was a blending of both. Anyway, as I saw it, Goldsmith caroused with Tom Jones, and Fielding discussed philosophy with the Vicar of Wakefield; Nicholas Nickleby made bold to speak to W. M. Thackeray, and to ask his favor in behalf of a poor artist named Turner; and "Boz," as he passed through Longacre, was tripped up by the Artful Dodger and fell into the arms of St. Charles Lamb on his way to call on Lady Beatrix Esmond. No doubt my London was in large part a dream, but it was enchanting. It is said that if you live in London five years you will never be happy anywhere else, and I lived there long enough to feel its endless fascination.

RAINBOW CLUB

One of the first groups I attended was a meeting of the Rainbow Club, formed by Lady Stapley, who had the knack of making people feel instantly at ease and at home. Her idea was to bring together folk of all colors of thought—crusty Tories, rabid radicals, socialists, saints, sinners, all sorts, and have them discuss things; try to think of such a gathering on Fifth Avenue, New York! To hear such a group talk about the weather would be interesting, for each one would carry a different climate in his mind.

Next to me sat an American woman, wife of an English nobleman, and between ourselves we said snippy, saucy things about the English, as no doubt they did about us. Thinking that I could trust an American woman, I confided to her in a whisper the ungallant remark, "Really this is the homeliest set of people I have seen in many a day."

But, as Kipling would say, I learned about women from her. What did she do but tell the hostess what I had said, and I wished devoutly that I might drop through the floor or else evaporate. To my amazement the hostess beamed upon me, saying that I had paid her and her guests the highest possible compliment.

"You Americans," she said, "say such nice things; we knew you were homely when we met you." I tried to look pleasant and understand, but I was all in a fog. The traitoress at my side knew—what I did not know—that in England the word "homely" means cozy, chummy, companionable, pleasant. That was true of the group too, but it was not what I had in mind! It taught me a lesson, but it filled me with alarm, inasmuch as I was to preach the next Sunday for the first time as Minister of the City Temple. If ordinary, everyday words, I thought, have such different meanings in England from what they have with us, what would I be saying without knowing it?

Then there was an air-raid alarm, the lights were extinguished, and we sat next to the inner walls of the house, the while our hostess recited great passages from the Bible in the dark; it was most impressive.

The discussions of the Rainbow Club astonished me, showing that there is more freedom of thought in England than in America. Liberty, in fact, means a different thing in England from what it does with us. In England it signifies the right to think, feel, and act differently from other people; with us it is the right to develop according to a standardized attitude of thought and conduct. If one deviates from that standard, or pattern, he is scourged into line by the lash of opinion. We think in a kind of lock-step movement. Nor is this conformity imposed upon us from without. It is inherent in our social growth and habit. The average American knows ten times as many people as the average Englishman, and talks ten times as much—did not Heine say that "silence is conversation with an Englishman?"

We are gregarious; we gossip; and because everyone knows the affairs of everyone else, we are afraid of one another. For that reason, even in peacetime, public opinion moves with a regimented ruthlessness unknown in England, where the majority has no such arrogant tyranny as it has with us. When the subject of Anglo-American relations came up in the Rain-

bow Club, the fireworks began, and I was appalled by what I
heard. Journalists, labor leaders, radicals, conservatives, moder-
ates, all were there. They called a spade a spade; they were not
afraid of names and labels. They talked frankly and to the
point, they cracked the nut of every kind of idea to get the
kernel—"except in opinion not disagreeing," as Carlyle said of
his talk with Sterling. It was a new experience to me, refresh-
ing and at times infuriating, as when it dealt with my country,
in regard to which they exhibited such abysmal ignorance, if
not enmity.

There is, it is true, plenty of anti-British feeling in America;
it may be decried but it cannot be denied. Its roots go back to
the Revolution; it has been cherished, also, by folk of other
races in our midst. Far be it from me to justify it—my whole
life has been set against it. What is not known is that there is
plenty of anti-American feeling in England—it was to dog all
my days at the City Temple. It takes many forms—envy, fear,
sheer hatred, supercilious superiority, irritating condescension,
unbelievable pettiness, nagging nastiness. Before our country
went into the war it was almost unbearable; after we entered
the war everything was pleasant; ten days after the Armistice
my mail was almost unreadable. Even leading Free Church
ministers indulged in it—men of first-rate minds talking childish nonsense; their names ought to be recorded here, but I for-
bear. Younger ministers were not infected by it, nor the City
Temple congregation. But the press of London deserves to be
castigated without mercy—with some exceptions. Of this more
anon.

THE NEW MINISTER

No one may ever hope to receive a warmer welcome than
was accorded me upon my return to the City Temple as its
Minister, and it was needed. Something like panic seized me,
perhaps because I did not realize the burden I was asked to
bear until I arrived at the Temple. Putting on the pulpit gown
of Joseph Parker was enough to make a young man nervous,
but I made the mistake of looking through the peep-hole which

he had cut in the vestry door the better to see the size of his congregation. The Temple was packed, a sea of faces in the area, and clouds of faces in the galleries. It was terrifying. Pacing the vestry floor in my distress, I thought of all the naughty things the English people were wont to say about American speakers—how we talk through the nose, and the like; albeit I had a Southern voice. My sermon, and almost my wits, began to leave me. There was a vase of flowers on the vestry desk, and in the midst of my agony, as I bent over it to enjoy the fragrance, I saw a dainty envelope tucked down in it. Lifting it out, I saw that it was addressed to me, and, opening it, this was what I read:

> Welcome! God bless you. We have not come to criticize, but to pray for you and with you.—The City Temple Church.

At once my nervousness was forgotten; and if that day was a victory, it was due, not to myself, but to those who knew that I was a stranger in a strange land, and whose goodwill made me feel at home in a Temple made melodious by the richness of its memories and the challenge of its opportunities.

On Monday morning, following my first Sunday as Minister at the City Temple, a letter lay on my desk, written by Thomas Yates, a brother minister whom I had not then met. Of course we became friends, and remained so until his death; his book, *The Strategies of Grace,* is among my treasures. His letter came when it was needed, as he had guessed; it was a sacrament of thoughtfulness:

> Dear Dr. Newton: This note is timed to reach you on Monday morning, after what will be a trying day, when you may be feeling rather blue, wondering why you left your great country and came to us in our distress. It is to bid you a simple and cordial welcome, and wish you the blessing of God. Pay no attention to the reptile press like *John Bull;* ignore the polished sneers of *The Morning Post*—they do not speak for the real England. We need your voice and your vision. You are no stranger to us; many of your sermons have been read in England, as have your books. Long may you live and labor among us. Be as American as you like, and as heretical as you desire;

there are no strings on the pulpit of the City Temple. Little men will be little, they cannot help it. They will envy you, of course, but that will be a tribute. Read Psalm 27:13, 14. With Brotherly Love.

Turning to the Psalm this is what I read:

I had fainted, unless I had believed to see the goodness of the Lord in the land of the living. Wait on the Lord; be of good courage, and He shall strengthen thine heart: wait, I say, on the Lord.

How beautiful is the spirit of reverence which pervades an English church service, in contrast with the too free and informal air of our American worship. The sense of awe, of quiet, of yearning prayer, so wistfully poignant in those days, made an atmosphere most favorable to insight and inspiration. It made preaching a different thing. In intellectual average and moral passion there is little difference between English and American preaching, but the emphasis is dissimilar.

The English preacher seeks to educate and edify his people in the fundamentals of faith and duty; the American preacher is more intent upon the application of religion to the affairs of the moment. The Englishman goes to church, as to a house of ancient mystery, to forget the turmoil of the world, to refresh his spirit, to regain the great backgrounds of life, against which he may see the problems of the morrow. It is said that the distinctive note of the American pulpit is vitality; of the English pulpit, serenity. In the one more activism, in the other more otherworldliness. Perhaps each has something to learn from the other.

Talking to a dear Scottish friend about the matter, he said that an Englishman either reads an essay, or he talks nonsense, and neither is preaching; while Scottish preaching is expository and analytical. When I made bold to ask about American preaching, there was a glitter in his eye, and I dared not press the question. We did agree, diplomatically, that neither type of preaching was what it ought to be. The people are not astonished at the teaching, as of old, nor do the rulers tremble with rage. Nor, again, is the place shaken by the winds of God and

lighted by tongues of fire. We fail, all of us, dismally, and need
to sit in the Place of Hearing.

I took a day off to unwind my nerves after the tensions and
excitement of the City Temple opening. I went down to the
White Horse Hill, near Uffington, and lay on the grass for
hours near the head of the huge horse carved in the chalk.
What a panorama lay spread out below and clipped out on
the skyline. Just below was the vale of White Horse, which
Michael Drayton, no mean judge of such matters, held to be
the queen of English vales. The tide of life was at its zenith.
Everything was brimming with sap, scent, and song. Yet one
was aware of the infinitely old all around, of the remote and
legendary. The Horse himself, for instance—who carved him
out of the chalk? When? To what heroic or religious end?
There is nothing to tell us. How different Nature is in a land
where man has mingled his being with hers for countless generations; where every field is steeped in history and every crag
is ivied with legend. Such places give me a strange sense of
kinship with the dead, who were not as we are; the long, long
dead, the men who knew not life in towns and felt no strange-
ness of sun and wind and rain. Uffington Castle, with its huge
earth walls, was nearby. Perhaps the men of the stone age
fortified it. Perhaps King Alfred fought the Danes there.

But what was that faint, rhythmic throb? The guns in
France! How ghastly to try to preach the gospel of Christ to
the beat of those Drums of Death—the tomtoms of hell!

A. MAUDE ROYDEN

It was plain that I must have a colleague at the City Temple.
The strain of three sermons a week, with so many outside
demands, had taxed the strength of a giant like Joseph Parker,
who often enough "warmed over" old material for the Thursday noonday service, and it had nearly killed R. J. Campbell.
One year at the Temple was equal to five years anywhere
else. Besides it was my desire—with which the people of the
City Temple were in accord—to engage in a larger ministry of

interpretation between England and America, although I had begun to feel that I was talking against the wind which blew my words away.

However, English people loved to hear the story of Lincoln. To find a colleague was no easy task—so many preachers were away at the war that churches had to double up. As England was at that time a world of women, and they were entering a new, strange and dangerous life, it seemed to me that if a woman of genius could be found the problem would be solved. Woman had shown her worth in the war, taking the place of man even in hard, heavy work. There was need of a woman of vision to interpret the new life of woman, its spiritual vision no less than its obligations. Some of the City Temple folk hesitated, and a delegation waited upon me, led by a dear friend, who begged me in a rich Scotch accent to "bide a wee" before doing such an unheard-of thing. "It is sure to raise a row," she added; and she was right about the commotion which it created.

Who first suggested Miss A. Maude Royden as the woman exactly fitted for the venture, I do not know; probably the editor of *The Christian Commonwealth,* which published the City Temple sermons and news. Fortunately, I knew something about her through Miss Jane Addams, of Hull House, Chicago, and as a reader of *The Common Cause,* of which she had been editor. Devout almost to asceticism, Miss Royden was a leader of every cause that had to do with women and children in England; but she had never preached and had no thought of trying, knowing, as a daughter of the Church of England, that she would not be allowed to preach in her own communion. She did not know whether she could preach, nor did we, but, finally, not without much persuasion, she agreed to try. As I had a date to preach in the Cathedral at Glasgow, I let her have both services at the Temple. Hours before the service, long queues formed at all entrances. If some came out of curiosity, all remained to pray. Her subject was "The Laws of Life," her text the words of Jesus, "I have called you friends" —her thesis the trustworthiness of God, freedom from the bond-

age of caprice. "I preached the same sermon in the evening;
it was the only sermon I had," she exclaimed, gaily, when I
returned. A good sermon, I explained, ought to be preached
more than once, and I told her about a manuscript of a sermon
by Beecher, among my treasures, on the margin of which he
noted fourteen dates when it had been preached; and that
helped.

The secular press, for the most part, welcomed the innova-
tion with joy, though some—notably *The Morning Post*—regarded it as a part of the common calamity. In private, I had
to bear the brunt of the criticism in a flood of letters, some
angry, some ugly, with many a stinging sentence about Yankee
impertinence. The words of St. Paul about women keeping
silence in the church were worn threadbare—so few knew
what they meant. The gibe of Dr. Johnson about a woman
preaching being like a dog walking on his hind legs, was not
forgotten; and so it went, with much talk about "petticoats
in the pulpit."

A jolly letter said, "My word, old chap, what are you doing,
anyway? A woman in the pulpit—as if we are not upset enough
already! It takes Yankee nerve to do it. Of course it's nonsense; but after hearing the lady, I am bound to admit that it
is the right kind of nonsense. Here's luck to you both."

The Bishop of London, when I met him, was concerned to
know whether Miss Royden actually stood in the pulpit of the
City Temple, and, most important of all, whether she wore a
hat—oblivious to what she was doing with the brains under her
hat! In fact Miss Royden wore a dress resembling a cassock,
with a cap to match, making her look very like Savonarola.
Later, when we confronted a moral atrocity which only she
could handle, a series of Sunday evening sermons made her even
more like the flaming preacher of Florence.

Slight, frail, with a limp in her gait, as a preacher Miss
Royden was unique in her simplicity, direct, forthright, winsome, always practical. Rich, mellow, well-modulated, her voice
was singularly revealing, her articulation distinct, and, without a trace of sentimentalism, she spoke to the heart. There was

no shrillness in her eloquence, no impression of strain, no affectation. She spoke with the inevitable ease of long practice, as a spiritually-minded woman in sensitive contact with life, guided by a rich culture, a lofty faith, and a sanctified common sense, joined with a rippling humor. She was most at home in an assembly when the people could talk back, conversational rather than oratorical. At the City Temple she usually had an after-meeting in which her hearers could discuss questions suggested by the sermon, or the problems in their minds.

Some of her epigrams were very striking in their swift summing up of situations, as when she said, "The Church of England is the Conservative Party at prayer." A passage lives in many minds in which she described the moral chaos of the times, its spiritual fatigue, its restlessness of heart, closing with the words, "So lies a sick world in the arms of God." During the first World War Miss Royden was an ardent pacifist, like W. E. Orchard. I was not; I accepted war as the horrible alternative to something more horrible. Yet no one even thought of asking her to muffle her testimony—she was left free to speak her own heart. By the time of the second World War she had altered her attitude. There was no "pious pap" in her preaching, no prettified rhetoric decorating a candied Christianity. She was the greatest woman preacher of her generation, and the City Temple gave her an opportunity equal to her genius, to which she measured up magnificently; it was a joy to work with her.

Later, in *Some Living Masters of the Pulpit,* I paid tribute to the ministry of Miss Royden more in detail, along with fourteen other British and American ministers. Her book, *Sex and Common Sense,* was notable, both in its frankness and in its restraint, coming when it was "sex-o'clock" in literature. *Here and Hereafter* was rich in insight and practical wisdom, as were *Political Christianity* and *Prayer as a Force. I Believe of God* was, so far as I am aware, the first book of theology by a woman, up until that time. She did not accept the Virgin Birth of Jesus as a literal fact, but she did avow for faith in his physical resurrection. Woman can comfort woman, and in her "clinic," as she called it, she helped multitudes of women in a desperate time. For a picture of the City Temple in those days, see *The Greatest of These,* a story by Archibald Marshall. Like Wesley, she remained an Anglican, but only in her private capacity, and her influence was centrifugal. She had a chapel in her home and practiced in private what she preached in public. Recently she was married, but her husband lived only a few months.

LETTER FROM HELL

A letter from a City Temple boy came to me one day, written from "Somewhere in Hell," as follows:

> Dear Preacher: The luck is all on your side; you still believe things. It is topping, if you can do it. But war is such a devil's nursery. I got knocked over, but I am up and at it again. I'm tough. They started toughening me the first day. My bayonet instructor was an ex-pug, just the man to develop one's innate chivalry. They hung out the bunting and gave us a big send-off, when we came out here to scatter the Hun's guts. Forgive me writing so. I know you will forgive, but who will forgive God? I cannot. This war makes me hate God. I don't know whether He is God of battles and enjoys the show, as He is said to have done long ago. . . . If so, there are smoking holocausts enough to please Him in No Man's Land. But, anyway, He let it happen! Omnipotent! and—He let it happen! Omniscient! He knew it in advance, and let it happen! I hate Him. You have been kinder to me than God has been. Good-bye.

Later a shell exploded where he was standing, and he was blown to bits. The religious reactions of men under the pressure and horror of war were often terrifying. The general rule, to which, of course, there were many exceptions, was that those who went in pious, with a kind of traditional piety, came out hard and indifferent, and sometimes militantly sceptical; while those who were careless emerged deeply serious—religious, but hardly Christian, with a primitive pantheism mixed with fatalism; not church-minded. Many, to be sure, were confirmed in the mood such as haunts the stories of Conrad, in which good and bad alike sink into a "vast indifference," or the mood of

Hardy, in whom pessimism is mitigated by pity, as bitter as the salt sea, as black as the hour before dawn. Others fell back upon the "hard, unyielding despair" of Russell, and their heroism filled me with awe. Huxley, I know, thought the great Force that rules the universe a force to be fought, and he was willing to fight for the moral rights of man. It was magnificent, but it was not war. The odds are too uneven, the fight too futile. And still others learned, at last, the meaning of the Cross. Men cannot be dragged through a jungle of blood and violence and remain the same.

PETRIFIED MINDS

My colleague, Maude Royden, was prohibited from taking part in a Good Friday service in the Church of the Holy Sepulchre—the Church in which the City Temple congregation now worships, since the Temple was blasted to ruin. The rector moved the service into the parish house to escape the edict. Apparently Miss Royden would desecrate a church, not being an ordained priest—so would Jesus, who was only a layman. People were not allowed to meet at the foot of the Cross, at a time when the world was shaken by the thunder of universal war! The tragedy of it was appalling!

About the same time the Bishop of Manchester suggested that there ought to be a great gesture of goodwill, a new dimension of fellowship between all the churches, if only to dramatize the spirit of co-operation among Christians, and appeal to the nation in behalf of the spiritual life. But no; Bishop Gore thought it well that Anglicans and Free Church folk should pray together in times of national peril, but such meetings should be held "on neutral ground, either out of doors or in some building other than church or chapel!"

Merciful God, if people could not pray together, except on some spiritual No Man's Land, talk of a new fellowship was futile. Bishop Gore was a man of simple, unforced goodness— one never met him without carrying away a sense of holiness, but his mind was petrified; his faith had become a fixation—

alas! fixed on old ecclesiastical regulations which made the will
of God of no effect. Such fixations defeated the very purpose
of the church and delayed the answer of Jesus that His followers should be one in Him and for the fulfilment of His
dream. In the first World War the Church "fumbled the ball,"
missed the bus. An unchanging church—unchanging, that is,
about little rules and rubrics—in a changing world, awry and
in agony, was hard to know from blasphemy; fellowship broken
by pettifoggery; a static church in a dynamic world. The Bishop
said that certain "sacramental values" had to be conserved, as
if Christian fellowship were not the supreme sacrament, the
value of which no one could estimate or even imagine.

Here was the same old thing which I had fought from the
beginning. Put starkly it meant, "You have got to think as we
do, use our forms, submit to our dictation; we alone have the
truth—only our forms are valid"; which was—and is—the apoth-
eosis of vanity and futility. As if identity of opinion about
Jesus and church customs, not sympathy with His spirit and
the wish to follow His way and learn of Him, should be the
basis of fellowship. Else we cannot worship together, cannot
work together—doing together what none can do alone. Even
today the spectacle of a divided church, divided about little
realities, and even unrealities, telling the nations to unite, is
an impertinence.

The Church, unable to set its own house in order, dares to
make a blueprint of a new world order—the impotence of it
amounts to impudence! If the Church cannot practice brotherhood, divided by barriers, both of creed and class, it makes
the brotherly life seem like a fourth dimension. To be sure my
attitude was rank heresy, I was called "an ecclesiastical polyg-
amist"—very interesting, if true. Really I was not aware that
Christ had more than one Bride. Which sect is the Bride of
Christ? And what are the others? Concubines? Deliberately and
of set purpose I have gone from church to church, from room
to room in my Father's House, leaving doors open behind me,
even when they were slammed in anger—the doors of Baptist,
Disciples, Universalist, Congregationalist churches. Not casu-

ally, but with the profound conviction that there is one Church of Christ which includes all our sects, or there is no Church of Christ at all—but a huddle of groups which in their blindness crucify Christ anew by their pettiness. These things I said in the City Temple pulpit—and have been saying in myriad ways since—but people only stared at me, thinking me dangerous, if not daft!

APRIL 6TH, 1917

Of course, there was much ado when the United States came into the war; everything was different. The Union Jack and the Stars and Stripes were intertwined in the pulpit of the City Temple. At the morning service we sang a verse of "God Save the King"; in the evening Miss Royden used a verse of "God Save the People"; and so the budget was balanced. Then we used another hymn, written, I believe, by Dr. Huntington, of New York, "Two empires by the sea, Two nations great and free, One anthem raise." At any rate the anti-American mud-guns were silent, for the duration, except for Dr. Selbie, who was implacable and incorrigible. It was now possible for me to go into a shop without receiving a nasty dig about my country before leaving. My mail at the City Temple was readable for the first time. Still, the insane jealousy of an American in the City Temple persisted among Free Churchmen; they could not forgive me. The Anglicans were never rabid, they were kindness itself, and my fellowship with them was delightful. At least they were gentlemen, and that was more than could be said of certain Free Churchmen, one of whom argued at length to prove to me that Bertrand Russell had a much greater and finer mind than William James, the childishness of it! Again I mention no names; they are all dead, and their folly should be buried with them.

In 1916 the first welcome given me, outside the City Temple, was by the National Assembly of the Brotherhood Movement, in the Bishopsgate Institute; I can still feel the warmth of it. Later, as a member of the National Council of the Movement, I came to know, admire and love its leaders: William Ward,

author of *Every Church a Brotherhood,* a dynamo of energy
and enthusiasm; Tom Sykes, a Yorkshire man with a bucket-
ful of brains and a heart of fire; Harry Jeffs, wise journalist
and noble Christian; and greatest of all Dr. John Clifford, the
Grand Old Man of the Free Churches. (He wrote lovely things
about me in his diary, parts of which were published, later,
in his biography.) Together, or in teams, we went to and fro
over England, at a time when the brotherhood of the world was
shattered, speaking in behalf of fraternal righteousness and
seeking to organize God's light. Springing up spontaneously,
the movement was in answer to a deeply felt need for a closer
fellowship in the service of a more practical Christianity. It
was religious, but not ecclesiastical; spiritual, but not sectarian;
positive, but not dogmatic—its sole object being to assert the
principle, spread the spirit, and promote the practice of brotherhood. It made no dogma, theological or economic, a test of fellowship, but invited every man of every rank and walk of life
to join hands and hearts for the common good. No wonder it
won my aid!

JUST AN AIR RAID

Of course there were many air raids; I lived through twenty-
eight, escaping death twice by a narrow margin. One remains
fixed in my mind, July 6th, 1917, because it has never been
referred to in print, so far as I am aware. After a party given
in my honor at "The Hill," the home of Lord Leverhulme, as
we walked to the underground station, we saw thirty-two planes
hovering over central London. Grouped in a triangular formation, they maneuvered leisurely to and fro, flying low, and we
thought they were English planes from their markings. Just as
we reached the center of the city, where the streets were full
of people watching the planes, suddenly, at a signal, a shower
of bombs fell, exploding with deafening thunder.

The crowds hurried and scurried, but too late. It was a complete surprise, and the havoc was horrible. Ambulances were
moving hither and yon, picking up the dead and wounded. In
Gray's Inn Road, not far from the City Temple, among the

many victims was a boy of eight, shockingly mangled. Regaining his senses for a moment he asked, "Is my mates all right?" and died.

No cry of pain, no thought of himself! Many were killed and maimed, but such a people cannot be terrified. At midnight, I was still too wrought up to sleep, torn between nausea at the sights and something else I could not define. It was neither fear nor anger nor excitement, but a vast tide of mingled thought and emotion, in which I seemed to float like a tiny boat on a deep sea—now submerged, now swept along, as if my individuality had been caught up into something greater than itself, yet it remained individual and alert. The feeling could not be analyzed. The sickening scenes haunted me—a cordon of police about the door of a shattered home, where two were killed and a little girl had her leg blown off. Calm good-nature prevailed. Officials were courteous and firm. Everybody was kind, helpful, practical. As long as I live I shall have from this experience a new sense of unity and fusion of purpose, an awareness of our common humanity, which drew us all together in a trustful and direct comradeship.

Once, later, when the air-raid warning sounded, I started to enter the shelter under the *John Bull* office—of all places! Happily, I changed my mind and ran to the next shelter, not wishing to be found dead in such a place. Alas, a bomb hit the *John Bull* building and did not explode until it reached the shelter, killing many, and drowning others by breaking a water-pipe; eighty in all. Again, while walking across Ealing Green a piece of steel, large enough to kill an elephant, fell three feet in front of me. In those days one was apt to be flirting with death any hour; a preacher began his sermon not knowing whether he would live to finish it. At the City Temple, an officer sent a note to me in the pulpit when the enemy planes reached the coast, which gave me time to dismiss the congregation and give a chance to go to the shelters—tube stations chiefly, since London had no such shelters as it had later in the second World War. Even in the first war, again and again I joined the pajama parade to the tube station near the Russell Hotel, which was sixty feet deep and safe.

AMERICA AGAIN

In August I went for a journey along the western front, as a guest of the British Government—to Abbéville, Arras, and on east, where we were guests of an officer in a huge dugout built by the Germans, with all modern conveniences. Then into Flanders where, on a hill, we became targets of German artillery and just missed being blown to pieces. On the hill we found a German gasmask, dated "1913!"

Then to Paris, no longer gay Paris, after which I went to America on a speaking trip and to bring my family to England. America had entered the war unprepared, as usual, and it took time for it to make its force felt. Never had I seen such an America before, or even imagined it. Everywhere one heard the sound of marching, marching, and I, who had just seen what they were marching into, watched it all with an infinite ache in my heart. It was an awe-inspiring America, new in its unity, its power, and its vision of duty. Time out of mind I had known Uncle Sam in his suit of nankeen trousers strapped under his instep, his blue swallow-tail coat and brass buttons, and his ancient high hat. It was not easy to recognize him clad in khaki, wearing a gasmask and a "tin lid," and going over the top with a Springfield rifle in his hand. That change in outward garb was a visible sign of much else. More sinister, more terrifying was the blend of alarm, anger, hate, knight-errantry, hysteria, idealism, cynicism, moralistic fervor and plain bafflement, which made up the war-mood of America. One felt the altruism and inhumanity, the sincerity and brutishness lurking underneath, long glossed over by prosperity and ease, until we had become scarcely aware of it. Down the streets of New York, at midnight, one heard long lines of men marching, singing "Over There." From New York to Iowa I went—in Cedar Rapids no building could hold the people—from Texas to Boston, where I preached in Dr. Gordon's church, and to and

fro, telling our people what the war was like; after which I
returned with my family to England.

My family had not gone with me at first, owing to war conditions and the settling of our affairs. I had lived at the Russell Hotel, and returned for them now, despite the dangers of
the sea. Back in England living conditions were extremely difficult, houses were hard to secure—we had to live in furnished
homes, and in hotels. Housekeeping was a puzzle, compared
with the simpler ways and myriad conveniences at home. Re-
strictions were many, the City Temple people were most helpful—but it all added up to living in a new way in a strange setting. We had many things to learn, and had a lot of fun learning to live in England—of which more later. It was indeed an
adventure, and youth is equal to anything new and exciting.
"The American way of life," we discovered, was not the English way—and English ways never change; so we had to adapt
ourselves to all sorts of strange habits and customs.

MR. LLOYD GEORGE

On my desk at the City Temple I found an invitation to
attend a private breakfast given to a group of Free Church
ministers by the Prime Minister at No. 10 Downing Street.
It was the most extraordinary function I have ever attended,
as much for its guests as for its host. Mr. Lloyd George spoke
to us for more than an hour, and we saw him at close quarters
in the intimacy of self-revelation most disarming. What a way
he had of saying, by the lifting of an eyebrow, by the shrug of
the shoulders, by a gesture in a pause, volumes more than his
words told. He felt that the Free Church brethren were
estranged, and he wished to explain matters and set himself
right.

His address was very adroit, but one felt a suggestion of
cunning even in his candor, despite a winning smile. He talked
like a man in a cage, telling how he was unable to do many
things he would like to do. As he spoke, one realized the enormous difficulties of a man in his place—the pull and tug of

diverse interests, his incredible burdens, and the vast issues with which he had to deal. No wonder time had powdered his hair almost white and cut deep lines in his face. Behind him hung a full-length painting of Pitt, and I thought of the two together, each leading his country in an hour of crisis. I thought him worthy of such company—though hardly in the Gladstone tradition—a man of ideas rather than of principles, but lacking something of the fascination of Disraeli. Such men are usually regarded as half charlatan and half prophet, and the Prime Minister did not escape that estimate.

At the close of his address there was a disposition to heckle the Prime Minister, during which he learned that Free Churchmen were estranged, and why. One of the urgent questions before the country was an actual choice between bread and beer—about which I had made protest in a sermon—and the Government was unable, apparently, to decide. The food-hogging brewery interests seemed to be sovereign, using sugar when we could not get it for our tables, and the Prime Minister was tied—too willingly, perhaps. The liquor traffic is less open in England than it is with us, and those who profit by it are often the most aristocratic class, including the Church. Anywhere in London one saw baby-carts in front of "pubs," while the mothers were inside guzzling. Never before had I seen drunken mothers trying to push baby-carts! When the Prime Minister was asked why, unlike President Wilson, he avoided the use of the word God in his speeches, I thought his reply apt.

It was done deliberately, he said, lest he seemed to come into competition with the blasphemous mouthings of the German Emperor. His final plea was that, as Britain must bear the brunt of the war until America was ready—as Russia had carried it until Britain was ready—she must muster all her courage, patience and fortitude. As I left the house, a group of sleuth-like pressmen—good fellows, all—waylaid me and asked for some hint of the meaning of the meeting; but I was dumb. They insisted that "after a minister has had breakfast with the Prime Minister he ought to be a well-primed minister," but I declined to be pumped, and they let me go. When the supply of truth does not equal the demand there is a temptation to manufacture, and the guesses in the afternoon papers were astonishing—at least a million miles from anything resembling the truth.

A story must be added, if only to show another side of Mr. Lloyd George, his gay spirit, his homey charm and prankishness. Once I preached in the Welsh Baptist Church of which he was a deacon, a good deacon too, when his duties of state allowed him to serve. Naturally the visiting minister was invited to dinner by the senior deacon, and a more charming family group I have never known. After dinner we had a sing-song around the piano, and what singing! Tea-time came, and while the tea was being prepared I admitted that I had come to admire the tea-hour in England as a time to relax and indulge in chit-chat. It would be a good thing, I added, if America had such an hour, since our people are tense and in a hurry. Whereupon the Prime Minister put on a pretty act in his best oratorical manner: "But remember, we offered you Americans tea once and you refused it!" Looking as stern as possible, I played up to his lead: "Exactly, you did offer us tea, but, being a nation of shop-keepers, you put tax tags on it, and we dumped it into Boston Harbor." Then, as if by spontaneous combustion, all of us exploded in laughter. They agreed that we had played our parts very well.

Later in the tea-hour the Prime Minister confided to me a religious perplexity which bothered him greatly, he said. There was a twinkle in his blue eyes and I suspected a booby-trap. In his Church, he explained, there were two parties divided about a vital issue. One party held that we are baptized *in* the name of Christ, the other that we are baptized *into* the name of Christ. Having been brought up a Baptist, I had never heard of any such issue, but I awaited developments.

"Can the issue be very important?" I asked.

"Extremely important, and I belong to one party—I am ready to fight for it."

"Which party do you belong to?"

"That's the trouble; I can never remember which side I am on!"

"G.K.C."

I had a bite and a delicious chat with Chesterton—"G.K.C.," for short—who apparently regarded the Dogma of Beer, or the right to drink it, as an article of the Christian faith. Every time I met him I thought of *The Man Who Was Thursday*, a story in which he drew a portrait of himself. He was not only enormously fat but tall to boot, a mountain of a man, with a tiny, squeaky voice. "The mountain labored and brought forth a mouse," he said—happy is the man who can laugh at himself.

His head, seen from behind, looked larger than any human head has a right to be. The soul of good-fellowship, as the wine went down in his glass, one witnessed an exhibition worth going miles to see. He led words into the arena, first in single file, then four abreast, then in regiments; the feats they performed were hair-raising. If he talked in paradoxes, it was for the same reason that more solemn people talk in platitudes— he could not help it. From the Gospel of Beer, our talk turned to H. G. Wells and his new theology; and it was good to hear Chesterton laugh about a God unfinished and still in the making. His epigram hit it off to a dot. "The Christ of Wells is tidy; the real Christ is titanic."

We agreed that the portraiture of Jesus by Wells was in bad drawing, being too much like Wells; but we remembered other portraits by the same hand—Kipps, Polly, and the rest—extraordinary and alluring. If Dickens was the greatest American ever born in England—as I often said to the annoyance of my English friends—Chesterton is the best England has given us since Dickens went away. One loves him for his uproarious faith in God, his strength, his sanity, his divine joyousness. When he came to America he promised not to write a book about us. Happily, he recanted and wrote one of the best books any Englishman has written about America—not sniffing at un-English things, but trying to understand them, or leaving them for "Father Brown" to unravel. Who can ever forget his description of the star-spangled chief of police of Oklahoma City!

GEORGE BERNARD SHAW

Having met Bernard Shaw and heard him lecture, I think I have solved the riddle of his personality. There is a dual Shaw and a duel is always going on between them. The private Shaw is physically finicky, almost old-maidish, shy, blushing like a schoolgirl when you meet him. Gentle, generous, full of quick wisdom, he suggests lavender and China tea in dainty Old World cups—he is kindly, without the shattering wit.

The Public Shaw—well, we know what he is—aggressive, vastly conceited, saying old truths backwards, laying claim to an omniscience that would astonish most deities—a genius with a jazz mind. He frankly tells us that he is far greater than Shakespeare. He is a literary acrobat standing on his head to attract attention or walking the tight rope in the top of the tent; the father of the wisecrack, whereas the truth is that if a man is truly wise, his wisdom does not crack. Smitten with the curse of cleverness, his darts of wit are nearly always tipped with the acid of cynicism. Whether prophet or harlequin, he has shot his bolt—and missed the mark; Public Bore No. 1. This is said without malice, for the sake of the truth—he has no word of comfort or command.

Two memories of Bernard Shaw are worth including here. At a huge meeting in Queen's Hall, in London, I happened to stand beside Shaw on the platform, celebrating the alleged "peace." The vast audience, led by a massed choir and the great organ, sang "Our God our help in ages past," the Isaac Watts hymn, which is almost the religious national anthem of English-speaking folk. As the volume of voices blended and swept over us, the majesty of the hymn was felt—it is really a paraphrase of the 90th Psalm, singing of the Eternity of God and the fleetingness of Man, swept away by the flood of years.

Looking out of the corner of my eye, I could see that Shaw was deeply moved, and I remembered a page in one of his books in which he made a kind of inventory of his soul, which included, he said, "a cathedral." As we sat down at the end of the hymn, he whispered to me, "Doctor, I would rather have written that hymn than all my foolish plays." Of course, his plays were not foolish, but dazzlingly clever.

A few evenings later, at a meeting of the London Society for the Study of Religion, a small but remarkable group, it was Shaw's turn to read a paper, review a book, make a speech, or give almost any kind of performance he liked. We had learned to expect the unexpected, and we were always surprised. On that evening he chose to review, in a most solemn manner, a German Dictionary of American Slang, in which some old pedant, with German thoroughness, had actually tried to dig out the derivations of such words as bunk, punk, flunk, skiddoo, and the rest. The results were fantastic, and it lost none of its picturesqueness in the review. Some of the words were new to Shaw; some of them were new to me, when he appealed to me for aid. The mortality among slang words and phrases is very heavy. Shaw pointed out that some of the phrases go back as far as Shakespeare, for example, "not so hot." Slang is language in misery, said Victor Hugo, and yet some words are recruited from slang, cross from the wrong side of the railroad tracks, and enter the dignity of the dictionary; for example, "tote" and "wangle." What Shaw did not realize was that slang phrases are often ordinary phrases given a new twist, or accent, like *"Listen* to the bird," which happened to be the title of a song sung by a lady following an address of mine at the close of a school in Iowa. She herself did not realize it, but the audience came near exploding in laughter. But the review by Shaw was not all fun—he pretended to be solemn, but he was serious—and it brought up the question whether Jesus used any slang phrases of His day, as He certainly did puns. Baron von Hügel settled the argument by saying, "Jesus played upon words, but He did not play with them."

LONDON SOCIETY

"The London Society for the Study of Religion" was a small group with a big name. It had a limited membership and few rules. The Dean of St. Paul's, the Minister of the City Temple, the chief Rabbi belonged to it automatically, so to speak. Chesterton, Shaw, Montefiore—scholar and saint—and Baron von Hügel, a Catholic layman, a philosopher, writing English in the German idiom, were among other members. One evening Dean Inge read an essay on "Immortality," which made the afterlife so abstract, so tenuous, that it seemed unreal. Whereupon Shaw, in a whisper—the Dean being quite deaf— moved the organization of a Suicide Club. He did so with impish delight, on the ground that such a life was undesirable, and also he is never more happy than when he can gibe a Dean or a Bishop.

The Dean, of course, heard none of this extraordinary parliamentary procedure, nor was the motion put to a vote. The Dean, Shaw said, had a fine mind, but his education was unfortunate, as if a surgeon had forgotten to remove his sponges and instruments and sewn them up inside the patient.

The soul of the Society was von Hügel, frail, his face looking as if it had been carved out of old ivory. He was the greatest spiritual thinker and personality it has ever been my joy to meet. It would be impossible for me to analyze, much less describe, his influence upon me, both by his personality and his writings. He saw that science and mysticism are the two wings by which the human spirit flies, and that either without the other is almost fatal. In ways too deep for words to fathom he altered my inner attitude, giving me a sense of the reality and art of prayer, of the Church, of the mystical life, such as I had not known before, in his essays and in his letters of counsel. He did much to help me to where I am thus far down the ways of life, clarifying and fortifying faith.

FOUR ARCHBISHOPS

It has been my honor to know four Archbishops of Canterbury. Davidson was the first. We often met and spoke together during the first World War. A short, stockily built man, he could use more simple words in preaching a great sermon than any man I ever heard. The first time I sat beside him at a luncheon, I remarked about a Scot being the Archbishop of Canterbury. He said he would tell me a story, if I would promise not to tell it. I promised, but now it can be told: Sandy went to London from Glasgow on business. When he returned he was asked whether he had seen any of the English, and he replied, "No, I saw only the heads of the departments!"

The Bishop chuckled as he told it. "Of course," I said, "you know the English reply to that gibe—they call themselves a race of lions ruled by asses."

With my wife and daughter I attended the funeral of Archbishop Davidson in Westminster Abbey in 1930—a service stately in its simplicity; the audience was like an album of the great men and women of England. At the Mansion House I first met Dr. Lang, who was Archbishop of York, when he spoke upon his return from a journey to America. He followed Davidson at Canterbury, and he in turn was followed, years later, by Temple, who was both a philosopher and an ecclesiastic; he was infinitely kind to me when I flew to England in 1941. His sudden death, later, was an irreparable loss to the Christian cause; he was so forward-looking, so courageous, and no man knew the dialect of every class in England in quite the same way that he knew it. The present Archbishop of Canterbury, Dr. Fisher, formerly Bishop of Chester and then of London, I met one day after he had preached in St. Martin's in the Fields. His sermon was simple, direct and unforgettable, alike for its matter and for what can only be called the athletics of its delivery. In the pulpit he reminded me of my late friend, Dean "Barney" Phillips of the Cathedral in Washington City.

THE MIDLANDS

As one of many such journeys all over England, I record a trip to the Midlands. At Manchester I preached on Sunday in the Cavendish Street Chapel, where Joseph Parker ministered before going to the City Temple, and lectured on "Lincoln" the following Monday evening. No one ever had a more cordial welcome anywhere—the Midlands are very like America, and I felt at home. As a preface to my lecture I paid tribute to the Manchester *Guardian,* expressing gratitude for its sympathetic and intelligent attempt to understand my country in the difficult days of our neutrality. The American Consul, in seconding a vote of thanks to the chairman—a part of the ritual of an English public meeting—told an interesting fact found in the files of his office. A group of Manchester citizens, knowing the admiration of Lincoln for John Bright, a Manchester man, had a bust of the Quaker statesman made, and it was ready to be sent when the news of the assassination of the President arrived. They cabled to Mrs. Lincoln, asking what they should do. She replied telling them to send it to Washington, and it is now in the White House.

As a fact, I did not see Birmingham, because a heavy fog hung over the city, like a dirty, yellowish blanket, and had not lifted when I left. I could hardly see my audience when I rose to speak, and felt half-choked all through my lecture. As it was my first visit to Birmingham, I began by recalling the great men with whom the city was associated in my mind. The first was Joseph Chamberlain. No sooner had I uttered the name than there were hisses and cries, "No, no! John Bright!" I had forgotten that Bright had ever sat for a Birmingham district. The next name was Cardinal Newman. It was received with silence, then with a few groans. When I mentioned Dr. Dale, there was loud applause; for he was not only a mighty preacher, but a great political influence in the city. I reminded my audience that, when Joseph Chamberlain was accused in the House of Commons of representing Dr. Dale, he retorted that he had no mean constituency. The last name mentioned was J. H. Shorthouse, the author of *John Inglesant*—a mosaic and one of my favorite books. If the name was recognized at all, there was no sign of it.

Returning from Edinburgh, I broke my journey at the ancient city of York, to conduct an institute for ministers in the Monkgate Methodist Church; also to lay flowers on the grave of John Woolman, the sad St. Francis of the New World, who died while on a preaching mission to England and was buried at York.

AN AMBASSADOR

Dr. Walter Page was not well near the end of his ambassadorship to England. More than once I served as his understudy, so to put it, especially when he was to speak to some religious assembly. The American Y.M.C.A. had given a sum of money to aid the British Y.M.C.A., and as he wanted me to go in his stead, I went to see him, asking how I should act and what I should say.

"Remember," he said, "an ambassador is a man with a ball and chain on his foot. His business is to look wise and say nothing in particular, and do it eloquently—using plenty of soft soap. Can you fill the bill?" he inquired.

"But how can I represent you unless I tell a Negro story? The English people are fond of your stories, which are also parables. If I am to make your speech, you must furnish the story."

My suggestion started him telling stories, making him forget that he was ill. It was a bitter time, in the awful waterlogged winter of 1917-18; the English people were depressed, their armies in Flanders were floundering in infinite mud, and we wanted to cheer them up. Here is the story Dr. Page told me to tell, showing how long America expected to stay in the war.

Sambo and Rastus were on trial, as usual, for various kinds of mischief, and after they had been sentenced were on their way back to jail.

"What did you git, Sambo?" asked Rastus. "I gits six months. How long is you in fur, Rastus?" asked Sambo.

"*Oh, I is in frum now on!*" said Rastus.

Armed with such a good story, I went to a great meeting in Stoke Newington, an "official" of my country for the first time. The Ambassador himself could not have had a kinder reception, and he said next day that, judging from the reports, I had not disgraced him. But it was the story that did it—all the papers had editorials about it.

It was no easy job, preaching to soldiers, as I did in rest-camps—the Canadian Camp at Whitley and the American Camp near Winchester and along the front, often with Studdert-Kennedy, the greatest preacher to soldiers in the first World War. (One night, when Westminster Abbey was packed with troops, I heard him preach a sermon in slang, talking soldier slang and making it sing! Some of the words I did not understand, but the soldiers did.) A whiff of poison gas injured his lungs and hastened his death—the war had already broken his heart; but he left us poems that still sing, despite his sorrow. The difference in preaching to men who had not seen the war and those who had been in it for a year or two, was very great—one could tell the difference blindfolded.

Never can I forget an evening at Camp Whitley, the eager, earnest, upstanding men, bronzed by war and weather. Only now and then did one know the thrill of digging under or breaking through the wall of adamant in which men sheltered that shy and lonely thing they dared not lose.

At Winchester, of course, I had a chance to speak to our American boys by the acre; also to see the Cathedral where two of my best friends sleep, Izaak Walton, and Jane Austen, "the miniature Shakespeare." It is the city of Arthur and the Round Table, of the Saxon Chronicles, and of King Alfred. In the Cathedral, less a cemetery than the Abbey, even an amateur can trace the old Norman style of architecture, then the early English, enshrining the history of a civilization, an emblem of that eternal resolve to love rather than hate, to hope rather than despair.

ARTFUL DODGER

The Prime Minister spoke again in the City Temple, and it was an astonishing performance, as much for its wizardry of eloquence as for its moral camouflage. For weeks he had been under a barrage of criticism, as he always was when things did not go well; the audience was manifestly unsympathetic, if not hostile. As no one knew what might happen, it was arranged that he should enter the pulpit during the singing of a hymn. When he rose to speak—his stout body balanced on tiny, dwarf-like legs—I sat on one side and Dr. Clifford on the other.

"I do not come here as the first Minister of the Crown, but as an humble Free Churchman," he said. "Dr. Clifford and I have fought our battles together all over the kingdom"—which was true.

In ten minutes he had captured his audience. It was pure magic. I felt the force of it. But, after it was over and I had time to think it through, I found that he had said almost nothing. On the question of bread or beer he had turned a few rhetorical tricks, and nothing else. The *Evening Star* called him a *stuntsman,* and I was half inclined to agree with it. Referring to an intimation of peace from the German Emperor, he said, dramatically, "It is a dagger wrapped in the Sermon on the Mount!" His genius just then seemed to consist in his agility in finding a way out of one tight corner into another, following a zigzag course. An enigmatic and elusive personality, if he never left me with a sense of sincerity, he did give me a conservative thrill. Despite his critics the record of his actual achievement was colossal, and I knew of no personality in the kingdom that could take his place. Like Theodore Roosevelt, he knew how to dramatize what he did, making himself the hero of the story; and it was so skillfully done that few saw that the hero was also the showman.

At the Thursday noon service, March 21st, we had news that a great battle had begun, but we little dreamed what turn it would take. Instead of the long-expected Allied advance, it was a gigantic enemy drive, which seemed to be sweeping everything before it. The Allied lines were first bent, then broken, and it looked as if the Channel ports might be captured. All internal dissension was hushed; one saw once more the real quality of the British people, their quiet courage shining most brightly when the sky was darkest. London was tongue-tied; people looked at each other and understood. Resolute, all-suffering, unconquerably cheery—it was magnificent!

The City Temple was jammed on Sunday; people were gathering up their final reasons for holding on in the battle of life, seeking the ultimate solace of the Eternal. Not one of that vast, eager, earnest congregation, with their aching hearts, knew what happened in the soul of the preacher. The sermon I had prepared for the day vanished from mind; never have I been able to recall what it was. Instead, a new sermon flashed into my heart, full grown, and preached itself, I was only the voice —twice that has happened to me since. It was duly reported and published; it was the title sermon of a book which appeared in the autumn, *The Sword of the Spirit*. If God allows a preacher to be truly eloquent half a dozen times in his life, he ought to be satisfied—that is enough.

PRIME MINISTERS

In the old Guildhall I heard four Prime Ministers speak when, after "the Lord Mayor's Show," following a parade through the streets of the city in his gilded carriage, a banquet is given in the evening. Asquith, speaking in calm and weighty words, in a style as lucid as sunlight and as colorless; Lloyd George, picturesque, persuasive, with little literary quality in his speech; Bonar Law, a quiet, matter-of-fact, business-man orator; Ramsay MacDonald, earnest, eloquent, in the manner of a lay-preacher, as indeed he was, only more polished in phrase.

Also in the Guildhall I heard President Wilson, slim, neat, graceful, speaking with the magic of phrase of which he was master; and General Pershing, reading a carefully prepared address, when he was given the freedom of the city. Either in the same Hall or in the Mansion House—I forget which—I heard Arthur J. Balfour, tall, handsome, with glorious dark eyes, speaking with inevitable ease, using no notes. (When he gave the Gifford Lectures in Glasgow, I was told that he used only the back of a large envelope, on which he jotted down headings on his way up from London on the train. I saw the envelope, but could make little out of the headings.)

Three times, in the Mansion House, I heard Winston Churchill—and met him often—in the days when he was regarded as too unpredictable, if not explosive, "too much like his father," to be entrusted with power. In those days he had a decided lisp in his voice, which he seems to have overcome later. In one address he spoke of "pious America," referring to our Prohibition Law, which made his hearers squirm in their seats, wondering what effect it might have on American opinion. Yet to this "dangerous" man England turned in her hour of greatest crisis and need, and his voice rang out over the world like a trumpet.

A DAY'S WORK

As my study was in the City Temple, I had to guard my morning hours for study—our home was in Ealing, to get away from air raids—and the Verger, Mr. Linton, my dear friend and helper, protected me. He was an adept in weeding out crackpots among the many who came to see me in the afternoons; but he could not turn down American soldiers, many of whom came for counsel, some as mere panhandlers.

Take one day as an example. When I arrived at the Temple, the Verger said there was an American minister in the church, "I think he said his name was Fosdike."

Of course I knew who it was, and when I asked where he was, the Verger said, "He is sitting in the pulpit." It was a weekday, and the church was closed and empty. Up the pulpit stairs I climbed and for the first time met Dr. Harry Emerson Fosdick. He had been speaking to the American boys in France, and told me what was going on in their minds. We talked of the old Temple and the voices it had heard, of the agony of the war and its crucifixion of Christian ideals. What days to read the Bible, we agreed. Itself a book of battles, its simple, flaming words found new exposition in the awful exegesis of events. Once more the Four Horsemen were riding down the world. The challenge of Job was fresh every day; Jeremiah was justified in his sorrow; the Suffering Servant of God was a liv-

ing Figure. He promised to preach for me at the next Thursday
noonday service; it was a notable sermon, which I could preach
again today—if it were not against the law. Later he entered
upon a ministry, spiritually influential to a vast degree, and
every honor awarded him added to my happiness.

After Dr. Fosdick left there were others, among them Bishop
Brent, head of the Chaplain service of the A.E.F., who wanted
me to speak to a large company of our army officers at the
American hut in St. James' Place. Of course I agreed; then
followed a talk, intimate and unforgettable, with one of the
really great spiritual leaders of his generation, a practical mystic, competent and consecrated. I never saw him again, except
when he thanked me for my talk to the officers—but the memory of him is an unending benediction. Then followed a
preacher who had lost his faith and felt that sad sinking of
heart when the bottom drops out of life; a dear man, desolate
of heart, whom I tried to comfort—that is, to give strength and
faith again. Then a woman, about whom the Verger was in
doubt, but I asked to see her. Of British blonde type, as a girl
she must have been very beautiful—English women change so
terribly about twenty-five or thirty. She was hesitant and ill
at ease, saying that she had attended a few services at the City
Temple and wanted to talk with me, provided I would talk
with her.

"Somehow I felt that you would listen to me," she said. "In
spite of the fact that until recently I was a woman of the street."

"How did you come to enter such a life?" I asked. "Of course
you need not tell unless you want to—what you say to me is
buried in my heart."

Then followed a pitiful story of a happy girlhood in a Mid-
land city, how she was married, had a child who died, how her
husband was first unfaithful and then went to the war and was
killed. "It was foolish, I know," she added, "but I gave up
and let go, and when a woman falls she goes to the bottom."

"What about your manner of life hurt you most?" I inquired.

"Apart from its sinfulness, I dreaded most the awful loneliness of it—I was an outcast, shunned, except by men who had evil passions."

" 'Until recently,' you said. What arrested you in your way of life? I should be interested to know, if you care to tell me."

"In Piccadilly, Sir, one evening I saw a woman with a little girl, the most heavenly human being I ever saw, with big blue eyes and a crown of golden curls. The child smiled at me— and my evil life collapsed."

" 'And a little child shall lead them,' the Bible tells us. Have you found work; can I help you in that way—we do such things."

"Yes, I am employed; but what I want to know is whether God can forgive me for the life I have been living?"

"Yes, indeed; He can and will forgive any sin but one, and if you had been guilty of that sin you would not care about it, would not know it. Jesus forgave a woman, saying, 'Neither do I condemn thee; go and sin no more.' Let's ask Him."

Together we prayed, beginning with the Lord's Prayer—she sobbed her way through it. Then other prayers followed, and we parted. Often I saw her in the Temple service. Later a tiny note from her lay on my desk, saying simply, "You taught me that the love of God has no limit; it saved me. Thank God —and you."

MAISONS TOLÉRÉES

Once more it was shown that a woman can do some things in the pulpit which no man can do with the same effectiveness. When the question came up as to the *Maisons Tolérées*—that is, houses within the bounds of the British Army in which women were herded, under medical supervision, for the uses of the soldiery—I had a conference with Miss Royden, telling her that the question was hers. As an American, I could not attack the British Government, as I had done on the issue of bread and beer. No man could deal with such an infamy properly. The Master of old Temple Church told me that he had tried and failed.

My colleague agreed, and the manner in which she dealt

with it was magnificent. First, as always, she got the facts, then
delicately, yet plainly, disguising none of its beastliness, she put
the case with the flaming wrath of outraged womanhood at the
degradation of her sex. To those who defended the system—
I had heard it defended in a group of Christian ministers!—
after describing the tolerated house at Gayeux-sur-Mer, she
said, "Girls who are visited on the average by twenty or twenty-
five men a day, do not long retain any of the youth and attrac-
tion which will bring men to them. Soon their places have to
be taken by other girls, and the state becomes the procurer!
To any women who believes the sacrifice necessary, I would
say that she herself ought to volunteer. The men who urge
regulated prostitution on grounds of national or patriotic necessity, ought to invite their wives and daughters to fill the
places left vacant by the women who are worn out! I use words
that sear my heart, but as a woman in a Christian pulpit I
cannot be silent in the presence of such an infamy."

Soon the Government began to wince under her attacks,
and the abomination was abolished. The next time I saw the
Bishop of London he was so full of praises of Miss Royden
that he forgot to ask about her hat!

No spring drive could equal the drive of spring in England,
when April comes marching down the days. Kew Garden was
like a bit of paradise, and neither war nor woe could mar its
glory. How the English love flowers—even in the slums of
London, the most gaunt and God-forsaken on earth, in the
windows tiny flowerpots add a touch of color to the drab scene.
Each English home, in the better districts, is walled in for
privacy, and has its flower garden. At the front, in dugouts,
one found old tin cans full of flowers, gathered from no one
knew where. And such bird-song! It began with a morning
concert, and there was an anthem or a solo every hour. They
sang as if the heart of the world were a mystic, unfathomable
joy; even Thomas Hardy wondered what secret the "Darkling
Thrush" knew that he did not know, and, further, what right
he had to sing in such a world. After listening to the birds,
one could not despair of man, seeing Nature renewing her life.

His war, his statecraft, his science may be follies or sins; but his life is only budding—the flower is yet to be. So one felt, in those desperate April days, with a lilac beneath the window and a bird singing. An English officer told me of hearing a little bird singing in the midst of a battle, as if trying to drown the din of war.

UNSEEN FIGURES

In times of crisis, when the soul is near the surface, astonishing things happen; how little we know of what is in us! At the communion service in the City Temple, on the first Sunday of the month, we read the names of our own boys killed during the month. Never can I forget the service that evening when I preached on "The Voice of the Dead," not for the sermon, but for what the congregation did to the preacher. My text was, "He, being dead, yet speaketh," but I soon felt, in the way a speaker senses the mood of the people, that, while I was talking in terms of communion, my congregation, in their love and loss and longing—three of our boys had been killed that week—were thinking of communication, or the possibility of it, with those gay and gallant lads. Suddenly, as if a veil had dropped, I saw the pain in the eyes of my people—like the pain in the eyes of French women in Paris, as I had seen it, as they looked through an iron fence when a troop train was leaving for the front; it will haunt me as long as I live. Again, the same bright, brave pain in the eyes of my people pierced me, and their great heartache swept over me like a tidal wave, almost sweeping me away. But I reminded my people that Jesus did not think of death as we do. Indeed, he first came to teach us, and then to show us, that death is not what we fear it may be—not a stone wall, but a vine-covered gate. Therefore, the text as He would revise it would read, "He, not being dead, yet speaketh." The result was electrifying; it healed many a deep hurt, including my own.

After the service, among many who came back to the Vestry to speak to me, was a woman of striking appearance.

"Who were the two men in the pulpit with you tonight?" she asked.

"Only one man was in the pulpit with me," I explained, "the Honorary Church Secretary, who made the announcements."

"Yes, I saw him, of course, but there were two other men," she insisted.

"Can you describe them, please?" I requested.

"The first one," she said, "was unusually tall, thin of chest, with a shock of coarse hair a bit tousled, with beard, and a mole on his cheek, wearing a Prince Albert coat."

"A very good description of President Lincoln. Now the other man, what was he like?"

She said he was not so tall, but had the mouth of a man who could have been sensual, had he not been restrained. He had a curious gesture—which she tried to imitate—rather awkward, unlike anything she had ever seen. "That is a good picture of Professor David Swing, especially the gesture which a Chicago newspaper man said reminded him of 'a country undertaker inviting the second cousin of the corpse to take a last look.' It so happens that I wrote biographies of both Lincoln and Swing, and it may be that studying their lives, brooding over their words and works, so stamped their very images upon my spirit that they were, somehow, reflected from my mind; the more so because my text was 'He, being dead, yet speaketh.' Would you think that in the nature of an explanation?" I asked.

"As a remote possibility, Sir, perhaps, but not as a probability," she replied, after some hesitation. So it ended, leaving me perplexed. Evidently she was unconvinced by my attempted explanation.

So powerful was this mood at the time that some thought that a new religion was at hand, with Sir Oliver Lodge as its prophet and Sir Conan Doyle as its evangelist, both of whom lectured to my Literary Society at the City Temple. Neither, however, dealt with psychic matters. Lodge talked about "The Structure of the Atom," so simply, and with such lucidity of exposition, that my daughter, then a little girl, listened as if it had been a fairy story. Sir William Crooks talked of Psychic

Facts, as a man of science, objectively, telling what he has seen with his own eyes, in broad daylight; not making a religion of psychic phenomena but asking that they be studied.

A dear friend of mine, a famous judge, decided that we would investigate; our experiences need not be reported—I want to keep what reputation I have for truth and veracity.

Finally my friend said, "Padre, we have gone far enough. I'm going to stop. There is something there beyond a doubt, but what it is I do not know. Anyway, it is knowledge which the human mind cannot bear. We are not ready for it; perhaps we are not good enough to know it. God does not let us know the truth unless and until we are in sight of the ability to use it. We live in a guarded universe; if one dares to seek the final truth, he may lose all truth—he may even lose his sanity. I'm going to knock off and call it a day. But, if you go on, please tell me what you find out!"

PATIENCE WORTH

Years before my interest in such matters had been awakened by an unusual case in St. Louis, the more so because those involved in it were friends of mine. One of them called me "an addict of the occult," only "occult" was not the right word. Here, briefly, is the story. Two ladies were playing with a ouija board, and suddenly odd things began to happen. The ouija board took things into its own hands and spelled out, "Patience Worth my name. Many moons ago I lived."

She went on, using an odd archaic style of speech, seldom a modern word—a quaint dialect until one got used to it. She claimed to be a Quaker maid, but when, where or how long ago she had lived she refused to tell. She declined to be a fortune-teller, "a witch," she called it. Instead, she wrote poems, epigrams, stories: unusual stories studded with shining phrases. The poems were so lovely, the epigrams so striking, the stories so remarkable, that all were astonished. One of the stories was a full-length life of Jesus, telling how a Greek slave-girl gave birth to a child on the same night on which Jesus was born—

only her child was the incarnation of Hate, as Jesus was of
Love; hence the title, *A Sorry Tale*. The two lives ran parallel;
their paths crossed—and the child of the slave-girl was the un-
repentant thief who died on one of the three crosses outside
the city gate. Such was the literary device; the version of the
Sermon on the Mount in the story was a thing of unearthly
beauty—I read it with a bowed mind.

The woman—Pearl Curran—who served as amanuensis for
Patience Worth, was a wholesome, delightful person, but utterly incapable of the range of thought and magic of phrase in
the poems and stories she recorded. The poems and stories were
published; nothing was done in a corner. Dr. Prince, research
officer of the Boston Society for Psychic Research, studied the
case for months, comparing the poetry of Patience Worth with
that of Tennyson, Arnold, and Wordsworth, not to her disad-
vantage. How explain it? *The Case of Patience Worth,* by
Walter F. Prince, is a hard book to get today, but a more enchanting book—quite apart from the issues involved—I can
hardly imagine. For sheer beauty there are few like it. Mr.
Yost, editor of the St. Louis *Globe Democrat,* wrote a book
about Patience Worth. My dear friend William Marion Reedy,
of *The Mirror*, tried to interview her, but she poked fun at him,
calling him "Mr. Fat-awide"—he was almost as large as President
Taft. However, he described her keen humor, her sweet spirit,
her rich wisdom, as if describing a distinct and charming personality. He did not commit himself, but he was astonished
beyond words at the quality of her literary genius. My friend
Mrs. Curran was as much astonished as anyone else at the
stories and poems she reported.

Dr. Prince did not attempt explanation, albeit he mut-
tered a few words about the unexplored depths of the subconscious mind at the end. There he left it; there I leave it—
except to say that no body of writing known to me is more
worthy of the dignity of spirit-speech, if that was what it was.
Unfortunately, the report on the case was not finished, and I
could only give an outline of it to my friend, the judge, who
joined me in my studies. Years later I sent him a copy of the

final report by Dr. Prince, only to learn that he himself had passed to where, beyond these dim shadows, there is light; where, as an English officer said, we learn more in five minutes than all the saints and sages of all the ages have ever learned, or even dreamed.

ROYAL FAMILY

Few Americans realize what the Throne and the Royal Family mean in the life of the British people. Our idea of the King is colored by our republican preconceptions, not to say our prejudices—not knowing that England is in many ways more democratic than we are; politically she is more democratic than we are, socially we are more democratic than she is. The other day, in the City Temple, an American minister spoke of the King as "an animated flag," little dreaming of the thing of which he is the symbol and the profound affection in which he is held. There is something spiritual in this devotion to the King, something mystical, and the Empire would hardly hold together without it. The Royal Family is really the exaltation of the Home, which is ever the center of English patriotism. Of every Briton we may say, as Bunyan said of Greatheart, "But that which put glory of grace into all that he did was that he did it for pure love of his Country." This sentiment finds incarnation in the Royal Family, in whom the Home rises above party and is untouched by the gusts of political passion. At a time when thrones were falling, the King and Queen moved freely among their people, greatly beloved, and all who knew the value of our civilization rejoiced and gave thanks.

In August, 1918, in spite of dangers at sea, I took my family back to America for the duration; we crossed the bar at Liverpool in the glow of a miraculous sunset which haunts me still. It was a quick trip, but I preached in the Fifth Avenue Presbyterian Church, New York, and the following Sunday in the Church of the Divine Paternity. Returning to England, my ship was one of fifteen loaded with American troops. It was at the time of the influenza epidemic, and the funeral flag was kept flying most of the time. Off the north coast of Ireland we witnessed the sinking of an enemy submarine—saw the depth charges explode and finally the oil on the water. Once more, on a Thursday noon, I took up my work at the City Temple, in an address entitled "The New America," in which I tried to describe my experience in rediscovering my own country. During the rest of the war and until the spring I lived in the home of John Wilson and his daughter Janet— they were like father and sister to me, whose loving-kindness and laughter never faltered. Mr. Wilson was a member of the Church Council, along with Dabbs, Dawson, Stoba, Weeks, Cornforth, and others who were my friends and fellow-workers. The City Temple did not have a rectory or manse until after my time, and then only for a little while. Pew rents were few and at small rates; no American church would attempt to operate on such a basis—that is, largely upon the English penny.

Soon after my return I was asked to speak to a group devoted to Anglo-American friendship, but I did not mention the subject, except casually. It was as useless as rain at sea, since all were utterly convinced already; anyway, somehow we never got beyond the courtesies and commonplaces of after-dinner eloquence. All of us felt that the war was nearing its end, and we dreaded a tragic reaction driving England and America farther apart than ever. Not much idealism was left after the long struggle, and even that was worn thin. Already there were rumors of friction between our boys and the Tommies.

Little groups could do little; what we needed was a great gesture of friendship—and I did not know how it could be made. On all sides there were whispers of revolution in England, but I had no fear of it, except for a few flare-ups in Wales and among the hot-heads on the Clyde. As if revolution had not already come! As the Napoleonic Wars ended the rule of the aristocratic class—except in the Foreign Office—and brought the middle class to the fore; so, I was convinced, the war would end middle class rule and bring the man down under to the top. In any case, England believes in revolution by elections, not otherwise. Their non-explosive temperament stood them in good stead in those days, as always. Nearly all the leaders of the Labor Party were my friends.

Keir Hardie I saw but once, and the impress of his spirit remains with me. When I asked him if he had it all to do over again, would he do it in the same way, he replied, softly, "No, Doctor, I would enter the pulpit."

The band of young men who followed him—MacDonald, Thomas, Henderson, and the rest—had to decide whether they could do the best Christian work in the pulpit or in the Labor Party. They decided for the party and became lay-preachers, and good ones too, especially Henderson, who preached for me in the City Temple, and was my close friend to the end. They gave the Labor Party a spiritually-minded leadership, such as American Labor has never had in the same degree. Now, at this writing, the Labor Party is in full power, for the first time, and we shall see what we shall see.

LORD MAYOR OF LONDON

During my life in London, and my visits later, I knew five Lord Mayors of London. The old city proper is only a mile square, even Westminster Abbey is out of bounds. The King himself cannot enter old London without permission of the Mayor—it makes a pretty, antique little ceremony when the Lord Mayor, at a point where one of the old Roman gates used to stand, reads an elaborate document allowing His Majesty to enter. The first Sunday in June is Hospital Sunday in the metropolitan area, and the Lord Mayor always attends the City Temple in state with the Lady Mayoress and entourage.

Oddly enough, all the Lord Mayors I knew were Free Churchmen, and the Mayor often came to the Temple between state occasions—he would sit with me in the pulpit and read the first lesson. In 1933, when I was preaching for the summer in the City Temple, the Honorary Secretary said to me, "As you know, the Lord Mayor is coming to the Temple today in state; of course you know your duties."

He neglected to tell me who the Lord Mayor was. My duty

was to put on my pulpit gown and Doctor's hood and meet the
Lord Mayor and his party at the front door. When the Mayor
and his wife drove up in their gilded carriage—he was Sir
Charles Collett, my old friend—he greeted me cordially, and
we walked slowly down to his pew.

As we walked he said softly, "While you are in London you
must obey my orders. Which means that you must make the
sermon short, or at least 'snappy,' as you Americans say. This
robe weighs sixty pounds and it is hot. Also, you are going
home with us for dinner at the Mansion House, not only today
but every Sunday you are in London, and stay for supper if
possible. When we get home you must put on this robe, and
you will know the burden I bear." This he said, looking
straight ahead, both of us keeping our faces immobile.

After the service the Verger was at the door with my hat,
and relieved me of my gown, and I rode home with the Lord
Mayor where we had a rather elaborate dinner. He showed me
through the Mansion House, which has an assembly room for
public meetings, called the Egyptian Room—not so named, as
I had heard, because built of taxes imposed on Nonconformists,
and so called "the Egyptian bondage"—but because of its deco-
rations. There is a prison in the Mansion House and a court
room, where the Lord Mayor sits as a judge. The rest of the
Mansion is, of course, spacious and well appointed.

So, every Sunday during my visit, I dined with the Lord
Mayor and his family, and came to feel at home with them—
his gay spirit and bright smile never failed. That is, not until
the middle of July when, at the airfield at Hendon, the plane
which his son was flying exploded in the sky, and the boy was
burned to death. Seeing the headline in the afternoon paper,
I hurried to the Mansion House, and witnessed a pitiful scene
—I stayed most of the night. The gay smile was gone, deep lines
were in his face. Three days later there was a funeral service
in St. Paul's where, for the first time, I saw a Fascist salute
in England, made by a tiny group as the body was carried out.
Still, I went every Sunday to the Mansion House for dinner, at
the command of my friend—one of the gayest, now one of the

saddest, of men. Somehow, I was told later, he managed to finish his term of office in November, and then suffered a bad nervous breakdown; I never saw him again.

SLANGUAGE

One day I went to see a friend laid up in a hospital with a broken leg. The nurses, one of whom attended the City Temple, decided to have some fun with me—they were gay, dainty, and full of life. When I asked about my friend they said, "He is full of beans, and they are pulling his leg today." What "full of beans" might mean I did not know, but I had visions of my friend in agony while his leg was being limbered up after being in a cast. Gales of laughter followed, when they saw the blank expression on my face. They explained that "full of beans" meant that he was feeling fine, and "pulling his leg" meant that he was taking a walk. "Now, it is your turn to try us with some American slang."

My story was about a young American minister, a remarkable linguist, who was sent by our Secret Service into Switzerland to watch what the Germans were doing. The Germans suspected his business, and watched him as he watched them. If he took a room at a hotel, they were sure to take the next room, and tap his telephone wire and listen in. Finally, remembering an O. Henry story, he decided to show the Germans that he could get a message through in spite of them. Wishing to report the fact that an officer had absconded with the money of his office, he called American headquarters, and said, "The main guy here swiped the chink and beat it. Kept his dope-sheet in his bean. Do you tumble?"

Back came the answer, quick as a flash, "Sure, Mike!"

In the next room he heard the Germans swearing in all the languages they had ever learned. They got every word of his message, but it made no sense.

"What did the Secret Service man say over the telephone?" I asked the nurses.

"Sounds like Eskimo or Esperanto," they said, their pretty

faces all puzzled. "Mike is the only word we can make out—what did he have to do with it?"

"Any American child nine years old would know all the message," I said, rubbing it in. "You flunked the exam—I *am* surprised."

"What does 'flunk' mean? Is it something like 'bunk'?" they asked, bewildered. As the honors were even, I left the matter there—not translating the message, just for mischief, but they got my friend to help them, when I repeated the story.

ARMISTICE

From my Diary, under date of November 11th:

London went wild today. As a signal that the Armistice had been signed, the air-raid guns sounded—bringing back unhappy memories—but we knew that the desired, delayed, inevitable time had arrived. The war had ended; and humanity, on its knees, thanked God. Words were not made for such a time. They stammered and faltered and failed. Whether to shout or to weep, we did not know; so we did both. Something not ourselves had made for righteousness, and we were awed, subdued, overwhelmed. The triumph seemed wrought, not by mortal, but by immortal thews. But shouts of joy were muffled by thoughts of the gay and gallant dead.

The rebound from the long repression was quick, the outburst startling. Men danced in the streets. They hugged and kissed and sobbed. Flags flew everywhere, flags of every color. Women wore dresses made of flags. Shops and factories emptied of their own accord. At an early hour a vast host gathered at the gates of Buckingham Palace, singing the national anthem. The King and Queen appeared on the balcony—the applause was like the sound of many waters.

St. Paul's was crowded by noon, the Abbey jammed, the City Temple packed. It melted the heart to hear them sing, "Our God, our help in ages past"; there was an echo of a sob in their song. All knew that the secret of our joy was locked in the cold young hearts that slept in Flanders, and on the gray solitudes of the sea. Never was the world so coerced by its dead. They commanded; we obeyed. The old city became a cathedral, its streets aisles, its throngs worshippers.

The rush of events had been so rapid that men were dazed.

At first, peace seemed less real than war. From prayer the city turned again to play; no wonder after the long strain, the bitter sorrow. There was little hatred, only pity and hope and joy akin to pain.

No sooner had the Armistice been signed than there followed, not simply a rebound, but a collapse, which no one who lived through it can ever forget. Swiftly, tragically, the high mood of sacrifice yielded to a ruthless selfishness, the solidarity won by the war was lost, and most of the idealism which had stood the terror and stress of it. The moral demobilization was terrifying; the disillusionment appalling. Men had lived a generation in five years; and instead of the new world of which they had dreamed, they found themselves in a world embittered, confused, cynical, gray with grief—all the old envies working their malign intent. Such chaos offered free play to every vile and slimy influence, making the earth an auditorium for every hoarse and angry voice that could make itself heard. It was a time of social irritation, political reaction, spiritual fatigue, almost more trying than the war itself, the only joy being that the killing of boys had stopped.

The anti-American mud-guns started again in the reptile press. It was so in America too, as Annie Swan reported; she felt "a coolness, a new, subtle hostility, everywhere." My mail at the City Temple was frightful. One would have thought that America, not Germany, had been the enemy of England in the war. W. L. George, the novelist, put it in an epigram, "If the war did not make us love our enemies, it at least taught us to hate our allies." These things are not set down in malice— God forbid—but to show the mood of the hour. America was in the war just long enough to get angry; England had suffered beyond belief. In the midst of it all, Arthur Henderson said to me, prophetically, "If we have a national election in Britain, you will not get a Wilson peace."

COUPON ELECTION

A national election was called; "Coupon Election" it was named, since each Coalition candidate had to have the in-

dorsement of the Prime Minister, not to say the chief brewer
of the land, the organizer and wire-puller of the campaign. It
was clear that the Prime Minister intended to coin into political capital all the anger, suspicion, resentment and disillusionment burning in the public mind—to mobilize the least admir-
able elements of England, not the great, noble England—and
have them in solid phalanx behind him at the Peace Conference. The story was that, walking with a friend one day, he
suddenly stopped, tapped his breast, and said, "I sometimes
wonder if this is Lloyd George."

His wonder was shared by millions of people. Anyway, I
had the time of my life attending every sort of meeting; it was
better than a circus. The best speech I heard was by a Methodist preacher at a Labor meeting in Kingsway Hall. His sentences cracked like rifle shots, and they hit the mark. The
campaign made me first sick, and then homesick; it was so
like our way of doing it. That is, all except the hecklers—they
were quick and keen of retort. Also, the English can beat us
at mud-slinging. It is humiliating to admit it, but it is so.
However, we are young yet, and longer practice will no doubt
give us greater skill.

Mr. Asquith told me how he made a speech on world affairs,
and one of his audience said, "What we want to know is, are
we going to get a pier for our boats?" Always the local grievance clouded the larger issue. How familiar, as if a man had
gone out and encountered on the street what he thought, for
the moment, was himself! Men, otherwise sane, seemed to lose
all proportion and perspective. Wise men talked drivel, prom-
ising what no mortal could perform, inviting the scorn of history and the judgment of God. O Democracy!

Grouch Corner, in Hyde Park, always a menagerie, was a
whirling delight during the campaign. There anybody could
say anything he wanted to say—nobody could say him nay. For
five minutes I listened to a kind-faced old man with a beard,
but could detect nothing resembling an idea in his remarks.
The crowd became restless. One of his friends, no doubt,
pleaded, "Let us give our friend time to extricate his idea."

The crowd seemed willing, until, finally, a sailor said, "Balaam's ass had an idea, but this bloke has none."

Everybody left, but the speaker went on. Never have I heard sharper tongues or keener criticisms. The Prime Minister was skinned alive. My country was ridiculed and denounced. It had little or nothing to do with winning the war, apparently; we jumped in on the winning side. Besides it brags too much—in its own words, "too fresh." No man or cause was exempt.

"Why do you allow this sort of thing?" I asked a kindly policeman.

"It is a safety valve; better let them blow off here than blow up somewhere else," which is the typical English attitude. Anybody can say anything so long as he does not do anything about it.

"My business," added the Bobbie, "is to keep order and see that no speaker is molested, no matter what he says."

THE PRESIDENT

As soon as it was known that President Wilson was to attend the Peace Conference in person, the Tory papers in London began skillfully to paint a caricature of him in the public mind. He was described as a kind of Hamlet, living aloof in the cloisters of the White House, a visionary companioned by abstractions; a thinking machine so cold that one could skate all round him, having "as good a heart as can be made out of brains"; in fact, "not a man at all, but a bundle of formulae," and finally, by the *Morning Post,* as a "political Moody and Sankey" coming to convert Europe to his gospel of "internationalism," which it described as a "disease." Such was the reactionary attitude toward the man who made the only constructive suggestion seeking to prevent the "collective suicide" of war.

Not all the press was guilty of this black build-up. *The Times* —by virtue alike of its position, not only as a journal, but as an institution—secured from the President a memorable interview, in which he was shown to be actually and attractively human;

and, further, that he had no intention of demanding the sinking of the British fleet. The President arrived in London the
day after Christmas, and the greeting accorded him was aston-
ishingly enthusiastic. Really I have never seen anything like
the way in which he captured the English people; he swept
them off their feet. For a brief time his marvelous personality,
his unaffected simplicity of eloquence, his charm, seemed to
change the climate of the Island. No man in our history could
have represented us more brilliantly. In the Palace as guest
of the King, in the Guildhall as guest of the City, at the luncheon of the Lord Mayor in the Mansion House, his words were
not a mere formal, diplomatic response, but at once real and
appropriate. On the Sabbath, instead of going with the King
to St. Paul's, he went to the tiny Kirk in Carlisle, where his
mother had been a girl and his grandfather the minister. His
brief talk in the old pulpit was a gem, and it touched the people
deeply.

At the Mansion House luncheon we learned the election re-
turns, the result having been delayed to get the report of the
soldier vote. It was a Tory victory by a trick; the Liberal party
had been asphyxiated. Mr. Asquith had been defeated, Mr.
Bottomely, editor of *John Bull,* elected—which, translated into
our terms, was like the defeat of Elihu Root and the election
of Hearst. The Prime Minister got what he wanted, a Parliament hamstrung, with no moral mandate, and no effective
opposition, Labor having been almost shattered, and seventy
Sinn Feiners, who were either in prison or pledged not to sit.
The more the meaning of it became clear, the greater was
tragedy revealed—the victory of the mob, led by cunning reac-
tionaries, as distinct from Democracy. At the Peace Conference
an idealist, an opportunist, and a materialist sat down to put
the world to rights; it was not necessary to add a pessimist.
My heart was heavy, the more because of news from America,
and rabid partisan rancor running rife there. At any meeting
of Americans one was sure to meet Lord Bryce and sometimes
Lord Charnwood, whose "Life of Lincoln" had made that great
figure a common possession of the English-speaking race. Charn-

wood had once lived in Iowa, I was told. Both were depressed about the future of Democracy, and rightly so, because it was without a spiritual renewal to cleanse it, orient it, and give it direction and responsibility. Labor was restive. Down in Wales, where I went to lecture on Lincoln, I asked a Labor leader what was holding things together, and he replied, "All that prevents an explosion is the fact that these men went to Sunday School years ago; nothing else restrains them now."

In the national British election of 1945, Winston Churchill, a really great war-leader, intrepid, of bulldog tenacity, of incredible eloquence, a personality of world-wide charm, was crushingly defeated; and wisely so. Not always—not often—is a war-leader the man to make peace. Churchill lost perspective; he was unaware of what was going on in the minds of his own people—he was in fact walking backward into the future, thinking in terms of a vanished splendor, trying to keep petty kinglets on their tottering thrones. He did a great work in a great manner, but his mind was petrified in spots, strangely blind to what was before his eyes. He will be remembered and honored for his titanic labors and his golden eloquence. If Lloyd George, also a great war-leader, had been defeated in the same way in 1918, history might have been different—yet we cannot tell what would have happened if something else had not occurred. As Arthur Henderson—the dear Cassandra—said to me, "The President is defeated before the Conference opens; the cards are stacked against him." MacDonald was defeated; labor was left sullen, bitter, angry. It was one of the greatest tragedies of modern history—a Tory-brewery Parliament led by a facile opportunist, seeking temporary gain at the expense of permanent injury, which makes the word "politics" smell to heaven.

"If there is reaction here," said Henderson, "there will be reaction elsewhere, everywhere"; alas, he was right.

PEACE AND CHAOS

One evening I attended a remarkable meeting in the Royal Albert Hall in behalf of the League of Nations. Earl Grey—

one of the noblest men I have ever met—presided, and in a brief address, more impressive for matter than for manner, he stated the reasons for some attempt to organize the inner forces of mankind. The chief speaker was Lord Robert Cecil, whose character and Christian idealism made him an asset to civilization. One sentence of his stuck in my mind: "If we are to have peace, we must first obtain recognition for the fact that the good of mankind as a whole does actually exist."

No heckler intruded until he said, with emphasis, that the League must, at last, include *all* nations. At once there was an uproar.

"Must Germany be allowed to enter the League?" he was asked.

"*All* nations," the orator repeated.

"Traitor! Traitor!" was shouted.

Confusion reigned, the while Cecil stood as cool as an Alp, calmly wiping his glasses. The proceedings then went on until a woman in the gallery asked about Ireland. The speaker replied. "Ireland was ably represented, I hope, at the Conference by General Smuts and myself."

There were fist fights all over the Hall. We knocked each other over the head, some were thrown down stairs. It was the most militant peace meeting I had ever attended!

Much was being said betimes about the ultimate influence of the war on Christian theology. Much was cloudy, but some things were becoming clear. The war was an awful demonstration of the moral, social and spiritual purpose of God in history. Perhaps its most deeply felt truth was that God suffers with us, though the dogma of a Finite God, brought forward by Wells, Shaw, and by Rolland, in *Jean Christophe,* while valid as a protest against a God who lives aloof from humanity, was unequal to the deeper needs of the soul. The Atonement was now known to be a fact, not a fiction. We were not our own; we were bought with a price. Human nature had been revealed in an apocalypse, its good and evil alike. Christian faith must be thought out anew, involving not only the individual, but the bearing of nations to one another. Unless there was more security for everybody there would be less security for anybody. The "Gospel of the Kingdom of Heaven" was being rediscovered.

The Church must be not simply a house of holy mystery, but also a fellowship in which great social ends are realized under religious ideals. Secularism was bankrupt, and sectarianism a sacrilege, as all agreed. The missionary enterprise had new implications, and it must have new methods. The moral collapse must be stemmed—most of the crimes were bigamy. The Church had failed to deal with sex—in broad daylight in public parks were scenes of such vulgarity that one was grateful for the protection of garden walls. The fate of those fallen in the war—many of whom were "unconverted"—must inevitably modify our thought of the destiny of man. One thought of the lines of Chesterton, in 1906:

> The evil Power, that stood for Privilege
> And went with Women and Champagne and Bridge,
> Ceased: and Democracy assumed the reign,
> Which went with Bridge and Women and Champagne.

What was happening in America was hard to make out—I had lost touch with my own country—except that, under cover of a poison-gas attack on the President, a coalition of hatreds had been formed to destroy him. It was a phobia; even in England I heard Americans talk about the President as I had never talked about the German Emperor. At the Peace Conference he was the victim of a vendetta by men of his own country who, for partisan purposes, were stabbing him in the back. Then he was stricken at a time when he was most needed. It was appalling! Without him reaction would run riot. Though wounded in a terrifying manner, he still held the front-line trench of the moral idealism of the world. Whatever his faults —his errors of judgment and limitations of temperament—his world-vision was clear, though he lacked the political acumen to work it out. Later he was reported to have said, "It is yet too early in history," but he also said, showing his intrepid faith, "I would rather be defeated in a cause that will one day triumph,

than to triumph in a cause that will one day be defeated."
First a writer, then a maker, of history, he knew that it takes a
major operation to get an idea into the human mind. Today
we have lived to see the Senate which refused to ratify the
Treaty of Peace, and rejected the League of Nations, almost
unanimously sign, seal and deliver the Charter of the United
Nations, albeit not without blood, fire, and unimaginable horror and sorrow, just as President Wilson predicted, with seer-
like vision and searing words, in one of his last speeches at
St. Louis. Wilson has been vindicated; he fell as much a casualty of the war as any soldier who fell in the Argonne—a
victim of the partisan venom and horn-eyed stupidity of his
people.

YE OLDE TOWN

One day I went a-wandering just for fun. Near the Tower of
London I met a philosopher who was also a poet. A short,
ruddy-faced man, he stood on the bridge looking at the barges
in the river, and I ventured to speak to him.

"Your city is a magnificent mystification. It gives me the
creeps. It is made to get lost in. Can't find my way anywhere
unless I steer by the dome of St. Paul's. Never saw such a
crazy place. In New York the streets are numbered."

"So I have heard," he said; "all numbered like prisoners in
gaol. I should hate it. Often heard how Americans gush, but
had my doubts about what they said."

"Take a journey to America some time," I said, "and you
won't want to go to heaven. But tell me how to know London.
What is there to shout about in this charming, scraggly old
town, built without a plan? I've seen Kingsway and Buckingham Palace, and nearly choked in a fog."

"That is not London at all," he replied, "except for the
fog. Have you seen Covent Garden at 5 A.M. or the Parliament buildings at dawn? Have you heard Big Ben strike at
midnight? Did you ever know in the center of a city such clois-
tered quiet as you find in Inns of Court?

"The things you mention are new and awful," he went on. "They don't fit into the rest at all. Have you stayed in a Bloomsbury boarding house, or sailed the Thames in a ferryboat, or seen the babies in Kensington Gardens?

"Ah, my friend," he added, "have you bought muffins from a real 'muffin man,' while smoky sparrows twittered in smoky trees? You don't know London until you know such things."

"Tell me some one thing, if you can," I asked, "which will give me the London spirit, so I won't feel like a stranger. I love London."

"Go to the Tower at sunset," he said, after a pause. "Sit in the courtyard by the White Tower and hear the guard turn out and sound 'Retreat.' And watch the ravens, fabulously old, serenely confident, and incredibly wise. Then you will get a vague notion of what London is.

"You Americans are a people who chew gum and win wars," he added, giving me a dig at parting.

"Why not add 'and wear horn-rimmed glasses'?" I asked. He laughed as if to split, and so long as we can laugh at each other, and with each other, we shall be safe and sane, however silly we may talk.

HOMESICK

It was beginning to be plain that my work at the City Temple was done, although my people did not agree—they wanted me to live the rest of my life in London. But that was impossible. My children were becoming utterly English in voice, manner and spirit, which was all to the good, but they were also utterly American; it meant that they would not be happy in either country. Besides, I was homesick, ill at ease about America; it had resigned from the human race, leaving the world to stew in its own juice.

Looking back over my life in London, I can truly say that while I did not want to go there in the first place, and would not have gone at all except for the war, I do not regret that I did go. Nor do I regret leaving, though my ministry was a triumph from the beginning, in spite of my many errors and the terrible conditions under which I worked, and the horror and suffering which I pray God to be able to forget.

One of my joys at the Temple was the Thursday noon service for business men, because so many preachers attended it, among them some of the veterans of the pulpit, John Clifford, John Hunter, W. L. Wilkinson—men of the post-graduate school listening to a junior. John Hunter once held Glasgow in his hand, then came to King's Weigh House, London, but could not do what he had done in Glasgow. He went back to Glasgow, but could never recapture his old mastery of the city. Only once in my life have I known a man who made a second pastorate in the same church better than the first—Glenn Atkins, in the First Congregational Church, Detroit.

Young men no end attended the service; they had forgotten that I was an American—they were most brotherly, and I remember them with special affection. They were gallant and gracious, as were thousands of business men, many members of all kinds of churches, who came for a little hush amid the rush of trying days.

Anyway, I accepted the pastorate of the Church of the Divine Paternity, in New York City. My last Sunday at the City Temple lives in my mind vividly, especially the evening service, always the largest service in an English Church. In the morning the Temple was packed, in the evening it was jammed, people sitting on the pulpit stairs, and even in the pulpit itself. My text was from the Book of Revelation, "These things saith the Amen"—the Amen of God to the aspiration of man, the Amen of man to the will of God; seeking to make vivid the vision that sees through the shadows and affirms, not that all is well, nor yet that all is ill, but that all shall be well when "God hath made the pile complete." Later it was published in *The Truth and The Life,* closing with the lines:

> I heard it all, I heard the whole
> Harmonious hymn of being roll
> Up through the chapel of my soul
> And at the altar die,

And in the awful quiet then
Myself I heard, Amen, Amen,
Amen I heard me cry.

As long as I live I shall carry in my heart the faces of my dear English friends and especially the love and loyalty of the people of the City Temple—the memory of their kindness is like the sacramental wine in the Cup of Everlasting Things. Hung in my heart, also, are many pictures of the beauty-spots of that blessed land—glens in the highlands of Scotland; the "banks and braes o' bonny Doon"; mountains in Wales; stately old cathedrals, strong, piteous, eloquent, sheltering the holy things of life; the towers and domes of Oxford; Stoke Poges on a still summer day; the roses of Westcliff; the downs of Wiltshire, where Walton went a-fishing and Herbert preached the gospel—and practiced it, too; Rottingdean-on-the-Sea; St. Ives in Cornwall; scenes of the Shakespeare country; the church, the theater, the winding Avon; the old Quaker Meeting House in Buckinghamshire, where Penn and Pennington sleep together; great, gray London, in all its myriad moods; London in fog and rain; London in mist, haze and smothered sunshine, like the temperament of its people; London by moonlight from the dome of St. Paul's; the old, rambling city whose charm gathers and grows, weaving a spell one can neither define nor resist; London from Primrose Hill on a clear, frosty day; London from the Savoy in October, seen through a lattice of falling leaves, while a soft mist hangs over the River of Years.

····· 7 ·····

New York City

As we neared America all its history and legend throbbed in my heart, like a sweet habit of the blood. The very air was different, as if the spirit of home had run out to meet us on a gray, fluffy sea. Yet those years of tragedy had left in me a great veneration for the land whence our fathers came, and for its people. In America they would be saying ugly things about England, as in England they said nasty things about America; I was doomed to be hurt both ways, like a man torn between his wife and his mother, both of whom are adepts in snippy gossip.

Slowly our good ship crept through the gray mists of morning, passing Lady Liberty, to whom a British friend took off his hat, saying that She ought to stand with her back to a land of Prohibition—ashamed! Then, dimly at first, we saw the wonderland of New York, rising sheer from the level of the water, half fantastic in its airy lightness, like a range of fairy mountains, except that the skyline was broken with more precision than in the wild architecture of nature. Above all towered a peak which might have been the Matterhorn, which they told Cardinal Mercier was the spire of the "Church of St. Woolworth." The Cardinal, it is said, looked dazed, not remembering any such saint in the calendar, but ready for any adventure that might befall him in America. And so, home at last!

It was bewildering to pass quickly from old London Town, with its time-stained buildings and whitey-brown atmosphere, into the brilliant streets of New York, with its newness, its youthfulness, its lucid sunlight in which everything stands out

201

distinctly, and where the air is like champagne; from the land of day before yesterday to the land of day after tomorrow.

Still more disconcerting is the difference in psychological climate. One is all repression, the other all expression. "Hush! It is so rude, don't you know"—that is England. "Hello! Hurrah! Where do we go from here!"—that is America, the land of talk, where people tell all they know and live with the blinds up. Meanwhile, the first letter I opened, from William Marion Reedy of St. Louis, was not encouraging:

> Why stop in New York, if you object to living in a foreign city? New York is a polyglot boarding-house of the human race; just a place on the way to somewhere else; a railroad station. It is a meaningless conglomeration of humanity; an unhealthy coating on a stone tongue in the mouth of the Hudson—a wart on the nose of civilization. Its architecture, like its confusion of tongues, has the Tower of Babel backed off the map. The Jews own it, the Irish run it, the Americans visit it in rubber-neck wagons. It is bounded on the east by Blackwell's Island, on the south by Wall Street, on the west by Greenwich Village, on the north by Babe Ruth and the Polo Grounds. Its business is chasing the dollar, its diversion the leg-show, its political symbol the Tiger. When you land, buy a ticket for America!

Yet, despite my happiness at being home, I was deeply perplexed; I felt like a stranger in my own country—the shock of it was shattering. There was something new in American life, which I felt everywhere but found it hard to fathom—a wild, shuddering, half-hysterical fear. When I asked what it meant, I was told that we had been sleeping on a volcano, and that it was a fifty-fifty chance of saving our institutions. America afraid of itself—it was something new to me! Our people did not trust one another, and spoke in whispers, making the President a scapegoat of their phobia and nonsense. When I told of the freedom of speech in England, I was assured that it would never do here. The melting-pot had not melted; after fifty years of immigration we were still a heterogeneous people, with every European race and rancor represented.

Free speech might be possible in England, my friends argued, where everyone knows every twist of the public mind; but it is different when an Irish Catholic policeman has to listen to a Russian atheist on a soapbox at the street corner. It was all wrong—first fear, then hatred, then intolerance. No doubt there were undigested foreign groups in America, but repression was a poor aid to digestion. If our people did not understand their new neighbors, it was high time that they got acquainted with them. Wholesome fear is stimulating, but such paralyzing fear was absurd. No one can really injure America but Americans, and they can do it by their terror-stricken bigotry. A letter from an old friend showed how the war had revealed "the looped and windowed raggedness" of organized religion. His pessimism was the reverse side of his moral earnestness, and it gave me furiously to think.

Dear Padre: Often we have talked about preaching, you insisting upon its utility, I insisting upon its futility. While we do not agree, I honor your tenacity to tradition; the Church caught you young, and besides you are some sort of a mystic. To me the plight of the modern preacher is pitiful. If he is not a mere "seller of rhetoric," if he is spiritually alive and wants to speak for the whole community, he cannot do it. He is regarded as the spokesman of a sect, of which we have two hundred—some of them small enough to be insects. It is nothing short of a tragedy, and he is not to blame for it. I'll say we have made a grand mess of Christianity.

The Church in its present form is hopeless; its organization inefficient, its sectarianism a stupidity—as you agree—you have fought it tooth and toenail. If not dead, it is deadening, the odor of decomposition is in the air. Yes, I know what you will say about renewing it from within; but it cannot be done. Twenty years ago it turned its back upon the new science, and lost the leadership of thought. Today it rejects the social vision in behalf of a fine-spun mysticism, sits on the sidelines and does nothing. It not only fails to take Jesus literally; it fails to take Him seriously.

Look at New York. Where do you find the great churches, including your own? It is where wealth is most evident! There are churches enough on Fifth Avenue, but as you go east the spires are few. The old downtown churches are sold for vast sums, and the money used to build gorgeous religious clubhouses uptown—retreating from human need, leaving the masses in poverty and despair. Our church life is a gratification,

seldom a sacrifice. It coddles the prosperous, and forgets the
dwellers in the abyss. It skims the middle-class, nothing more.

Why waste your time on the sermon-saturated pagans in the
pews, who would be the same kind of persons without the
Church as with it? They are not hypocrites—not consciously so;
they are the conventional type, loyal to a tradition for family or
social reasons. They are the sort who put Jesus to death long
ago, and they are trying to embalm Him today. Stay in the
Church if you can; some of us stay out in order to keep our
religion. Come into journalism with me—what a stinging pen
you wield; let's knock the daylights out of humbug.

Would any New York paper print the letter my friend wrote?
Not one. It would scare any editor white. Freedom of the
press? It is gagged and wears hobble skirts. It will not even
report the sermon in which a preacher dares to tell the bitter,
old, and haggard truth—it might lose a reader or a nickel!
When I spoke of the phony hotel religions as teaching sanctified
selfishness, making a little tin god of the subconscious mind,
calling them "bootlegged religion," my friend Frank Cobb,
who endorsed every word of it, chided me for it in an editorial
in the *New York World*. A fine man he was too, brilliant, but
hamstrung, doing tricks like the monkey of an Italian organ-
grinder. When I spoke of the necessity of fraternity between
English-speaking peoples as the basis, at least, of any hope of
world peace and stability, my words were not reported. Knocking the daylights out of humbug—some people get the life
kicked out of them while trying to get a kick out of life. The
press is not a leader, but a follower—a cloudy mirror, reflecting
only what it is safe to reflect. No, the average editor is so shy
that he blushes when he sees himself in the mirror of his own
paper.

The night of my Recognition as Minister of the Church of
the Divine Paternity was an hour of fraternal courtesy and
goodwill. It is an old church, as New York counts oldness;
like other churches it has journeyed uptown with the years,
from Pearl Street, opposite City Hall, where Thackeray delivered his lectures on English Humorists, to 45th and Fifth

Avenue, where it was a shrine of patriotism during the Civil War, to 76th and Central Park West.

The present church, built in cathedral style, with a Magdalen College tower, has one of the loveliest chancels in America. A carved oak pulpit, an exquisite Tiffany communion altar, a mosaic of "Christ at the Feet of His Disciples," and to the right hangs an American flag from a staff cut from a rail off the old Lincoln farm. The Whitfield organ is a delight, with its myriad tones and keys.

Dr. Cadman spoke with incredible facility and felicity about the use of symbols in religion, and the ministry of beauty. My friend Major Putnam remarked on the appropriateness of having a liberal preacher with an orthodox heart in New York. Edwin Markham talked of the fellowship between poetry and preaching—a poet must not be a preacher, nor a preacher wholly a poet. He was one of the most radiant spirits I have ever known, my friend for many years. A disciple of Swedenborg in his faith, in the vestry before the service he wrote a quatrain which, he said, summed up my faith and his, as indeed it did; only, alas! it makes most of us Christians of the Left Hand:

> No soul can be forever banned,
>   Eternally bereft;
> Whoever falls from God's right hand
>   Is caught into His left.

CLIFF-DWELLERS

From an English home in Ealing, shut in by vine-covered walls, the drawing room opening into a garden, to a New York apartment house, was a novel adventure. The Rectory of my church was in the Hendrick Hudson at 110th Street and Riverside Drive, on the top floor. There we were, several hundred families, each living on a separate shelf, like doves in their cotes, piled up, jammed together, yet with no spirit of neighborliness—we had proximity without community. No one knew who lived above or below, and nobody seemed to care. A man was carried out in his coffin, tipped endwise in the elevator, and the fact of his death was the first knowledge we had that he ever lived. Opening the door of the dumb-waiter, at the risk of being guillotined, one gazed into a deep, narrow well, like the Bottomless Pit, hearing all kinds of languages. It was a new kind of life, requiring no little adjustment both of body and mind. Outside a roar of traffic amid dizzy heights, the whirr of invisible machines, the myriad lights of flashing and dancing electric signs—it was New York, at once the most cosmopolitan and the most provincial of cities, and a perpetual wonderland to me.

Below my window was the lordly, broad-breasted Hudson, as it nears the sea. Its moods were as many as my own, varying with the hours: now lucid and lovely, now overhung by a soft haze of dreamy meditation, now swept by a blue dust of rain. It became almost personal in its friendliness, and I felt its bafflement as the inflowing tide pushed its waters upstream, like the pressure of the Eternal Will thwarting my impulsive spirit, like the struggle in the heart of Everyman. Every evening the Divine Artist painted a sunset scene over the New Jersey hills, and I marveled at His masterpieces. One evening haunts me still. The whole sky was aglow with gorgeous colors, a mass of molten splendor, like Dante's rose of gold, with foundations of dark vapor. Gradually the gold changed to delicate, tender green, then to pale lavender, deepening into soft purple as night came down, like a shade drawn over a latticed window in the City of God.

HEARTACHE

And yet, and yet; in spite of my cathedral-like church, work I loved, and troops of friends, I was unhappy; my very soul was sore. The long-lived storm of great events, the awful war—the fact that it could and had transpired—the frightful scenes which haunted my memory, the seeming futility of it all, depressed me. Far back and deep down in my heart there was a dull hurt. Such a tragedy tells terribly upon the inner life, who can ever tell its ravages! No one can be dragged through a jungle of violence and not be wounded. My faith in God was not shaken —not for an instant—but the human scene was appalling, in its apathy, inertia, and blurred cynicism. One thought of the lines:

> To build and build and build on running sand—
> How terrible it must be to be God.

Of course we were bidden not to be idealistic but very "practical," but the world was not practical; it did not work, I was preaching in chaos; which was worse, iniquity or imbecility, my own included, was hard to know. Goethe was right when he said that in face of stupidity even the gods are helpless.

All about me was hissing hatred, race against race, raucous and rasping; no great poet set my soul dancing before God; it was sex-worship in literature. The churches ran along in old grooves deep enough to be graves, each edgy about its infallibility, sensitive about its sovereignty, senseless in its sectarianism; Christianity had become churchianity, a poor thing, since it could not have even fellowship. Worse still, there was an incredible emptiness of soul, a spiritual vacuum, in which people were trying to live, gasping for breath—a hollowness of spirit, as if, obsessed by day-by-dayness, inner values had been forgotten or lost.

The question faced me: Was Christianity enough? The answer was, emphatically, No—not in any content we had so far given it. Was Christ enough? No, not in any interpretation we had achieved of His life and teaching. A few great souls, a few small groups, saw the dismal situation; the rest did not see or did not care. Our greatest tragedy was in our group-life, and the Church, the most unique group on earth, was failing to give leadership. Salvation, if it be only individual, is merely salvage. Never shall I forget that black time, yet, like Pasteur, I found in God—in the still sense of His nearness—a "lasting provision of faith and fire." Once more that glorious dream, or vision, visited me, showing a stately old cathedral, the White Presence at the Altar, and the elect minds of the race listening and giving assent to those calm, unhurried, piercing "words of eternal life," and my hurt was healed, in part. I could go on. Almost I fell from God's right hand, and was caught into His left!

YOUNGER GENERATION

No doubt Adam and Eve were worried about the younger generation, and not without reason. Our young folk in those post-war days were as gay, as vivacious, as irresponsible, as superficial as ever young folk have been; only more so. Like everything else, the feud between youth and age was made acute by the war, which left the world neurotic, erotic, and in so many ways idiotic. Old restraints were thrown off, old standards upset. At best the mood of youth was an engaging sauciness; at worst a downright defiance—or else they played at the old game of Shock-My-Aunties. There was a new hypocrisy—once bad folk pretended to be good; now the nicest kind of youngsters posed as wicked! None the less, it was a mistake to think that youth was not serious just because it refused to be solemn. Most of the past was dead to them—blotted out by the red mist of war. They had as much Christianity as was embedded in the social order; and that was very little. A gifted and high-minded young editor, who wanted me to go on his staff, put it to me in this way, recalling his austere upbringing in New England:

It is like a nightmare to think of it. Sunday was as dismal as a funeral. Joy was a sin, an idea was an agony. Every happy impulse was trampled upon; every healthy instinct was suppressed, as if it were vile and shameful. God was a big policeman always on watch with a club. Facts about sex were unclean, and I grew up in ignorance of my own nature. If I asked a human question, the old extinguisher was brought out and applied. All inquiry about religion was squelched forthwith, as if one had touched a tabu. We had to swallow it whole, or leave it. Art was blasphemy and science an invention of the Devil.

No, it is all off. I'm done. They got God and the Devil mixed. They put the war over on us, but they can't put their religion across. They think we are a wild, godless set. It may be so, if they mean their petty, fussy little God, who is harder to please than a spinster school-mistress. We are not irreligious, but we want religion to make sense. What is the Church going to do about it? No preacher over forty can speak our language, and young fellows shy at the pulpit—it has no pull in it. No, I don't talk like this to the old folk—they would not understand.

As I "listened in," agreeing with much that he said, I wondered how the younger generation could make a worse mess of the world than we had made. Anyway, it would soon be in their hands, and my prayer was that the insight of Meredith might be fulfilled, when he saw youth and age uniting "to rear the temple of the credible God." Then I took from my pocket a letter from one of the grand old men of New York and read it to him:

> I am ill at expression in religious matters, my creed being a plain and practical one. I think if every person would every day do some kind deed to some one other than themselves, the burden of the world would be lifted; and I try not to wait for the others to begin. It seems to me that such a practice leads directly to spirituality. The step to realization is a short one, and the world is doing everything else but taking it.

"BAGDAD-ON-THE-SUBWAY"

One day I showed an English friend the sights of New York, and it was as good as a storybook. He had never seen the city before, and if I stretched matters a little, the Lord will forgive me. Of course there was no use dragging skeletons out of the closet, so I avoided certain sections of the city—those parts where it shades off into shabbiness. He was a good sport, pretending to accept my version of the facts; but when I said that the Pennsylvania Station takes the shine off Buckingham Palace, he had his doubts. Up Riverside Drive to Grant's tomb, through Columbia University, and lunch at the Russian Inn, where some artist had told fairy-stories in a riot of color on the walls. Down to Trinity Church, St. Paul's and Wall Street, and tea at a French café. Washington Square, the O. Henry Country, and Gramercy Park, and dinner at the Armenian Restaurant. To John Street and the mission, which is "the Mother of Methodism, ninety-nine steps from Broadway." Chinatown and the Joss House, followed by Greenwich Village. A Socialist meeting where an orator argued that "a living wage is one that keeps the soul of the employer alive!" A lighted elevated train running through the shadows, like a fiery serpent. A shoreless ocean of humanity tossing up to the astonished skies its gray billows of steel and stone—no wonder Blake was blinded by a vision of London; it charred his eyes. As we parted at the Prince George Hotel, my friend said, "Tomorrow, perhaps, you will let me see the American quarter!" The rogue! With other beings made in the image of God I was crammed into a car, thinking subway thoughts; "and so to bed," as a famous Londoner would have said.

Next day we tried it again, and I was astonished to learn how well my friend knew the O. Henry stories. But he argued that O. Henry was not a genius, as if anybody can say what genius is. What is it but the ability to see what others merely look at, to remember what others forget, and to fix its vision in the eternal repose of art? It was the last point that he doubted —he agreed that O. Henry saw "the great big city of razzle-dazzles" as no one else ever saw it, and that his stories are its best biography. Also, that he knew how to

> Turn to a woman a woman's
> Heart, and a child's to a child;

but he questioned whether he had the literary form to make his stories live—he was too eager for that sudden twist of surprise at the end. Only once, he said, did he venture as far uptown as Seventy-second Street and Riverside, and then he asked with an injured air if he had "not passed Peekskill!" Yet to him New York was a laboratory of human nature that held his insight and interest by its medley of comedy and tragedy; a perpetual Arabian Nights entertainment. From the lower East Side, where, in August, "kids on fire-escapes with their tongues out try to get a bit of fresh air that hasn't been fried on both sides," to the bright lights of Broadway, "calling moths from miles to come and attend the singeing school," he knew the marvel of New York, reveled in it, and wrote about it. Perhaps my friend was right, no mean judge of such matters, as to the enduring quality of his art. But of his rich humanity, his humor and pathos, there can be no doubt. "The Making of a New Yorker" is surely a classic, showing that the frigidity of the city is only a bluff, its garish glitter and shallow vivacity a veneer, its hardness a hoax, hiding a foolish kindness of heart. From my diary:

> What a picture lower New York makes seen from the river on a crisp, frosty day, when the purple wing of evening brushes the grime away. On the left a sky of pearl and old silver; on the right the city, shrouded in violet haze, with row on row of lighted windows rising like fairy-palaces, until it seems fantastic, dream-like, unreal. It is incredible that man should have uplifted such cliffs and peaks, here in shapes of stalagmites, there in slender towers. Yet he has done so, making his masonry rival the mountains of God. The sun sinks, the fog deepens, and as the soft night falls over the scene the elevated trains look like sinuous, slow-moving comets gliding to and fro through a human Milky Way.

TWO FAMOUS STREETS

Broadway is a parable of human life. Born amid the rocks of Spuyten Duyvil, it has an innocent, if rather ragged, childhood, and is ready for school by the time it reaches Columbia and Union Seminary—though one doubts if it learns much theology. Leaving the University, it behaves very well at first; but by the time it arrives at Columbus Circle, its mind runs to automobiles, which is not a good omen. Alas, between Broadway Tabernacle and the Flatiron Building, it is a gay and giddy-paced street, garish in manners if not in morals—all lit up and flashy—known as "the street of the seven sins," though not so bad as it is painted. By the time it gets to Grace Church, it is a sober, middle-aged street, the glitter of the White Way having faded into the light of common day. At the City Hall it learns politics, but to no good purpose. Gradually it becomes the Street of the Dreadful Height, until it ends in a Grand

Cañon, and thinks only of money, as if smitten with the avarice of age. Toward the end even its churches are very rich, which makes one ponder the words of Jesus about the end of a "Broad Way."

By contrast, Fifth Avenue, from Madison Square to the top of Central Park, is a fine lady, elegantly dressed and well-mannered, with the way of one secure in her social position. She has wealth and power, and the great churches she passes add dignity without solemnity to her deportment. If her skirts are cut as befits the fashion—alow or aloft—she is no flirt like Broadway, much less what Wells called a "paint-disaster of the street"; it is a difference not of inches, but of intention. She moves with fair grace, but without striking sinuousness. She dines at the Waldorf, worships at St. Thomas's or the Cathedral, as her heart inclines, reads at the Public Library, and keeps a museum of art for her guests. If she smokes it is in the seclusion of her stately clubs, any one of which would make the palace of an Oriental monarch look like a rummage sale. At times, methinks, she is haunted by the dreadful shapes of poverty hidden in the drabness into which the city sinks toward the east. It is a brilliant, gracious avenue, more high-heeled than high-browed, but kind-hearted withal; in short, a glorified Main Street.

BOOTLEG RELIGION

Once I made a study of "illicit religion" in New York, in hotels and halls where all kinds of cults hold forth. What strange philosophies folk run after, drifting hither and yon, seeking magic and the moon—anything to tickle curiosity. Restless, troubled, hungry of heart, they take refuge in the occult and the esoteric, in quest of some formula, some charm, to heal their ills and unify the disarray of the inner life. It would be grotesque if it were not tragic—this search for power without discipline and salvation without sacrifice. Which was the more interesting, the audiences or the lecturers, it was hard to know. Of course, the seekers after sensation were there, as everywhere; the kind of women who adore Wagner and Theosophy one week, and the next hang on the lips of some shop-worn celebrity from Europe or India, or the newest boy-violinist. But most of the audiences were serious, earnest folk, to whom religion had evidently become a tradition or a memory, and some of them had known bitter sorrow, for which they had found no healing. Wistful, unhappy, it was pathetic to hear them listening to strange, half-baked philosophies, most of which were plain frauds.

Many of the lecturers were just fakes, conjuring with the magic words, Health, Happiness, Success, harping upon vibrations of one theme: "How to get what you want." One posed as "a curative psychologist and personality-builder"; another offered "healing the involuntary way"; and still another talked learnedly of "the Hidden Giant"—the Subconscious—followed by "classes in Healing, Concentration, and Prosperity." Fortunately, a few were real teachers of spiritual truth, trying to help people to make use of spiritual energy in daily life.

Each of these cults betrayed some lack on the part of organized religion—chiefly its neglect of mysticism—and the penalty was exaggeration, or degradation. The tragedy of our time is the schism between the head and the heart, the divorce of science and mysticism; the failure to see that the inner life is a realm of law where order is the trophy of obedience. Alas! the Church seems able to deal only with the intelligent, the prosperous, and the healthy; with the sick of body and soul it is helpless. Has our religion nothing to say to physical beings who have a bodily life to live? Has the Church no help for the subnormal, the distressed, the over-burdened, and those whose minds seem scattered by the dizzy whirl of city life? Has it no art of healing, no technique of inner realization? Before the Church attacks these new cults, it ought to study how far its own failure to minister to human need has brought them into being.

TEA WITH TAGORE

Rabindranath Tagore came to New York. This was not the first time he had been in America, since he had a son in the Uni-

versity of Illinois. Having met him in London, he invited me
to take tea with him at the Algonquin Hotel. The room in
which he received me had a touch of Eastern light and color,
as if he had brought a bit of India to America. Standing beside
the tea-table, in oriental garb, he greeted me with a gentle,
stately simplicity of courtesy, friendly without being formal.
As he talked his exquisitely soft voice was like music—speaking
with the English accent, beginning a sentence in the treble key
and sliding down—and the impression of a great spiritual personality made an atmosphere in which one thought only of the
highest things. His oriental robes, his dome-like forehead, his
iron-gray hair and beard, his beautiful dark eyes, made a picture of singular winsomeness, as if some figure had stepped out
of the pages of the Bible. I remembered how Yeats, the Irish
poet, seeking someone with whom to compare Tagore, had gone
back to Thomas à Kempis, but I would add a touch of Walt
Whitman, and perhaps of Francis of Assisi. Also, I recalled a
happy argument with Alfred Noyes as to whether the poetry of
Tagore was poetry at all or not.

We talked—or rather he talked and I listened, putting in a
word or a question here and there—of how America needs some
of the mysticism of India, and India some of the activism of
America. There was a tone of pathos in his voice when he
spoke of the chaos in India, almost of heartbreak, yet he preferred it to the metallic, touch-the-button civilization of the
West. "The world does not know the truth," he said. "It has
no common idea about which its life may unite and cohere. It
has forgotten, if it ever discovered, that down below race, rank,
religion there is a fundamental humanity, which is universal
and everywhere the same. I am a man of India, as to my origin,
training and outlook; but I am something else—I am a human
being, a man of humanity. I have learned that, though our
tongues are different and our habits dissimilar, at bottom our
hearts are one. The clouds, generated on the banks of the Nile,
fertilize the distant valley of the Ganges. East is East and West
is West—God forbid that it should be otherwise—but the twain
must meet in amity and understanding. I do not think in terms

of nationality—not even of Indian nationality—but in terms of
humanity and its obligation to live by the law of love if it is
to live at all."

"In short," he interjected, "by what Jesus taught and lived,
the vision of the Kingdom of God as it is shown in His mind."

"Yes, Jesus was right," and he spoke the great name with
evident love and reverence; "and He was a man of the East.
His words are not whiffs of perfume—they are poetry indeed,
but poetry believed in—but also great laws of life and truth,
as much so as the laws of chemistry. But you do not believe in
Jesus—I mean your people do not. If you did, America would
be happy. But America is not happy; I see it in the faces of
your people. God is wanting—"

Of a sudden a light came into his face, as if he had seen a
vision, and he talked, more to himself than to me—about the
love of God. I shall never forget it. The rush and roar of New
York were hushed, and the room became a sanctuary. In this
far country his mind had found its native land of the spirit.
I might have been listening on the hillsides of Galilee, or beside
the sea, while Jesus taught. His words were simple, but they
had such radiance of reality as I had never heard before—I
dare not try to reproduce them. "May he give us the beneficent
mind," he said, softly, quoting from an old Indian poem. My
feeling, as we parted, was that I had met one of the greatest
lovers of God I had ever known.

SUNDRY MATTERS

Here follow certain items from my Diary, the dates of which
do not matter:

—How many influences play upon preaching. My sermon
today simply did not go; something was wrong. Water in the
carburetor, the spark dead, or something else. It was a fairly
good sermon, and not ill-considered, but it had no life, no fire,
no power. When it is so, preaching is the hardest work on
earth—harder than making brick without straw. It is baffling.
A dumb, dismal mood creeps out of the mists of the mind and

seals up the fountains of the spirit. One is helpless against it, unable to achieve release of personality. St. John was "in the Spirit on the Lord's day." He trod on air, his feet walked among the stars. Perhaps on other days it was not so. God keeps His sacred wine for the sacramental feasts of life. The wind bloweth where it listeth; today it was calm, and the oars were heavy.

—Heard a good story about dear Robert Collyer, showing his wisdom and humor. When John Haynes Holmes came to the Church of the Messiah, the old man became pastor emeritus, and he was in his pew at every service. No two men could be more unlike, but the old saint was loyal to the new prophet. After a while, when some of the older folk began to be ill at ease under the new teaching, one of them asked Collyer how he liked the new minister.

"Fine, fine," he said; "he is a bright young man and will do big things; we are very fortunate."

Not satisfied with such a reply, and feeling that there was something Collyer had not confessed, the questioner put the matter point-blank:

"Honest, now, Doctor; don't those sermons make the snakes run up and down your back?"

"Yes, they do," Collyer admitted, slowly, hesitantly; "but you just wait. After a while some young man will come along and make 'em run up and down his back, too!"

—Went down in Water Street to McAuley Mission, "dry dock of a thousand wrecks." What a carpenter shop for the making and mending of men—broken men, pieces of men, "Ex-men," as Gorki would say. They actually advertise for sots, bums, down-and-outs, and those who have no hope—like Christ writing a "Want-Ad," asking for the refuse of the world. And around Him, as He predicted, gather a strange, weary, forlorn company of men whom life has defeated—the sick of soul, the palsied of will, the demon-haunted—seeking, as of old, His healing touch, His forgiving word, His hand put forth in the darkness, which tells them that they may still hope—that the impossible is true. It is like reading a new chapter from the Acts.

—At the time when the modernist-fundamentalist debate was at its height—or depth—a group of journalists gathered in New York, Frank Cobb of the *World* presiding. I was asked to sit in the conference. The question came up, What is the matter with the Church? Why all this fuss and furor? The suggestion was made that the mind of the Church must be deeply divided in its thought about God. Then came the second question, In what terms does the Church think of God? Since no one could answer, I was appointed a committee of one to find out. The result was a remarkable symposium—as I can truly say, since I did not write it, but only edited it—called *My Idea of God*. Catholic, Jewish, Protestant, modernist, fundamentalist, Quaker, Ethical Culturist, Christian Scientist—all kinds of thinkers were asked, not why they believe in God, but in what terms they think of Him. The book was reviewed in the *New Republic* under the title, "Eighteen Gods," which was more clever than accurate. It had a wide reading for many years.

ELIHU ROOT

As I listened to Mr. Root speak one evening on the League of Nations, the words of Theodore Roosevelt came to mind: "The greatest man that has arisen on either side of the Atlantic in my lifetime." It was a large remark, and must not be taken too literally, any more than the estimate of Roosevelt by himself as "a mediocre intellect highly energized." It was very impressive—a little gray man, speaking in quiet, measured words, and a vast audience listening as to an oracle. It used to be said in New York, just for fun, "If you loot, see Root before you scoot"; and he is still an attorney, albeit having great causes and whole nations for his clients; having all the handicaps that go to make up wisdom, but lacking the spiritual quality. It means much to have a mind of such gravity, sanity and clarity devoted to the public service. For thirty years and more he has lived at the center of public affairs, without yielding to cynicism. Yet one misses in him a rare thing not easily defined. Manner, wisdom, wit? Call it, rather, the seer-like quality, the poetic touch, the haunting accent. Men admire Elihu Root; they love John Hay.

A few days later, on a train to Washington, I went into the dining car and saw Mr. Root sitting alone at a table for two, and I asked him, "May I share your table?"

"Certainly; it will be a pleasure," he said.

"Of course you do not know me," I said, "but I know you—in fact I heard you speak the other evening; I was deeply impressed. I see that you are reading a beautifully bound book;

I am curious to know what you read when you read what you like to read and not as a professional necessity."

"There it is, see for yourself," he replied, handing the book to me. "But be careful and don't drop it, because it has dynamite in it—it might explode."

Indeed, he was right—it was *Sartor Resartus,* by Carlyle, a story of spiritual struggle out of the night in which life says No, through a "center of indifference," to the dawn when life says Yes, told in what Meredith called "a wind in the orchard style." Then we talked of many things.

When he asked my name, I was surprised that he recognized it. "Yes, yes, I remember, you were at the City Temple in London. One of my English friends sent me a copy of one of your sermons, preached when the British Army was before Jerusalem; it was one of the finest things I ever read."

In regard to Anglo-American relations he had some good things to say, after I had told him that I did not get to first base on that subject. "There are difficulties," he pointed out. "The English think that God made them first, and then made the rest of us out of the scraps left over. But we have our stupidities too, plenty of them. We are really two peoples separated by one language. But it will work out right, if we give it time, because both peoples have sense and sentiment enough in common to make it work—at the moment the less said about it the better. If we are too anxious we may spoil it."

The slender spire of the Washington monument crept into the sky—we were nearing our capitol city. As we parted, I felt that I had met a man truly wise, not merely astute, a man of sound judgment, simple and kindly, as great men always are; and, above all, a great gentleman.

CARL SANDBURG

In New York, in the early 1920's, Carl Sandburg called up on Easter Eve: "Tomorrow will be a heavy day for you, I know; but I should like to ask you two questions. I'll not stay more than ten minutes, or twenty at the longest." Of course I asked him to come. What a fine face he has, rugged yet gentle; what a rich personality. Then, for the first time, I learned that he was writing a life of Lincoln. In preparing to write *The Prairie Years,* he had read my *Lincoln & Herndon,* and he wanted to make sure of the authenticity of a speech by Lincoln, printed for the first time in my book, delivered at Troy, Kansas, on the day that John Brown was executed—a rather stern speech, Carl thought, almost out of key with the spirit of Lincoln. Also, about some letters from Horace White, which added interesting information about some early biographies of Lincoln. The questions were easily answered. I was indebted to Horace White himself for his letters and for a copy of the Lincoln speech, for which he, in turn, was indebted to Robert R. Hitt, who had reported all the speeches of Lincoln in his debates with Douglas, and, I think, went with Lincoln on his tour of Kansas.

We fell to discussing the religious attitude of Lincoln, no doubt suggested by Easter Eve. Sandburg held that Lincoln, at bottom, was an agnostic, with which I did not agree—except in so far as all of us are, and must be, agnostics, since we can know only in part, and prophesy in fragments, as St. Paul said. But something more than an agnostic resignation to an inner decency was needed to explain Lincoln, especially his growth of soul which made his life, toward the end, a spiritual masterpiece. "I was driven to my knees because there was nowhere else to go," he said, under the pressure and tragedy of war. By prayer, the moral fatalism of his early years, I argued, became personal, and God became a Father and Friend. Sandburg still stood by his guns. Suddenly he looked at his watch, and it was two o'clock in the morning; we had forgotten about time. He apologized abjectly and left. Naturally I followed his work, reading first *The Prairie Years,* and, later, the four volumes of *The War Years.* It is an amazing piece of research and writing. The stories of the Gettysburg Address and of "the funeral procession seventeen hundred miles long," will never be surpassed by anybody.

LINCOLN STUDENTS

Of course my long study of Lincoln gave me a permanent interest in all books written about his life, and I came in touch with many Lincoln students; two of whom are still living. As a young man Rufus Wilson went to Springfield and met William H. Herndon, the law partner of Lincoln. Herndon was well along in years, a little the worse from too much drinking, but still a fountain of information about the early years of Lincoln, albeit rather garrulous, with certain fixations of mind the more firmly settled because he had been so roundly abused by myth-makers. All through the years Wilson has been diligently digging up new facts about Lincoln, and the people who surrounded him, which he has recently published in a fat book.

Then there is my dear friend, Dr. Edgar DeWitt Jones, minister of the Woodward Avenue Christian Church, Detroit, who has also been engaged, for years, in unearthing no end of new and valuable facts about Lincoln and those near him, which he is about to publish under the perfect title, *I Have Lived with Lincoln.* In his new and great Church, he has a Washington window and a Lincoln window, making it at once a shrine of patriotic lore and of religious faith, as befits a man of whom a brilliant journalist said, "Preachers regard him as a great historian, and historians regard him as a great preacher." He happens to be both; he is one of the noblest preachers of our generation and a former President of the Federal Council of Churches of Christ in America.

"EAST SIDE, WEST SIDE"

One day I went to the East Side of New York to offer a gentle prayer over a little child run over and killed by a car near the House of Service conducted by my church. Up four flights of stairs, in a narrow hall lit by dim gas-jets, over floors creaky and uneven, I reached the tenement "home," where I witnessed a heart-breaking scene. Half a hundred people had gathered in the rooms and halls, a testimony to the kindliness and neighborliness of the poor. After the service, as the little body was carried out, the children who had been playing in the streets assembled, their bright faces bestreaked with dirt, making a picture as they stood in the silence.

For hours I wandered along the dingy streets, littered with rubbish, where people were so crowded that life trod on life, and solitude was unknown. The sidewalks swarmed with children; the air rang with their shouts or curses, as they darted to and fro amid the rumble of wheels, playing their games. To one watching the scene, it had a kind of repulsive picturesqueness, but to be in it, with no hope of a better lot, would have made the best people in the city anarchists within a week—alas! it is harder to get the slum out of the people than it is to get the people out of the slum. It is accepted with patient fatalism by people whose dwelling-places are more like dens than homes. Only the joy of the children redeemed the drabness from utter desolation.

Rambling on into the Jewish quarter, I found the sidewalks thronged with peddlers and purchasers, everybody trafficking eagerly. There were little girls of Madonna-like beauty, with oval faces and olive tints, and clear, dark eyes, relucent as evening pools; and on boxes, in the doorways, old men with long beards of jetty black or silvery gray and the noble profiles of their race. Among such as these, I remembered, Jesus walked, and from among them chose His disciples and friends. As I walked homeward in the falling daylight, the scene was touched with the gentleness of evening, blurring its harsh realities with beauty—like the mercy of God softening the brutality of man.

Writing of my New York years, in his *Adventures in the Minds of Men*, Dean Lynn Harold Hough institutes a contrast between Dr. Fosdick and myself, as follows: "In the work of Dr. Fosdick there is none of that mellowness, that ripe grace of expression which gives charm to the work of Dr. Newton. Dr. Fosdick is often wonderfully brilliant. And he is magnificently alive. But he has not been alive very long. In some of

his deepest moods Dr. Newton makes you feel as if, like the
Sphinx, he has seen the whole pageant of the ages and through
centuries of meditation has grown wise. Dr. Fosdick finds the
keen phrase. His writing makes you think of linen of the very
best and most durable quality. Dr. Newton finds the haunting
phrase. He makes you think of rare old satin with here and
there a touch of royally beautiful brocade."

How gallant, how gracious; and yet, in spite of his praise
of my parts of speech, while he leaves Dr. Fosdick a "young
fellow"—as indeed he is in spirit—he makes me akin to the
Ancient of Days, sorting out centuries in my meditations and
wrapping them in lavender and old lace. Some time I mean to
tell how old Dr. Hough is, just for fun, or something equally
awful, to even the score; yet who could ask for a kinder friend
or a gentler critic?

Again my Diary:

SNAP-SHOTS

—David Swing was right. Snakes crawl, birds fly, and rabbits
run, but man talks himself forward. Having discussed a thing
for a century, he takes a cautious step in advance, and then sits
down and reopens the infinite conversation. Take the matter
of Church Unity, about which we have had a series of able lectures at The Brick Church. All agree that a divided Church is
wasteful, as well as stupid and ineffective; but the pace of a
snail is swift beside the progress we make toward unity. Indeed,
beyond the evil of overlapping, we do not know what we mean
by Church Unity, much less how to bring it about. It makes
one think of the saying of Rose Macaulay in *What Not:* "To
organize religion, a man must have the talents of the Devil, or
at least of an intelligent Civil Servant." Anyway, the sons of
darkness outwit the sons of light, and the cohesive power of
greed outruns the coherence of Christian enterprise. Must the
Church always be last—following the procession—riding in an
oxcart in a day of express trains and planes?

—One of the finest feats of "organized preaching" in New
York is the Madison Avenue Presbyterian Church, under the
leadership of Dr. Sloane Coffin. Standing on the borderline between a fashionable apartment house section and a gray, poly-
glot slum, by sagacious strategy it has brought the extremes of

society together, as few churches have been able to do. It is a notable achievement, as much for its tact as for its vision, uniting personal piety and social ministry. Within all its activities the genius of a great preacher is present to inspire, edify, and guide. A scholar, a teacher, a master of what Beecher called "executive Christian ideas," he thinks like a statesman and preaches like a prophet; persuades by his earnestness and ennobles by his compassion.

—The election of Dr. Manning, rector of Trinity Church, Bishop of the Episcopal Diocese of New York, reminds me of a scene. After a Sunday evening service in the City Temple in London, a number of people were waiting to speak to me. The Verger weeded out those whom he regarded as curiosity-seekers, or autograph-hunters, but he would never turn down an American. "Doctor, there is a lady giving her name as 'Mrs. Mississippi' who very much wants to see you. Maybe that means something to you, but it is beyond me," he added. "By all means show her in," I told him; I knew that she was a Southern woman. She entered, a tall, fine-looking woman, with gray hair and flashing black eyes. The story she told me was pitiful. She had married a brilliant man and lived in New York City; they had two little girls. Then, suddenly, her husband was smitten with a strange mental affliction. She loved him too much to have him put away—she could not bear it. "I could not have gone through it if it had not been for that little man of God at Trinity Church. He is a priest of the Most High, if ever there was one. He stood by me to the bitter end." After her husband died she went to London to live. Since I heard that story I have always loved Bishop Manning, even when I did not agree with him.

—Some of the folk I saw at Ellis Island yesterday haunt me, especially the face of an old woman, so gentle, so sad, such a face as one often sees on the East Side. It was a face charged with a pathos too great for one mortal life, telling of the harsh attrition of foregone generations. Moulded after a noble design, in pure lines, the broad forehead, the firm mouth, drooping, yet tender, a face in which Nature, the great tragic dramatist, had carved the sorrows of a race. Its chief feature was the eyes, large, dark, haunting, a little dulled by the film of years, as if the vision were inward rather than outward; eyes that brooded over their own depth, and saw things far away. She was startled when I smiled at her; then the deep lines of her face filled with the glow of a sunny kindness. There she sat, her bags at her feet, her hands—old, blue-veined, hard with toil—crossed in her lap, waiting at the gates of America.

—Really, there is no need for a minister of the Church of the Divine Paternity, but only the great organ, with its myriad keys, tones and echoes, played by a gentle-hearted, spiritually minded artist who, for twenty years, has made his instrument his altar—Warren Andrews. His music is both priest and prophet to me, uttering those wistful yearnings which well up in every human heart, but which no tongue can ever speak— white truths which mortal words discolor. When I hear it I begin to see a hint of a meaning in the turbid ebb and flow of human misery about me, albeit only a glimpse, only the shape of a reason that floats into my heart and melts as quickly away. But in rare moments, by the mercy of God, I feel a ground-swell of prophetic rhythm—an undertone of all-sustaining melody—running through our tangled mortal years, prophesy-ing a fair, far time when sorrow and sin shall cease and the soul of man shall be happy and free—learning in love the truth it has lost in hate. And sometimes, as my friend plays, for his joy and mine, the tumult of Time is hushed, Eternity murmurs on all my horizons, and a Presence is at my garden gate.

THEOLOGY

No doubt I ought to be telling of my development in theol-ogy, but there is little to tell. While I have kept track of such studies, all the way from St. Augustine, the Shakespeare of theology, and St. Thomas Aquinas, whose cathedral-like theol-ogy, built upon the basis of Greek philosophy and Christian revelation, still stands, despite the shock of ages, I have never attempted to make a system of theology. Any system, no mat-ter how magnificent, must of necessity leave out as much as it takes in—as well try to shut up summer in a garden or winter in a woodshed. Still, the insights of faith need to be set forth in an order of ideas, however inadequate. Many of the propo-sitions of theology are majestic, some are preposterous, because behind them is a wrong idea of God—and if we are wrong about God we cannot be right about much else that matters. For me, what counts is not the many things we try to make ourselves believe, but the few profound things we cannot dis-

believe and remain men—or only truncated men. Every time I
have thought of a system of theology for myself, I have remembered *Brand*, in the Ibsen epic, who started to build a temple
to house his thought of God; but, by the time he got his house
of God built, his thought of God had outgrown the dimensions
of his shrine. Once I spoke of this matter to my friend Baron
von Hügel, and he confirmed my feeling, saying that instead
of making a system, he was content to drop plummets as far
down as possible into the riches of Divine Grace and human
experience, without trying to weave them together into a system. To him I owe an unpayable debt, in spite of his curiously involved idiom; more, perhaps, to his personality than
to his books. It is said that Barth "rang the church bell in
Europe," but, alas! its tones were soon drowned in the crash
and thunder of universal war. He did recall us to the trans-
cendence of God, but he cut God off from history, leaving us
to wander in a wilderness—later, he modified his attitude.
Kierkegaard, the "melancholy Dane," is enjoying a temporary
revival, and no doubt he has some piercing insights to give us,
but he was so abnormal a man that no one can follow him far.

To be sure, once in a blue moon, one finds a book of vision,
such as *The World's Redemption*, by E. C. Rolt—a book unfinished and unpolished, written by a dying man away from all
libraries, its penetrating insight due, perhaps, to the ministry
of pain and the near presence of death. While not invulnerable
to criticism, it reveals more theological genius than any book
I recall; it deals with the Love of God in a manner unique and
profound, almost surprising the mystery into which the writer
was so soon to pass, lingering at the portal while he wrote.
Also, I may add that *The Human Situation*, by W. Macneile
Dixon, is one of the most remarkable books written in my
lifetime; it is dazzlingly brilliant, it shakes a man in his shoes.

SPEAKING AND WRITING

My friend Edgar DeWitt Jones, in his *American Preachers
of Today*, has a chapter on my work, written with the extraor-

dinary generosity of a friend. Among others he discusses Dr. S. Parkes Cadman, and in that chapter he quotes someone as saying, Cadman ought never to write, Newton ought never to speak, or words to that effect. While my friend does not endorse the saying, there is a real point to it just the same. Dr. Cadman was in his glory as an orator, a master of assemblies; his personality always reminded me of Theodore Roosevelt, only Cadman was the more brilliant of the two, having fabulous resources instantly at command, and an incredible facility of phrase. Yet Cadman could write magnificently, as witness his chapter in analysis and interpretation of John Wesley, in his *Three Religious Leaders of Oxford;* it would be hard to equal. By the same fact, while I have never tried to be an orator, since the very quality which makes oratory effective renders it unreliable, because a man is apt to say more than he sees, which is fatal to preaching, I can be persuasive betimes. Besides, spoken speech and written speech are two different things; they ask for different techniques. My sermons are never written until after they are preached, which gives me the benefit of what the congregation sends me in mist, which I try to return to it as gentle rain. In spoken speech there is, and must be, some repetition, for sake of emphasis, on the ground that "what I tell you three times is true"; but it must be "artistic repetition." Even then it has been estimated that the average congregation gets only two per cent of what the preacher says. Half a dozen times in my life I have written sermons and read them, but seldom with success. Only one was really successful, "The Crisis of Christ," delivered at the anniversary of the Colonial Missionary Society in the City Temple, in 1930; it appears in *Things I Know in Religion.* After all, each must do his work in the way best fitted to his gifts and his purpose in the pulpit.

My lectures on *The New Preaching* were given at the College of Preachers in Washington City, a unique College associated with the Cathedral—not a Seminary, but a place where men who have been in the service, and do not feel that they are doing their best work, can return and refresh, if not remake, their preaching. The lectures were repeated at various divinity schools of different churches. My intention was to follow the book with another on *The New Preachers,* studying Fosdick, Sockman, Sherer, Tittle, DeWitt Jones and others—not "an unco-squad," as Burns would say, but gallant fellow-workers; but alas! the book was never written.

In 1917, while on a speaking-tour of my country, approaches were made to me to give the Lyman Beecher Lectures on Preaching at Yale; but it was impossible for me to return from England in wartime to do it. Anyway, I have said all that I know about our preacher-craft, and more too, perhaps; yet I never fail to read a new book dealing with the art of preaching. It is endlessly interesting, since there is no form of speech on earth like it. Of course there is only one sermon really worth talking about—the Sermon on the Mount, the Mt. Everest on the landscape of the soul.

MANHATTAN

New York is an amazing human encampment—nowhere else on earth, perhaps, do so many people of all sorts and conditions, so many races, colors, creeds, and tongues, live so close together, piled up on top of each other. If Jerusalem is the city of faith, Athens the city of art, Rome the city of law, Paris the city of fashion, London the city of liberty, New York must be the city of fraternity—or else an inferno! Fortunately, the old Dutch settlers planted the principle of toleration on Manhattan Island, and it is still active and alive. Even Peter Stuyvesant, whose personal theology was as unbending as his wooden leg, knew how to live and let live, to think and let think.

Today New York is a great Jewish-Catholic city, and it is almost as difficult to conduct a Protestant Church on Manhattan as it would be in Paris. One preaches to a procession; as many pass through the church during the year as enter it. Neighborhoods shift swiftly, baffling the shrewdest forecast; and a church finds itself a lonely island in an alien sea. Old families break up or move away, and young folk seek the suburbs to rear their families. The tempo of the city is terrific; home ties give way to hotels and apartment houses—poor substitutes—making the tie between the church and the home tenuous.

Many who come from smaller communities, not finding the old informal fellowship in the city, abandoned the church, or else became "church tramps."

At one time a group of churches on the West Side made a canvas of our neighborhood, and when we could get into the apartment houses—without being arrested—we found no end of people who either had their church-letters in the trunks, or had left them in their home towns. They begged us not to report them to the churches of their own faith in New York. One day I made eleven calls and found only one man at home, and he had a broken leg and could not get away. All the while, vacations lengthened and the church year was shortened, and parish life became more difficult—some of my Official Board did not live on Manhattan Island. The glitter of the city fascinated me, its rush and hurry wore my nerves to a frazzle. What will be the fate of our city churches—except those that stand on old foundations, like the Dutch churches—is hard to know. No ordinary methods of work apply, yet the need of spiritual fellowship in the crowded loneliness of city life is appalling.

A dear lady in my parish, Mrs. Washington Cooper, had a horror of a girl being in New York without money. So she set up a fund, and it fell to me to administer it. One evening a handsome girl came in and asked if I would let her have fifty cents. "Certainly," I said, "but a girl who needs fifty cents needs more than that." Then I told her the story of the fund. "Take five dollars, and if you need more come back. Remember it is not my money, and you are under no obligation to me." She kept back tears with difficulty. Months later, while I was preaching in Cleveland, she paid back the five dollars with interest—one of the few who did so out of thousands who have "borrowed" from me—not because they were dishonest, but because the condition which made them ask aid prevented them from repaying.

Some New York customs tried me, especially the funerals at night, as if in our reck-and-neck race for the nickel we did not have time to pay respect to our dead. No wonder Jesus wept over a city, knowing its brutality, its black wickedness, its nameless possibilities, and its aching pathos!

JEWISH PREACHERS

Rabbi Adolphus Moses was the first great preacher of the Synagogue whom it was my honor to know, in Louisville, Kentucky, in my student years. Later, in St. Louis, both Dr. Sale and Dr. Leon Harrison—he of the magical eloquence—were my friends; I attended the Bible classes of both. In Chicago I knew Dr. Joseph Stoltz and Dr. Emil Hirsch—who that heard his lecture on "John Ruskin" can ever forget it, even the manner in which he pronounced the name of Ruskin? In London I knew the chief Rabbi, Dr. Herts, but was never able to get close to him. In New York I knew the late Dr. Enelow, and, of course, Dr. Stephen Wise, and his remarkable wife, who is a painter.

Here is a most unusual story as Mrs. Wise told it. She and the Rabbi were spending a part of their vacation in northern Italy. Each day they went for a walk, exploring the countryside. One day they came to a wayside shrine, in which there was a picture of the Christ. They paused and studied it, but did not like it, "because it was too much like Henry the VIIIth!" If there is to be a Christ, they agreed, He must not look like that beefy, heavy-jowled figure, whose name smelled to heaven. They decided to do something about it. At the inn where they were staying there was a young English curate with a heavenly face—fine, firm, tender, exquisitely wrought. They told him of their dilemma, and he agreed to allow Mrs. Wise to paint his portrait. When the painting had been finished, the three went to the shrine, took out the Henry the VIIIth cartoon and put in the English-curate Christ.

"Now, did you ever hear of the wife of a Jewish Rabbi paint-ing a spiritual Christ for a Catholic shrine?" she asked.

"Never; but what kind of robes did you put on him?" I inquired.

"Just his surplice, which I arranged to suggest an oriental robe," she explained.

"That was perfect," I told her; "a stole would have been out of place. Jesus never wore a stole—he was a layman and had never been ordained! It is important to get things straight."

The late Felix Adler, founder of the Society of Ethical Cul-ture, who came out of the Synagogue, bringing its profound mysticism, was my neighbor and friend. His books have influ-enced me deeply, especially *An Ethical Philosophy of Life*, which gives us a new version of the Golden Rule, and *The Reconstruction of the Spiritual Ideal*, in which much that has been written later was anticipated. How often the word "frus-tration" appears in his writings.

In Philadelphia Dr. Fineshriber—he and I were young men together in Iowa—and Dr. Wolsey, are my neighbors, in whose synagogues I have preached. They are a good company of bril-liant men, in whose fellowship I have found inspiration and joy.

But the Rabbi I knew most intimately was the late Joel Blau, of Peni-El Temple, New York, in what someone called "the steam-heated slums of upper New York." He was my neighbor, my friend; we read together, we played together—he was a man of myriad moods, but gifted and charming. He wrote a book of essays, entitled *The Wonder of Life*, which I reviewed with enthusiasm but not with exaggeration; the re-view was syndicated in the Jewish press, as well as in other papers. One day he was in my office, when I was editing the annual book of *Best Sermons;* the book had to go to press within two days, and there was no Jewish sermon. A telegram came from the secretary of Rabbi Harrison of St. Louis telling me that the Rabbi had been taken to the hospital, and would not be able to furnish the Jewish sermon. Passing the telegram to Rabbi Blau, I said, "Here is your hat, too. Go home, pull out all the stops on your organ, and give us a great piece of music; please!"

Glancing at me quickly, he asked, "Do you really mean it?"

"Them's orders," I replied.

The next day at noon his son brought me the manuscript of a sermon entitled "The Great Hunger," which out-topped almost every sermon in the book. A former rector of my present parish liked the sermon so well that he decided to preach it in his own pulpit. He calmly announced that Rabbi Blau of New York would preach in the Church of St. Luke and Epiphany next Sunday. At the appointed time he entered the pulpit, told the story much as I have told it, and read the sermon—read it well, too, as he knew how to do. In telling me the story he added, "Do you know it nearly ruined me; for months my people kept asking, 'When is Rabbi Blau to preach again?' "

Whether my syndicated review of his book and his sermon in the book of *Best Sermons* had anything to do with the call of Rabbi Blau to the West London Synagogue, I do not know. Anyway I do know—what I did not tell him until later—that I had a letter from an influential man in that synagogue asking about Rabbi Blau; and he did not suffer in my hands. In due time he was called to London and came down to Philadelphia —where we had moved, meantime—and we spent the day talking it over. Very earnestly I urged him to go, telling him the while what I knew about how to get along with the English people. He went, and after a few years, alas! died, a victim of cancer. His old congregation in New York had merged with another congregation, and a new synagogue was finished shortly after the death of Dr. Blau. A memorial meeting was arranged, in which I was asked to take part. Wearing the cap of a rabbi and a Genevan gown, I paid tribute to a man in whose "desert-born soul," as he described it, there was a spark of the God-fire we call genius.

A NEW ADVENTURE

In the meantime, the stress and tension of New York City had begun to tell upon my health; I doubt if I would be alive and writing these words if I had remained in the city. Besides, I was doing too many things; or rather I was doing one thing in too many ways—conducting a great parish, editing *The Master Mason*, an eighty page monthly, editing the annual book of *Best Sermons*—I read so many sermons that I almost lost my religion; going all sorts of places to preach or speak, preaching in colleges and universities, Harvard, Princeton, Cornell, Vassar, all the way from Maine to Mississippi, and again and again to the University of Iowa; not forgetting the Chicago Sunday Evening Club in Orchestra Hall, led by my close friend Clifford Barnes.

Anyway, I happened to be giving a series of Lenten talks in the foyer of the Academy of Music in Philadelphia, at the invitation of Edward Bok. Bishop Garland attended the first meeting and introduced me to the group, but had to leave for another engagement. Then, as he told me later, he "camped on my trail"; he just missed me by minutes at the First Reformed Church, where I had preached. Finally he caught up with me and invited me to enter the Episcopal Church—a thing I had never considered; he put his case skillfully, turning my own logic against me. We had been friends for many years, and he was a brother Mason.

"More than once," he reminded me, "you have said that there is only one Church of Christ on earth, and that it takes all of our churches to make that Church. If that is so—and I fully agree—then the Episcopal Church is at least a part of the Church of Christ. I deplore the fragmentariness of the Church as much as you do. You belong to us, you will be happy with us —we know your record, we have read your books; and I will smooth the road."

"Really, my dear friend, I had never thought of such a thing, although in England I saw the Church at its best; its men were very kind to me—they were gentlemen. Of course I accept the Apostles' Creed as a statement of Christian facts, and of the faith based upon those facts, but some of its phrases I interpret in a different way. In my preaching, at least, I have always added two phrases to the Creed, between the phrases 'Born of the Virgin Mary, suffered under Pontius Pilate,' in my heart I have inserted the words, 'preached the gospel of the kingdom; went about doing good'; so as not to leave the life of Christ out of the Creed."

"Exactly," he replied—I can still see his slight figure, his luminous blue eyes, the eyes of a poet who was at the same time a fine executive, "I fully agree. But, so far as I know, Doctor, the Episcopal Church has never issued an official interpretation of the Apostles' Creed. I have read your little book of sermons, dealing with each phrase of the Creed, and while I would have said some things in a different way—you are entitled to your interpretation, and I to mine.

"As to ordination," he went on, "years ago when you were a very young man you were ordained to the ministry, and your lifework has shown that that ordination was authentic and valid. In the Episcopal Church you would be ordained a priest —it is a different thing; it does not contradict or invalidate your former ordination; not in the least degree, I assure you."

"Yes, I quite understand, Bishop," I told him; "if the word 'priest' had been used at my ordination in years gone by, there would have been trouble. Nothing would make me happier than to be ordained by every Church in Christendom, by Bishop, Presbytery, or any other authority; but I should insist, in my heart at least, on having the taxi-driver, the washerwoman, the ditch-digger, the flapper with her painted fingernails, the baker, and, not least of all, the chubby hand of a little child laid upon my head giving me their human blessing. Then, perhaps, I might be a priest of the human soul, healing its hurts, uttering its deepest desires, answering even its unasked questions, and also a prophet of the Love of God, which is all that matters."

When I looked at Bishop Garland his eyes were misty with

tears; I had packed the whole passion of my life and ministry into my words. And so it was agreed; I was ordained later in Old Christ Church, Philadelphia, and in due time became Rector of the Memorial Church of St. Paul, Overbrook, the first and only suburban church it has ever been my honor and joy to serve.

The Bishop did what he said he would do; the statement issued by him welcoming me into the Church was extraordinarily generous; too much so to be quoted here. I came to know his wife, so stunningly beautiful, so gracious, so vivacious; in the Diocese they called her the Archbishop, and I dare say she was a good one. Of course I was denounced roundly, oddly enough most furiously by the alleged "liberal" sects, who called me "a lost leader," and other endearing names. But letters came from great Christian leaders—Dr. Arthur Brown, Dr. Cadman, Dr. Morrison, and not a few laymen, saying that both Bishop Garland and I had done a wise and beautiful thing. A statement issued for me by the Diocese of Pennsylvania was published from end to end of the land, in gist as follows:

Something deep in me responds to the sweet and tempered ways of the Episcopal Church. Its atmosphere of reverence, its ordered and stately worship, its tradition of historic continuity, linking today with ages agone; its symbols which enshrine the faith of the past and the hope of the future; its wise and wide tolerance; its old and lovely liturgy—like a stairway, worn by many feet, whereon men climb to God—and, still more, the organized mysticism of its sacraments—all these things of beauty and grace move me profoundly.

More vital still, if possible, is the central and strategic position which the Episcopal Church holds in the confused religious situation of our time. It is the roomiest Church in Christendom, in that it accepts the basic facts of Christian faith as symbols of transparent truths, which each may interpret as his insight explores their depth and wonder.

Midway between an arid liberalism and an acrid orthodoxy, it keeps its wise course, conserving the eternal values of faith while seeking to read the Word of God revealed in the tumult of the time. If its spirit and attitude were better understood, it would be at once the haven and the home of many vexed minds torn between loyalty to the old faith and the new truth.

After all, there is one Church of Christ. It may wear many names, but its faith is one, and finally, or soon or late, it will be one fellowship, drawn together by creative desire, or driven together by sheer necessity of facing the forces of destruction in our day, which, if they have their way, will end in materialism and futility. Each man should labor where he can do his best work in behalf of our common Christian enterprise; and I look forward to happy and fruitful service in a great and gracious fellowship.

Naturally, small groups, in the Episcopal Church, and outside, took exceptions to my statement. Those inside objected to my saying that the dogmas of the Church were mere symbols, as if they could be anything else! Liberals repudiated the word "arid," and some orthodox leaders the word "acrid," but, alas! both words fitted the actual facts.

My old friend Burris Jenkins, a great preacher and a great editor, reported in his paper, *The Christian*, that I had become an extreme high churchman. "Hey, there," I wrote him, "by what right do you say such a thing? As you well know, I have always been a high churchman—tall enough of soul to see over any wall of sect or party fence ever built. In the Episcopal Church there are three kinds of people, as an old saying puts it, 'low and lazy, broad and hazy, high and crazy,' and I do not belong to either group. In fact, I am just what I have always been, only I hope a bit better, and, alas! much sadder. A debate about ideas can be exciting, if the ideas are important; but an argument about millinery is as dull as ditch water. A man may have all the candles he likes—they are pretty—he may dress in any kind of vestment, so far as I am concerned, so long as he knows what he means by it and what he means makes sense. A sacramentalist, yes—only I would say that there are five thousand sacraments; a sacerdotalist, no. I am not interested in apostolic succession, but in a succession of apostles. Now, will you be good?"

He was good; he published most of my letter and apologized abjectly.

One man, the editor of *The Congregationalist*, tried to understand; he said that the war had done something to my heart, as indeed it had. To preach the gospel of the Love of God in a world black with hatred and drenched with brother-blood was agonizing beyond words. Frankly, I understood why the British Tommies sang ribald words to sacred tunes. The war bombed down the last vestige of interest I may have had in the differences which divide religious communions. The withering words of Thomas Hardy came to mind:

> After two thousand years of Mass
> We've got as far as poisoned gas.

Also, it was plain that religion, as then organized and interpreted, was not equal to the problem of redemption in its tragic and gigantic modern setting. The lands of Luther and Wesley blasting each other to bits! Pacifism was no solution. It only meant that if one did not aid his country in dire plight, he aided the enemy by so much. The dilemma was terrifying; it was a crucifixion.

Yes, something had happened in my heart, and as these lines are written a second World War, more frightful than the last—total war, global war—has just come to an end, amid confusion and terror. Started by a megalomaniac, leading a docile and frustrated people, it plunged the race into a holocaust such as history has never known, even unleashing the basic energies of the universe, under whose threat and menace we must now live. It brought cruelties unbelievable, obscenities unmentionable, and sorrow unfathomable; a sob follows the evening sun around the world. It remains to be seen whether even the Atomic Bomb can crack an impervious, petrified sectarian Christianity and make it a living force. Two world wars in one lifetime are more than enough; rather than go through another I should prefer to stand against a stone wall and be shot at dawn. Anyway, I shall wear crêpe on my heart until Death hangs his sickle at my garden gate.

····· 8 ·····

Philadelphia

"NEXT TO AMERICANS, I like Philadelphians best," said the late Bishop Stewart of Chicago, with his irrepressible sense of humor. Anyway he liked one Philadelphian well enough to marry her. Just the same there was a point in the jolly gibe of the Bishop. Philadelphians are a folk apart; they have their own ways of doing or not doing things; they do not work very well together. If one begins anything in Philadelphia he must use one of two tools or both—politics and family influence—and he must begin it in the days of Benjamin Franklin; then nobody can stop it. It will go on automatically, so to say, forever. There are spots in Philadelphia where one would swear one is in London—for instance they kept up cricket in Philadelphia longer than in any other American city.

Someone has said that Philadelphia is less a city than a collection of villages, but the same is true of London, too—it is a cluster of twenty or more towns sewed together without pattern. In some degree it is true of New York—there is little Syria, little Italy, little Armenia, little Bohemia, Harlem, and a new Jerusalem: a patch-work of races. Few American cities are beautiful downtown, but the suburbs of Philadelphia are among the most beautiful in the country—if the Main Line district were in England, tourists would travel there to see it. A museum of history in peacetime, a munitions factory in wartime, always a center of medicine and music, the politics of Philadelphia is rancid and its religion static. Withal it is a cozy, comfortable, delightful place to live. Its tempo is not tiring but it is implacably conservative, appallingly complacent.

To be a Philadelphian proper, of course, one must have

237

lived—or his family must have lived—between Vine and Pine Streets and the two rivers, which was the city as Penn planned it.

The delightful sketches of Philadelphia by Christopher Morley show the picturesqueness of the old city. *Along These Streets,* by Struthers Burt, in spite of its monkey business and its cardboard characters, makes one aware of the history of Philadelphia and its spirit. Also, his *Philadelphia—Holy Experiment* adds to our obligations, although the "holy experiment" of William Penn did not refer to Philadelphia as it is today, but to the Christian Commonwealth, which he set up in 1680, and which continued for seventy-five years, until 1756— the first such Commonwealth to be set up anywhere, so far as I am aware; certainly more Christian than the Puritan theocracy in New England. At first only Quaker folk were allowed to vote, then members of other communions, and finally, by the logic of their own principles, everybody; then it ceased to be a Christian Commonwealth. One often wonders what Pennsylvania would have done if it had remained a Quaker Commonwealth until the War of the Revolution—but it is useless to speculate about what might have happened if something else had not transpired.

Naturally, in Overbrook, I was a kind of outlander, but I had a grand time. My people were all about me. There were swarms of young folk, and we had not only a Church School, but a Junior Church, into which young people were confirmed from the School. The Junior Church had its own Vestry, wardens and service—Staats Cotsworth, now active on the stage and in radio, was my warden, and a good one. At 9.45 I preached to the Junior Church—I took them through the Life of Jesus and the Life of St. Paul, giving them a consecutive knowledge of the Bible; quite unlike the hit and miss, hop, skip and jump method of the Sunday School lessons. Many of their parents attended the service—they could get to the golf courses sooner! No Rector ever had a better warden than Harry Lineaweaver; he was a high churchman in background and training—he knew all the things that I needed to learn.

"An Episcopal parish is a complicated contraption; it has

a lot of machinery about it," he said. He taught me the parts and how to run it; a sweeter soul never lived.

A lovely, jolly woman, full of gay mischief, said to me one day, "You just wait until this honeymoon is over, and we'll go after you with hammer and tongs; you have no idea how tough Episcopalians can be."

It was all bluff, just spoofing; besides the honeymoon never ended. My work went on betimes, editing *The Master Mason,* editing the annual anthology of *Best Sermons,* and writing other books; eleven books were edited and written in my Overbrook days. No man could have asked for a better Vestry or a kinder congregation. Johnson Ward was on the Vestry; indeed he has been on the Vestry of every Episcopal Church I have served; I could not do business without his keen financial insight, his quick humor, his brotherly kindness—it would take a book to tell how much I love him. He backed me up to the hilt in my campaign of preaching in colleges; he saw its importance.

Temple University conferred upon me the degree of Doctor of Laws, due in large part, I have always suspected, to the ingenuity of Harry Lineaweaver, and other members of the Vestry of St. Paul's Church, Overbrook. Years before, Coe College in Iowa had made me a Doctor of Literature, after the publication of *Lincoln & Herndon,* and my work in conducting a popular Lectureship in English at the State University. During the World War Tufts College, near Boston, added the Doctor of Divinity. Finally Hobart College made me a Doctor of Humane Literature, along with Bishop Fiske. It fell to my lot to give the address; the Bishop "survived" the address, in gay spirit congratulating himself on his powers of endurance.

On our way home we rode part of the way together, and he told me many interesting and unusual experiences in his life. Finally I said, "Bishop, if I am ever elected President, Justice of the Peace, or even Dog-Catcher, I mean to have a law passed requiring every man who has lived a rich and varied life to write the story of it; and you will be the first one I'll put in jail if you don't obey that law."

He pretended to look very serious. "But that is like a man building his own tombstone," he said.

"Nonsense; you know your own life from the inside, and you know how to write as few can do. "Cellini was not an old man when he wrote his life-story," I added.

"Heavens and earth, you do not compare me with him!" he exclaimed.

"Not at all; only I would not put you past a good deal of mischief. Indeed, I'd love you more for it"; and I told him a Lincoln story to prove it. Finally he promised to do it, but unfortunately, death did not allow him to finish the story. He was a brilliant man, a noble preacher, and a gracious friend.

COLLEGE PREACHING

It was indeed a queer time, odd to the point of eccentricity—those lush days before the crash and chaos of the Depression. In the mind of youth there was a kind of theophobia, due in part to its heralded "revolt," its resentment of parental authority in other connections, directed against parental religious ideas by way of retaliation. H. L. Mencken was much in vogue, blasting "the boobs of the Bible belt" with vitriolic violence, amid roars of laughter, as Robert Ingersoll had done years before. The American Association for the Advancement of Atheism was in full swing, financed, it was said, by a famous Brewing Company. At every university there was a Chapter of the A.A.A.A., as it was called for short. I made it a point of getting in touch with the group. One evening, after the routine business, I was introduced by a charming young man, who said, "Now the university preacher will speak to us about that glorified guess, called God." How delightful—the Lord had delivered him into my hand. The adolescent mind is a terrifying thing; it is so cocksure, if not cock-eyed. In beginning my address I thanked the chairman for his phrase "glorified guess," pointing out that Columbus made such a guess and found America; that every scientific discovery had its origin in such a "guess," as Marconi had told me when we rode from London to Paris one day.

When I said to him, "It must be a satisfaction to you, Sir, to know that your discovery has saved so many lives," he had a faraway look in his eyes—he was a simple, friendly man—and replied, "Yes, it is, Doctor, I guessed right, but my work is only a beginning."

But, I added, if we are to discuss anything, we must have some agreement as to the meaning of the words we use. Then I turned the tables on them, asking, "What kind of God do you deny? Or, as you say, does not exist?" I put the question point-blank and pressed the issue. One after another they told me. "Are you all through?" I asked. "If that is the kind of God you deny, I want to file an application for membership in your chapter. Such a God is no more like the God in whom I trust than a kangaroo is like an archangel, and discussing the matter would be like shaving a pig—a lot of noise and no wool."

They were taken aback by my approach. "But can you prove your God?" one asked.

"Certainly not; if I could prove Him, in your meaning of the word 'prove,' He would not be God to me. Little things we can prove; big things do not need it. Honestly, I cannot prove that I exist, if anyone denies it. Descartes, the father of modern philosophy, did the best he could when he said, 'I think, therefore I am'; but he might just as well have turned it the other way round, 'I am, therefore I think.' What kind of a God could my little mind 'prove'? How would I go about it? Outside of mathematics and certain demonstrations of physical science, there is no such thing as certainty on earth. But there is something better, Certitude—every day we act on things of which we are more sure than any man can be of anything in a laboratory of science or a court of law."

Then I told them about Robert Ingersoll, whom I had heard often as a young man. I described his golden voice, his amazing eloquence, a positive mind on the negative side of religious faith. His father was a minister, narrow, dogmatic, bigoted, and Robert revolted against his father and the God his father preached—Luther could hardly call God Father, because his own father was so unlovely. Then I quoted to them the words of St. Paul, "When I became a man I put away childish things," and spoke to them earnestly, but very pointedly, about growing up religiously, as well as in other ways. No man wishes to live by the negation of the faith of other men—he must have a faith of his own, won and owned by himself. The childish thought of God as a Big Man in the sky, with long beard, is gone; it does not fit into the universe as we know it, and, having lost that faith, as they must inevitably, many think they are atheists. In fact, I said, rubbing it in, this Chapter is more dogmatic than Athanasius; only your dogma is different. Because a few get God and the devil mixed, it is no reason why we should move out of the house of God into a bleak orphanage. As a country editor might say of a party, "A good time was had by all." Anyway, I was never again asked to attend a meeting of a Chapter of the A.A.A.A., to my deep regret; they must have passed the word along.

THE EPISCOPAL CHURCH

The longer I worked in the Episcopal Church, the better I knew it, the more I loved it. What I said in my statement on entering the Church was true. Bishop Garland wanted me to take a more active part in the politics of the Diocese, but I was too busy, and, besides, as a politician, my fingers were all thumbs. Always the Episcopal Church makes me think of a Southern plantation home, ages old, rambling and roomy, spacious and gracious, built and built upon, some floors higher than others; rather dignified and formal, where everybody dresses for dinner, and a misplaced collect is a breach of etiquette; it is friendly withal, in a distant and diplomatic manner; too often a holding company rather than an operating concern, to change the imagery for a moment.

It can be terribly stuffy and snobbish at times, and I have often observed that as its clergy become more "catholic," they become more exclusive—but maybe I do not know the meaning of English words. It does not matter—yes, it does, because it retards the growth of the Kingdom of God and makes His will of no effect. But no church is ideal; one must do as the old Greeks did, "take a second voyage" and find the place where one can do his best work, refusing, as I have always done, to build barbed-wire entanglements about the Altar of God. Our clergy lean too heavily upon a lovely liturgy, forgetting, as Melville said, that the pulpit is the prow of the ship, all the rest is in the rear; the pulpit is the first to meet the winds of God, and the bow must bear the earliest brunt, fair or foul. Ritual is not enough, not all people are symbol-minded—the priest is useful, but the prophet is a necessity, if religion is to live.

Three times I have been urged to allow my name to be presented and voted on for the office of Bishop, but I have always declined—not out of disrespect for the Office. God forbid! In the American Church, No; in the English Church, Yes, perhaps. The Bishop of Portsmouth said to me, " 'For the love of Mike,' as you Americans say, never be a Bishop; it is a dog's life."

But he was tired and ill, and had been one of the great executives of the Church of England. Alas! he slumped on his desk, dead, three days after I was his guest over the weekend. Bishop Williams of Michigan called himself "the trouble-man of a corporation"; his work irked him at times. For such labors I have no aptitude, no skill, no desire—my work is of a different sort. It ought in all fairness to be added that many of the best preachers in the Episcopal Church—not all of them, far from it—came into it from other churches in which more emphasis is laid upon preaching.

Phillips Brooks, a great, golden-hearted preacher, was an exception to all rules, as genius always is—like Topsy, he "just growed." He ought never to have been made a Bishop. Once he heard that people were not going to church, and he went out in his Diocese to find out. Of course, wherever he went no place would hold the people, and in his innocent humility he concluded that the rumor was wrong. There are noble preachers in the Episcopal Church—for example Dean Emerson, of Cleveland—I gave him the last push which put him into the Church, telling him that he would be as lonely as the dead at first, and then ridiculously happy; and it came true. He knows how to make a sermon, and how to preach it, putting handles on it so people can take it home and use it.

The late Bishop Fiske was a grand preacher; so is Bishop Scarlett of Missouri, to name no others. Among the younger clergy there are men of fine promise. But the sacrament of preaching is not emphasized in the Episcopal Church as it should be; there should be higher standards for men entering the ministry—personality standards, I mean; we need men who would not be failures outside of the pulpit. But who am I to be lecturing the Church—the older I grow the less I know about preaching, and the more I love to try it!

PARROT PATTER

My college preaching went on, accompanied by group discussions with charming young people, and everywhere I heard the same patter about religion as "sublimated sex"—no wonder when there was sex-obsession in literature—prayer as autosuggestion, and the idea of God a projection from the human mind. When everybody is saying the same thing, we may be sure that nobody is doing any thinking. In fact, I was speaking to a generation spiritually illiterate—the mind-set of the time was supposed to be scientific, even if few of the young people with whom I talked could pass a high-school examination in any branch of science. Except for a few trained in the Church tradition, they did not know the Bible—few of them knew it in any real way —and the language of the Church was an unknown tongue to the rest.

It made me see how utterly the Church had failed to teach its own Book to its own people—the Bible is not easy to understand, except a few great passages, and few there be that know how to interpret it. How well I remember a day in the glorious chapel of a famous university whose high pulpit the students called "the speak-easy." I spoke about what life is all about and how to think of the meaning of life as well as the means of living. After the service the President of the University said to me, very earnestly, "I make it a point to attend the chapel services, but that is the first sermon I have heard in a long time that I understood. Men come here to argue about God, trying to prove something that nobody denies until they try to prove it. As a layman I am not up on theology; but you talked about life—your sermon was not academic but human; it went places and took everybody along." This is reported, not in praise of my little sermon, but to point out that college preaching needs to be very simple, direct, and in contact with life—if the President is bored, how about the students?

One day I preached at Mt. Holyoke in the morning and was to be at Smith College in the evening. When I arrived at Smith College, I found that someone had telephoned from Mt. Holyoke suggesting that they ask me to preach the same sermon; and I did. It was about spiritual law, showing that the inner life is a realm of law, that we cannot live at random and hope to get anywhere; then I dealt with the law of faith, the law of prayer, and so forth. Apparently, it had not occurred to those young women that there may be a science of the spiritual life, and that the saints were masters of that science—not visionaries, emotionally unstrung if not nervously unstable. The idea of "law," as one of them said, "the economics of the inner life," apparently was novel to them and also something they could put to the test; they did not want a purely emotional religion. A most interesting group discussion followed the service in one of the college parlors; the girls filled all the chairs and spilled on the floor. I told them the story of St. Teresa, her fine executive ability, her rippling humor, her stern spiritual discipline, and how it took her eighteen years to learn how to pray. Some of the girls did not like the word "saint," but by the time I had finished, they saw the point—the saints, I told them, did not know they were saints; the sinners elected them to be saints after their death. But why should not religion have its experts no less than music and science? Many of the girls had swallowed "the new humanism," hook, line and sinker; and I had the happiness of showing them that it was in fact very unhuman. Let me add that of all student groups, medical students were the most responsive to religious appeal—barring a few who were purely materialistic.

GREAT CHANGES

William James said that the greatest "revolution" in his generation was the discovery that human beings, by changing their inner attitude of mind, can alter the outward aspect of their lives. Happiness depends, he said, not so much on what happens to us, as on what happens in us, how we take a thing, how we lay hold of life, lightly or sadly, and what we do with it; whether we are positive and active or passive and pessimistic. No doubt this "discovery" had much to do with the health-mysticism which ran rife in his day, since, as Dr. Mayo said—and he should have known—that the percentage of psychogenic diseases, due to wrong thinking, the wrong slant, and mismanagement of our minds and loss of religious faith, varies from between sixty-five to seventy-five. What an astonishing disclosure; what a show-up of the efficacy of bread-pills, and other devices for curing people who are not ill, but only imagine they are. This state of facts gave the psyche-sciences—even religion—a very great opportunity to serve twisted and clouded human minds, and bodies too. Clear thinking, in fact, is as much a duty as clean living; it is a part of it. Much of the old, fear-haunted religion has gone aglimmering, and it will not be missed. The Real Presence is not a terrifying thing—albeit searching and subduing—but a consecration, enduing us with courage to live and comfort to die. It is not work that hurts, but the worry that weakens and wears us down, if we let it do so.

By the same token, one of the greatest changes I have seen in my lifetime—an extension, perhaps, of what James saw— has been the new attitude toward old age. There are more people in the world over sixty-five than ever before, but they are younger and gayer of spirit than their parents were. Lincoln wrote of himself as "old and withered" at forty-eight, two years before he was elected President, before his great work arrived. After that date he did not speak of his age; he was too busy. People today do not let go, let down, and give up to be old as early as they did formerly. James Martineau, who was so frail that he was not expected to live to be thirty, wrote one of his greatest books at eighty-five. Wesley, who thought himself old at fifty, preached with power until he was nearly ninety. They were exceptions in their day, but their attitude and achievement are not exceptions today. Fifty may be the old age of youth, but it is also the youth of old age, and if the winter has come to our heads it is only because the summer has gone to our hearts, where there is still blossom and bird-song. No one is exempt from the infirmities of age, but he need not grow old of spirit—if he gets old of body he can grow younger of soul.

MIND READING?

The Master Mason, of which I was editor, was published in Washington City, and my duties took me there once or twice a month. The manager of the magazine, Andrew Randell, and his wife, Vera, were old childhood friends of mine in Texas. One evening Vera told of a "psychic" she had seen, who told her things that made her hair stand on end. She dared me to see her, quoting the old saying, that "A man who is afraid to take dare will steal a hog and eat the hair." So, naturally, I had to go—little did she know how interested I was in such matters. She went to the telephone and made a date, out of hours, that evening, for "Mr. X." She drove me to the modest home on Ontario Street and sat in the car outside while I went in for a "reading"; on the way to the house she told me some of the things the psychic had told her—one thing, that she would be a widow within three years, which, unfortunately, came true. In a medium-sized room I greeted a tall, portly, fine-looking woman, with gray hair and wonderful dark eyes.

"Good evening, I am Mr. X," I said, and sat down across a

long narrow table from her; I said nothing more until the end of the interview. In front of her she had a crystal ball, covered with a handkerchief, which she did not take off, at one side of her an astrological chart. She gave me a pad of paper, asking me to write on one sheet the names of half a dozen people, then living, in whom I was especially interested. I wrote the names of my family and one or two friends. Then I was to do the same, on another sheet, with a like number of people who had passed away and not let her see the names I wrote—I know she did not see the names. Then I was to make paper balls of the two sheets, put my right hand over them on the table, and she looked at my left hand. She did not go into any trance, but began talking, telling me my name, and saying the last name I had written had given her a powerful "vibration," as she put it.

"It was either Lelia or Delia, it will clear up presently. She was your wife's sister, who died while you were living in England. As girls she and your wife had a ring which they owned together and wore alternately. If your wife will write to her sister's husband, Mr. Cox, in Pittsburgh, he will be glad to send her the ring, because he knows that she wanted your wife to have it." If I had ever heard of the ring, I had forgotten about it— still, I may have heard of it.

Then she told me about my father and mother, giving their names correctly; about my wife, whose health at the time was a little uncertain, saying that it would not be serious, but telling what it was. My two children she described, not only their physical appearance, but their qualities of mind and temperament; that my son was an instructor in English at the University of Pittsburgh, but that he would enter the American Foreign Service and be sent abroad in 1931. I was dressed in a business suit, without clerical attire. "I see you wearing two kinds of robes," she said, "the vestments of an Episcopal clergyman and the cap and gown of a university—you are preaching a great deal in colleges. You live in a rectory attached to a church, but within eight or eighteen months—it is like looking down a corridor, one cannot gauge the time exactly—I see you living in a house with trees in the yard and the garden walled in. Before that time, however, you will be invited to a dinner by a group of gentlemen, at a club downtown in Philadelphia. There will be a big round table, and after the dinner, when the dishes have been removed, papers will be laid on the table. They will make you a proposition you have not even imagined. Of course you do not have to accept it, but I think—I may be mistaken, to be sure; I only see what will happen—but I think you would be wise to accept it."

Then she told me things I had never mentioned to anybody —one that I had always wanted to write a religious novel, as indeed I had, going so far as to select the name of the hero in my mind, Robert Ligon. She warned me against doing too much, against trying to swim too far at the seaside, and about my health—not to imagine that I was made of iron. Many other things, little more than vague dreams in my heart, she seemed able to dig up and express. For example, "You can go back to New York City, if you care to do so, and you can end your ministry in Washington, if you so desire. You will also be called back to London; I hope you do not go." Then she added, "I know they wanted you to be a Bishop, but I hope you will always dodge it. Have I told you anything interesting?" she asked.

"Yes, indeed; all that you have told me about things past is quite correct—I do not remember about the ring my wife and her sister owned jointly; but I can find out. All names you have given accurately. Of course, as to future events I must wait. Yes, I have always wanted, intended, to write a novel— a great love story, not only the love of a man and a woman, but the love of God. Tell me, how do you do this?" I asked.

"To tell you the plain truth," she said, "you know as much about it as I do. I grew up as the only child in the only Catholic family in a Kentucky county, and that meant, as you can imagine, that I was left much alone. But I was never lonely; the White People were all round about me. They told me things, and I told my mother what they said; she began to see that what they told me came true. That is all I know about it.

Many people come to see me—Congressmen, members of the Senate, men of the F.B.I., all sorts of people. I tell them what I see, charge a modest fee, and use all the money, beyond my meager needs, to help young women through college, or in any way they need help."

We became great friends, and I am under promise to say a little prayer for her when she passes away; which I hope will be a long way off, because she is a noble woman and has done no end of good.

ST. JAMES' CHURCH

When I told my family about it, they teased me terribly, especially my son, who said, "Just to think, Dad, you of all persons, going to see the Witch of Endor." My wife said that she was right about that ring, and shortly afterward, while visiting her old home in Kentucky, her mother said, "Mr. Cox was here the other day and left the ring you and Delia used to own and wear; here it is!"

About twelve months later I was invited to dinner at the Rittenhouse Club in Philadelphia; there was the big round table, and after the meal, papers were laid on the table, and a group of gentlemen from the Vestry invited me to become co-rector, with Dr. Mockridge, of St. James' Church, at Twenty-second and Walnut Streets. As I had begun to feel that my parish at Overbrook was too easy, lacking challenge, after thinking the matter over, as I was to be Minister of Preaching, so to put it, and could go on with my writing and editing, I accepted, my work to begin in the autumn of 1930. For a change, my wife, daughter and I went to Europe, where I was to preach in the City Temple, in London. My reception in England was especially cordial; the fact that I was now an Episcopalian—to them an Anglican—made no difference.

Indeed, I went to London at the invitation of the Congregational Union of England and Wales, of which I was still reckoned a member, to preach the sermon on the Anniversary of the Colonial Missionary Society. In 1918 I had the honor of preaching the Anniversary sermon before the same Society, but at that time I spoke as a Free Churchman. In 1930, having entered the Episcopal Church meanwhile, I spoke in a dual capacity, so to put it. Even the secular press sensed the uniqueness of the occasion and commented on it. The sermon was entitled "The Crisis of Christ," one passage of which was quoted and discussed all over England, and may be set down here as one of the focus-points of my entire ministry, since my habit has always been to practice Christian unity as well as preach it:

> For half a thousand years on this Blessed Island the Body of Christ has been torn by a profound schism, the story of which we know, and the tragedy of which has been carried to the far ends of the earth even in its missionary labors! Let me humbly bear my witness in the pulpit of the City Temple, speaking both as a Free Churchman and as an Anglican, *knowing both sides from the inside,* and treasuring the precious thing which each seeks to conserve. Before God and this company of my brethren, I testify that in my own heart they are not divided, but are as the two hemispheres of one Christian world, and what God has joined together we must not forever keep asunder! Let us treasure both traditions and reckon them equally holy, equally vital, equally precious; but let us keep in our hearts the warning words of the Lord Jesus how He said: "Ye do make the will of God of no effect by your traditions!"

After finishing my engagement, we went for a brief tour on the Continent, crossing by way of the Hook of Holland to Cologne, where we spent several days—the home of Meister Eckhart, one of my profoundest teachers of faith. One evening we went to a motion-picture show, where Government films of the fierce fighting on the Western front were shown; many people cried out, and some women fainted, recognizing the faces of kinsmen in the hell of war. The Germans had no ill-will against Americans, only they thought we should have stayed out of the war and attended to our own business. The Cathedral haunted me, blessed me. Then we went slowly up the Rhine by boat to Weisbaden, where we paused, then by rail to Munich, where we stopped for a week. I tried to get into a Hit-

ler meeting, but it was impossible—the place was packed with
young people; but I could hear his voice, not a German voice,
but the voice of the greatest rabble-rouser in history. At the hotel I asked an old German judge who understood English if he
did not fear such a man, and he replied, "Can you imagine a
staid, conservative people like the Germans being led away by
the blatherskite like that?" Yet three years later he came into
power!

Then we went by "wagonlits" to the wonder city of Venice,
for a week, where, in the San Marco Cathedral, on the day of
Pentecost, one of the saints tried to pick my pocket, but my wife
was too quick for him. Soon we learned that nobody spoke the
name of the Dictator except in a whisper, and then not without
looking around to make sure that no one heard the whisper.
This hush-hush attitude continued as long as we remained in
Italy. Next we went to Florence, a city of art, haunted for me by
thoughts of Savonarola, who was also a psychic and foretold
what was to befall his city years ahead. His "Bonfire of the Vani-
ties," and his "Bank of Pity," came to mind; what he foretold
came true, and they killed him. He went to his death walking
lightly, singing softly, while Machiavelli looked on! Then to
Rome, but the glaring, blinding heat was too much for us. Still
everything was hush-hush, but I happened to be an honorary
member of the Anglo-Saxon Masonic Lodge—long since closed
—and some of its members were kind to me on the sly. They
would not be seen with me, lest I get into trouble; but in all
sorts of indirect ways they showed their thoughtfulness. We
headed north to Milan, to see the cathedral, a poem in stone,
where we saw the Cardinal ordain a group of young men to the
priesthood. Then into Switzerland where we played snowball
on the Jungfrau, to get cool, and fell in love with the Swiss
people. Then to Paris for ten happy days, then back to misty
England and down to Carbis Bay and St. Ives, in Cornwall, to
rest after our tour.

TWO MEMORIES

When we returned home we learned that my son had been studying all summer at Crawford School in Washington, and had passed his examinations for the Foreign Service—he was waiting to get his first post. Also, as Dr. Mockridge occupied the Rectory at St. James' Church, they rented a rectory for me at Merion, a house with trees in the yard and the garden walled in.

My last sermon at St. Paul's Church, Overbrook, had for its text the beautiful, unending benediction with which the offices of Morning and Evening Prayer close. However, before I leave that lovely, gracious parish, I must record two memories, one sad, one happy. It was in the spring before I left St. Paul's that my little mother died, suddenly, without any warning illness, in Dallas, Texas, where she lived with her youngest sister—the last two of the family except her brother who lived near. The death of my mother left me with a profound loneliness, at first, followed by a sense of the eternal world as near, dear, and home-like, because she had entered there. In the next to the last talk with her I mentioned her favorite text, which I had heard her quote for many years. It was from the Epistle to the Galatians: "I live by the faith of the Son of God, who loved me and gave Himself for me."

Sometimes she emphasized the first part; sometimes, with awe-struck wonder, the second—"gave Himself for *me*"—which made her religion profoundly personal.

"And so you are going to preach on my text?" she asked, becoming suspicious, looking at me with her great dark eyes.

"Yes, you have lived that text; perhaps if I preach about it, I may learn its meaning," I had to admit.

"How many points will the sermon have?" she inquired.

"Three, so far," I told her.

"What is 'Firstly, my Brethren?' " she asked with a twinkle in her eye, knowing the unctuous ways of old-time preachers.

"First, it must mean that to you Jesus is the Son of God in a unique, supreme, satisfying way or degree," I said.

"Yes, my faith began in that way, but that is only the beginning. Jesus is all I know or need to know of God—all of God that can dwell in human form, 'He himself with His human air,' as Browning said."

"Of necessity," she went on, "we live by a borrowed faith, at first—borrowed from our parents, our teachers, chiefly from our church. Later, as we go on in life, it becomes a participating faith, as we share it in our hearts. It may be mysticism, as you call it—it is not a Bible word; I do not like it.

"And the second point?" she persisted—she who knew how to make a sermon better than I did.

"It is that you believe in what Jesus believed in—God the Father—because He believed in that truth." She looked at me closely—nay, she looked through me, beyond me.

"Do you remember the Tennyson line, 'He laid his mind upon theirs, and they believed in his beliefs?' " she asked. "Yes, I have faith in the faith of Jesus not only because Jesus believed it, but because He tested it out up to the Cross—and beyond! Surely that is proof enough!"

"The third point?" she asked.

"Well, is it not true, Mother, that you believe in Jesus because He believes in you—believed in you before you believed in Him—believes in you when you do not believe in yourself?"

"Yes, my son; if it had not been for Jesus, if He had not believed in me"— She never finished the sentence. The alternative was unthinkable, for both of us. Our faith in God may any moment falter and fail, but His faith in us does not fail, His love "will not let us go!"

Then Mother added, "If only I could say, with St. Paul, 'For me to live is Christ'—He is living my life for me."

But if she could not say it for herself, I can say it for her—she would not have wanted me to say it; the sermon was not preached in her lifetime. She would have thought it sentimentalism. Anyway, by that faith she lived her heroic and dedicated life; in it she died suddenly, alone, at dawn—no pain, no struggle. She woke up early, went in and wakened her sister, saying, "Get up, lazy-bones, and let us have some coffee." Then she went back to her room nearby and passed away noiselessly—only God heard the soft, ineffable, homeward sigh of her spirit.

F.D.R.

My other memory was of the first time I saw and heard Franklin D. Roosevelt. It was while he was still Governor of New York and gave the address at Vassar College when my daughter was graduated. Going early to the chapel, I found a seat up in the gallery, which was well filled. Then the Governor and his party came in slowly, he wearing those heavy steel braces without which he could not walk at all. A special ramp had been built so he could ascend to the platform, not without assistance. There he sat down, while the students and faculty filed in. After the opening ceremony, the Governor gave one of the most charming addresses to which I have ever had the joy of listening. Assisted to his feet by his aides, he held to the pulpit desk and talked simply, lucidly, in a friendly, fatherly manner, with that golden voice which millions were later to hear all over the world. He made his points clearly and told stories to make them vivid—stories chiefly from his experience as Assistant Secretary of the Navy.

For example, we need to understand the language of the people with whom we deal. An American warship was convoying some British vessels, and the American officer noticed a light on one of the English ships. He came alongside and said, "Put that light out!" The British promptly put it further out. Whereupon the American officer picturesquely—not without some profanity —got the British to understand: "Beg your pardon, Sir, we did not understand that you wanted the light extinguished." Again, it is one thing to know from books and another thing to know how to apply our knowledge in practice. Two young naval cadets were aboard a warship, and the captain sent them aloft to take reckonings and determine the exact location of the ship. In due time they returned with their report. The captain, looking at their figures, said, "Take off your hats, boys; this is a very solemn occasion. According to your figures we are in the chancel of Westminster Abbey!"

Little did I imagine, listening to his address, that that crippled man, who had not walked for years, would ride into power as the President of the United States and hold the office longer than any man in our history. Still less that he would lead us first through an awful depression, then through the most ghastly war in history; in peace, planning for a war he knew was inevitable, in war, planning for peace far ahead. It so happens that I do not belong to the party of the President—not since the days of W. J. Bryan; but I am an American first and a party man last, if at all. Nor have I ever belonged to any hate-brigade, either. However we may debate the policies and personality of President Roosevelt, two things are sure, he was one of the greatest leaders of mankind, and of his fame there will be no end.

CENTRAL CITY CHURCHES

There was no lack of challenge in the situation of St. James' Church—now, at last, I had become a Philadelphian, in the heart of the city. The office of co-rector, if not canonical, was efficient, and it ought not to be unusual for two Christian ministers, with equal authority, to work together without friction, much less feud; Dr. Mockridge and I did it under great difficulties, not of our own making. No sooner had the Diocese decided not to build a cathedral on the Parkway, but at Roxborough, than Dr. Mockridge decided to do cathedral work in the center of the city; hence the invitation to me to join him, which cut down, somewhat, my preaching in colleges. Our plan was to have every type of service in St. James, High, Low, formal and informal, and all the rest. If such different services were held in the Church at large, why not have them in one parish? Why allow different types of churchmanship to make a little sectarianism within a sect, like wheels within wheels in the vision of Ezekiel? How often I have thought of what a dear old Scot, a member of the Church Council of the City Temple, in London, said to me one evening, after a sermon which he liked very much, "Laddie, the Gospel of Christ is a big thing; we must pray God to stretch the skin of our minds so we can grasp more of its grandeur."

For years Dr. Mockridge had worked to do away with the pew-system at St. James', and had finally won out. The third oldest church in the Diocese, many of the pews were owned outright; the people had deeds to them, which they cherished. None the less, at last all the deeds were laid upon the Altar, and pew-owning was abolished. This policy cut the revenues of the church very little at first, because the people were still there, but with their children, most of whom had migrated to the suburbs, it was different. They did not feel the same family tie holding them to the old church.

In these despites, our project got off to a good start, at full speed, just as the Great Depression descended upon us, "like a thousand of brick," as they say down South. Indeed, it well-nigh flattened us out. To add to our sorrows, a group of people, each of whom had given one thousand to two thousand dollars to the church each year, died one after the other, in a short space of time; we were almost desperate. Spiritually our work was a triumph; financially it was precarious, if not impossible —to the great delight of a lot of people—static stick-in-the-muds —who thought that because a thing had never been done, it ought never to be tried. It was clear that our only salvation lay in forming a union with some other Episcopal Church. While at St. Paul's, Overbrook, I had proposed a union with the Church of the Holy Apostles, in South Philadelphia, where ninety-five percent of the population was colored. So many of that parish lived in and about Overbrook and often attended our services. The idea was to make the Holy Apostles a great colored church, enlarge the building at St. Paul's—we were already pressed for room—and make that a great white church. The name St. Paul and the Holy Apostles would not have been incongruous, since St. Paul himself said that he was one "born out of due time"—a kind of Divine after-thought. The two

Vestries met and discussed the matter, but we had not yet hit upon the idea of a co-rectorship. I am sure that Dr. Toop and I could have hit it off together in good faith and fellowship.

Anyway, this idea came back to mind, and again we proposed union, or federation, between St. James, Holy Trinity, and the Holy Apostles, to be called the Church of the Holy Trinity and the Holy Apostles; again the Vestries met and discussed the matter. Dr. Floyd Tompkins, Rector of Holy Trinity—an Episcopal Moody, greatly beloved in Philadelphia—was heart and soul for the project, and he could have carried his Vestry with him. Unfortunately, he died at the critical moment, and the plan fell through. Then a proposal was made to unite St. James with the Church of St. Luke and the Epiphany, which was itself a union of two parishes, brought about in 1898, when the exodus from the city to the suburbs had begun. The two parishes went so far as to worship together for a year, and I preached for the two congregations in one. Then, suddenly, that plan blew up. I know why, but it is a "military secret," and, I may add, to my infinite regret.

Forty years ago there were eighteen flourishing Episcopal churches between Vine and Pine Streets and the two rivers; now there are seven—yet more people live in that area than lived there forty years ago. Most of those churches simply "folded up," evaporated; not one would now be open but for its endowments. As Homer said of the shades in Sheol, "They are alive enough to know that they are dead." Dr. Mockridge and I saw this situation clearly; we felt it deeply; we tried to do something about it, but the Depression defeated us.

A situation of a sort similar faces the central city churches in nearly every American city. There is a "Fifth Avenue psychology" in New York City, which even Grace Church cannot overcome. Does the Church appeal to only one stratum of society, and is it helpless with other strata? The Presbyterian Church in Philadelphia has done no better than we have. They did put the old First Church on Independence Square with Calvary Church, and apparently it killed both churches!

It is a serious plight for all churches. St. James' Church, the third oldest in the Diocese, was the last to vanish; it hurt me deeply to see it go—the most churchly church in the city. But if churches live largely by endowments, they are kept alive, or at least kept open, by the dead. A proposition to unite St. Luke and the Epiphany and St. Stephen churches, using St. Luke for a Sunday church and the other, St. Stephen, for an everyday church, because of its location, was voted down by a majority of one in the Vestry of St. Stephen's Church, I was told.

If churches of the same faith and order cannot unite for the common Christian worship and witness, why talk about Church unity at all? If church people had as much sense as they claim to have sentiment, it might be worth while. But no; churches will stand and die in their tracks rather than join with brethren of their own communion in behalf of the common good. Such stupidity was appalling to me, beyond my comprehension, and I was done with it. In the meantime, I had started a daily Feature in the American press, which was at once so successful and so interesting that I had no wish for another parish, cluttered up with quibbling ecclesiastics. When one preaches every day to three million people, why bother about a parish anyway? Calls for my time came from all over the land, more than I could answer; for a time I accepted service with the National Preaching Mission of the Federal Council of Churches, organized in Philadelphia in 1908, and was making haste slowly toward getting Protestant Churches to do together what none can do alone.[1] From Denver to Portland, Maine, we went, a glorious band of fellow pilgrims, flying much of the time from city to city, holding great meetings and, I think, doing something for America.

While I did not want another parish, my friends of the Church of St. Luke and the Epiphany—they knew me, I knew them, we could "talk turkey," as we say—had put the plight of the church to me. The young rector had left, and he had left the old church in a bad way. Charles Stewart Wurts, the Ac-

[1] *Origin and History of the Federal Council of Churches,* by E. B. Sanford.

260 of RIVER OF YEARS

counting Warden, put the facts before me; it was a black picture: the church had been borrowing from its own funds, not from its endowments, to keep the ship afloat. The young rector was a Cambridge don, an able man, with a keen mind and a devastating gift of sarcasm, a real scholar, but it was the first parish he had ever held, and he had done the wrong thing at the right time, almost without fail. Worst of all, he turned Communist, spent his summers in Russia, learned the language, and wrote a rather interesting book about his experiences, entitled *An Unholy Pilgrimage*.

He might just as well have put a bomb under the church; one Lenten sermon on "The Futility of Prayer" lost him three vestrymen. After all, people do not go to church to hear religion reviled or at least ridiculed; they go for worship, as the word means, to find the worth of life, its meaning, and inward sustaining in its often pitiful broken beauty. At last the young and very unwise radical left, and asked to be demoted from the priesthood.

A GRAND OLD CHURCH

Such was the situation at the Church of St. Luke and the Epiphany; there was a motion before the Vestry, so I understood, to close the church; the Vestry was a skeleton of its former strength. During the year when I was preaching for the two congregations, we lost Dr. Klopp, a great surgeon, who had long been on the Vestry, as Dr. Redman, Dr. Thornton, and Dr. Currie, and so many physicians had been in a church dedicated to the Beloved Physician. Anyway, I could not see a beautiful old church closed, and I agreed to try to see what I could do, provided they would not spend any more of their funds and let me do it in my own way. They agreed: "Of course, if you do all the work and spend no money!"

But they did not let me do all of the work; they were wonderfully loyal and responsive. Soon, alas, three vestrymen died, five in fact, in quick succession: Dr. Currie, son of a former distinguished Rector; Mr. Sewell, an old-time gentleman, who used to dress in his Sunday best and call on me in my office, formally sending up his card; Mr. Walter Wheeler, tall, handsome, devoted to the church; Dr. Theodore Grayson, of the Department of History of the University of Pennsylvania; and Mr. Clay, who had retired from business and intended to take a desk at the church and help me to reorganize the parish. He suffered an injury, and by the time I reached him at his summer place at Bay Head, New Jersey, he was unable to speak to me, but gave me the sweetest smile.

Thus we were left with only a shadow of a Vestry, but not for long. Judge Charles Sinkler and Dr. Russell Boles—one of the greatest physicians in the land, who has saved my life twice— transferred from St. James' Vestry to my Vestry, as did Johnson Ward, without whom no Vestry of mine would be legal. Dr. Thomas Stewart—whose father, as a young man, had been the architect of the church, in 1840, in a style which he duplicated in St. Paul's Church, Richmond, Virginia, a few years later— came on the Vestry, where he should have been long before; as did Mr. C. F. Bonsor, who had been attending my services even in my Overbrook days, and in whose home I am utterly at home.

Mr. Dodd Bryan tells me that his father had been a pewholder in St. Paul's Church, Overbrook, but that neither he nor his lovely wife had attended a service there. They became "church tramps," as they admit, and dropped into the Church of St. Luke and the Epiphany one Sunday to see and hear what was going on; they came the next Sunday and the next, then they took a pew, and he came on the Vestry, to my great delight. Later, when Mr. Norman Brock, who followed his father on the Vestry, moved to California, I commandeered Mr. John Mason, who has been a vestryman in some church most of his life and knows the part by heart, and he accepted. These gentlemen joined those gentlemen still on the Vestry when I became Rector: Mr. Arthur V. Morton, Mr. Malcolm Lloyd, Jr., whose father was a vestryman before him, Mr. Charles Stewart Wurts, who also followed his father in office—now on leave of absence as an officer in the Navy, where he has received four citations for distinguished service—Dr. Redman, who claimed to be "the world's worst vestryman," but is not entitled to that distinction. These names I record with pride and affection; they are not only my vestrymen, they are my friends. There is nothing I would not do for them; there is nothing they would not do for me. This autobiography—a "tombstone," as Bishop Fiske would say, or he might call it "a tall story"—warns them that I do not intend to overstay my time; but I mean to knock some home runs before the end of the game.

REMAKING A CHURCH

In spite of severe illness which laid me low the first week my ministry began at St. Luke and the Epiphany, the church was soon a going concern, due to the loyalty of my friends all over the city; not only Episcopalians, but folk of many communions, including a group of young professional men and women. The gap between a few old families and a goodly company which came from the Epiphany Chapel on Summer Street, now occupied by an Albanian Greek Orthodox congregation, was filled up, and we had a sustaining congregation. The fabric of the church had disintegrated, the floor of the church itself had sagged, and the outside had been painted to resemble a gray warship, heaven knows why! The old wooden girders in the floor had to be replaced by steel, the roof fixed, and the whole building redecorated outside and inside. All this was done, and we paid back the money which the church had borrowed from itself under the former rector. A windfall in the form of a legacy pointed up the endowment fund after the ravages of the Depression, and the sale of the Church Farm on West Chester Pike added its part. In every way possible I tried to make a church of free and tolerant faith, of friendly spirit and homey atmosphere, by intimate chancel talks and personal contacts. Our congregations grew, people coming from a distance; many who had been alienated from the church, for one reason or another, returned. We owed no debt; the church was liberal in thought and orthodox of heart; there were no old feuds to settle—there had been many in times agone, I learned, but they had passed away. Unfortunately my college preaching had been cut down, because, if I left home, the congregation "played hookey" in a scandalous manner.

THREE BISHOPS

To go back for a moment. Bishop Garland asked for a Bishop Coadjutor—that is, one who would succeed him automatically, in case of death or disability. He was slim, trim and wiry, but few knew how frail he was—a case of arrested tuberculosis. It was not difficult to elect a man, but the Diocese had an awful time getting anyone to accept the office. One after another declined, until the situation would have been ridiculous if it had not become tragic. The first to decline was Dr. Henry Sherrill, Rector of Trinity Church, Boston. Shortly afterward I happened to be preaching the annual Phillips Brooks sermon in Trinity Church, and referred to the fact that Brooks had declined to be Bishop of Pennsylvania, then I added, "which seems to have become a habit with the Rector of Trinity Church"—to the amusement and solid satisfaction of the congregation. When I went further and called it "a very bad habit," I found myself in a minority of one. Even my old friend Dean Scarlett, of Christ Church Cathedral, St. Louis, turned us down. Finally we turned to a man in our own Diocese and elected Dr. Francis Taitt, for many years Rector of St. Paul's Church, Chester. By his gentle ways, his sweet Christian spirit, his homey wisdom in which there was no cunning, and, no less, by his gorgeous gift of humor, he was a gift of God to the Diocese and the city.

Bishop Garland died suddenly, a victim of pneumonia, and Bishop Taitt came into power. Whether he was a manufacturer of stories or a retailer, I could never quite make out; perhaps he was both. Some of his stories were parables; others, well, just stories told for fun. An old man when he was elected, after a notable service, he in turn asked for a Coadjutor, at the same time naming the time of his retirement—All Saints' Day. Undismayed by two defeats, the Diocese elected Dr. Oliver J.

Hart, Rector of Trinity Church, Boston, and, happily, by his acceptance, he broke the "bad habit" I referred to in my sermon. With his soft Southern voice, his genius of faith and friendship, and his constructive Christian vision and practical capacity, Bishop Hart has already done great things for us. He will do even greater things if he is not stymied by church politicians, who are a nuisance and a pest. In the old days of Philadelphia—far, far back—there was "the Christ Church crowd," as it was called, who ran the Diocese and tried to run the city too; and they almost did it. We do not want such a gang, nor do we wish a return performance; we do not intend to have it. Something in Bishop Taitt haunts me still; I never met him without being better for the contact—even a casual greeting in the street. The same quality is in Bishop Hart in rich degree, and it will ripen with the years—a simple, unforced goodness which is the greatest thing on earth.

OXFORD GROUP

From the first I was interested in the "Oxford Group," but at no time was I actually identified with it. Something always held me back, yet it was one of the few rustles among the dry leaves of religion in my time. Nor was I ever able to make out why the name "Oxford" was tacked onto it. It was in fact a purely American invention, a kind of synthetic movement in which many elements were blended, chiefly things which the Church had neglected or forgotten. For one thing, it was unsectarian, and that attracted me—it cut across all sects; it had no rules; it recited no creed; it observed no sacrament, in the usual meaning of the word. For such things members of the Group went to the church which each loved best. Some churches were disrupted by Groupers, it must be added, who had more zeal than wisdom.

"To have a changed world we must have changed lives," was one of their slogans—manifestly valid, since the world can be no better than the people who live in it. Truth to tell, in the average church a "conversion" would be an astonishing thing; the good people would not know what to do about it. The minister himself would be puzzled. Oddly enough the Group made its greatest gains in the Episcopal Church, especially in the High-Church wing, and among the Quaker folk, perhaps because it adopted so many things common to the Meeting House—its "quiet time," its quest for "daily guidance," and its impromptu informality. A Group "house party" was a gay and happy assembly, serious but in nowise solemn. Everybody was free to take part; there was no "preaching"; there were talks, testimonies, "confessions"—one man left the Group because he objected to "swapping sins before breakfast"; and some of us can understand his feeling. Instead of old creeds mechanically recited, there were affirmations of certain Absolutes, quite new in a day of relativity—absolute integrity, absolute purity, absolute devotion—a rather tall order, as all will agree, but better than the droning of dogmas with no meaning. Unfortunately, the Group got off to a bad start, due no doubt to overenthusiasm. It was driven from the campus of Princeton University —it was said—because of an overemphasis on "sex," somewhat remarkable in a day when sex was well-nigh supreme and instinct was magnified, not to say glorified, in literature and life. Every movement has its frayed edges, and as the Group was largely a movement of young people, it made its mistakes.

GROUP TECHNIQUE

For three reasons I was interested in the Group, in spite of its faults, one of which was that it seemed to mistake familiarity for fellowship. In a Group meeting, never large, everyone called everyone else by his first name, as in a Rotary Club—the late Right Reverend Logan Roots, for many years an Episcopal Bishop in China, became just "Logan," and he liked it. To me such a thing seemed artificial; at any rate no one ever called

But one thing must be said, in an age of mass-mindedness me by my first name—evidently I did not "belong."

and loud speakers, the Group recaptured the values and uses of the group; a most significant fact, when "fellowship" had almost disappeared from the churches. The crowd thinks—if it does think—with its fears and hatreds, not with its brain and heart. Massed passion does not make for wisdom, but for terror. Only in the group, where men think freely and in fellowship, does truth reveal itself.

First the man—the seer with his vision—then the group, where his insight is discussed pro and con and tested by experience; then the multitude; that has been the order of advance, alike in poetry, in painting, in science, no less than in religion. Prophecy began in little groups of men "whose hearts God had touched." First Jesus, then His disciples, whom He trained, whose stupidity and misunderstanding He endured; then the Church and the multitude. It was so with a band of poets led by Wordsworth, a group of artists led by Ruskin; as it had been of the "holy club," led by Wesley. The group which gathered about Wesley were called "Methodists," in derision, because they sought to devise a "method," a technique, of the religious life, without which it is lived at random. Another such group came later, also called the "Oxford Group," led by the shy and awesome figure of Newman. Some of us think that, intellectually, it was a gallant advance backward, but it illustrates the group-principle. The latest "Oxford Group" was also derided and criticized without mercy, but they made themselves "taunt-proof," to use their fine word, and went on their way bravely. Even the old Methodist "class meeting" had passed away, and my hope was that religion might be reborn and made intimate by the use of its ancient technique.

VITAL RELIGION

Also, the primary emphasis of the Group was upon "personal religion," and that interested me profoundly. It is obvious that personal religion is the permanent fountain of the spiritual life—if that spring dries up, as it has well-nigh done in our day, religion is a mere form, a shell, an echo. This note had hardly been heard for years, due in part to the decay of the old evangelism. The emphasis in religion had shifted from theology to sociology and then to psychology. There can be no doubt about it, that in the Group, religion, as an inner experience and emancipation, became a living and vital reality for many to whom it had been only a tradition, or merely a word or a rite. They "found themselves," or were found by Something other than themselves, to which they gave themselves in dedication; life passed from frustration to faith, freedom, and an intimate sharing of the deepest experiences. As a boy I used to love to hear people talk of "what God had done for them," to use their phrase; but such heavenly gossip had been hushed for years, as if we had been smitten mute about the inner life.

It was not "good form" to talk about God and the soul, it simply "was not done." The Group broke down that reticence, and it was a new experience to me to hear a band of young people talking freely about spiritual affairs. To be sure, they used a new vocabulary; they spoke the language of their day, but the silence had been broken and they were no longer dumb. The Group, never giving up anyone as hopeless, tackled the worst cases, and its work in dealing with alcoholics—always a discouraging undertaking—is worthy of remembrance and admiration. If, often, they seemed to toady to "high society"—the country-club crowd—it must be admitted that that "set" needed attention, since they paid only a lip-service to the Church, more for social than for religious reasons. On the other hand the Group sought to influence influential people—which was good strategy—and it did so to a remarkable degree; not forgetting the while to play up famous names in its publicity. Indeed, it became an adept in publicity, as modern in its methods as business tries to be. If a famous tennis champion became a Grouper it was news, and people are as hungry for news as they are for food. Let me add, what I happen to know, that the Group, instead of living in luxury, as many have said, was actually operated "on a shoe-string," as the saying goes.

MORAL REARMAMENT

In its second phase the Group became the Moral Rearmament program, and this too awakened my keen interest. In other words, while not giving up its emphasis upon personal religion, it extended its strategy to social problems and causes, especially to the stability and integrity of the home and to right—that is, Christian—relations between management and labor in industry. This change, or extension, of emphasis lost the Group many of its followers and some of its leaders, who seemed unable to see that religion has anything to do with social and business affairs. In its new adventure the Group took a page from the life of St. Francis of Assisi who, when he visited a certain town, found that the Mayor and the Bishop were enemies—they were not even on speaking terms. Francis knew that a sermon would do little good, if any; even if both the Mayor and the Bishop heard the sermon, each would apply it to the other. Being a saint of the order of poets, and a wise man besides, he put on a show, in which, with gay laughter and good spirit, he showed up both. They saw the point, apologized to each other, and peace was restored. Such has been the method of the Group in dealing with labor difficulties—to dramatize the situation so that all could see it for what it was. It has not always been successful, but for every strike it failed to stop, there are a half dozen which it prevented—only we did not hear about them.

The tactics of the Group are very simple and direct. Through its "teams" it personally gets in touch with the leaders of both management and labor, presents the Christian case, and asks that it be given a trial. Much depends on the skill and spirit with which the Christian alternatives are offered, and the way it is carried out when it is accepted. Thus the Group has fought Communism on its own ground, and cold-blooded materialism and violence, and the testimony of the leaders of both management and labor cannot be ignored. To say no more, the Group sets out to find what is at the bottom of a labor dispute, and they find that it is not always economic, but often moral and personal, springing from a lack of contact and understanding.

One thinks of Annie Jaeger, a saint of the Group, whose motto was, "Do it on the door-knob," that is, meet and talk with the men themselves, and discover what the real issue is— the personal equation is important. Annie was a tiny woman of intrepid faith and tireless labor, who once had kept a shop in a rather dismal English town. Set on fire by the spirit of the Group and its service to industry, she became a towering personality; her story, if written with insight, would be an epic. She died in Philadelphia and was buried from the Church of St. Luke and Epiphany. Never, in my whole life, have I attended such a service. After the lesson and prayers, men of the CIO and AFL, journalists, ministers, workmen, men of the sporting world, all sorts, spoke of her nobility of character and winsomeness of spirit. It was less a funeral than a celebration, an hour of victory in which death had no sting—such a service as the old church had never seen in its long history. Some days later I received a long cablegram from England, signed by labor leaders, titled folk, Members of Parliament, thanking me for allowing the Church to be used for her farewell—as if any thanks were needed.

"SLEEPING PERIODS"

The "Oxford Group" was and is significant, chiefly, for its effort to devise a method of spiritual contact and social strategy suitable and workable in the age in which we live. What its future will be remains to be seen—the immediate religious future is dismal in a weary, hungry, devastated and frightened world! Emerson speaks of "sleeping periods of the soul" into which the race falls now and then. Such a period seems to be upon us today, and it has been so through my entire ministry. Often in the past a single God-illumined, love-anointed soul has led a spiritual advance and resurrection. Francis did it in the Thirteenth Century, so rich in lofty and haunting personalities. Wesley did it in his day. But no spiritual world-figure has

walked the earth in my lifetime, except Gandhi in India, whose
fight to enfranchise millions of "untouchables"—to accept them
as members of the human race—was one of the most magnificent crusades in history. He has commanded the homage of
hosts of his own people and the admiration, but not always
the agreement, of the people of all lands. No human being
in my day has exercised an influence more incalculable and
immeasurable, alike in political and spiritual affairs. Also, in
my lifetime there has been no classic of the religious life like
that spiritual mosaic wrought by a man "in a little nook with
a little book," known and beloved far and wide over the world
as *The Imitation of Christ*. No such book could be created in
our age. The tempo of the time, its preoccupation with things
external, its hurrying day-by-dayness, its whirl and swirl of
events, make the arts and offices of the spiritual life seem remote, if not unreal.

The spirit of brooding meditation, of deep and still thinking, of humility and inward wisdom, is well-nigh lost, not
merely for lack of time to practice it, but from lack of disposition. Instead we have a tedious egoism, a "science-save-us-cult,"
a curious faith that organization can substitute for inspiration,
a dearth of that rich inwardness which was so consecrating in
days agone. In such an atmosphere my ministry has been exercised, in the face of odds beyond reckoning—but I have tried to
keep faith with the truth that makes all other truth true; and
my hope is unshaken.

London Again

IN 1934, or thereabouts, when W. E. Orchard resigned from the King's Weigh House Church in London to enter the Roman Church, the officers of the Church made overtures to me to follow him in that famous pulpit. They intimated that they were thinking of carrying the Church, an old Free Church Foundation, into the Anglican communion. Anyway, just for fun, I went to London to talk it over with the Committee and the Bishop of London and everybody concerned, although at the time I did not want to go back to London permanently. Happily I sailed on the good ship *Samaria* and caught the same boat coming back; the skipper, Captain Malan, the Commodore of the Cunard Fleet, became my good friend. He,showed me all over the ship, and, being a lay-preacher, he preached me a sermon on the subject, showing how the ship could not be navigated without Unseen aid. He found out my birthday and gave me a party. He was to retire the next year, and I asked him what he intended to do. "I have two hobbies, raising roses and my church, a perfectly good Baptist Church, in spite of what you haughty Anglicans may say." When I told him that I had been brought up a Baptist, he wondered how I ever became a black-sheep. He made me sit at his table in the dining room and spend much time with him on the bridge.

In London I found a bewildering muddle. The Bishop of London, who entertained me as his guest in his palace and beat me playing tennis—or rather, I, of course, let him do it —declined to give me a license to become Minister of the King's Weigh House Church, if it remained a Free Church—what he called a "chapel." He even intimated, indirectly, that he was not happy because I had preached a whole summer in the City Temple. Whereupon I told him plain and flat, albeit with a smile, that it was none of his business about my preaching in the City Temple, and that I would never kick my Free Church friends in the face; never!

Then I went to Dr. Sidney Berry, Secretary of the Congregational Union of England and Wales, and laid the matter before him. "Doctor, we can do nothing with the King's Weigh House. It has been entirely unco-operative with us since Dr. Orchard started his New Catholic movement. If it wants to join the Anglican Communion we cannot prevent it, and would not if we could. However, to do that requires a unanimous vote of the House of Commons, a thing seldom seem in England. But we would be happy to have you back in England, and if you say the word we will undertake to canvass every Free Church member of the House, and maybe it can be done. No doubt it would want to enter as an Anglo-Catholic parish, if that is what you like," he added.

"I quite understand," I told him; "some of the Official Board have been telling me of their faith in the transubstantiation of the elements in the Communion, whereas I prefer the word 'transvaluation,' if any word is used."

At the last moment the Church Board decided not to attempt to enter the Anglican Church, and that settled the matter. Settled it happily for me, because I had no desire to return to London, much less as the Vicar of an Anglo-Catholic parish, although I have the greatest respect for every type of churchmanship. While I had made no definite commitments to the Church Board, yet I had gone so far as to make withdrawal difficult, or at least embarrassing. In 1941 I went along Duke Street to see the famous old church, only to find it bombed to ruin, except for the small chapel.

Soon after my return from London, Dr. A. T. Robertson, Professor of the New Testament in the Baptist Seminary in Louisville, Kentucky, was preaching in Philadelphia. In the afternoon his host brought him in an automobile to my home in Merion, and we spent a happy afternoon together—one of the happiest visits of my life. He was a little older, with the same little impediment of speech, but as charming as ever. We talked of the old days and the old boys, especially the men of my time and class; he had kept track of them. Some had gone, in particular, George Burlingame, in the midst of many sorrows. It was plain that he wanted to know whether I was going to the King's Weigh House Church, in London; the matter had been played up in the religious press, with the intimation that I might follow W. E. Orchard into the Roman Church. Robertson did not want one of his "boys" to go that route. He asked timidly, almost slyly, about the state of affairs. I told him the whole story, and he seemed greatly relieved. Bless his heart, he need never have had any fear; there was not the slightest possibility of such a thing. Being more catholic than the Roman Church—since I do not exclude them, while they exclude me— I could see no point in going to London to be Vicar of an Anglican Church when I had a church of the same order in America. Dr. Robertson was in high spirits when he went away, waving me a hearty farewell; I never saw him again.

FLYING PARSON

It is only fair to tell something more about my flight to England in 1941, as a guest of the Ministry of Information, although in *Live, Love and Learn* I gave some sketches of my experience. Often I had thought that my grandchildren might fly the Atlantic, but I had never imagined doing so myself; however, everything has been speeded up these days, even the velocity of history has been accelerated until we are dizzy. Now it can be told—at the time I could not even tell my wife when I was flying nor where I hoped, "with journeying mercies," to land. It was at dawn that we took off from Baltimore in a British plane that looked like a flying Pullman car, a hundred and fourteen feet long, with a wing-spread of a hundred and sixty-five feet, the seats to be made up as berths or bunks if needed; with thirty-seven passengers and seven members of the crew.

It was a cosmopolitan group of people, including my friends

Rabbi Lazaron, of Baltimore, and Dr. Henry van Dusen, of Union Seminary, New York. One woman was aboard, the wife of the Prime Minister of a Balkan state, and she was the only one who suffered from seasickness, or perhaps we should say sky-sickness. A good lunch was served, and we took tea, in the English manner, in Newfoundland, where we also refueled, and at dusk headed straight across the Atlantic, arriving in ten hours or thereabouts. No sleep for me; all night long I talked with interesting people—one who had lived for years in South America and another who knew China from end to end.

Much of the time we flew very high—say twelve thousand feet —in the early morning we were above the clouds, as if sailing in an arctic sea, flying a hundred and eighty miles an hour, but there was no sense of going at that rate. A German fighter plane nosed its way up through the cloud—there was no mistaking it—it could easily have knocked us down. At once our plane dived into the cloud and flew, the mist lashing the windows, then, at last, lower and lower, until we could see land— a farm looked like a pocket handkerchief, a house like a postage stamp. We landed softly in an inlet at Foinge, in West Ireland. Three of us, not liking the bus provided to take us across the Island to Dublin, hired an automobile, and rode on the edge of eternity. It went so fast that I soon gave up all hope of ever seeing Dublin. But, evidently, the driver "knew his stuff," for we arrived safely ahead of time. Most of the country through which we rode gave me an impression of drab, dismal poverty, except a few big houses and great estates. The driver, as a kind of extra dividend, took us over Dublin to show us the chief places of interest, including the university, and then to the Royal Hibernian Hotel. Next morning we were "flown blind," the windows of the plane sealed up, so we could see nothing, to an airfield near Bristol, England, where we caught a long, slow, crowded train to London. At the Paddington Station I was met by the Reverend Hugh Martin—now a Doctor of Divinity—of the Ministry of Information, wearing a top hat and a Prince Albert coat; and by my friend Dr. Daniel Poling, of Philadelphia, who had flown over on an American bomber.

WOUNDED LONDON

London was a skeleton city, all the children had been evacuated, and what a difference it made not to hear their merry voices—a city of grown-ups is a dull place. Everywhere we could see what the blitz attacks had done—houses blown to bits or their roofs burned off. At the Russell Hotel, where I had lived for months during the first World War, one of the old doormen greeted me cordially—another, he told me, had been killed by a bomb. The manager was the same, and much of the help, only a bellhop had been promoted to run the elevator. The hotel had been badly damaged, its two top floors ruined by incendiary bombs; the manager told me how he was playing his piano during a raid and suddenly a piece of concrete, as large as a water-bucket, crashed through his window, blown from the University of London Buildings, two blocks on the other side of Russell Square. Wandering through London was a desolate experience; going along Kingsway and down Holborn, I saw the City Temple, my old church, a mass of ruins, and next to it St. Andrew's Church, a thousand years old, in the same plight. It seemed as if churches had been special targets, picked out for destruction. One could trace the four great blitz attacks, like furrows ploughed through the city, in December, 1940, March, 1941, April 16th, and May 10th.

Of course I reported at once to the Ministry of Information, located in the University of London Buildings nearby; new buildings they were, and so stood up to the bombings better. They had arranged an all-Anglican program for me, which I promptly smashed, saying that I had not come to England as an Anglican, but to preach in all kinds of churches and meet every sort of group. Accordingly, we got in touch with Dr. S. W. Hughes, a good friend of mine, Secretary of the Free Church Council, and between them they worked out a program tough enough to break an iron man, and kept adding to it—including preaching in the Abbey, St. Paul's, St. Martin's in the Fields, City Road Chapel—where Wesley spent his later years—Central

Baptist Church, a meeting of clergy; and it was the same all over the country, with discussion groups, no end, over the teacups. These included two Bomber Commands of the R.A.F.

While I was at the office of the Ministry of Information, a telephone call came from the Foreign Office, asking me to drop in that afternoon, if possible. When I arrived, to my surprise I met a Mr. Law who had worked on the Philadelphia morning *Public Ledger* at one time, had lived at Wayne, and attended my services at St. Paul's, Overbrook.

"Of course, Doctor," he said, "we know you and you know the English people; here is a card from the Foreign Office permitting you to go anywhere and see anybody; it will save your time. I'll tell you almost anything you may want to know, except about Hess, and everybody has his Hess guess."

As I was not interested in Hess, we talked of many things, and all during my stay, in every part of the country, besides the card from the Foreign Office, I was assured by officers of the police and of the Home Defense: "Doctor, the country is yours; go when and where you like."

As I went to and fro over England, I discovered a new England, new, especially, in its attitude toward my country; a desire, for the first time, to know America and its people—none, absolutely none, of the nagging, irritating anti-American feeling I had known during the first World War. A law had been passed requiring that any school receiving a grant of money from the State should teach American History, and I was greatly interested in how they did it. Hitherto, the English schoolboy knew nothing of American History; his textbooks stopped, some of them, with Columbus, while others came down to the War of the Revolution, which they described as "the disruption of the Empire." The making of the Constitution, not to speak of the stupendous period of our development, was all a blank in the mind of the schoolboy. For the first time I did what I had never expected to do—I conducted two Institutes in American History; one of them for a group of Workingmen's Educational Associations; they had been reading the *Life of Lincoln,* by Lord Charnwood—and, knowing that I was interested in Lincoln, they asked me to speak to them. For an hour I talked about Lincoln, and for another hour they asked me questions, to bring out things not clear in their minds— quick, keen, pertinent questions. Later, a group of educators and professional men asked me to tell the story of our Constitution, how and why it was made as it is, the influences which played upon the men who made it, comparing it with the unwritten Constitution of England; all of which was on my ground, and I enjoyed doing it.

The English people were more approachable, more talkative than they had been in the days of World War I. Going into Liverpool, I saw among my fellow passengers a man whom I thought I knew, but was not sure. I hesitated to speak to him —I had tried that in the old days, and the man I spoke to handed me a newspaper to keep me quiet. He then picked up a paper himself, but I saw he had it upside-down, and I wondered how much news he learned. Anyway, taking my life in my hands, I spoke to my fellow passenger.

"Glad to see you in England again, Doctor," he said; "I was not quite sure that it was you. In the old days I used to attend your services at the City Temple, occasionally, even if I am a member of the Society of Friends."

"Yes, I thought I knew you," I said, "and I remember that you are a Quaker; it must be a terrible time for you, as it is for all of us. I know the books of Fox and John Woolman from end to end; some of my ancestors were Quakers."

"A terrible time is putting it mildly," he replied; "we are fighting 'the powers of darkness,' stark and undisguised; if this evil genius wins, there will be no Society of Friends. Do you think America will come into the struggle?"

"Yes, inevitably; and I think the President realizes the fact."

Then he told me, what I had learned at the Foreign Office, how the President had rushed every available rifle and round of ammunition to England when, after Dunkirk, it had nothing with which to defend itself. Again and again, all over the country, men of the home guard, with tears in their eyes, were to show me those rifles.

"Did it ever occur to you, Doctor, that the blow which will bring your country into this awful struggle might come from the West? The Japanese always strike before they declare war, as when they attacked Russia years ago."

"Yes, as a possibility, but hardly as a probability," I answered. "My son was for nearly four years an American foreign officer at Nagoya, Japan, and in his letters to me he reported wave after wave of anti-American feeling. They hate us, he said, and if they ever get a chance they will stab us in the back. If the Japs should do such a thing, in the end there would not be enough left of their Empire to fill a hollow tooth."

"No doubt you are right," he agreed; "but it would be a nasty fight. Nevertheless, if the Japs should strike, it would bring you into our war, and us into your war; but I am sure you could finish off the Japs left-handed—they are a sly, tricky set. What brings you to Liverpool, if I may ask?"

"Tomorrow afternoon, in the service in honor of the Battle of the Atlantic, I am to preach in the Cathedral and in the evening in the Cathedral at Chester; then, on Monday morning, I am back in Liverpool to speak to the Constitutional Club, and also to a large group of war-workers."

"Back at your old tricks, I see," he commented; "doing the work of five men; may the Lord have mercy on your body, whatever becomes of your soul. Look for me tomorrow in the Cathedral congregation."

The morning service in the Cathedral had been in thanksgiving for victory in the Battle of Britain, in honor of the R.A.F., of whom the Prime Minister had said, "Never have so many owed so much to so few." As has been said, the afternoon service had to do with the Battle of the Atlantic, then not yet won. The Cathedral is a vast place, with the largest chancel I have ever seen—the choir sang the whole Litany as a processional hymn. At the foot of the chancel, at the request of Dean Dwelley, I read a Litany which he had prepared, made up of lines from the Atlantic Charter; it was superbly arranged, and most impressive. Then followed the sermon, in one paragraph of which I argued that Northamptonshire ought, really, to be annexed to the United States as the 49th State in the Union, because it had furnished the ancestors of five of our Presidents, to say nothing of Benjamin Franklin, Longfellow, and no end of other famous Americans. Washington, of course, was the first, his family lived at Sulgrave Manor; the Adams family, which gave us two Presidents; the Harding family—there is a street in Northampton named Harding Street, and the Coolidge family. After the service a member of the Royal Family who attended the service came back to thank me for the sermon, and Dean Dwelley, pretending to look very stern, said:

"What does your Royal Highness think of the notorious proposal of aggression by Dr. Fort Newton, suggesting that Northamptonshire be given up?"

"In view of the evidence as presented," said the Duke, "I cannot honestly interpose any objection. But it does occur to me that, since America has taken the best of Northampton, it ought not to bother about the rest!"

HEART-TO-HEART

A Canon of the Chester Cathedral, who took part in the service, was ready with his automobile to drive me to that ancient city. Chester, as the word means, was an old Roman camp; the walls built by the Romans are still standing; people were walking to and fro on the wall—lovers hand-in-hand—as we entered the city in the long-lingering glow of a summer evening. In the evening the Cathedral was jammed. It is a small cathedral, cosy and warm, parts of it eight hundred years old. After the service I spent the evening and night with Bishop Tubbs, formerly Bishop of Rangoon and acting as Dean of the Cathedral; never shall I forget the heart-to-heart talk we had. He was a tiny man, physically, but a great, beautiful soul.

"Our Bishop has recently been made Bishop of London," he said. "Why cannot you become our Bishop? It could be easily arranged. You would be happy in the Diocese of Chester, and we would be happy with you."

"If I wanted to be Bishop at all," I replied, "I should prefer to be Bishop in the Church of England—the office is more a spiritual office than it is with us. But I remember how Bishop Gore was irked by his labors as Bishop of Oxford, and gave it up. But I do not want to be a Bishop anywhere; my work is of a different kind. Besides, to be a Bishop of the Church of England I should have to give up my American citizenship."

"Who knows, we may have a common citizenship some day," he said; "at least I devoutly hope so."

Then we talked of our two peoples and our common civilization, and we agreed that the two pillars on which our society rests are the Holy Scriptures and the Common Law, the Bible and Blackstone; if either pillar totters the whole structure will topple. Together, too, we wondered whether our civilization would be able to achieve spiritual culture enough to break the ghastly cycle which other nations and peoples have followed: first wealth and prosperity, then culture and lush luxury, then moral dry-rot and the fading of religious faith; finally the slip into seas of sodomy and alcohol, as happened in Persia and Babylon, which made Egypt a mummy and Rome a shell. We honestly did not know; we could only hope. Next morning I was back in Liverpool.

"You missed a big show last night, Doctor," said the Lord Mayor, referring to a vicious air-raid.

"Is the cathedral safe?" I asked.

"Yes, but in the dock district the damage is appalling," he replied, as indeed it was when he drove me through it later in the day.

PORTSMOUTH

Next Sunday I spent the weekend in Portsmouth, going to Leeds, Leicester, Manchester, and a Methodist gathering near Birmingham between times. The Bishop of Portsmouth, who was my host, lived four miles out of the city at Farnham; his garden was ten acres in size. At that time we were rationed to one egg a month, but the Bishop talked persuasively to his hens, asking them to be more liberal in behalf of an American guest. Apparently they understood and obeyed orders, as we had two eggs each next morning. As we drove to the cathedral, the Bishop said, "Take notice, Doctor, of the type of face you will see in the cathedral congregation. It is different from any type of face you will see anywhere in England. Here live the Jutes, a tribe which came from Jutland, along with Angles and Saxons, in the Fifth Century!"

The cathedral was crowded—it was Home Defense Sunday, and one type of face did stand out above all others, a very pleasant face; after fifteen hundred years it was still distinct. They are utterly English in their thought-forms and in their religious faith, but they have preserved their racial identity. The pot has not melted them down.

After the cathedral service, the Lord Mayor gave a luncheon in my honor, attended by perhaps twenty-five men. During the luncheon I said to him, "Mr. Mayor, we have a slang phrase in common, but we use it in different meanings, 'pulling his leg.' You mean, I understand, taking a walk; our meaning of the phrase is nearly a synonym of your word 'wangle,' coined during the first World War."

"I see, Doctor, what do you want to wangle out of me," said the mayor.

"If it is not a military secret," I said, "I should like to know what is the exact extent of the devastation in Portsmouth? In America everybody thinks that Coventry is the worst wrecked city in Britain, perhaps because it was the first to be blitzed and got the publicity. But I have been to Coventry, and it is as nothing to Portsmouth, albeit bad enough as heaven knows."

He took a moment to answer. "It is not a military secret, but the picture is like this. In normal times Portsmouth has a population of three hundred thousand people—to be exact, sixty-four thousand houses, of which 57,600 have been destroyed. Of course Portsmouth is a naval base, but the guns at the naval base were too hot, and so they blew up the city. If what little hair I have is well-nigh white, you will understand when I tell you that for twenty-four hours we had no water, no light, no gas—all the services were knocked out."

After the luncheon I spoke to a great Brotherhood meeting in a large Methodist Church, followed by a discussion at tea-time; and in the evening I tried to preach at a Harvest Festival in St. Mark's Anglican Church—alas, my voice was nearly gone. By the time I reached the home of the Bishop, I could hardly speak above a whisper. The Bishop came in later after a heavy day of confirmations. He was alarmed at my condition and sent for his physician, nearby, Dr. Stevenson. The doctor, a short, stockily built man, with blue eyes and reddish hair, looked down my throat. "Now say Ah, as in Ah-men, like a good Anglican," he said, and after his inspection he said, "The only thing wrong with you, Dr. Fort Newton, is that you have been talking too much. My orders are that you go back to London and keep your mouth shut for three days, and this condition will clear up. Otherwise it may hinder your trip, and you are a kind of religious Wendell Willkie."

The Bishop followed the doctor to the door, and as long as I live I shall see those two old heads in a huddle, concocting some remedy for me. As we parted for the night, the Bishop said, "Doctor, you will find some medicine on the table beside your bed." What the remedy was is off the record, but it did the work.

Back in London, I did keep quiet, using the interlude to be vaccinated in order to return home by the Clipper plane from Lisbon. It was an American regulation, as I learned at our Embassy, of which we should have been told before leaving home. Anyway, I took a taxi to see a doctor at Alford House, Park Lane, and talked to the driver, as I always did. Taxi-drivers are a race of philosophers; they see some queer things, and they are wise. We spoke about England and America, among other things.

"About all the difference I can see between us," he said, "is that we count money in pounds and pence and you in dollars and cents."

Quite casually I remarked that I was going to see a doctor.

"A doctor? You look very fit to me," he said as I got out of the cab.

"Yes, I am entirely fit. In fact, I am going to a doctor in order to get sick."

There was a twinkle in his eye. "There you go again—nobody can tell what you Americans will say next."

When I explained that I had to be vaccinated against small-pox, he said, "Nasty business. I don't hold by that idea. To stick a needle in a man and poke poison into him takes him off his dignity. It is like asking a reptile to help one do a mathematical sum!" What fun to tell that to the doctor!

BIRMINGHAM

My vaccination did not "take," and so I was off to Birmingham to preach for my old friend, Canon Guy Rogers, Rector of St. Martin's Church. He told me how, during the blitz, the roof of his church had been burned off on a Saturday night, and next morning it was raining, as it does in Birmingham and Manchester, by force of habit. None the less, the Rector stood in his pulpit under a huge umbrella, and his people stood in their pews under umbrellas. The services of an ancient church must not be interrupted by a little matter like that. After the evening service—held early on account of the blackout—I was a guest at a dinner at the Rectory, to meet some University friends. At the close, Canon Rogers took me down to the tram and told me to go to the end of the line and then walk four minutes to Queen's Hotel, "Since you will not stay at the Rectory; serves you right."

It was in vain that I told him that I had to be off early next morning and did not want to upset the ritual of the Rectory. At last I reached the end of the tram-line and walked and walked in the blackest "blackout" I had ever seen, but could not find Queen's Hotel. Finally I touched a gentleman on the arm and asked him if he would be good enough to direct me to the Queen's Hotel. "Certainly, I'll be delighted," he replied; I was not twenty feet from the door, and he soon showed me in.

"How did you manage it?" I asked.

"It was really very easy, I am blind—day and night are alike to me!" I looked at him and saw that expression of serenity and gentleness one so often sees on the faces of the blind. "Yes, I was blinded in the first World War, and I had hoped that the world would not be so blind as to go into another war."

CORNWALL

Off again for a four-day tour of Cornwall, where I used to take my vacations when I lived in London. Once I was called back to London on a sad errand, and a Cornish friend asked, "Going up to England today?" The Cornish people are Celts, akin to the Welsh, independent, kindly, rich in legend, and charming to know. Leaving London by sleeper, I woke up at Plymouth Junction. After breakfast, I went to the Station Master and showed him my card from the Foreign Office and asked if I might see Plymouth.

"You do not have to show me any card, Doctor; I used to hear you preach in the City Temple. In fact, I sat on the pulpit steps and heard the last sermon you preached as Minister of the Temple. Being a lay-preacher, I have preached that sermon more times than the law allows since. As you Americans say, It was a 'dandy!' I intend to hear you preach in City Road Chapel next Sunday. I am, you see, a Methodist. I'm sorry I cannot show you Plymouth; it does not exist. If you will hop in my car, I'll take you around the headland, and you can see where Plymouth used to be."

We rode a little way, and before me lay the ruins of a city. The desolation was complete; an earthquake could not have done a better job. As we returned to the Junction, my friend said, "Cheerio, Doctor; do not be so dejected; all this horror will be over some day. For years you have gone to and fro between your country and mine, talking of the necessity of friendship. Nobody took you seriously; but now, at last, I think they will listen. I have heard you every time you have been in London, in 1932, '34, and all the rest."

At the station I caught the train for Truro, where I spoke at noon in an exquisitely beautiful cathedral, of Fourteenth-

Century architecture. In my address I told of what I had seen at Plymouth, of what the Station Master had said about Anglo-American friendship, of certain things I had talked over with Bishop Tubbs at Chester. The address made a deep impression; I know because a speaker can always feel such things; and in England the more deeply people are moved the less they say about it. Emotions are given to an American to express; to a Britisher to suppress. At Falmouth, in the evening, there was a great public meeting in the Town Hall. The city had been badly bombed; across the street from the Town Hall a large Methodist Church had been shattered. A prayer-service was going on at the time of the bombing, and some people lost their lives. After my speech in the Town Hall, a little man came to me and said, "Do you know that you are standing near where our Lord once stood?"

Of course I knew the Cornish legend—if it was a legend—that Joseph came to Cornwall for tin and brought the boy Jesus with him.

"And remember, when the *Mayflower* put out from Plymouth it ran into a storm and put into Falmouth for repairs. This was the last port at which it touched before reaching New England."

As if, in his own heart, he were linking the Boy Jesus in Cornwall with the romance of my country, almost as if those sacred feet had touched our New World shores, to consecrate our history! The next morning I was driven to a seaside resort some miles away; it looked at first a little like Asbury Park, New Jersey, a city of children evacuated from various places, swarms of them everywhere. A young Methodist minister, named Price —a friend of the late Dr. Cadman, who tried to lure him to Brooklyn as his assistant—was having a grand time with the children. He had arranged for me to take tea with a Bomber Command of the R.A.F. nearby.

Never have I seen a finer-looking group of young men, one in particular, about whom I asked an officer.

"Yes, he is the son of former Canon Elliot of St. Paul's Cathedral, in London." The fliers were much interested in a racial map which I drew of America, showing where the different racial groups had settled, and how seventeen different nationalities, or races, had part in the settlement and development of our central Eastern states. These boys, and others like them, had been climbing the English skies to fight for freedom, justice, human dignity, and kindness. In the evening there was a large public meeting, after which I was driven across the country to catch my sleeper for London.

The following Sunday I did preach in City Road Chapel, London, where Wesley spent the last thirteen years of his life, and where, at five o'clock every morning, he celebrated the Holy Communion—at once an Anglican and a Methodist to the end. Wesley sleeps in the yard behind the church; his mother in the Dunhill cemetery across the road, along with Isaac Watts, John Bunyan, and Defoe. The old church stood like an island in a sea of desolation—most of the buildings round about it down; the church itself was hit by a fire-bomb, which, happily, was extinguished. My friend, the Station Master of Plymouth, was in the congregation, true to his word, along with many of my old friends, and a great group of young ministers of all sorts. To stand in the pulpit of John Wesley was an honor and a consecration. He was a man in whom God kindled a white fire which swept through England and saved it from something like a French Revolution. If only we could have another spark of God-fire today to match the Atomic Bomb and free us from its threat and menace, under which we are doomed to live. But, maybe, war itself has committed hara-kiri—it is too terrible to fight.

The largest congregation I had in any London church was at St. Martin's in the Fields. It was a Harvest Festival service—like our Thanksgiving Day—only in England no one day is set apart, and each parish observes any Sunday in the autumn, as best suits its purpose. St. Martin's is the parish of His Majesty, the King, but evidently he played hookey that day. Vegetables and flowers were in the chancel and about the pulpit, which stands out in the church. The church was packed, and I could see many old friends, my publishers, journalists, not a few friends from the City Temple. After the service I held a kind of impromptu reception on the front porch of the church; it was almost like a family reunion.

Following the service, I went home to lunch with the Vicar and his wife; we had a good talk together. He told me how nearly St. Martin's came to being blasted to bits, and how he could see Westminster Abbey and the Parliament buildings burning and the water system of the city failed—clogged with mud. How St. Martin's escaped he could not imagine—many buildings around it went down. Even Charing Cross Hospital, nearby, was badly damaged. Of course the robot bombs came later, almost doubling the damage done to London and the South of England; some of them falling as far north as Manchester.

Still London stands, scarred and scornful, after such a dreadful experience; subdued too—but wise with long years of proud and honorable history; more like a village than any great city I know, the home of a people to whom life without liberty is not worth living. Long live London!

EXIT FROM ENGLAND

If to get into England in those days was difficult, to get out was more difficult; but my friends of the Foreign Office smoothed the way. But some things I had to do myself, one of which was to report to the Alien Registration Office. A group of folk from many lands were gathered there; some could speak broken English, others could not—all were afraid. As my passport was from a friendly land it was soon cleared, the more easily because the officer in charge was an old friend of mine —he used to stand guard at the rear of the City Temple and send warnings of air-raids to me in the pulpit. "Doctor, we are always glad when you come to England, and sorry to see you leave," he said.

A shabbily dressed, bewildered old couple, whom life and the war had badly battered, came in, tense and trembling. For them, dealing with the "authorities" had been a nightmare, and they shrank from it. My officer-friend saw the situation, went to them and put them at ease. They were shown chairs. He patted them on the shoulder gently, and smiled. Their fear was relaxed. They were amazed, doubting what they saw.

"Listen," I said to the officer, "it is none of my business, but the way you treated that old couple made me feel good all over. The Bible says something about dealing with the other fellow as you would have him deal with you, does it not? Look, they are smiling; they feel like guests, and in a police station too!"

"Well, you see, Doctor," he said, "I've been thinking a lot about the mess we are in and how we got into it, and if there is one thing about which I am sure it is that there hasn't been much of God's work done in Europe lately. As you know, I am not much on religion," he went on, trying to clear himself of piety, as so many do, "but if I can manage a bit of it here, it can't do any harm, can it?" That officer—burly, apple-cheeked, shy—has written no book to show how to make a better world. He has attended no conference of brain-trusters to discuss the subject, nor will he be invited. He has no blueprint of Utopia, but every day at his job, often humdrum, he is practicing the blessed art of treating people as if they were human, like himself.

A minister-friend told me of an awful evening he spent in an air-raid shelter during the blitz. Coming off duty after a hard day, he lay on the floor of the shelter too tired to read, much less to sleep. No one was allowed to leave the shelter; the din was deafening. Suddenly from behind him came a small voice, speaking in the Cockney accent, "Wouldn't yer git orf to sleep better if I was to tike off your boots, sir?"

Looking around my friend saw a boy—fourteen, not more— with an elfin face and bright smile. Good manners? Yes; but something more. Honest-to-goodness religion too. He thought of the other fellow, when everybody else was thinking how they could escape alive. If we are to build a better world out

of the scorched salvage and seared souls after this war, my
friend thought, we shall need all the courage and kindness we
can get—people who care and seek to share.

FLYING "SOMEWHERE"

Leaving London with regret, as I always do, I went to Bristol
for the night. In the morning, in an Egyptian darkness, we
were driven to an airfield, where we took a small Dutch plane,
which would carry eighteen people. As I climbed on board I
saw across the aisle an old friend, a London health-officer,
sitting in seat number twelve.

"Where are you going?" he asked.

"I'm going to Lisbon on my way to God's country," I replied.
"Where are you going?" I inquired.

"To Lisbon on business," he answered. "Why are you looking at the number of my seat so carefully?" he wanted to know.

"Your seat is twelve, and I was afraid that mine might be
thirteen," I told him.

"Still superstitious, are you?" he asked. Then we made search,
and we found no seat thirteen. Off we went in due time, es-
corted by a fighter plane through the war zone—it went over
us, under us, on either side, like a king bird protecting a crow.
Within a few hours we landed at the Lisbon airport, some
twenty miles out of the city. Nearby stood a German plane,
not far away an Italian plane; we were on neutral ground.
Dr. Porter and I hired an automobile to go into the city; it
went like the wind, and I could see that he was nervous. On the
way he had told me that he had come to Lisbon to advise with
the Government of Portugal about building a hospital. He
was met by State Officials, to whom he introduced me, and went
away with them; I went to the Avenida Palace Hotel. In England I had been warned that the Lisbon hotels would be exor-
bitant in their charges, but it was incorrect—the rates were reasonable, the food excellent, the service good. How good to see
a lighted city again—a pink city, all aglow at sunset. Gay throngs

from many lands mixed and mingled; the city swarmed with spies and refugees—one had to be careful to whom one talked and what one said.

THE WHITE CITY

My friend Dr. Porter spent much time with me at the hotel; we saw the night-life as well as the day-life of the city. Fortunately, the Clipper time-table had been upset by storms on the Atlantic, and I had four days and a half in Lisbon. The Doctor arranged a luncheon for both of us with an upper-class Portuguese family, and I was very glad to see a better type of face than one sees on the streets. As the Doctor spoke French fluently and the family understood French, he acted as my interpreter. Our host was a merchant in nuts. He had forgotten more about the nuts grown in my own country than I had ever known—hickory nuts, walnuts, and the rest. On our way to the luncheon I told the Doctor that in American slang the word "nut" had become a synonym of "daft" in Scotland and "balmy" in England. Accordingly our host was "a 'nut' about 'nuts.'" The Doctor doubted whether he could get that across in French—"It is tricky," he said, "and I might slip up"—but to my amazement he did get it across, and our host laughed heartily. They were charming people, and it was a happiness to have met them.

In the lounge of the Avenida Hotel a young Englishman recognized me. Years ago I had preached in the church of his father in Southampton and had been a guest in his home when he was only a lad. He had spent some time in Spain betimes, admired the people, knew their language, and was enthusiastic about their literature. He was in fact on a secret mission to Spain at that time, taking his vaccinations against typhus the while, to attempt to divert the fruit being sold to the Germans to England, where it was sorely needed; I had seen fruit only once in a while in England—a few English apples. The Doctor, my young English friend and I made a team; we slept very little—the city was too interesting, we might miss something or somebody. John Gunther turned up from "the inside" of somewhere; Erskine Caldwell and his remarkable wife arrived, on their way home from Moscow.

Lisbon was at once a gangplank to America and a gateway to the vast concentration camp of Europe—a city where gilded wealth and ghastly poverty lived side by side. We explored it all; the night clubs were too garish and not at all to our taste, crowded by foreigners, chiefly. It was odd to go into a moving-picture theater and find it jammed, while Ginger Rogers and Clark Gable spoke Portuguese, the people roaring with laughter at the things they said and did. Also, it amazed me that so many English and American books had been translated into Portuguese, as we saw in the shop windows, such as *The Story of the Bible,* by Van Loon, a life of the President, a biography of the Prime Minister, and no end of detective stories. There was no doubt about the sympathies of the people of Portugal, for window after window was decorated in honor of the R.A.F. The nation might be officially neutral, but it was also an ancient friend of Britain. Thousands of people were waiting for passage to England and to America and had been waiting for months.

A TRAGIC STORY

One day, as I stepped out of the Avenida Hotel to take a stroll, a neatly dressed woman was coming across the courtyard. Suddenly her suitcase came unfastened and an avalanche of things poured out. Hastening to her aid, I rescued some papers about to be blown away, while she replaced her things—what amazing things ladies carry in their bags! A little confused, she recovered her poise.

"Thank you so very much," she said in broken English.

"A Free French woman, if I may judge by the badge you wear," I said.

"No French woman is free until France is free," she replied, with flashing eyes.

"I am an American clergyman," I explained, "returning

from England to America; an Anglican clergyman, as you might say. I saw many badges like yours in London, bearing the word 'Résistez' and the old Huguenot slogan. I wonder, if by any chance you know Madame van der Vaulgt?"

"Yes, she is my friend," she replied, startled. "Is her husband alive?" she asked eagerly, searching my face for a hint of a reply.

"Alas! whether he is living I do not know." Then I told her how I had met him in London during the first World War in a Masonic Lodge.

"Yes, Eben was a Mason, I often wondered why," she said; "his wife is a French woman, and was editorial writer on the Catholic daily paper *La Croix* until France fell; I have not seen her for months."

"But there is nothing wrong or unusual about a man being a Mason and his wife a Catholic. In English-speaking lands Masonry is never involved in affairs ecclesiastical or political. 'Dr. Van Der,' as I called him, as you know, was a brilliant Dutch barrister. I was interested in the journal he published, *The New World;* it appeared, simultaneously, in French, Dutch, and English; he planned to carry it into German and Italian. It advocated the League of Nations and all liberal and humane principles for the re-ordering of the world. Years passed, and I returned from England to America and lost track of the Doctor."

It seems, I went on to tell her, that he was in Rotterdam when the Germans flattened out that city, after the Dutch people had surrendered in the second World War. Knowing that he would be a shining target for Nazi venom, he fled to the Dutch East Indies, by way of America, where he had a transit-visa. At Ellis Island he became desperately ill and had to undergo a major operation. As soon as he was able, he made contact with the Rector of the French Church in New York and with me. He wanted to land in America for six weeks, long enough to make contact with American business firms, whom he might represent in Java, where he expected to teach and practice law. At once I went to Ellis Island and talked with the shadow of the man I had known years before.

Fortunately, the Rector of the French Church in New York and I were able to arrange with our American authorities for Dr. Van Der to land; he was to be a guest at the French Church rectory. But, at the last minute, our plan was upset by some enemy of his in the Dutch Consulate, and he was deported and sent on his way to Java. Meanwhile, I did send a long cablegram for him to his son in the South of France, who had been a machine-gunner in the French Army. Whether he received a reply to the cablegram, I do not know, nor have I had a word from him since. It has puzzled me much, because it was not like him not to drop me a line and let me know what and how he was doing. She was depressed by the story I told, and so was I.

Later, in the lounge of the hotel, she told me and my young English friend many stories, comic and tragic, about what her people were enduring in France under the German rule. The slow-witted Germans were sorely vexed by the tricks and pranks played upon them by French students. Some things she told made her blood boil and her eyes blaze; also, as she became excited, she dropped into French, and I did not understand everything she said. We both warned her to talk softly, since no one knew whether people who would not hesitate to do away with all three of us were listening. She did not tell her own story, but such hints as she dropped added up to a bitter, long-drawn tragedy. Lisbon haunts me—hurts me—still, because of the nameless sorrows underneath its glitter and gaiety. The French lady made me think of General de Gaulle and his speech I heard in London—a man of flame—only she had more of the grace of humor.

HOME AGAIN AND WAR

As I had "priority" on the first Clipper plane leaving Lisbon, in due time we took off in the morning, stopped at the Azores for tea, and at Bermuda next morning. There we were held up by storms over New York, and we caught up with our sleep, in part at least. Then on a Sunday we flew to New York, and home again. Having spoken seventy-eight times in two months, and having gone all over England, I was tired to the bone. In fact I had gained a pound while in England, but it must have been an English pound, because I lost it, with two American pounds in weight, on my way home. The United Syndicate, handling my daily feature in the press, had reached the bottom of the barrel, and I had to begin to get ahead again, while conducting a great parish without any assistance. The tensions of the trip had been terrific from the nervous energy expended, to say nothing of the drain upon my sympathies at sight of the devastation of places I loved. Within a month after my return came December 7th, a "day of infamy," and my country was plunged into cataclysmic calamity of universal war, which we did not want and for which we were not prepared. Disaster followed fast and followed faster, such defeat as America had never known. Our boys went off to a new war, Red Cross units went to work, stars began to appear in windows of homes and shops, and service flags full of stars in the chancels and pulpits of churches. Who can ever forget those days?

Again the old hurt and heartache pierced me, which I had known all through the first World War—the ghastliness of preaching the gospel of Christ in a world at war. A thousand times I thought of the Raphael painting of "The Transfiguration of Christ," at the top of the Mount "the glitterance of Christ," as Dante would say; at the foot of the Mount, the father with his epileptic son, whom the disciples could not heal. Just so, there stood the Sermon on the Mount, high, white, eternal, and at its base a world torn by the torture of war—the agony of it was excruciating to the Christian mind and heart. Also, what my Quaker friend had said to me on the train going into Liverpool, "May the Lord have mercy on your body," began to be justified. Somehow, I stumbled through the winter, but early in April I had a bad crack-up, just as I was preparing to go to Iowa City for the Vesper service at the University and to visit Cedar Rapids next day. Instead, I went to the hospital, my body ablaze, my nerves threads of fire. However, I crawled out of bed to take the three-hour service on Good Friday and to preach on Easter Day, talking of immortality, looking like a candidate for it about to be elected. My old friend W. R. Boyd, of Cedar Rapids, suddenly remembered that he had "business" in Philadelphia. He came all the way from Iowa to see me, and his visit was better than any dose of medicine could have been.

THE PAY-OFF

Such was the first instalment of my pay-off for having done too much in England and long before. John Ruskin said that there is no bad weather, but only various kinds of good weather, and no doubt that is the best way to look at illness. Francis of Assisi called his body "Brother Ass," but he rode it too hard and died at the age of forty-four, albeit leaving a fragrance as of the winds and flowers of heaven in the Galilee of Italy. Somehow, I managed to go on. My physicians ordered me to stop all activities outside of my parish, they even threatened to stop my daily feature in the press. Their orders I obeyed to the letter, almost; if I cheated a little, it was only a wee bit.

This meant that I could not go preaching all summer as I had been doing—one whole summer for Dr. Russell Bowie at Grace Church, New York, where the church was full of people, not New Yorkers, but folk from all over the land. A whole summer for the United Churches of Montclair, New Jersey; a blistering summer at Pittsburgh where twenty churches united in a service in Carnegie Music Hall, with days so hot that one could fry an egg on the sidewalk. Then a summer for Bishop Manning in the Cathedral of St. John the Divine, New York, during the World's Fair; and at the Church of the Ascension on Fifth Avenue, during the second year of the Fair. Such things I did, not because I had to, but because I loved to do them—and they were worth while.

Slowly, the tide of battle began to turn; the miracle of American production began to make itself felt. Allied strength gathered and grew; the enemy made enormous mistakes. Petty alien bundists, and subversive elements on "the lunatic fringe" among our own people, were rounded up and hushed up. The attack of Germany on Russia was a fatal error, and turned out to be her undoing; at first it seemed to sweep everything before it, but it shortened the war. In February, 1943, I signed the third five-year contract with the United Feature Syndicate for my daily talks in the press. By that time Monte Bourjaily had retired as manager, in favor of George A. Carlin, a gracious gentleman, a superb critic, a dear friend. The contract was duly signed, but with a gentlemen's agreement that if my health should go bad, I could be relieved of my labor with proper notice. Unfortunately, later in the year, my health went to wreck, owing to a disintegration of my blood—there was an explosion, and I was laid aside. It was a choice between my feature and my church, and to give up my church during the "duration"—when clergymen were so scarce—would leave it in the lurch. My feature ended in January, 1944, and it remains for me to tell the story of it, somewhat in detail, for its sheer human interest, and because it is unique, so far as I am aware. To tell the story I must go back to the depths of the Depression, when it started, and while the story runs parallel with the story I have been relating, it is in fact a different story.

SIGNING OFF

It must be obvious that I can touch only the fringes and highlights of eleven years of work; it taught me more than any seminary or any number of books could teach me. My readers were really my collaborators. They sent me stories, suggestions, parables, hints, and all sorts of material; but best of all they told me what was in their hearts. If I made a mistake, a slip as to a name or a date, it was quickly corrected. Some wrote to me regularly—people of spiritual insight—and I looked forward to their letters, many of which I have kept. Often I have been asked what type of article I liked best to write. It is hard to say, since all of them had one central purpose: to give good thoughts in a bad time, to help folk over a hard place, when just a little push meant much; to open a window in a stuffy life and let in light and air; to "kid" somebody out of a dismal mood; to note some vital fact in a dreary situation, which had been overlooked—often a case in court is lost, for lack of one fact more; to bind up the broken-hearted; to set free those made captives by fear, shyness, and that old fake "inferiority." In short, to show that one can live a rich life on a shoestring, as Jesus did, as St. Francis did; and that no matter what our lot may be, life can be a winged, singing thing, if we have the grit, grace and gumption to take hold of it firmly, handle it lightly, and give it discipline and direction.

A thousand times I have had in mind the three questions which Emily, in *Our Town,* by Thornton Wilder—a play packed with spiritual understanding—brought back with her, when she passed out of her body far enough and long enough to see life in better perspective. First, "Do any human beings ever realize life while they are living it?" A few do, a very few; some people do see the sheer wonder of just living, seize it, and enjoy it; they do not put off living as so many of us do. Most of us are afraid to live, afraid to take the risks; we are too tame or too timid or too lazy to make the venture. We do not see life until it has passed, and it is too late to live, as was said of a greatly beloved President of our country. Youth does not see the beauty of youth—its boyish grace, its maiden magic —as age sees it. A boy does not see himself as his father sees him, still less as his grandfather sees him, with the kinder perspective of the years.

The second question is equally penetrating: "Are we always at the mercy of one self-centered passion or another?" Most of us are most of the time—even romantic love is often a self-centered passion, when it seems to be centered in another. Any self-centered passion—love of money, political ambition, or the many varieties of vanity—blinds us to the beauty of life. Some one thing gets so close to us that we cannot see anything else, not even life itself.

The third question is profound and searching: "Don't we ever really come close to another?" Is it impossible to get out of ourselves into the lives of others? Must we be shut up as prisoners in the solitary confinement of our tiny cells? The fight against loneliness begins early and stays late. We can get just so close to other people, even those we love best, and a door is closed, and we are stopped. In reality we can get closer to God than to anyone else, if we know how and take time to do it. And so religion—or whatever word we may employ to describe this inner necessity—is not simply vital but important, and we had better learn the art and knack of it. But enough; a great poet has told us that life is just an opportunity to learn how to pray, and prayer cancels loneliness.

After reading I know not how many letters—we counted thirty thousand the first four years, and then lost count—many impressions remain. One thing is plain—the human heart is everywhere the same, and love is the way to it. Human beings are very much alike, whether white or black or brown. In spite of differences, which they exaggerate and think important, they have faiths, fears, hopes, needs and dreams in common—and love and loss and longing. If only we knew one another, trusted one another, helped one another, what a world we could build out of wrath and ruin. How strange that our first attitude toward the Other Fellow should so often be one of suspicion, of distrust, if not of hostility, or else a deadly indifference. Yet we have only to look into our own hearts to know what lies hidden in every human heart. All of us are a little weak, a little strong, a little good, a little bad, foolish when we fancy we are wise, and wise, often, when we fear we are foolish. My final impression is one of profound compassion for my fellow men, since each fights a hard fight against heavy odds, and all need the fellowship of man and the mercy of God, or, as *John Inglesant,* one of my favorite novels, puts it: Only the infinite pity of God is equal to the infinite pathos of human life.

..... 10 .....

Everyday Religion

FOR MORE THAN ELEVEN YEARS I listened in on human lives.
For that length of time I conducted a feature, a daily talk, in
the American press, called "Everyday Living," which reached
an enormous audience. It was a kind of Everyday Church, in
which the people talked back at the preacher, as no doubt they
often want to do in other churches. They said many lovely
things to me, but they also told me where they thought I was
wrong, and why. They spoke very plainly at times, and that
did them good and it taught me many things that I did not
know. Indeed, if I had known years ago what I have learned
from my readers, my ministry would have been different—
whether better or worse I do not know, but more simple, more
intimate, more direct, more full of pity. No experience in my
life has been more instructive, more revealing, or given me
more insight into humanity and the things with which men
and women face and fight day in and day out.

It all came about accidentally, as we say, knowing not what
we say. For some time Malcolm Bingay, of the Detroit *Free
Press*—my great friend for many years—had wanted me to conduct a column of counsel in his paper. It was hardly possible,
since I lived in a distant city, and I thought that such a column
ought to be syndicated in many papers. One day—I tell the
story as it was told to me later—Monte Bourjaily, Manager of
the United Feature Syndicate, dropped into the office of the
Free Press. While Bingay was called out of his office on an
errand, Bourjaily picked up my little book of prayers, called
Altar Stairs, which Bingay kept on his desk. He read it while
he waited. When Bingay returned he asked about the author,

saying that he had been looking for someone to conduct a
column of practical inspiration, and that the little book, both
by its simplicity of style and breadth of spirit, had put an idea
into his mind. Bingay told him of his effort to induce me to
write a column for the *Free Press,* and then, with the generosity of a long friendship, gave me a character which an archangel would have found it difficult to live up to.

Nothing more was said, and Bourjaily went on his way.
Later I received a proposal from the United Feature Syndicate
—an auxiliary of the United Press in New York—to undertake
such a service. It was agreed that I should write a dozen or
fifteen pieces of a kind and in a style I had in mind, handling
the actual problems of life with "the spiritual touch," as they
put it. I did so on one condition: that those great journalists—
"newshawks," I called them—would go through the little essays
with red or blue pencils, criticizing them without mercy, since
we wanted to "put it across," in the lingo of the group. The
pieces were written and sent in. They took me at my word,
with devastating results. The more or less literary style of the
pulpit was definitely "out"; my tiny articles, about five hundred words long, covered with the markings of red and blue
pencils, looked like our national flag torn and tattered by a
cyclone. Here a graceful opening sentence had been decapi-
tated; there what I had regarded as a rather good phrase had
been amputated. Nothing had been added; it was a matter of
subtraction. The pieces, as edited and transcribed, were re-
duced to a clipped simplicity, almost austere, without the waste
of a word. Here ended the first lesson, and one which I wish
I had learned years before—to put things so that anybody can
understand, and then everybody can understand.

AN ASSIGNMENT

"Write religion; do not write about it," was my assignment.
The two things are quite different, as all agree—most religious
writing is "about" religion; it does not communicate the thing
itself, most of which is incommunicable; as Patmore said, "In

love and divinity what's most worth saying cannot be said."
Jesus could write religion, or rather speak it, since He did not
write. Others have been able to do it occasionally, in an hour
of clear insight, in a mood dross-drained and luminous. Sometimes, but not often, I was able to approach it—in parable, in
story, or in a line that was close akin to poetry. Anyway, this
assignment is really the job of every preacher, at once his ideal
and his despair. For months after my feature started pieces
would be returned, with a notation on the margin, "No, too
preachy." They had to be recast and rewritten, and even then
they were sometimes "chucked."

The name of my feature came up, causing a most significant
discussion. My suggestion that it be called "Everyday Church"
was turned down decisively and unanimously. It was in vain
that I accused some of the men of being afflicted with "an anti-
church complex." In the same way, my proposal that it be
called "Everyday Religion" met with thumbs down, but, after
some argument, it was accepted as an alternative title, leaving
it to the editors which to choose. In point of fact, a number
of papers did call the feature "Everyday Religion," among
them the Detroit *Free Press* and the St. Louis *Post-Dispatch*.
However, the title most in favor was "Everyday Living," on the
ground, as one of the group explained to me, that Jesus never
used the word religion in His life, so far as we have record;
He talked only of life. Thus, what to do with life, how to take
it, how to make it count, in spite of all odds and obstacles,
became the central topic of my talks about all sorts of subjects.

A DISMAL DECADE

Now consider the period covered by these tiny talks about
everyday living. The first one appeared on October 17th, 1932;
the last one on January 8th, 1944. It would be hard to pick out
a decade more troubled, more tormented, more terrifying. The
feature began in the depths of the Great Depression, and no
one who remembers that time can ever forget those dismal
days. From the heights of an inflated "boom" we plunged into

a bottomless pit. Many papers "folded up," leaving my feature high and dry. Nothing was certain but uncertainty. Securities became insecure. Values evaporated. Whereas, in the old days a check might be returned marked "No funds," during that devastating time it was often returned marked "No bank." Thousands of people who had made life drizzly, slaving and saving against a "rainy day," suddenly found themselves penniless, facing old age, with no time or chance to make a new start.

No one need tell—indeed, no one can tell—how such conditions reacted upon the lives of men and women, not only on their material fortunes but far back in the secret places of the soul. What fears, what gnawing anxieties, what dark forebodings beset human beings, like a plague the havoc of which no one can measure or describe. One saw long lines of the unemployed, and, what was even worse, multitudes of the unemployable. The Depression was spiritual as well as economic. Men who wanted to work, and knew how to work, began to feel that they were "unwanted," not needed—there was no place for them, especially if they were over forty—and these facts did things to men which words were not made to tell. To be "on relief" hurt all but the incurably indigent and lazy. Yet people had to eat, otherwise hungry-mad mobs would have swept through our city streets. The church, one may add, saw aspects of this situation invisible to others, if time allowed me to describe it.

"The giants of industry did not giant," said Will Rogers, whose untimely death was a bitter loss—he whose humor was so bright and so free from acid. Savings melted away, homes were lost, many families were broken up, rich men became poor overnight; weary feet pounded the streets seeking jobs—I signed the application for night-watchman for a man who had been vice-president of a bank. Gray hairs began to appear on the heads of men still young; deep lines were carved in the faces of people who had recently been prosperous, if not happy. There was a story telling how a man applied for an outside room in a hotel, and the room-clerk asked, "For sleeping or for jumping?"—so incorrigible is the American sense of humor, which makes a jest out of the stuff of tragedy. At a funeral in my church, at least a thousand dollars' worth of flowers were brought in the front door, while, at the back of the church, a long line waited to get into the soup-kitchen! Shabby shapes shuffled along our city streets, ex-men, down and out.

WAR CLOUDS

No sooner had we begun to climb out of the Depression than a cloud "like a man's hand," in the Bible story, appeared on the horizon, and in the distance we began to hear its muffled thud, and then the thunder, of approaching war. It seemed incredible, at least our people did not believe it possible—we did not realize the kind of world in which we were living. In spite of all endeavors—including the League of Nations and the Pact of Paris, "outlawing war," every effort and influence that men and nations could invent or evoke—the cloud of conflict gathered and grew. "Unfinished Business," someone has called it; because the first World War had not been finished, another war was in the offing. Alien ideologies began to be preached and enforced; dictators strutted to and fro, swollen with vanity. At last a megalomaniac, a monster of iniquity appeared, whose cunning was only matched by his cruelty, and the world was ablaze. Again war, total war!

Such, in swift survey, was the period during which my little essays about living every day were written, and read near and far by all sorts and conditions of folk. In short, at a time when faith was dim, when the direst predictions of the pessimists seemed justified, and the hearts of men and women were haunted by a sense of futility and frustration, I was engaged in the great business of cheering people up. Actually I was trying to give my readers a faith and a philosophy of life— not philosophy in the technical sense, but rather a "life-wisdom" long tried and trustworthy. Not in a cheap manner, not by "pep-talks," not with the expansive sentimentalities of the booster, still less with the galvanized absurdities of the "bunkshooter"—a most expressive word. Far, very far from it. Instead, with every resource at my command, by every art I could learn or contrive, I sought to show that life *does* have meaning, that it *can* be made to count for something, if we have faith, courage, wisdom, worship and kindness. A few words from two of my tiny essays sum up the substance of my teaching:

My message has been very simple. To live well we must have a faith fit to live by, a self fit to live with, and a work fit to live for—something to which we can give ourselves, and thus get ourselves off our hands.

We cannot tell what may happen to us in the strange medley of life. But we can decide what happens in us—how we take it, what we do with it—and that is what really counts in the end. How to take the raw stuff of life and make it a thing of worth and beauty—that is the test of living.

Courage is the first virtue, as kindness is the final joy—to be "a little kinder than is necessary." To take life for granted, grudgingly, is to spoil it; whereas to take it for gratitude, bravely and without fear, is to enjoy it, despite all its aches and ills.

To be happy is easy enough if we give ourselves, forgive others, and live with thanksgiving. No self-centered person, no ungrateful soul can ever be happy, much less make anyone else happy. Life is giving, not getting.

Life is an adventure of faith, if we are to be victors over it, not victims of it. Faith in the God above us, faith in the little infinite soul within us, faith in life and in our fellow souls—without faith, the plus quality, we cannot really live.

To faith must be added a life-wisdom, which may be summed up in six words, the three greatest maxims of the race. Two we owe to Greece, two to Rome, and two to Judea: "Know thyself, control thyself, give thyself."

For the rest, hope much, fear not at all, love with all your heart, do your best, seek the best in others; take life and dare it, have a little fun and share it; and put your trust in "the veiled kindness of the Father of men," in whose great hand we stand.

A CONFESSIONAL

The response to my daily talks was immediate, and most astonishing to me. Having never done such work before, I did not know what to expect. Certainly I was not prepared for the flood of letters which poured in upon me from all directions, from all kinds and conditions of people. They dealt with every sort of life situation, asking questions no mortal could answer and putting problems no one could solve. Urgent, eager, intimate, friendly, many had to be answered by letter; and there were interviews no end—examples of which will be given later in these pages.

Of course it had its amusing side, as when a little girl asked me to help her sell some kittens. Tabby had brought in more kittens than she could use, and she offered to divide the profits fifty-fifty. In 1933, in the depths of the Depression, such an offer was tempting. Then, there were weird, fantastic letters, from people off center and clearly eccentric. One man wrote a long intricate thesis, with maps, charts and a maze of figures, proving that the world is hollow and that we live on the inside of it—which explained to me the kind of hole we were in at the time, in 1934. Later I learned that the idea that we live on the inside of a hollow world is an article of faith in one of the smaller religious communions.[1] It is queer to what odd ideas religious sentiment attaches itself.

One was struck by the gift of strong, simple, vivid writing shown by people untrained. Often the grammar was off key and the spelling was awry, but the matter was good, the very stuff of life itself, racy with its reality, salty with the tang of its humor and tragedy. My letters were from folk of every station and walk of life, doctors, lawyers, college presidents, preachers, but also from housewives, servant girls, truck drivers, working girls, boys in school; a prisoner in his cell awaiting execution; people who deemed themselves misfits and failures; young folk who had not found themselves and did not know what to do with life; people perplexed in faith, not as to particular dogmas, but as to the worth of life itself. They told me things which they would never tell anyone else, they assured me.

Many of my letters—many of the most regular and valuable —were anonymous, but not because they were ugly. No one ever

[1] *The Small Sects in America,* by Elmer T. Clark.

wrote me an unkind letter. To be sure, some of my letters were angry and bitter—angry at life, bitter about God, critical of the whole scheme of things. After the war began, I had a long series of letters, written in red ink, ridiculing God as asleep, or gone on a journey, as drunk, or perhaps dead. Suddenly the letters ceased, and a daughter of the writer dropped me a kind little note, asking me not to take the letters of her father seriously; he had passed away. For years I received regular letters from certain readers, anonymous, rich in spiritual insight, often full of fun, telling me many precious things, often teasing me—one such series will be described later, because of its worth and charm.

ANONYMOUS LETTERS

The advantage of writing anonymously is that a human being can tell all, keeping nothing back, with freedom and completeness. Some of these letters were human documents of rare interest, life-stories which, if I had a right to print them, would make a real Book of Human Life. It is an awesome experience to be taken into confidence by thousands of people of all sorts and conditions: the business man at the end of his wits; the mother whose daughter is running wild; the father in hopeless desperation trying to make ends meet and hold his family together; the man who is old and "unwanted"—how often that word was used; the shut-ins and the shut-outs; the minister whose faith had been blunted, if not blasted; people who have been "on relief" and hate it, fearing that dry-rot may have set in; sensitive souls who feel that hardness of life and detest its humdrum; those who reckon themselves defeated, and are at first dazed and then numb; those who seemed unable to adjust themselves to life at all. They uncovered for me the real issues of life, the inner enemies of human souls, the problems with which men and women wrestle in the secret places of their hearts; things they were aching to talk about, but seldom had anyone to talk to, much less to give counsel. Much of our daily talk only skims the surface of life and does not plumb its depths.

Not counting notes of thanks and goodwill, most of my letters were from people in dire plight, under terrific strain and pressure. For this reason, no doubt, marriage muddles loomed large in my letters. Family friction—between parents and children and those awful "in-laws"—revealed itself in undisguised horror. Economic factors played their part too, along with the changed spirit of our uprooted age. The clash of youth and age was acute, often ruthless in its cruelty—letters told of family "scenes," of cutting words uttered, of threats made; the tragedy of parents trying to live the lives of their children for them; of children who were trying to wean their parents, as "old-fashioned" and totally "out of date," unable or unwilling to understand the new standards, which are in fact hardly standards at all. And so it went, a bitter war of generations!

UNTHEOLOGICAL

Out of mountains of letters only a few—not more than one in a hundred, and later none at all—brought up any question of theology, such as the differences which divide religious communions. The eternal questions, Why is evil? Why do men suffer, the innocent with the guilty, often the innocent and not the guilty? were always present, or never far away. But the issues which divide the churches did not seem to signify in the actual life as people struggle with it, hand to hand, perhaps because those issues are unrelated to the realities of everyday living. No matter how tormented my readers were by untoward experience—often heart-shaking and baffling—it did not occur to them that religion could help them or that it had anything to do with their woe. A generation ago it would not have been true in the same degree, but people today do not know how to use spiritual faith and energy in daily life. They have no techniques for doing so, having neglected, if they ever knew, the arts and offices by which such reality is made real. For example, the church has told people to pray, but it has not taught them how to pray today, in the speech of today, in key with the needs and conditions of life as we live it today.

A man goes to church—if he does go—and the preacher talks about salvation, as he should. But it seems far off and unreal. The thing real to him is a nagging, fretting wife who makes his soul sore or a boy who has brought him grief. Nearby sits a woman whose girl has decided to "live her own life," and she is helpless. She is not thinking about eternal bliss, but of how to get through the day without a "scene." Two pews away is a girl who finds it easier to take aspirin than to pray. The one helps her to sleep, and the other seems to do no good at all. What does the word "salvation" mean to such people, if it does not touch their problem or perplexity, much less save them from the "red hell" in which they are living here on earth? If this is true of church folk, more or less trained in the tradition and habit of the Church, what about those who know nothing of the Church, who seldom, if ever, enter its doors, except to attend a wedding or a funeral; people to whom the stately language of the Church is as unintelligible as Eskimo or Choctaw? For these reasons, and others of a sort similar, my daily talks avoided the old, familiar, lovely vocabulary of the Church. Instead, I tried to write about everyday living in everyday language.

CERTAIN RULES

As my daily talks went on and my letters piled higher, it became clear that I must lay down certain rules. Otherwise, I would have found myself conducting an employment agency or a matrimonial bureau, and I had no ambition to undertake either. For one thing, I did not want to divert attention from my main purpose and topic by dealing with debated issues unrelated to it. "Hot potatoes" was the phrase used by my journalist friends, samples of which will appear later in this story. However, some questions, widely discussed, I returned to again and again, such as Christian unity, the old bigotries which break and blight the brotherhood of man, and, after the war started, the impossible attitude involved in absolute pacifism.

Often I allowed my readers to deal with these and other debated questions, putting in a few words to show my own point of view, then dropping the "hot potatoes."

Another rule I had to make, and that was never, except in the most unusual situations, to give one reader the name and address of another reader. The pressure on this point was often strong, but I had to be firm, albeit with a few exceptions. No sooner had I made the rule than I broke it. A truck-driver wrote me a forthright letter, telling me "the heck of a fix" he was in—only he used a stronger word than "heck." He had been in charge of a fleet of trucks and was doing well, when, unfortunately, the trucking company failed, leaving him flat. He got a job with another company, which failed in turn. He had no interest in alien ideas hawked about the land, and no faith in the panaceas peddled by subversive agents; he was just a plain American who wanted to work, knew how to work, and wanted to know—"What in H—— has happened to America that a man cannot find work to do?"

One letter came from the office of Mr. Henry Ford, if one should use any prefix to a name so well-known and well-beloved, asking to know more about that truck-driver; and I gave the information. Mr. Ford read my articles regularly, it seems, in the Detroit *Free Press,* and every now and then I received some token of his appreciation and goodwill. He sent me a set of McGuffey's Eclectic Readers, which he had had reproduced in the format, type and binding he had known as a boy, and was good enough to autograph the First Reader. In common with a whole generation of American youth, he owed an unpayable obligation to those well-worn and widely used schoolbooks, which did so much to shape the mind of America in days gone by, giving many a boy and girl their first glimpse and taste of good literature.

TALKING IT OVER

In the matter of interviews it was not easy to lay down rules. They were many and interesting; they took time, tact, patience—for one to look at his wristwatch, as if he had no time, or very little, is deadly. To do all the talking is fatal. One must learn to listen, and that is a fine art, as will be shown in due time.

"Please forgive me for seeming to barge in," said a woman, about forty, or nearly so, I should judge. "I am a Catholic, but I want very much to talk to you, if you will allow me."

"The fact that you are a Catholic makes no difference to me," I assured her. "But why not talk it over with your priest? I am sure he would listen and give you the benefit of his wisdom and kindness."

"We have never met before, but I have seen your picture," she said, ignoring my suggestion. "Besides, I have read your daily talks for six years and know your spirit. I'm sure of two things—that you will not be shocked at any story, however horrible, and that you will help me if you can."

The story she told, leaving out no details, was dreadful enough; but it was possible to make suggestions which have been of help—the case is not closed. The very next day a Jewish woman laid before me a problem different, but hardly less difficult.

Here is as good a place as any other to say some things that need to be said. Since 1916 my ministry has been in great cities, London, New York, Philadelphia, and city life often does things to people. Its rush, its crowded solitude, its loss of fellowship, tend to distort human souls.

It became necessary for me to learn enough about psychiatry to know when a psychiatrist is needed—that much every minister should know. In time I was able to spot among those who came to see me, even among my readers, people who ought to see a psychiatrist; but it was hard to get them to do it.

A vestryman of mine, who had had a terrible time, refused to see a psychiatrist, calling him a Nut-doctor. At last he was persuaded to do it, with happy results. But I will have no dealings with a psychiatrist who is a materialist; he must be a man of the spirit.

At the same time, a clergyman ought to know the limits of psychiatry, as all wise psychiatrists do. They can go just so far

—they often do marvelous things, as I can testify from cases which I have sent to them. But some things they cannot do, which they know well enough. Great psychiatrists have sent cases to me, saying, "Religion must do the rest, if it can be done."

Exactly; the gospel—religion—can do things which psychiatry cannot do. The preacher must never forget that fact, and he must know how to apply spiritual faith and energy to life situations. His seminary ought to have taught him techniques to that end, as seminaries are now trying to do. He must not tinker with human souls; he must know his job and how to do it.

A servant of souls—"ourselves your servants for Jesus' sake" —that is surely the commission of a clergyman, who must be both a prophet and a priest or at least a human being who has faith and knows how to apply it to actual needs and concrete cases.

Some time later a girl, having journeyed by bus from another state, staggered me with a story of the most awful thing which can befall a woman. She had been outraged by a man whom she had a right to trust—a religious teacher; the man had died soon afterward, mercifully for himself. Her life was shaken, her faith shattered, and it was not easy to pick up the pieces and put them together into a pattern. It takes time to rebuild a lost faith—time, and a contagious faith on the part of the one who undertakes the task. It took months to work out the cure, but we did it—I kept in touch with her, writing her letters, sending her things to read. At last she was herself, despite a devastating experience.

Here is a different, an unforgettable example. An attractive young man hitch-hiked his way from a mid-western city to discuss with me the question: How could he make the best use of his life? He had many capacities, loads of personality; he had thought of the stage, of advertising, of writing. It was amusing to see how puzzled and hesitant he was upon entering my study in the parish house of the church—he did not know, he said, that I was a clergyman. Otherwise, as he admitted later, he would not have come to see me; then he hastened to add, "But you are different; I have read your talks." He meant to praise me, but he slandered my brethren in the ministry. He said that he had seldom attended church, and when he did it had nothing to say to him—which may have been his fault or misfortune, as he agreed. He was a very intelligent lad, but not a member of the intelligentsia—"those educated beyond their intelligence," as someone has said. He wanted guidance, and, unlike the "smart-aleck," was willing to listen and discuss.

WHAT TO DO WITH LIFE?

Hour after hour we discussed the question: What to do with life? How to invest our talent and influence to the best advantage? There are, in fact, only four things a man can do with his life. First he can run away from it, or try to, as Peer Gynt did in the Ibsen epic. It is futile, of course. If we dodge any duty or difficulty, we have to come back and face it, sooner or later, and pay the interest compounded by our cowardice. Second, we can run along with life, hunt with the pack, think with the herd, in obedience to the stupidity so well expressed in the phrase, "Everybody is doing it," which may be the very reason why we should not do it, if we have any standard or any character. Third, we can, if we will, take hold of life, with some faith and purpose, undergoing discipline, practicing courage, and run it to some end. All great lives show us men and women doing just that thing, which makes biography at once so interesting and valuable a study, endlessly fascinating.

But there is one other thing we can do with life, which I ventured to suggest to my young friend. "For me to live is Christ," said St. Paul. A man can give himself up utterly, in self-surrender, to a Person or a Cause, in complete dedication, and let Someone, or Something, else run his life. That is, perhaps, the nearest to happiness we can attain on this earth. To emphasize my point, I quoted the saying of Dwight Moody, which meant so much to me as a young man, when I heard him utter it: "Let God have your life; He can do more with it than you can." Unfortunately, that sentence from Moody did not "click" with my young friend; he looked at me not in disgust but in dismay—it was, apparently, an unknown language to him. At last, after talking it all over, I advised him to go into journalism, and he did so. Several years later, when he had become a city-editor, he wrote me a "report" of his experience.

Oddly enough, as his long letter showed, my friend had changed his attitude toward the Church; he even hinted that he had thought of entering the ministry. A journalist sees what goes on behind the footlights in the drama of community life, but he also knows what happens backstage. He knows what is printed in the paper, and why. He also knows what is *not* printed, and *why*. He is a realist; if he is not careful the edge of his idealism may be blunted, as my friend said. Not many journalists are cynics, although many must be tempted to try that "dope." But not my friend, the city-editor—he said that the Church has the secret and the medicine for the healing of humanity, if only it had the courage and wisdom to use it! Alas, he complained that the Church—perhaps unconsciously— had placed preservatism and resignation too high on the list of canonical virtues. Sectarianism, he said, is actually silly; such issues do not touch life at all.

RELIGION AND SEX

More specifically, he said that the Church—again without realizing it—is hamstrung by the fact that it is too closely tied in with a social and financial system which, so far from being infallible, will hardly bear inspection. One sentence in his letter was very striking: "We say that true religion must never go into politics; they said the same thing in Germany—but they let a false religion go into politics and set the world afire." Who can deny the facts in the case? George Eliot coined the deadly word, "Other-worldliness," to describe most of the religion of her day; alas! the word is not yet obsolete. But he was still further specific. He said that the greatest abdication of the Church was its unwillingness, or its inability, to face up to the facts of sex, and deal with one of the greatest drives in human

life, except by a method of hush-hush and repression. And that
too at a time when literature is so sex-obsessed. In reply I
sent him a copy of a sermon by a preacher-friend of mine, entitled "The Challenge of Sex to the Church," which he said
was a step in the right direction. But neither my journalist-
friend nor my preacher-friend could tell how to do the thing
which they agree—as most of us do—ought to be done, without
doing as much harm as good. Prohibitions and repressions are
not enough.

In the meantime, take another interview, as transcribed from
one of my talks:

> All of us listen in these days, when the radio makes the
> world a whispering gallery. What odd things we hear, news,
> previews, stories, comments no end, and tiresome talks about
> soap and vitamins.
>
> To listen in on human lives is different. In one of his stories
> Victor Hugo said of a man, "He had the art of sitting down
> and holding his tongue for hours by the side of a man who had
> lost the wife he loved or of a mother bereaved of her child." At
> such times silence is wisdom.
>
> Not long ago a woman sat across my desk, talking rapidly.
> She was almost stone deaf and could hardly hear a word I said.
> The story she told was pitiful, heart-breaking, and she told it
> in minute detail.
>
> Seventy years of age, she poured out her pent-up heartache.
> Seldom have I listened to a sadder history—due, largely, to a
> quirk in the mind of her father, and to the callous facts of life.
>
> While she talked—her voice soft, sometimes sinking into a
> sob—I thought of the agony wrought in the life of one person
> by a crotchet in the mind of another; how we hurt others by
> wrong thinking.
>
> The father did not want his daughters to marry—an odd,
> absurd idea. Something in his own life had made this twist in
> his mind, which well-nigh wrecked the life of the daughter he
> loved so deeply.
>
> If only we were wise enough to love our children and friends
> truly enough to allow them to live normal, wholesome lives—
> or let them alone. So I mused while I listened and wondered,
> as the story unfolded.
>
> The father had gone to his grave long ago, without knowing
> the hurt he had caused; the husband had followed later. The

woman both had loved was left alone, old, deaf, unable to take care of herself, and in dire need.

What a tangled tragedy—no one had intended, or foreseen, such an end. Yet she spoke so loyally, so lovingly, of both her father and her husband—so strange is the love of woman, passing all understanding.

"You have helped me so much," she said at last; "I just had to tell somebody, and you were kind enough to listen and give me sympathy." Yet I had said hardly a word, and I doubt whether she heard what I did say.

Anyway, I had shared her loneliness and sorrow, and that helped to lift, or lighten, the load; she gave me the sweetest smile as she left. A shower of letters followed this talk: readers far and near wanted to help the woman in her need, offering hundreds of dollars in aid. This confessional aspect of my little talks surprised me greatly; I was not prepared for it. But I was not surprised at the compassionate goodness of my readers, who were so quick in their sympathies and so eager to help. Life is often very hard; perhaps it was meant to be so, if we think about it aright, in order to harden what is soft within us and to soften what is hard.

11

Listening in on Human Lives

SOME THINGS are audible only when others are still. In Nablûs, the ancient city of Shechem, in the Holy Land, the traveler is told that underneath the city there run perennial streams of water. The hurried tourist listens in vain to hear them amid the busy hum of the day. He must wait until the bazaars are closed and the children have ceased to play their merry games in the streets and the grave-like silence of night has fallen over the city. Then, standing almost anywhere, he can hear the sound of running water.

Just so it is when we listen in on human souls, even our own souls. All of us chatter and sputter a lot, without saying what we mean, much less meaning what we say. We are busy about many things—often just busy being busy, without getting anything done. "Woman is a dark forest," said a Frenchman, but so is man as regards himself—how little we understand ourselves. We are so absorbed watching other people, wondering what they are thinking and saying. Our motives are mixed, and sometimes we do not see our real motive at all, especially when it is rather shabby. He only is an honest man, and truly brave, who can face the actual facts about himself.

When we hurt other people—when we say cutting, catty things about them and do unkind acts—in nine cases out of ten it is because something is hurting us. We may not know what it is. We may not want to know. We may even refuse to admit it when it is pointed out. Few people are willing to admit that they are envious, jealous, or afraid. They go on playing a game of hide-and-seek with themselves and others, and even with God. Only when some blow cracks the crust of our conceit—

or in a moment of lucid self-knowledge and self-revealing—does the veil drop and we really see ourselves and speak our deepest thought or fear or faith or dream. What strange things human beings are, wearing masks, play-actors, deceiving themselves more often than they deceive others; pretending to a virtue, or sometimes a vice, they do not possess.

Life for many today is deflated, a thing to be endured rather than enjoyed, and our problem is not so much to add years to our life as to add life to our years. All of us have a sense of unfulfilled possibilities; we are people of whom more might have been made. We are living below our possible selves, and we are unhappy, thwarted, frustrated, unable to find a way out. Yet, as many great lives show us, there is a way of thinking and living which, if we can master it, will set us free to use our powers to the full. As it is, William James tells us that we use only a tiny part of our possible power. What are the things that hold us back from the larger life we want to live? What is it that inhibits us, cripples us, making us victims of the morbid fatigues that spoil our joy and defeat our dreams? After reading piles of letters, "human documents," telling the naked truth nakedly, in which people have poured out their souls, some things have been burned into my heart.

PRIVATE ENEMY NO. 1

The first thing taught me is that Private Enemy No. 1 in human life is neither sin nor sorrow, bad as these can be. Sin can be forgiven and sorrow healed. Nor is it stupidity, not quite, since some forms of stupidity can be enlightened—even if an old classic writer did say that "in face of stupidity even the gods are helpless." No; as Kipling wrote of the shadow that leaps so swiftly through the jungle, "He is Fear, O Little Hunter, he is Fear!" It is not too much to say that human life is a battle against fear in which there is no truce. No wonder Montaigne said, "The thing in the world that I am most afraid of is Fear"; and that is the fact we must face and the force we must harness and handle, else we may be wrecked by it. Some things, of course, we ought to be afraid of; some things are dangerous. Two fears, in particular, should follow us through life, Robert Frost has told us: fear lest we prove unworthy of the One who knows and loves us best—that is fear of God, yet we are not to be afraid of God, as much religion has taught, or religion itself is destroyed. The other fear is fear of Man—lest he misunderstand us and withdraw his fellowship from us, making the loneliness of life unbearable. These fears—and other dangers of the common day—are real and valid, useful and wholesome, and they ought to be the end of all other fears. But, alas! we know well enough, it is not always so, not often so in fact.

Today we have a thousand other fears, less real but no less terrifying, which torment us by day and torture us by night. Never has the world been so full of fear, and it takes all sorts of subtle, shadowy shapes. A lot of our fear is a hangover from the past, and this surplus fear, unless mastered and directed, is apt to turn inward and work havoc. Sensible fear stimulates us, makes us alert; it is normal and protective. Foolish fear paralyzes us, makes us helpless, if not hopeless, with its imaginative forebodings. Oddly enough, the fear most rife today is not fear of death, but fear of life, not only fear for ourselves, but fear of ourselves; and that is not healthy. Self-fear projects itself outward and attaches itself to things not dangerous and which can do us no harm. The fear that benumbs man—and still more women—today is fear of failure, of breakdown, of loneliness, of drabness, of illness, of poverty; fear lest we be unequal to the demands made upon us. So few have any material security; and we have set so much store by such security that the lack or loss of it has assumed hideous forms and gigantic dimensions in the night, robbing us of the rest needed to do our work. It is this self-fear which makes life an agony for so many sensitive souls. As one of my readers put it plainly, in a self-revealing letter: "When the supply of fear does not equal the demand, we manufacture hobgoblins."

Such a state of mind—or mindlessness—is the result of many facts, forces and failings working in myriad ways, too many to

name, much less to analyze, here. It confronts religion with a
new problem, not yet solved. Up until the first World War our
religious teaching and appeal had to do, chiefly, with a "guilt-
situation," as it has been called. It told men of their sins and
called them to repentance. Such teaching and appeal are still
valid and sorely needed, but it is not the whole fact by a long
way. Today, in addition, we have to do with a "fear-situation,"
the full meaning of which we have not measured, much less
mastered.

I have considered this problem in *His Cross and Ours,* the
Lenten book which I wrote, in 1941, for the Presiding Bishop
of the Episcopal Church. Also, *Our Gospel—Or His?* by B. C.
Plowright, a remarkable book, by an English minister of vital
mind, which ought to be brought to America. Much has been
done and is being done to meet the new and desperate human
need; further discoveries in religion are being made. The words
of Jesus, who said more about fear than He said about sin, are
being studied anew. Since we soon hate what we fear, both
fear and hatred are listed among the sins of man, which is only
partly justified; but it gives one furiously to think.

This new fear is not the old-fashioned cowardice; it is a
nameless terror which leaves mental and spiritual wreckage in
its wake. As there are physical conditions which destroy the
spiritual life so there are mental states which make it as unreal
as a dream. The Church must not fail here—it must teach, and
show, "the practice of salvation." Much is being done in this
direction; more—much more—remains to be done. Jesus was
not only up to date in this matter; He was—He is—far ahead
of us.

Out of the horrors of the World War and the period of
spiritual fatigue, moral chaos and social confusion following
it—all of which are and are sure to be increased by the Depression and the second World War—a plague of new fears
swarms over the earth, spawning other horrors. It is a new fear,
the most devastating and disintegrating mankind has known.

How can we fight our fears, real and unreal, and win the victory? Must we always be a race of creepers, cringing, cowering

before life, like prisoners in a cell? No; provided we use the bright weapons at hand. Courage we need, of course; it is the first virtue, if not the root of all the virtues—courage to "take it" and come back, courage to meet defeat and not be defeated. The plain pluck of people is astonishing, as my letters show. Many a frail little woman faces disaster with a grit equal to that of a soldier going over the top. But even the finest courage wears thin unless it is supported and fortified by the "something beyond courage," of which Lady Montague wrote in a letter. What is that "something?" Is it some mystical, occult power, beyond the reach and use of ordinary mortals and bestowed only on the elect? Not at all.

WHAT FAITH CAN DO

"My appeal is to nothing more difficult than religious faith," wrote William James, whose letters tell of a terrible time through which he passed, when the issue was uncertain. As Walt Whitman put it,[1] "Faith is the antiseptic of the soul"; it disinfects us of our fears and those dark dismays, akin to despair, which make us long for some "honorable discharge from the bankrupt business of living." When faith fades out of the heart, fear crawls in, a vile and slimy thing. By the same token, when we win faith, which is "reason grown courageous," fear is driven out of our hearts. As a friend of mine put it picturesquely, "Fear knocked at the door. Faith opened it, and lo! there was no one there!" We hate a thing because we fear it; when fear is dead, love lives and life begins—then we know the loveliness of the night and the mercy of the morning. We live in an enchanted universe.

But we must be more specific. Faith is more than belief, more than opinion, more than tradition—useful and valuable as these may be. Many church folk who believe they have faith are victims of fear—"fears in the night," which even the wisdom of Solomon could not drive away. First, we must face our fear and find out what kind it is—real fear, or self-fear; that is not

[1] Preface 1855 Edition *Leaves of Grass.*

easy to do, because we are so seldom honest with ourselves. If
we isolate it, bring it out into the open, and find that it is self-
fear, admit it. To know the facts is not weakness: it is wisdom.
Half of our trouble in life comes of not facing the facts, especially the facts about ourselves. Since most of our fears have
been learned, so they can be unlearned, if we take the time to
do it, changing negatives into positives, and building up better
habits of mind in place of old ones we have drifted into. Also,
if we really understood ourselves, we should be afraid of very
few things in the world.

Carlyle noted how people turn to the past, talk about it, try
to go back and live in the days gone by. He wondered about it,
until he discovered the reason—"there is no fear in the past."
It is over and done and gone, whatever may have been its
hazards and displacements, as when old soldiers walk backward, living in the past. We know the things that have happened, and no matter how freighted with grief or other dis-
maying happenings our experiences may have been, they are
nothing to be feared any more. They have come. They have
gone. They are no longer uncertain. They may have done their
worst, but we lived through it. But we have no knowledge of
what lies ahead, and it is fear of the unknown that clutches
at the hearts of men and women. The past at least is secure;
the future is hidden. Yet today is the future of years ago;
memory ought to come to the aid of faith.

LIFE'S ANXIETIES

Next to fear, if not a form of it—a first cousin, so to speak—
is the nagging anxiety which wears us out. It eats like an acid
into the very souls of men and women, weakens them, and un-
fits them for living. Worry is a kind of subconscious fear, a
tiny rivulet of fear seeping or trickling into the mind, like slow
poison, until it paralyzes us. Unless it is checked, it cuts a channel into which all other thoughts are drained. Some things we
ought to be concerned about—using the word "concern" in a

different sense from the way the Quakers use it—but worry very easily becomes a habit of anxious, fearful, fretful thinking, and that is bad. The shuddering insecurities of the last decade have told terribly on the inner lives of people, as my letters show.

It is easy to pass, before we know it, from a thoughtful "concern" to a wasting worry. Worrying is thinking with our emotions, not with our minds; with our imagination, it would be more accurate to say. In any contest between the imagination and the will, the imagination is sure to win, because it is an artist; it makes pictures. We pop awake in the dead of the night, rigid and in a cold sweat, and the imagination puts on a motion picture of the thing we fear, and we are forced to see the show until we are worn out. It is a lack not only of faith but of emotional control. Our emotions are like the gas in the engine of our automobile, and we must remember that gas was rationed as worry ought to be. We must not leave the engine running without putting in the clutch. A wise reader gave this bit of counsel, a kind of technique worth pondering:

> The time to deal with worry is early in the morning, when the cares of yesterday and today come crowding into mind; and the method is to line them up, look at them squarely, and take their measure. Let me add that I am speaking of little nagging worries, not great sorrows—the shattering blows of life are something else, yet my method has value in dealing with them too. However, I am speaking of the little worries which we can master if we take time out and deal with them one at a time, carefully.
>
> Take one old worry always hanging around, "Let me see, I've met you before, and I think I managed to beat you very well, didn't I?" To another worry I say, "You seem to be smaller than I thought, now that the light is clear." To still another I say, "Why, you're not half as big as the worry I saw a friend wrestling with yesterday!" Anyway, I call them on the carpet, so to say, and when I begin to question them, they disappear. Having put each worry in its place, I turn to the little prayer Jesus taught us to pray. Then it is time to start the day; it is amazing what a difference it makes.

One of my readers—a dear lady eighty years of age—taught me two things which have helped me greatly. She learned them, she said, slowly, amid a hard lot, at great cost, and they prolonged her life. One is that we must learn to forgive people for what they are as well as for what they do; because what they do grows out of what they are. We cannot make people over, as the old button-moulder wanted to remake Peer Gynt, and if we could we might make them worse than they are. Besides, our business is to make ourselves better and others happy, as Stevenson taught us in his gay and gallant manner; and that is enough to keep us busy. If only we attend to our own business in this respect as well as in others, it will make for our own peace and the happiness of others.

The other thing my reader learned by living is that we must wait and see what happens and not worry till it does happen. In nine cases out of ten the thing we are afraid of and worry about does not happen. But if it does happen, as it does at times, other things will happen too which will change the setting and modify the result, making a different picture from the one our fear paints now. By a little effort, a little practice, we can learn the knack of putting things from us, throwing them off far enough to see them more clearly, and think of them as they matter—many things do not matter and are not worth the bother of worrying. Also, we must never believe our night-thoughts; they are the biggest liars on earth. Then, she added, be patient enough to live one day at a time, as Jesus taught us, letting yesterday go and leaving tomorrow till it arrives—which is really all that is asked of us. Then strength will be given us to bear what is laid upon us and to do what is required of us. Here is real wisdom, learned by long life, if we are brave enough to obey it.

PRIVATE ENEMY NO. 2

If worry is a child of fear, and never quite weaned—or, as someone put it, interest paid in advance on trouble which may never come—then Boredom may almost be described as Private

Enemy No. 2 today, of all days, when the world is turned upside down. In spite of the pageant of great events—perhaps because of it—people are bored to extinction by the petty round. Big things, which make for crisis, we can endure; they have a certain dignity about them; they thrill us, excite us. But little things, which make up the most of life, get us down. Hunting elephants is fine sport; fighting mosquitoes is a dreary and annoying business. Some routine, of course, we must have in life, else it would be chaotic; but too much, which becomes a ghastly grind, infuriates us, destroys us.

For boredom is sameness where sameness ought not to be—in the things of the mind and the spirit. Sameness in nature rests us; sameness in the soul ruins us. Banality is the blight of our age. In a machine age men tend to think of themselves as machines, if they think at all. The rich variety of life is flattened out under the steam roller of crowd-mindedness, and we feel not like living souls, but so many robots struck off a machine-made pattern. The advent of the collective mind, foretold with forebodings by Spencer, makes the individual seem insignificant. We think—if we do think—in the mass; we move in the mass; we mill about in a crowd; it is no wonder that people get tired of life, tired of the whole bag of tricks. Up until thirty life comes to us; after thirty we must take hold of life, or it begins to take things away from us. In middle life there is a sag, a let-down, very hard to bear.

Ruskin and Morris warned us of this horror long ago. They said that beauty is not a luxury, but a necessity, and that loveliness is as cheap as ugliness. We may sacrifice too much for civilization, they said; we may sacrifice culture, or even civilization itself, as the Romans learned too late. Above all things, Morris said, men hate dullness. They prefer danger to drabness. He foretold a cumulative disgust, from which men will revolt in violence, accepting almost anything to escape it; even war will be a joy. Until recently, life has been growing duller, in spite of more exciting amusements, games, gambling, drugs, and drink. To put it starkly, life amid the glare of neon signs and the blare of publicity—the same old slogans repeated parrot-like—with no ideal beyond safety first, a five-day working week, an auto, vitamins, the movies, a poodle, and at last a pension, is intolerable and unbearable. Does anyone imagine that such a dismal life can go on forever, or ought to go on? With no adventure, no glint of greatness, no gleam of spiritual vision? Just to get and beget, dreaming only of cushy comfort— no wonder vitamins do not vitalize!

The way out is by creative living. The remedy for banality is beauty. When everything is ready-made, life sours. One of my readers, a surgeon in a medium-size mid-western city, has solved the problem for himself. After all, surgery is a kind of high mechanics and did not satisfy. So, deliberately, he began to add new interests to his life, making for a variety of experience which saves one from the blight of boredom. He learned all about birds—he knows almost every bird-call. He is an adept about trees and flowers and always has a flower garden. He set up a shop and makes all kinds of things with his hands, useful things, toys. He reads widely, in regions remote from his work. He has many facets to his life and is never bored. He does not twang away on one string of the harp of life with maddening monotony. Even nature, for all its seeming sameness, has an infinite variety; no two leaves on a tree are alike. Human nature, too, is a medley of all sorts of souls—if all Chinamen look alike to us, it is because we do not know any of them. God never repeats Himself; like His works, He is permanently interesting. If we are bored, it is because we are blind or dumb or lazy!

EVERYBODY'S LONESOME

To judge from the letters which reached me, another inner enemy was brought home to me overwhelmingly, and that is the appalling loneliness of human beings. If one of my talks touched on this topic, a deluge of letters followed, as when I referred to the Thomas Wolfe essay, "God's Lonely Man." Never were human bodies so jostled; never were human souls so much alone, especially in the "man-swarm" of great cities, where life treads on life. Many, to be sure, living to great age, are left alone, and they must learn to be alone and not be lonely, a fine and difficult feat which some of them achieve. Others are isolated, but the loneliness most keenly felt is the loneliness of insulation, lives locked up, inhibited by fear, by shyness, by flatness of life, by a sense of inferiority, unable to get out of themselves into other lives. They have a craving to be liked, a hunger for intimacy, but shrink from the emotional contacts needed, unable to enter into other lives or to allow others to see into theirs. They are made prisoners by bolts and bars they cannot break, and one feels the ache of it. Yet we must not expect perfect unity with any human being, or complete understanding, even between lovers:

> Oh, we are forever divided,
> Despite what love has done
> To draw us close together,
> For we are two—not one.

Loneliness is one thing; solitude is another. Loneliness is thrust upon us; solitude we seek at times if we are wise. *Some Fruits of Solitude,* by William Penn, was a golden book to Stevenson, who found it by accident, and to others beyond counting. Loneliness hurts; solitude heals. Our religion is what we do with our solitariness, a great philosopher tells us. We can do two things with it—try to get away from it by "going places," doing things, hunting escape; but that does not work for long. Or we can make contact with One nearer to us than our own souls and turn loneliness into solitude, if we learn the law and art of doing it. It is not easy to do in an age of speed and shattering noise, but it can be done. Otherwise, we are broken off from the Center and Whole of Being and left isolated and adrift; life becomes ingrowing, not outgoing, and we get on our own nerves. As Bertrand Russell put it profoundly, "We are suffering not from the decay of theological beliefs but from the loss of solitude." Such an insight goes down to the very roots of our restless, feverish life, anxious, fear-driven, bored, and haunted by a sense of the futility of existence.

But we also need the fellowship of human beings, with needs

and hopes like our own, if we are to escape self-centeredness: not organization, but fellowship. To get out of ourselves, to get ourselves off our hands, is the first step toward health and joy. Some know the knack of it; others are inarticulate, awkward, inhibited, held by some secret bondage which must be broken. The Church, said Newman, is "the home of the lonely," and one wonders why more lonely souls do not find it so. Perhaps it is because the fellowship of the Church is not as rich, as real, as warm and fruitful as it ought to be. Here, no doubt, is the reason—one reason—why so many are seeking today in outside groups, of one kind or another, a freedom and intimacy of fellowship they do not find in the Church. One may regret some of the uses of such groups, and pity other uses, such as calling each other by their first names, mistaking familiarity for fellowship, but they do tell of a deep need when a new loneliness has settled down upon human souls.

LET'S BE KIND

One other thing my readers have taught me in a startling way. It was amazing to me to learn how many people go limping through life, crippled souls, owing to some hurt or humiliation, some injustice or cruelty, suffered in childhood. The stories told me were staggering—of starved souls, of people looking for something lost, of stabbing hurts and devastating frustrations. We do not realize how sensitive children are and how easily they can be injured, even when we do not know it, much less intend it. They feel the tension of a home even when they do not understand it. Humor we need in dealing with them—yes, but not satire, not sarcasm; these may make deep wounds and leave ugly scars. Teasing, when it becomes a torment, is a form of cruelty which ought not to be tolerated. In small doses it may be fun; in large doses it is poison. How often, when one of the primary instincts is thwarted or bruised, it may mar a whole lifetime, unless it is healed. As a mother wrote, "My boy fails in nearly everything he undertakes, and he seems to expect it." Exactly; something or someone broke down his faith in himself, and he was defeated before the battle began—self-defeated by a negative pattern of mind, which time and tact will be needed to alter. Else he may become a poor derelict drifting to and fro among the unburied dead which litter the world, to be dropped at last into the wastebasket of humanity.

Reading so many records of little lives mutilated by unkindness, it seems to me that kindness is the greatest thing in the world, if not the final joy of life. Also, it adds a terrible meaning to the words of Jesus about those who cause "one of these little ones to stumble"; His gentle words flash like lightning. One thinks, too, of what Dr. Johnson wrote to his friend Taylor on the last Easter Monday of his life: "In the meantime, let us be kind to one another." It may not be "all that this sad world needs," as a later poet said; but the world does need kindness as never before, and all the time. Indeed, it is the central and supreme simplicity of religion, as Jesus taught it and lived it. In a rough world we hurt each other so sadly; let us learn to be kind, very kind, "a little kinder than is necessary," as the young husband said in the Barrie play. What else can we do in this crazy, cruel world? Little indeed, so little that it looks like giving pills to cure earthquakes.

Fear, Anxiety, Boredom, Loneliness, Unkindness—these things make human life horrible; and the worst of these is Fear. It is the cause of most of our wickedness, our unhappiness, and our strange stupidity which passes belief. There is not as much sin in the world as many of us think; there is enough, as God knows, but most of our brutalities are the blows and blunders of blindness. We hate, we hurt, we rob and wrong each other, making life hateful to ourselves and our fellows, because we are afraid. "I was afraid," said the man in the Parable of the Talents, and he lost even his one talent.

Yet there is a Truth in life, a Truth about life—a Truth that makes all other truth true—which, if we are true enough to grasp it and brave enough to follow it, will set us free from the torment and terror of Fear. Man was not meant to be a cringing being, eaten up by anxiety, shut up a prisoner in silent loneliness, living in blind cruelty. He was meant for great adventure, if he has the insight to see the laws of life, and the key of kindness to unlock doors; and in his quest for the best in others he will discover something in himself not guessed before. For each of us, though we may not be clever or commanding, but only average and unknown, life can be winged and wonderful, full of meaning and music, if we have the faith to trust the God who made us, and the wisdom to live, love, and learn.

12

Grab-bag Mail-bag

As HAS BEEN STATED, my assignment was to write about life
with the human touch and from "the spiritual point of view."
What the editors meant by the last phrase they did not say;
perhaps it was not clear in their own minds. But it is important to know what we mean by the words we use. It is especially so with the word "spiritual," which has been so badly
handled, so abused, that it has become slippery, tricky, a mist
in the mind. A Chinese student said to Stanley Jones, "Do not
tell us to love our enemies; preach spirituality to us"—as if
spirituality were merely a soft, pious emotion which made him
feel cosy on the inside, whereas it is something much more
vivid and vital.

Many kinds of life have to be lived, and we must have a
care when we call one type of life spiritual and another not.
What is spirituality? Who is spiritual? When is a man spiritual
and when not? Audubon studying birds was not less spiritual
than Jonathan Edwards pondering theology. John Woolman,
the Quaker saint, was not more spiritual than Washington
at Valley Forge, fighting for the liberty of his people. Music
is not more spiritual than mathematics. An "interior" medita-
tive life is not necessarily more spiritual than an "exterior" life
of social ministry. A sanctuary and a laboratory may be equally
spiritual, since in both men seek the truth. In short, spirituality
is not only a sacred awe, a reverence, an inward aspiration; it
is also insight, action, doing or suffering the will of God. It is
not one type of temperament.

Jesus was the supreme Spiritual Mind, as all agree. When He
said, "Seek ye first the Kingdom of God and His righteousness;

and all these things shall be added," He revealed what the
spiritual mind is. It is a right sense of values; it puts first
things first—and so has a right estimate of everything else. By
"these things" He meant food, shelter, politics, art, science,
sport, all that man seeks, uses, and needs. These things are
valuable and have meaning when they are added to the thing
of most value. The world is all agog and awry, because its sense
of values is wrong—it puts power, money, fame, at the top,
whereas these things belong lower down in the scale. The most
valuable thing in life is a right sense of values; without it we
mix things and make a muddle. If we have it we are not fooled
by noise, fads, fashions and unreality.

THE SPIRITUAL LIFE

Man is a spiritual being, by virtue of being a man. He par-
ticipates, in some degree, in the spiritual life of his race, even
when he is unaware of the fact. He sees, dimly or clearly, the
values which give life its value. Man cannot live without bread,
but when he tries to "live by bread alone," he ceases to be a
man and sinks to a sub-human level. In some men, to be sure,
the spiritual quality is undeveloped, or so deeply interned that
it hardly seems to exist at all. But it does exist; it is there awaiting an awakening, if only by the tragedies of life. If some men
profess more than they possess, others possess more than they
are willing to profess. They are more spiritual than they seem
or are ready to admit. Many of my readers were church folk,
many were not. The fact that a man belongs to a church does
not always mean that he has a spiritual mind. Far from it. One
reader, a life-long churchman and even an officer in a church,
said frankly, "I do not know what it is all about. I have not the
slightest idea what Jesus meant when He taught us to pray,
'Our Father.' " Yet he was himself a father, and a good one too
—his own heart should have instructed him.

Some of my readers had a violent anti-Church complex, due,
nearly always, to some unhappy experience with the Church.
Others, outside the Church, were highly spiritually minded—

they seemed not to need fellowship, or they balked at saying a creed they did not understand or could not believe, reciting ancient phrases which had no meaning, thought-forms alien to their minds. There is a Church Outside the Church, so to name it; people kept out of any church by rites which they do not deem necessary—like Lincoln—who do not understand dogmas and cannot accept them. After all, there is no commandment requiring us to think alike; we are only asked to love one another—and sometimes we ought to love people well enough to let them alone. If only the Church had not made dogmas and rites tests of fellowship, it would be very different. Many people, many minds, and my task was to interpret spiritual reality to all.

ALL LIVE BY FAITH

Some of my readers were materialists, or said they were—but when their attitude was analyzed, it was not so. Others were atheists, or thought they were; at any rate they said so with a kind of glee. But when they described the kind of God they denied, He turned out to be no God at all or one in which no one ever believed or could believe. Their attitude was more emotional than reasonable—a bitterness due to some laceration in life, some disillusionment profound and devastating. One thing became clear to me: any faith, or unfaith, that is intellectually impossible cannot be spiritually satisfactory. We must love God, if we love Him in reality, with all our heart, all our soul, and all our mind, as the first and great Commandment tells us. The man to whom Jesus told the Parable of the Good Samaritan seemed to think that it is easier to love God than it is to love man; but he was wrong. To love God is the greatest adventure of the human soul and the most rewarding. But we cannot love God whom we have not seen unless we first love man whom we do see.

Furthermore, man lives by faith, even when he does not realize it. Indeed, often enough he "lives by the faith the lips deny, God knoweth why," as a famous poem tells us. Actually he has more faith than he knows, more than he uses. He never makes a journey, never starts a business, never gets married, except as an act of faith. He does not know that his journey will end safely. He cannot "prove" that his business will be a success. He cannot be certain that his marriage will be happy. Yet he makes the venture and takes the risks by faith. The same is true in his spiritual life—that is to say, his whole life. He cannot "prove" God, as we ordinarily use that word; nor can he prove the immortal life. Certainty is possible only in mathematics and some demonstrations of physical science. But we can have something better. We can have certitude, an insight and attitude of heart, as when Pascal—a man of mathematics, and a man of the spirit—said in a memorable sentence, "The heart hath its reasons which the reason knoweth not." Faith, certitude, is not believing things without evidence; it is doing what we see and know to be right and good regardless of consequences.

"THE CUP OF QUESTIONING"

It was against such a background and in view of these facts of mind and heart—obvious, but not often recognized—that my daily talks were written. For the same reason, it seems wise to give a number of the little talks, examples of questions asked, and problems stated in order to show what my readers were thinking and what they really wanted. After reading thousands of letters some things became clear as to what was in the hearts of men and women, even their unasked questions. They wanted to know how to think about God. Strangely enough—yet not so strange, perhaps—they wanted to know how to pray. They wanted to know something of the meaning of life and how they could handle it wisely and bravely and make it count. In dire need, they wanted to find something beyond courage—which is apt to wear thin—something to cleanse them of fear and heal them of hate—of all negative and debasing emotions.

Anyone who writes such a column as I was conducting must drink of "the cup of questioning," as Meredith put it. The human mind is a question-box and, sooner or later, every kind of question is fired point-blank at the writer. If, as Plato said ages ago, it is the pressure of the answer that puts the question, this is a wise arrangement, if we have the wit, the patience, the humility to seek and wait for the answer. Jesus did not answer many of the questions put to Him—albeit He often gave wise answers to foolish questions—but He did say to His disciples, "at that time ye shall ask me nothing." As if to say, all questions will finally be answered. If we were told the answers now probably we should not be able to understand them, however simply stated. Out of my grab-bag mail-bag I take a few examples.

UNANSWERABLE QUESTIONS

Here is one:

> My wife lost her sister recently. They were near of age and very close to each other. At the parting my wife called to her sister—did her sister hear her cries? There was only silence, so far as any of us could make out. It upset me terribly.

Take another:

> We lost a baby many years ago. No doubt he has grown in the life beyond, as he would have grown here, had he lived. He must be an adult now. Will it be possible for us to know him when we pass over? Or will he have grown so much faster that he will be a stranger?

Just once more:

> If those who "pass on," as we say, see what is taking place here below, and are aware of the agony of tragedy we are going through, how can they be happy? It must surely cloud their joy to see our sorrow, or else they may see with other and clearer eyes than our own.

William James was right. Nearly always, when people speak of religion, they really mean immortality, and nothing else. No immortality, no Christianity; and, we may add, no Christianity, no immortality—at least not in the sense in which we use the word, and as it is used in the questions just asked. Jesus was very restrained in what He said about the conditions of the afterlife—or life further on, as some of us prefer to say. There is no future life; it is all one life. That Jesus seems to have assumed, as when He said to one of the men who died with Him, "Today thou shalt be with me in paradise"—He never used that word elsewhere; it means a palace garden. "Today," the continuity of life is unbroken. He made a picture for the man, as He did when He talked with His disciples, "I go to prepare a *place* for you." When He spoke of His own death He merely said, "I go to My Father"; what a sublime version of death. But it is beyond the reach and grasp of most of us. It is helpful to remember that we could not have imagined the conditions of this life before we entered it—how mutton and ale, eaten by Shakespeare, could be transmuted into the thoughts of Hamlet or the airy dreams of Ariel.

NO RACIAL RANCOR

Some things, alas and alack! we have not achieved in America, as the following letter makes us feel. Indeed, the letter makes us squirm, alike because of something untrue in it and something tragically true:

> I am a Jewess [a reader wrote]. Of the sensitive, shy type. I have not put on the hard shell of aggressiveness that so many of my fellow Jews have donned to protect themselves from the daily abuse—in the form of "kidding," if nothing else—we are subjected to by Christians.
>
> Don't you think it would be much simpler for all concerned if you Christian ministers admitted that Christianity and anti-Semitism are synonymous? There is ample proof of the fact. We do not hear of anti-Semitism among Buddhists, Confucians or Brahmins. We do hear of anti-Jewish riots among the Mohammedans, but these are more in the nature of territorial disputes.
>
> I have many Christian friends, but they tell me I am acceptable because I am different. I am not different. I have a charming mother and father and my sister and brother are kind and generous. Surely we do not have any monopoly on the virtues, nor do we on the vices. I have even been welcomed as a guest by Christian friends at a certain summer resort, which is a

mighty fortress of Christian faith, where people of my race are not allowed to buy property, and are not received in hotels.

As I read the above I realize that I sound bitter. I do not mean to feel that way, but it would be much easier if Christians were not so hypocritical about their lessons in the brotherhood of man. Surely they must know that Jesus was a Jew and that His disciples were Jews too. No, that would not be Christian teaching. Do you know what it is like to be hated, to try to meet people half way and then be insulted?

Of course, my reader is wrong in thinking and saying that anti-Semitism is an article of Christian faith—it is simply not true, however far short of the Christian spirit Christian people, even Christian ministers, may fall. As all of us know, some Jews are acceptable, and some Gentiles are not acceptable. The Jews—the organized religion of that day—did have much to do with putting Jesus to death. But other peoples have dealt harshly with their prophets, who were too far ahead of their times, as criminals are throwbacks to a past no longer tolerated. What if the Jews had not been involved in the death of Jesus —where would our Christian faith be, since it is based, largely, upon His death and His victory over death? The situation does not make sense either way one puts it. There is no reason why a Jew, a colored man, or a man of any other race should be insulted; it is both un-Christian and un-American no matter who is guilty of the atrocity. All human beings are sensitive, shy, and easily hurt, as we know in our own hearts, and we must never forget that fact in our contacts with our fellows of whatever race.

AS NEVER MAN SPAKE

Hear now one of the most astonishing letters that reached me during the whole eleven years of my experience. It is so honest in its spirit, and so naïve withal, that it makes one wonder and think many thoughts betimes. Later I came to know the writer, who, for the reason stated in his letter, never attended a religious service until middle life. He did not know how to act in a church, until the usher told him to stand when the hymns were sung, to kneel in prayer, and to sit and listen to the sermon. He followed instructions and went to church many times thereafter.

> My story may be hard for you to believe, but it is true. It must be rather unusual, and I hesitate to tell it, but perhaps it will do good. My father, due to some sad experience, reacted angrily to all religion. Anything having to do with the church was taboo in our home. My sister and I were not allowed to go inside a church. So far as we were concerned, religion did not exist. Our father was a high type of man in many ways—we loved him, we respected him; our mother was dead—and we obeyed his wish in regard to the church. Often I wondered what a church service was like, but did not attend one until after my father died.
>
> It may seem incredible that a man of my age—I am forty-two—never read the New Testament until recently. Nor can I hope to tell you the effect which the book had on my mind. Especially the reading of the Gospels—I did not care so much for the rest. In fact I did not finish it—the book of Revelation was a mystery. But the story of Jesus, quite unknown to me, startled me, stunned me, stirred me as nothing else ever did.
>
> What I say may seem trite, even banal, but something deep and real has taken place in me. I hardly know how to describe it, except to call it a shift of interest, a new focus of life. The fact that thrusts itself upon me, after reading the story and words of Jesus, is that we are all wrong in our way of thinking and living. We are seeking the wrong things, following false goals—things that do not matter. No wonder we are bound by fears, anxieties, and forebodings. We could be free of all these things if we kept in the way that Jesus taught us, which is the road of faith and love and helpfulness. Above all things, Jesus had no fear, and having no fear, He knew no hate—that is life indeed!

One almost envies the experience of my reader in reading the Gospels for the first time—no wonder it did things to him. The greatest of all stories came to him with a freshness, a vividness, an overwhelming majesty of simplicity and power never to be forgotten. Alas, we read, or hear read, the flaming poetry of the prophets and the calm, unhurried, piercing words of Jesus, who spake as never man spake before or since, and the words are too familiar to work a revolution in us. We hear but we do not really heed, much less obey, and our lives are short-circuited, so to speak; a profound sentiment, not acted upon, ends in sentimentalism. We do not realize what manner of speech it is, "words of eternal life" in a world of conflict, confusion, and darkness. If only we could hear those words for the first time, they would shake us like a passion and show us what life can be!

"HALF-PEOPLE"

It seems to me, sometimes [a very different kind of letter said], that you aim too high in your daily talks. No doubt we ought to have high ideals, but I think you over-shoot average, everyday folk. We are not bad really, but, like people everywhere, we are lazy and selfish. The two hardest things in the world to find are true unselfishness and honest, clear thinking. If all of us thought as much—or even half as much—of the good of others as we do of ourselves, if we thought straight and did not let sentiment and self-interest muddle and confuse us, this world would be a beautiful country tomorrow, and no mistake.

But we are all afraid—you and I and the rest—afraid of our safety, afraid someone will rob us, or laugh at us, or hurt us, or make us feel small. We are not cowards about big crises—it is the little things that get us down. Life has dealt poorly with us; opportunity has not come our way—maybe we could not have taken it if it had. We lack grace, influence, and power. If we have felt a dim call to do great things, a peevish fortune has hedged us off. We are the man with one talent, if that much, and too often we hide it for fear.

Maybe we are only "half-people," as you once said, or even less. But life is rough at times, and ill-health, dull work—if we have work—and things hard to face up to do not make it easy. As you seem to have more practicality than theology, I'd like to ask a lot of questions. I've heard a deal of talk in my time, but I have never heard the answer I want to hear. To tell the truth, I haven't much faith in the evidence of things not seen, but I have faith in people who have faith.

As a description of the attitude and point of view of everyday, "average" folk, this letter is very remarkable. To them life is a riddle, and they try to find what joy they can as the days pass. If a fortunate thing happens, they seize it and enjoy it;

when disaster befalls, they shrug their shoulders and bear it
with the best grace they can muster. They take things as they
come, eat their "peck of dirt" without wincing, and try not to
be a problem, a burden or a bore. Arthur Clough summed it up
in his lines:

> The world is very ill, we see,
>   We cannot comprehend it;
> But in one point we all agree—
>   God won't, and men can't, mend it.
> Being common sense, it can't be sin
>   To take life as we find it;
> The pleasure, to take pleasure in,
>   The pain, try not to mind it.

It is a kind of Stoic philosophy adapted to modern need
under the name of common sense; and it has its value and uses.
How widespread it is we do not know; but if everybody took
such an attitude—wingless and alien to the sky—there would
never have been any great religion on earth. Such people,
kindly, gracious, cautious, often charming, simply lack the faith,
the courage—lack the "extra effort," as Bergson said—needed to
live the life of the spirit. There are those—God be thanked—
who refuse to take life "lying down": refuse to accept fear,
inferiority and frustration as final, and dare to live by an *uncommon* sense which looks at life in a big way, lighted by faith
and spiritual vision. To be sure, for most of us most of the
time, life is made up of little things; but we dare not let life
itself become a little thing. All of us are "people of whom
more might have been made," as God knows; but we can be
other and finer than we are, despite all handicaps, if we overcome our inertia, our dull lethargy which holds us in bondage,
and try for the highest, even if we fall below it. But to be
content with spiritual mediocrity—to accept it fatalistically, and
almost be proud of it, or else use it as an alibi—as my reader
almost seems to do, is fatal. We sentence ourselves to a low-
vaulted life, bereft of all greatness. If we dare to live daringly,
death will be a little thing, because we think of life in a big
way.

PSYCHIC FACTS

The response to my story of Patience Worth, in one of my daily talks, was overwhelming; it brought a deluge of letters. They came from all directions, from all kinds and conditions of people—most thrilling experiences, even dreams no end, intimations, "hunches," visits to psychics whose accounts of coming events had come true—often tragically true. Some of my readers pounded me terribly, as "a stubborn old die-hard" unwilling—afraid—to face what to them was the obvious explanation. One story—one out of many—I venture to transcribe here, since I was not sworn to secrecy about it, as I was about so many others; and also because it is so clear a case of the existence of these unusual, and unused, powers of the mind:

Sir, I am not an investigator of the occult, but I should like an interpretation of the following experience, if possible. Years ago I was the superintendent in the installing of some machinery in a building owned by a corporation in a city near here. The weekend was the time when most of my work was done, and I remained in the building from Saturday until Monday, sleeping on a couch in a remote room and making inspection tours at irregular hours much as a watchman.

One Sunday morning, about nine o'clock, I was walking along a gallery facing a line of elevators, twelve in all. The gallery was well lighted. The elevators had been inspected by myself Saturday night, and all levers were on the down motion, and locked. The only key to those elevators was in my pocket. The elevator pits were forty feet below the gallery where I was walking.

My attention was drawn to a car at the far end, about half of its upper section above the gallery landing. The doors were about half open. A woman, about middle age, was bending forward from the waist at the floor level with her right arm extended, waving to me. She was as much a human or natural person, as you or I. There was nothing unearthly about her. She was a stout woman, about five feet seven inches in height. She wore a polka-dot dress, with large white spots in it.

I wondered at her presence, as all persons admitted to the building on weekends were by my permission, and one entrance only was available. I had a trusty man at that entrance. As I approached the car, the doors closed, leaving a space of about six inches between them. When I was directly in front of the car, I saw that other persons were in the car. I looked them over.

There was a middle-aged woman, a younger woman dressed in a red waist and dark skirt, a woman of Italian or Spanish type. She smiled at me. On my right, as I looked into the car, was a tall, well-built man of about forty, with a fine, clean-cut face—a man of refinement. He was looking toward the eastern side of the building. On his face was an expression such as I have never seen on a human face. It was strained, drawn with inward thoughts, as if his very soul shone through with suffering.

Two other men were in the car, one in each of the far corners. They were men of ordinary appearance and dress. Both of them smiled as I looked around at the group. I asked them who they were and why they were there. They simply smiled at me. I was puzzled in every way, and insisted on them telling me how they had entered the building.

I received a few smiles and nothing more. Suddenly the knowledge that I was in the presence of something unearthly was driven home to me. I made the sign of the Cross and prayed. To my surprise, I felt no fear. To make sure, I went to the entrance, and the man there—my friend and helper, and I walked back to the car. He saw what I saw. I knew then I was not insane. We did not discuss the matter, for he thought they were natural persons. I told him I would attend to the matter, and he went back to his work at the door.

I endeavored in every way to get some of the persons in the car to speak. I received only smiles from all of them, except the tall man who never looked at me and never changed his expression. I went to my office to ponder. Again and again I went back to the car, and found them still there. Early Monday morning I visited the car and they had not moved. At seven they were gone and the car was in the pit, locked.

My reports of my work were signed and delivered. At nine I took the same car from the gallery landing of my office. The car was well filled, not with my visitors of the day before, but with workers, as I thought. Suddenly, on my right and left I saw two men of most striking appearance of the night before. The tall man was still looking toward the east, but the strained expression was absent from his face. The man on my left smiled and bowed.

We stopped at the street level, and the man on my left stepped out and waited for the other to join him. As they met in the aisle, the man who had stepped out first, turned to the other with a smile and said, "The Captain." The tall man looked and gave me a slight nod, and, as I looked, they were gone.

What did I run into that Sunday? It was something I did not expect, but through some law not known to me I witnessed an extraordinary happening—one of a number of experiences I have never cared to discuss with anyone. Did I have a glimpse into another dimension? Your friend said there was a line it was not safe to cross. He was right. I am not a spiritualist or any other kind of "ist." I am a good Catholic, trying to do my best. I would appreciate an answer, in your way and time.

As soon as this letter appeared in one of my talks—even more severely abridged than it is here—a telegram came thanking me for "the grandest lie anyone ever heard, and the best told." Other readers accused me of making up a tall story, but they were wrong. They paid me too high a compliment. The story was not a lie. Anyone familiar with the subject knows books full of such stories—*Phantasms of the Living,* by Edmund Gerney, for example, to name one out of many; *Sight Unseen,* by Frederick Leib, and his charming wife, is very interesting in many other ways. My point is that these phenomena are facts; when all allowance is made for trickery, the powers of the human mind are amazing. Too many cases are too well authenticated to leave any doubt, as in the life of Emanuel Swedenborg, for instance, who was very restrained in using such gifts. He wanted to meet John Wesley, and Wesley promised to meet him when he returned from a preaching tour—how busy Wesley was, unhasting and unresting, to the end. Swedenborg dropped Wesley a note expressing regret at not being able to meet him, because, before Wesley returned, he would have passed out of this life, giving him the date. And so it came about, and two great, but very different men, never met on earth.

POT CALLING KETTLE

"One of our neighbors, a nice person, a mother just under forty, with a little girl, the wife of an officer in the service, told us a startling bit of fact some days ago," a letter related. "Her husband, when he was at home recently, out of a clear sky, said that he wanted a divorce, in order to marry a Catholic girl, with whom he is infatuated. He further said that their marriage, according to Catholic teaching, is invalid, and their little girl was born out of wedlock. Is that what the Catholic Church teaches?"

So far as I am aware, the Catholic Church has never said in so many words that all Protestant marriages are invalid and all Protestant children are illegitimate. But it seems to imply as much by its attitude and acts. It reminds me of the story of how Phillips Brooks once startled the people of the Church of the Holy Trinity in Philadelphia, by saying that "God is not an Episcopalian." Of course no one had ever said it in exactly that way; it was not necessary—it was taken for granted by the people in Rittenhouse Square. We do not see what we take for granted; we see through it. Our Catholic friends will not worship with us; they will not be buried with us. To put it plainly, any church, old or new, large or small, which assumes, or claims a monopoly of the love of God and the sacraments of His grace, is guilty of something close akin to blasphemy. As Bernard Shaw once said—and no one can talk as much as he does without saying some good things, now and then—"The Church is in the hands of God, not God in the hands of the Church."

But, good reader, some Protestant churches come very near to the same absurd idea. An old proverb talks about "the pot calling the kettle black." In the church in which I was brought up no one was allowed to take communion—the word "sacrament" was never used—in another church of the same faith and order. On the theory, logical enough, that one should commune only in the church under whose discipline one lived;

and in those days church discipline was a reality—do I not know? As for churches of other rites and orders, they were, by implication, synagogues of Satan; they were excluded from thought, without the pale, as if they did not exist. Such narrowness, which is straight, sharp-pointed, and one-eyed, like a needle, is not confined to the Catholic Church, which, with an amazing flexibility, has ways of getting around its own bigotry when it wants to do so.

STARK TRAGEDY

Down upon my desk fluttered a letter, written on plain paper, in short gray sentences, telling a story of grim tragedy. It asked for help in a very delicate situation, and I tried to do what it asked:

> I am a young mother, thirty-five years old, dying of cancer. It is a bitter business, but I can take it. How much faith I have left I do not know; very little I imagine. Of course I hate to leave my husband, who is a good man, always kind. What troubles me is my little boy, eleven years old—my pal and joy. Should I break the news to him? If so, how should I do it? If you can help me I shall be eternally grateful.

In reply I wrote her a long letter—not easy to write—telling her that I had lost my own mother not long before, and how, after a period of aching loneliness, the Unseen World had become nearer, more real, more homelike, because she had entered it. To which I added two truths which we ought always to remember—in the Land of the Spirit there is no distance and no time—"a thousand years are as a day." By the same token, I told my reader that she could do more for her little boy than anyone else, and she owed it to him to tell him. Then I tried to write out how she could tell him, making a very simple statement, interwoven with many of the words of Jesus, about "many dwelling-places" in the House of God, never far away. Some time later a letter came from her husband, telling how his wife had kept a scrapbook of all my pieces, very neat; and how she had followed my counsel about her little boy almost exactly. "Then a wonderful thing happened," he said. "My wife regained the faith she thought she had lost, first as a tiny spark, then as a white flame. You helped her to die happily, and you have helped me to live bravely; thank God, and thank you." Yes, it is worth while, sharing our faith with others.

BLACK BROODINGS

For months I have been on my back in a military hospital [a striking letter told me]. Naturally I have had time to think, and perhaps some of my thoughts have been rather dismal. But, honestly, I want to ask a question which has often been in my mind, long before the war. In view of the facts of life, have I any reason to love God?

Perhaps this will illustrate my point of view: my bed is out of doors part of the time. Before me is a little patch of grass. Assume that I have powers of creating. I people the grass with little beings; give them free will, minds to think, and a capacity to suffer. They never asked me to be created. I placed them there, giving them no choice in the matter.

Then I create, or permit to exist, an evil power which influences my little people against me. I give them only slight proof that I exist at all. And then I tell them to worship me, love me, do my will, or suffer torment—perhaps eternal torment. I am here beyond their power of vision; my little people know nothing for certain except that they suffer. I created them, therefore am I not in a degree responsible to them as well as for them? What right have I to expect them to love me?

Many might hate, but how many would love me, no matter how much I loved them. I could, of course, put it stronger. But you will follow my line of thought. My going down amongst my little people to "save" them does not alter the case. God exists, I believe, but will you be good enough, sir, to tell me why I should love Him?

Why should we love God? The Bible tells us, "Because He first loved us," because love alone is creative; because man was born out of the far depths of Divine Love, and is neither an alien nor an exotic in the universe, but its child, dust of its dust, spirit of its spirit. Yes, God takes responsibility for man, else He were a being whom it were an act of worship to despise.

The idea of an arbitrary, irresponsible almightiness is a fiction. He does not put man here, amid these short days of sun and frost, for fun, still less for torture. God is under obligation to man, to every man, to all men, under all the obligations of His nature and character. His love does not, will not, cannot let go. Surely my officer-reader, in spite of his wound, can bring himself to believe that God is as good as a good man—is that asking too much? Yes, we love God, in the end, when the clouds are off our souls, because He is infinitely lovely, fairer than any poet-dream.

HOW TO GET FAITH

The two questions most often asked me, both profoundly important and practical, were these: How can a man get faith who does not have it, and how can he regain faith if he has lost it? By faith, of course, we mean more than opinion, more even than belief—a fire and force in the soul giving unity, drive and direction to life. Seldom, if ever, is faith the fruit of argument. True, the mind must be convinced, but the heart must be warmed and the will moved, which is a good description of a real sermon. Either one, without the others, may end in dogma, sentimentality, or fanaticism. The best way, the surest and most vivid way to get faith, or to regain it, is to make contact with a man or woman who has faith. Faith is gloriously infectious— there are more good infections in life than bad ones—like courage, like hope, like love. These divine contagions are the health of our spirits.

Often one man of faith can electrify a whole generation and alter an age. St. Francis did it in his day. John Wesley did it. Phillips Brooks did it in his time, albeit in a more limited way. One day a man went to see Brooks, bowed down by some burden, perplexed by some problem. Overflowing with life and zest and confidence, Brooks talked to the man out of his heart. The man was transfigured, uplifted. At the door, as he went away, he paused and said, "It is odd; I've forgotten what I came to see you about. Very well, no matter; I think I see the way through it."

Brooks had not argued; he had opened a window and let in fresh air.

"I believe in God because Marcus Dodds believes in Him," said a student in the University of Edinburgh. It was a borrowed faith, as all our faith must be at first. As a reader put it to me: "Please let me use your faith—tell me that it is so, and I'll take your word for it; since I seem to be all in a mist, and cannot see my way." It was agreed, and it worked. Not many of us could pass a high-school examination in any branch of science; yet what utter faith we have in science and in men of science. We have not checked their findings; we cannot verify their experiments. It is so in the life of the spirit, which is what my little mother meant when she said, using the words of St. Paul: "I live by the faith of the Son of God." He had laid His mind on her mind, and she believed in His beliefs.

TANGLED LIVES

So much for a few samples from my mail-bag; the story might go on, almost literally, without end. There was a letter from a young man in prison, awaiting execution: "I never trusted anybody, and I was never happy a single hour in my life. You did not preach at me; you gave me Christ—both a faith and a philosophy of life; I go to my end, justly, cleansed and without fear." There was a letter from parents who had adopted a child, and wondered whether they should tell her she was adopted, and when. Of course, they ought to tell her, else she might find it out to her hurt. There was a letter from a woman who wanted to know whether she should tell her sister that she had cancer. If her sister asked, yes—one has a right to know such a thing. If she does not ask, there is no need to tell. "Did my cousin know that I was not present at her funeral?" asked a reader. Long ago Lessing taught us that if we knew all things, it would mean the end of growth and unfoldment.

However, I must add one letter, which brought a deluge of letters from my readers when it was printed—letters offering aid, with plenty of plain speaking about two boys and their attitude toward a tired little mother who was made to feel that she was unwanted. If only we remembered the next to the last sentence in the following letter and put in a cheerful word for each other—how much better it would be:

Never miss one of your pieces [wrote a little mother]. Sermons, I call them. They buck me up. Wonder what you could tell me in my fix. Poor parents. Sent to work at eleven years. Married at sixteen to get away from it all. Husband died. Four children to raise. Two were fourteen and sixteen, both dying in four days in Municipal Hospital.

Eldest son married a wife. Wants none of me. Young son, twenty-one, all I have left. We live now in two furnished rooms. One year ago fell while working at house-cleaning, trying to make living. Now my right hand is useless. Loss of two bones. Can't use it. Had to learn to write left-handed.

Young son goes out a lot. Sees other homes. Girl he goes with has well-to-do people. Hates to come home. Fights with older brother on help to keep me. They went to court, but they showed they were in a lot of debt. Court told younger son to carry on. He don't eat with me on Sundays. I sit alone.

Am so lonely, wishing I was dead. Is there any way for me yet? Weigh one hundred pounds. Can't work any more. Am in the way. Hope you can put in a cheerful word some day. I close.

LITTLE SACRAMENTS

"Where now," asks Thomas Wolfe, "are all those things which a man scarcely dares to think he has remembered, all the flicks and darts and haunting habits that flash across the mind unbidden?" Little things, chiefly, he explains. Quiet steps that came and passed along a leafy street in summertime down South years ago; the voice of a woman in a sudden burst of tender laughter.

Life, as Thackeray wrote, can be tiring, burdensome, even terrifying, as we all know, just a humdrum grind—repetitions, the old conversations over and over again; but it does have its pages of poetry, now and then, between long passages of dull, plodding prose; "delightful passages, the dear, brief, forever-remembered."

Here follows a list, which might be endless, such as each could make, of memories that return at unexpected moments, evoked we know not how or by what—mayhap by a sound, a scent, making us often happy, often sad. They start up suddenly, mysteriously, in the mind, seize it and sway it.

Years ago on the streets of London I heard a voice—I am sensitive to voices—the voice of a police officer when I asked his aid to direct me—the kindest voice I have ever heard in my life. How many times I have heard it, like a sweet-throated bell in the back of my mind, ringing.

Or a face that flashed in the street, in a passing car, seen in profile, or lit by a smile—like a little girl I saw on a New York street, her head crowned with golden curls, her smile like an angel. I did not speak to her, did not know her name, I never saw her again, yet she lives in my heart.

The way the sun came and went, sifting through the trees; the silvery moonlight falling on the path of a boat on Spirit Lake in Iowa thirty-five years ago—dim, pale, almost ethereal as we sped, making me think of the line in the lyric-hymn, "O light that followeth all my way."

One recalls a wife, a mother, a child, a friend, not in all their acts, but at some one moment, when they pause in some pose, happy or pathetic, and their very image is imprinted upon our soul—we see that picture, like a photograph forever; hands folded, the head atilt, the very essence of their personality.

One recalls a thousand things—or they come without being called; he does not know, always, if what he recalls is fact or fiction or a fusion of the two; nor does he care. Yet those fleeting, furtive, soft-footed memories touch us deeply, like the tones of Vesper bells, shaping our lives.

Not all our memories are happy, but the evil and the ugly tend to drop out of mind, like falling leaves of yesteryear. An artless act of kindness, a word of cheer, the touch of a friend, an old hymn humming in our mind, the loveliness of a child, or the lift of a prayer—they are the little sacraments.

PICK-UPS

My idea of a hard life—harder than riding in a jeep—is to live without a sense of humor, which blunts the sharp edges of things and cushions our jolts and jars; and yet very great men have lived without any trace of humor—for example, John Wesley and Count Tolstoi.

Luther called the Golden Rule a vest-pocket edition of the gospel, yet in my whole life I have never heard a sermon on that golden text, except such as I have tried to preach myself, which do not count; and I have read only one sermon on it— preached by David Swing. The Golden Rule is not as simple as it sounds.

For twenty years I have been a clergyman in Philadelphia, and have served three parishes, yet in all that time I have buried only one baby, a lovely little boy accidentally infected by some error in a hospital. What a tribute to the triumph of medical science in its care of child-life!

"We watch others too much, we ought to watch ourselves more," wrote Beryl Markham, in *West With the Night,* an autobiography with only two dates, yet packed with excitement and adventure—she was the first woman to fly the Atlantic from East to West—written in a style that is pure magic.

Typographical errors are thorns in the flesh. In one of my books I wrote of "legitimate inquiry"; the printer's imp made me say "legitimate iniquity," and my friends exhibited an inordinate curiosity on the subject, wanting to know, specifically, what kinds of iniquity were legitimate.

In the City Temple there was a Prayer Union, led, largely, by Marion Pyle, and it meant much to know that it existed— just to know that people were praying for me or even thought of me. No wonder St. Teresa had bands of her sisters praying all the time, especially at midnight when evil prowls the world.

When I was a lad an old colored man said, "If you could jest set on the fence and see yourself pass by, you'd die laughing at the sight." Self-humor saves us from egotism; to laugh at others is one thing, to laugh at ourselves is wisdom. It frees us from many a blunder and foolish notion, as Robert Burns learned.

After all the years, having heard most of the famous preachers in England and America—and some great preachers who are not famous—"Christ at the Feet of His Disciples," by Dr. Frank Gunsaulus is the greatest sermon I have ever heard; it is still vivid in my heart, not only the portrait gallery of the Disciples in the Upper Room, but the image and the organ-like voice of the preacher.

Let us hope that the new post-war generation will not be blinded by a blurred cynicism, like the first post-war generation, when "Dancing in the Dark" was the popular song—singing of the loneliness and futility of human hearts—to be followed, all too soon, by "Brother, Can You Spare a Dime?" Also, that they will learn other adjectives besides "swell" and "lousey."

The Ph.D. fetish was blasted by William James long ago as a thing stuffy and silly, since a thesis on "The Love Affairs of a Mouse" is no assurance that a man is a teacher; it has made the teaching profession a closed shop affair, a trade union in which a degree which does not exist anywhere else is a card of admission.

On our way back from the University of Missouri, where I had given the address, and my friend Washington Cooper, the famous engineer, had received a degree, we paused at Niagara Falls. He looked at it with the eyes of an engineer, itching to get hold of it and harness its power.

"Doctor," he said, "there is the greatest unused power on earth."

"No, my friend, the greatest unused power on earth is the spirit of God," I said.

"You are right," he agreed; "if only the Church were a school of spiritual technology, we could remake the world."

Every man has a maggot in his mind, a wise man tells us. That is to say, there is a point where his sense frazzles out into nonsense; his insight becomes cloudy and absurd. Sir Isaac Newton discovered the law of gravitation, a feat of genius unsurpassed; but he also wrote a book on the topography of Hell, about which he knew nothing. Indeed, no such place exists, as he used the word. Yes, I have my maggot—I may not see it, but my friends do—provided they are not bitten by the same bug.

John Dewey is the most overrated thinker of my generation. A slow, soft-spoken, farmer-like man, good to know, in the field of education he has made valuable suggestions. But in philosophy, when he is not incomprehensible he is utterly commonplace—his instrumentalism does not make sense. Years ago a reporter on the New York *World-Telegram* tried to describe a dim, misty, murky, half-foggy day, with faint gleams of sunlight, but he gave it up as a bad job. Then he quoted a long sentence from *The Quest for Certainty,* by Dewey, a sentence long enough to make a paragraph in which there was nothing resembling an idea, so far as anybody could discover. Then he added with delight and amazement, "Gosh, John Dewey can describe such a day!" With the greatest respect for Dr. Dewey personally, the reporter expressed my feeling regarding his writings.

SNAPSHOTS

Once a month, sometimes more often, my daily talk was a series of epigrams, some sent by readers, others gleaned from my reading, and some struck off myself, accidentally.

Praise does not hurt a man unless he inhales it. If he inhales it too freely, it makes his friends very nervous.

Thomas Paine wrote words for today—"If there is trouble, let it be in my day that my children may have peace."

William Penn was right when he said, "We can never be the better for our religion if our neighbor is the worse for it."

Tact is telling a person what you think of him without letting him know it—knocking him down with a feather.

If you are not made for happiness, do not let that be a reason for making others unhappy—keep the secret to yourself.

Big things show what a man can do—his power, his skill, his genius; little things show what a man is.

Women who are too unselfish make the best wives and the

worst husbands—if we are too good we make others good for nothing.

Aristotle said long ago that man is an animal that laughs— better still if he is able to laugh at himself.

Samuel Butler wanted someone to invent an assinometer—a gadget by which a man could tell just how big an ass he is; a million dollar idea.

Some things cannot be measured—we do not think of a ton of truth, a bushel of beauty, or an aspiration a mile long.

It is one of the laws of gravity not to laugh at our own jokes; but if we cannot laugh at ourselves we are a joke—and a bad one.

"A man is just about as happy as he makes up his mind to be," said Lincoln; but he himself never quite made up his mind about it.

We must give ourselves, forgive others, and live with thanksgiving—else we bypass life, and die without having lived.

SILENCE, PLEASE

"Be still, and know that I am God," we read in the 46th Psalm. Martin Luther had a lovely version of those words, "Be silent before God, and let Him mould you." Silence is the mother of truth, said a seer.

Some people are afraid of silence; it frightens them to think of it. They must be doing things, going places, endlessly talking—the radio turned on from ten to ten. They must have noise in order to live.

"All man's miseries," wrote Pascal, "derive from his not being able to sit quiet in a room alone." Yes, to learn to be silent and listen, to know how to be alone and not be lonely, are two of the finest arts of life, if it is to be deeply and wisely lived.

Silence, say the men of the East, is more than the absence of sound, more than stillness. It is creative; it is revealing; it tells us those things for which words were never made, if we have ears to hear.

Like the moment after the song is sung, like the Amen that follows prayer—silence is a silken web holding precious echoes which may else elude us; things we sorely need to know for the health of our soul.

It is a green valley in a desert place, a mountain top above the clouds, a blue sea under a sky full of stars, a cool hand laid softly upon a heart restless, alarmed and alone.

If we learn to be silent, its breaking is also a joy—like the cracking of brittle snow underfoot, or the falling leaf which stirs the stillness of an autumn evening, or the first bird-song of spring waking the heart after the white silence of winter.

Speech is of time, silence is of eternity,—a gift of God offered to heal the blows of sound. The silences of Jesus are eloquent; out of them came words of eternal life.

In quietness and confidence shall be your strength, it was said of old; a loss of solitude is a loss of sanity. When man listens, God speaks; when man obeys, God acts.

These are specimen pieces—a few tiny "talks" out of more than four thousand written—intended to show the spirit of my work. They may explain, in part, why so many people gave me their confidence and goodwill, told me their secrets, and helped me to write my talks. How to live is the main matter, just now it is how to keep alive—how to keep faith. The world is in a mess because we do not know how to live with ourselves, much less with others. We cheat, rob, and hurt one another because we are afraid, making life hateful to ourselves and others. It is "time to do away with all baseness," said Dante; time to learn how to live. We need more light, more love, more understanding—a lot more humility and plain common sense, and also uncommon sense. Indeed, our advance into the new and strange future, of which we can now see only the fringes, will be achieved by the uncommon sense of today becoming the common sense of tomorrow.

····· 13 ·····

"A Reader," for Example

SOON AFTER my daily talks started, letters began to reach me, at first almost weekly, then regularly twice a month, from a woman in Michigan. They were mailed, in the beginning, now from one town, now from another, but they finally came from Lansing. They were signed "A Reader" and gave no street address, so I could not reply. As the writer explained, "I do not want you to know me personally; nor do I want to know you, except as your spirit is shown in your talks, and that invites confidence." They were long, chummy, charming letters, with now and then a touch of Irish brogue, gay, saucy and serious by turns. They poked fun at me; they teased me. Sometimes she agreed with my talks; sometimes she disagreed and said I did not know what I was talking about. They were rich in insight, too, racy betimes, often hilarious, then again very sober, even sad, and I looked forward to them eagerly as the years went on.

She wrote to me for over eight years. In the early period, it seems, she suffered atrociously—the nature of her illness I could not exactly make out. There were "bouts with death," as she put it, when, by all the rules, she ought to have died; but she refused to do so. Her intrepid faith carried her through, and she would come up smiling and unconquerable. In time I came to know not only her innermost thought and faith, but her husband, her daughter, and even her dog and his odd ways. No one knew that she was writing to me; it was "one human soul talking to another," as she described it. In fact, the letters, taken together, were a kind of diary, deeply interesting and delightful.

A devout Catholic, her religion meant everything to her. Two of her letters told, in a remarkable manner, what the Mass meant to her, how she could not go on without it. If I had a right to publish those letters, they would do no end of good, as showing many people what a different expression of religion means and what it can do for a human being. How strange that religion, which ought to unite people, divides them by deep chasms. If only people would break up their faith into dollars, dimes and pennies—keep the dollars and let the small change go, how much better and wiser it would be.

MYSTERY OF SUFFERING

While preaching in Pittsburgh, as I often did in those days, I had met a woman and her daughter: two lovely people. Some time later the daughter married and was killed in an automobile accident on her honeymoon; and her husband was badly injured. "She was so young, so beautiful; she loved life—so gay and gifted," her mother wrote me. "Do you believe that God willed that my little girl should come to such an end? In my state of mind I cannot think straight. What have I done, what did she do, to deserve such a fate?" Of course I tried as best I could to comfort her—pointing out that all sin is evil but all evil is not sin; that neither she nor her daughter deserved such a tragedy. God wills good, only good, but there are many things in life which He does not wish, much less will. It was a mistake to drive fast of a foggy night, and often a blunder brings worse results than a sin; and so on.

"How could you say such a thing?" wrote my unknown reader in Michigan. "How do you know that God did not will that tragedy? Did He not will, or permit, the afflictions of Job? If God chooses to afflict us for our good—to test our faith and give us a clearer vision—why do you say He does not? We who are privileged to suffer know that you are mistaken—you do not know God as He wants you to know Him. If we did not know that God wills our suffering, if we did not take the cup of pain as a sacrament at His hands, we could not endure it. Nor does it matter what our suffering is. It may be physical suffering, or the loss of loved ones, or things worse than either. No matter; God sends our crosses, and if we bear them bravely, we share His suffering, and He shares ours. Yes, we suffer—do I not know?—and sometimes we feel overburdened, for we are only human. But even in great suffering we can know joy, if we know that God wills it. Did not God will the Cross?"

Who was I to say a word, in face of one who had won such a victory over suffering? My theories were as nothing alongside what she had learned of the way and will of God for human souls. Her letters, often interrupted by spells of agony—were aglow with faith, gallant of spirit, triumphant. If ever, in the awful goodwill of God, great suffering falls to my lot—which may include suffering for my sins and the sins of others, but also suffering unmerited, wherein agony becomes an opportunity—my hope and prayer is that I may be as brave and wise as my reader has been through years of torture. Indeed, after reading her letters, and the letters of many others, I have come to realize the meaning of the words of the prophet Ezekiel, when he visited his people in captivity by the river Chebar, when he said, "I sat where they sat, and remained there astonished." The dignity with which people receive heart-breaking blows, the patience with which they endure adversity, the hidden nobility of our race, fill me with amazement.

HIDDEN FRIEND

In the meantime, I went to Detroit to preach for a week in Lent. The *Free Press* arranged an interview, with a flashlight picture, in which I was shown seated at a typewriter, as if writing one of my daily talks, "looking up to heaven for a word," as Mark Twain would say. My unknown reader saw the picture, and it set her off in a rollicking letter in which she teased me unmercifully: "Is it really as bad as that? It makes you look like a wall-eyed pike. It is not at all like the picture of you I had made in my mind, such as we always make of those we read or read about. It's awful!" And on she went, having no end of fun at my expense, to which I was unable to reply, since I did not even know her name.

She began to worry, apparently, wondering whether I was getting her letters at all or not. To find out she suggested a "code" between us: "Begin one of your talks with the question, 'Can one do everything?' and I'll know that you are getting my letters." I did so gladly, because it gave me an opportunity to thank her for her letters, and to express my delight in reading them, and how much I had learned from her; appreciation, too, of her fun and frolic, her faith and philosophy. The piece was entitled "Charming Chatterbox." She wrote at once, pretending to be mortally offended, but between the lines one could see that she was as pleased as could be. The word "charming" had saved the day. "Anyway, you did not spill the beans," she said; I had not even told where she lived or given any hint by which she could be identified. "After all, maybe that picture was not as bad as I thought. It is younger than I had imagined; you would look fine in a garb of a Catholic priest"; which was the highest compliment she could pay me—she had often tried to convert me to her faith.

Then followed a silence, weeks long, when no letter came from my unnamed friend. My fear was that she might have been defeated in one of her "bouts with death," as she described her spells of illness. But no. Instead, she had been completely healed, she wrote me in a kind of awe-struck wonder, telling me at the same time how much work she had done the day before writing, the places she had gone; it was truly remarkable.

How did it happen? The doctor disclaimed any part in her recovery. "God did it, praise be to Him," she said very simply. She added, as she had often written in her letters, that she always knew it would come true—such was her unconquerable faith in face of all facts that seemed to belie it. Whatever the nature of her long illness, it was now gone, and she was both glad and grateful—a joy which I shared to the full, only I could not express it to her. Happily, her letters continued to arrive, taking new turns, surprising and delightful.

THE BOTTOM FACT

Some time later one of my talks told the story of a bad fairy who, to avenge herself on human kind, had erased from the speech of men and women three magic words, "I love you." The result was disaster—lover's lane was a desolation and all life awry—even for the fairy herself, who fell in love with a poet who because of her meanness could not tell her that he loved her. To save herself, the fairy had to relent and repeal her edict about the three magic words. Then came a letter from my unknown friend: "Years ago the man I loved married another, and I married a man I did not love, thinking, hoping, that, somehow, marriage would bring love. But it did not; what a nothing life is without true love—how empty and lonely! What a strange, wonderful thing real love is. But when one mistakes sex appeal, or what have you, for true love one reaps misery and unhappiness. To be married to one who is alive, but not living! I've never told this to anyone else."

Nor had I imagined such a thing, after reading her letters for eight years—she was so gay, so high-hearted, so brave. How many hidden tragedies are all round about us and we do not know it. What burdens, what disappointments, what secret sorrows people bear, keeping all to themselves. They are so sensitive, so shy, about what hurts them most deeply—it took eight years to uncover the bottom fact of the tragedy of my unknown reader. At bottom it was a frightful marriage muddle.

14

And Now Tomorrow

"WASTE LAND" was the title of a famous poem by T. S. Eliot, describing the havoc wrought in his soul by the first World War. Even its jagged and uneven lines recalled those wind-swept, rain-drenched battlefields, where nothing was left standing—splintered stumps of trees, shells of houses, and piles of pulverized brick which once had been towns and villages. These scenes were the outward and visible signs of an inward desolation, of blasted faith and searing cynicism, which no words could tell. For war not only destroys the lives and cities of men; it destroys human ideas, emotions, attachments, spiritual vision, taste, culture, everything that unites men into a unity more important than themselves; war is social suicide. But no poem could portray the far-stretching waste land of today, the devastation in the cities and the souls of men, where little is left standing of the world we knew. No tribe, however remote, is untouched by the universal disaster.

After a tragic interlude of wild inflation and economic chaos, war came again, total war, ruthless, without law and without mercy. The desperate decade now ending was a ghastly slip into "the old backward and abysm of time." No one foresaw, no one could foresee, the vast irruption of barbarism in the modern civilized world, putting out the spiritual lights, making morality a mockery, and turning human life into a phantasmagoria of horror, such as Dante never dreamed. Even yet we do not realize the enormity of it. It seems as unreal as a nightmare. The soul of man seemed to disappear, and when the soul goes man goes, he becomes a monster—a menace to himself and to his fellows. Docile and frustrated peoples, led by megalo-

maniacs, plunged the race into a shambles, and now that the
shadow is lifting the earth is a blasted and shattered ruin. It
was an apocalypse of treachery, terror and torture; man must
now pick up the debris of the civilization built up since the
fall of the Roman Empire and put it together in some kind
of pattern. The outlook is dismal; over wide areas the physical
conditions of the spiritual life do not exist.

DARKNESS AND DAWN

The year 1936 was the fateful year, as all agree. The world
passed from a post-war to a pre-war epoch; hoarse and hysterical
voices began to be heard. The world seemed to go into a tail-
spin, as if headed for the bottomless pit. Think, for a moment,
of the array of facts and the disarray of mind. Hitler had established himself in power by murder and terror. Fascism had become entrenched. The League of Nations collapsed. The policy
of sanctions failed. The Germans marched into the Rhineland.
As a consequence the Treaty of Locarno was torn up; the
attack upon the Treaty of Versailles redoubled—"the machinery
of peace" was wrecked. King Edward VIII abdicated, shaking
the British throne. The bitter, bloody civil war began in Spain,
as a kind of training ground of a new world war. Our own
Republic as we had known it almost ceased to be; democracy,
pushed to new limits, took its place—a process that had been going on for years. Alien isms, wild and bigoted, began to flourish,
finding fertile soil. Strange figures appeared from nowhere,
preaching hatred as the new gospel for man—race-hatred became a kind of black religion. The age of reason seemed to be
ending; instinct, and every form of the irrational, was glorified
in literature. Religion was in eclipse, except the new wild worship of "race and blood and soil." Faith gave way to fanaticism;
insanity reigned. Not principles but personalities came to the
fore, and they were twisted and distorted "leaders" from the
slum and the back-alley. The air vibrated, as the rival "holy
men" worked their incantations. Regimentation became a kind
of religion. The lights went out all over Europe, and flickered

everywhere else. The democracies were asleep—lulled by false security, cushioned by comfort, careless of danger. It was "the twilight," as Sholem Asch called it—not a morning twilight.

By contrast, 1945 was a dawn year—a year of "the right hand of the Most High," albeit not without black shadows. Early in the year President Roosevelt—our second world-minded leader—died suddenly at his post, busy to the last with plans for finishing the war and making the peace—a casualty of the war as truly as if he had fallen in battle. The President died of a "massive hemorrhage," as if the red tide of the war had flooded his brain and his heart. The Conference, which he had called, assembled in San Francisco, debated, and at last drafted a Charter of the United Nations. The Germans were beaten on their own soil, in their own sky—without an alibi— their navy destroyed, their armies captured, their cities blasted to rubble, their leaders made prisoners to be tried as war crim- inals before a high court. The Charter of the United Nations was signed, ratified, and sealed—by our own Senate, which had refused to ratify the Covenant of the League of Nations. All eyes then turned toward the Pacific War, where Japan, already blockaded, was being blown to bits by a rain of bombs. Then, without any warning, an Atomic Bomb was dropped on the city of Hiroshima, Japan, and the city went up in smoke and dust. It was as if, having had so many horrors, we had become a little callous.

"War is war," we said, and this is "total war"—a city blotted out did not matter. Russia entered the Pacific War, as agreed, to even an old score. Another Atomic Bomb was dropped, and another Japanese city disappeared, leaving only a brown splotch on the landscape. Japan, already defeated, and now stunned and stupefied, surrendered unconditionally, and the most ghastly of all wars passed into the annals of the race. Truly, the year 1945 divided modern history into before and after and set a new date in time.

"OUR LAST CHANCE"

To have looked upon such a pageant of stupendous events, moving swiftly to a focus in a single year, is not to have lived in vain. To have had a part, however tiny, in such an overturning of history, is an unforgettable honor. The conquest of the vilest tyranny ever contrived against mankind was complete and crushing; a federated evil, militant, arrogant, cunning, unscrupulous, was utterly beaten. But something more happened—one age ended and another age began, the meaning of which we cannot yet guess. The Atomic Bomb did more than punctuate a new period in history; it may have made modern man obsolete, his forts flimsy, his fleets useless, his whole civilization too precarious to be endured. To unleash the basic energies of the universe was a terrifying thing; it put into the hand of man a weapon which he is neither good enough to use nor wise enough to control. At the moment the destruction, the suicide, of humanity is a possibility; it may become a probability, unless man finds the soul he has lost. Either we are on the eve of the greatest era in the human story, or we are on the edge of the greatest of disasters. After receiving the surrender of Japan, the supreme Commander made a brief, timely, impressive address—seldom has so much been said in so few words. It sounded like a funeral oration over War itself; and if that is true, it was fitting that a soldier should utter it at such a time and place:

> Military alliances, balances of power, leagues of nations, all in turn have failed, leaving the only path to be by the crucible of war. The utter destructiveness of war now blots out this alternative. We have had our last chance. If we do not now devise some greater and more equitable system, Armageddon will be at our door. The problem is basically theological. It must be of the spirit if we are to save the flesh.

Here were true words, grave words, fitly spoken. All my mature life I have watched the incredible advance of man in applied science and his tragic inability to rule his own life, wondering what the end would be. Twice, in my generation, it has ended in catastrophe unimaginable, and it will do so again un-less man, under God, can lift his moral and spiritual life some-where near the level of his technical achievement. Here lies our deepest need and our greatest opportunity, if we can meet it. Let us hope that the discoveries of the future will be in the field of human relationships and the use of spiritual energy. Never-theless no one has yet found the secret of stepping-up the moral growth of mankind. In the human soul there is a hidden power more unbelievable than the Atomic Bomb, which, if unlocked, can make that frightful weapon a wand of blessing, if it is re-leased. Whether we can ever go beyond the height of thought and vision achieved, or received, in "the great thousand years"—that is, between the birth of Buddha and the death of Mo-hammed—may well be doubted; so far we have not gone an inch beyond it. But, if scientific technology can go so far and so fast, spiritual technology can go still further and faster, both in shap-ing personal character and social creation.

SPIRITUAL RESOURCES

In closing a life story devoted to the things of the spirit, it is natural to ponder the spiritual resources of our race, as a basis of hope for the future. One fact emerges—religion, as it is or-ganized and interpreted today, is inadequate; it is unequal to the human situation. Judgment is upon it. The story is aston-ishing, even ironical. From 1813 to 1914 the Church made its greatest advance, carrying its gospel to the far corners of the earth—ahead of the aeroplane, which is a fact of major import. Then came the explosion, the human earthquake, of the first World War. Something had gone tragically wrong; the lands of Luther and Wesley were tearing each other to pieces! Then, in 1920, began a series of great Church Councils—ecumenical assemblies—such as had not been held for centuries: Stockholm, Lausanne, Jerusalem, Oxford, Edinburgh, Madras, Amsterdam. The result was a rediscovery of the "Great Church," long hidden and lost, and, at last, the formation of a World Council of Churches, an effort to realize a world-wide Christian community. New hopes were awakened, new dreams, and a wider fellowship dawned. But other forces were growing and gathering power, sinister, savage forces, such as men had not imagined still existed. Then, a second human earthquake broke upon the race, shaking human society to its very foundations, leaving an appalling desolation in its path. Yet, God be thanked, the Church stood against the new tyranny, and could not be broken.

In spite of its defects, in Protestant Norway and Catholic Bavaria, the Church held the faith in bleeding hands, in face of a tide of terror, at a time when all holy things seemed to be erased from the earth. The Church in those tormented lands was truly great, alike in its resistance to evil and, in the end, in its forgiveness of evil. The story of its tenacious and triumphant faith, yet to be told, will be an epic to make the heart beat faster. In our own land, meantime, the most disturbing fact about the Church is that it is not disturbed about anything, as if it were both dumb and numb. Something deeper, more drastic, more creative is needed to awaken the Church and quicken the soul of man with a sense of those values and quests which save life from being a fleeting futility. It will come, strangely enough, out of the heart of religion itself, which is full of surprises no man can predict. Again and again, in the past, just when religion has been thought dead, it has brought startling renewal and resurrection, with lengthening vistas and lifting skies; and it will be so again, or soon or late, when we are ready and worthy and willing to have it so. No one can tell what religion will do next.

Just before the first World War a great teacher said, "If darkness shall ever come over the world, and God and every spiritual virtue grow dim, it may be that the Personality of Jesus will save us." Darkness did come over the world, darkness and confusion in which the face of God was hidden in a red mist. Only the Personality of Jesus was left, in which the highest that man has dreamed and hoped for is real and living, both ultimate and intimate; and the race of man was saved from utter despair. Today a deeper darkness lies upon the world, a confusion worst confused, in which not only spiritual values but the moral sense seem almost lost for multitudes, even whole peoples. Again the Personality of Jesus, "the lonely Greatness of the World," is our most precious possession; ever He stands ready, waiting to show us the Way, the Truth, and the Life— not the Christ of our subtle creeds but the Friend of our bitter needs. Not "despised and rejected" indeed, but worshiped and unobeyed, patronized but not followed. If men will not follow Jesus as the first deliberate choice, they will be driven to do so as a last desperate resort, as of old His disciples said, "Lord, to whom shall we go? Thou hast the words of eternal life." Those words—calm, simple, piercing—still tell us the one way to go, if we have ears to hear. Other way there is none out of the abyss into which we have fallen, following blind leaders of the blind.

What is the issue before the race? What is the crux of a dilemma which we must face and resolve? Not wages, or taxes, or boundaries, or charters. No, briefly and basically, it is the issue between a materialistic, fatalistic, nationalistic outlook and the vision of spiritual reality, the ethics of moral freedom, and the winning of world-fellowship. To put it otherwise, it is whether man is hereafter to think of his life in terms of cosmic meaning and concern, or as a mere accident, transient and pathetic, signifying nothing eternal—such is the issue as I have seen it take shape in the days of my years. Upon the way in which this issue is decided lies the future of man and the life and death of society as we know it. If the stone which God meant to be the head of the corner is again rejected by the builders, the house will once more collapse. A decision for materialism will be fatal to civilization; if the die is cast in behalf of spiritual reality, no one can set a limit to our hope for the days ahead of us.

FELLOW TRAVELER

As a young man I was eager to measure the meaning of Jesus, to fix His place in the human and cosmic order by some tapeline of reason. It is often so when we are young and do not yet see that Christ is a revealed mystery, not a mystery revealed, too vast for our tiny minds to grasp. Always Jesus eluded my mind;

He escaped logic and language and refused to fit into any neat category. He baffled me while He blessed me. Later, with the deepening of life, through the appeal of beauty and the teaching of sorrow, I was drawn into the mystic way, due to something hitherto unrealized in my nature. From St. Paul to St. John of the Cross, from John Tauler to George Fox, I followed their shining path, finding a new glory in the Life of Jesus and a new fellowship with the Eternal Christ, the same, yet ever new, "yesterday, today, and forever." Some things became crystal clear: one may accept all the creeds, with their majestic propositions, and not be a Christian. Indeed, one may believe in the resurrection of the body and be dead of soul and never present his own body as a living sacrifice. The creeds, I discovered, do not create discipleship, but are the records of intellectual struggles to interpret it; which, of course, is a useful thing after its kind—but not vital.

Due to many causes, no doubt, but untraceable, in my riper years I find the highest faith, the clearest wisdom, the sum of the duty and discipline of life, and the ideal of its dedication, in the words of Jesus, "Follow Me." After all, I am not asked to understand Jesus, but to follow and obey Him. Ever the mystic quest goes on. Ever the reason toils to fathom and estimate the wonder of "the human life of God." But life becomes simpler, more practical, more serene, at once easier and harder, more complex in its demands and more compelling in its persuasions, when I hear Him say, "Learn of Me; take My yoke, and ye shall find rest unto your soul." No other test of fellowship ought ever to have been made. Here is a way of unity and loyalty open to the wise and the simple alike, plain enough for the first steps of a little child and profound enough for the last meditations of old age. Someone has said that the varying interpretations of Jesus are like different men ascending a mountain and destined to meet on the summit. But I find that I have walked a winding way, a spiral ascent, which has led me to many points of view, but always climbing, seeking a wider fellowship and a clearer outlook—and ever a Friend has been at

my side. Once I tried to put my life into a tiny poem, which
was set to music:

> Will not our hearts within us burn
>   On the darkening road,
> If a White Presence we can discern—
>   Despite an ancient load?
>
> Whither goest Thou, pilgrim Friend?
>   Lone Figure far ahead,
> Wilt Thou not tarry until the end—
>   And break our bread?
>
> Follow we must amid sun and shade,
>   Our faith to complete,
> Journeying where no path is made—
>   Save by His feet!

IMMORTAL MAN

During the first World War, when things looked rather dark
for the Allies, a great public meeting was held in New York
City. Among the speakers were Arthur Balfour of England and
Henri Bergson of France. My feeling is that Dr. Walter Page,
our Ambassador to England, was one of the group, but my
memory may be at fault. After the meeting the speakers were the
guests of Joseph Choate, who had presided. For hours on end,
until far into the night, those brilliant men talked. What did
they talk about? The military crisis? No. The possible results of
the war? No. Peace? No, not a word directly. They talked about
the immortality of the soul. With clear insight they saw that
down below war and peace and public affairs, there is another
question that determines the rest. Small minds may think that
politics and religion are things apart and do not touch; but
they are profoundly wrong. Without God and immortality,
those men saw, our politics end in tyranny, brutishness, and
degradation. For, what we do for man, what we do with man,
depends upon what we think man is, whence he came, and
whither he is going. If man is not immortal—if he is merely a
clever animal—he has no eternal value we need to respect, no

signature of God upon his fleeting life; he may be used as a mere "hand" in industry, as a tool, or as so much cannon fodder. Leave out God and the immortal life, and human life loses its significance and sanctity; all its music drops to a lower octave. Man may become only a pawn in a game in the hands of a tyrant, a shirt in a parade, a cog in a ruthless collectivism. The answer to the question of the eternal life reacts, as those men talking into the wee hours of morning knew, upon the State, upon education, upon marriage and the home, upon business, upon all culture, upon all that has to do with the unity, beauty and stability of human life. Nothing in my lifetime has been more appalling than the dimming down of this faith in the worth and dignity and destiny of the soul of man, and the inevitable results which follow. Far worse than the cost of living is the cheapness of life, its seeming insignificance; never were human beings so devaluated and life so blunted.

Truly I can say that I have never doubted the immortal faith in the immortal life, though I have gravely doubted my worthiness of it—as every man must, unless he is better than the best man knows himself to be. Nor have I ever tried to prove it. Not once, even in my darkest moods, have I imagined, much less feared, that soul is less precious than slag, or mind less valuable than mud. This unquenchable faith is a part of life itself, its prophecy, the account which life gives of itself. Jesus did not argue about the Eternal Life; He lived it. By the law of love He made our everyday life, with its sunny and its seamy side, a radiant wonder; He gave it new depth, new value, new meaning, lifting it to a new level and rhythm. He "abolished death," as the radio abolishes distance; death remained a physical fact, but it was transcended by the triumph of spirit. Here, too, we must follow Him and not be afraid. "He is not here," in these dogmas we debate, in the rites we say by rote; "He is risen" and goes before us, as He said, a Pilgrim Christ, leading us into adventures we have hardly dared to dream. Still less can I conceive the conditions of life further on, any more than I could have imagined the conditions of this life before I entered it, which would indeed be incredible. Since the old scenery of faith has faded today, many people, finding the going hard, mistake a breakdown of imagination for a failure of faith and give up "the glory of going on and still to be." One thing is plain: without God and immortality human life is frustrated, stymied, and ends in futility; there is a vast vacuum in the human heart— and when man loses high religion, he easily becomes a victim of the lowest.

THE HUMAN SCENE

As one looks out over the world today it is foggy, misty, the smoke of battle not lifted, the clouds tattered; no one can see far or see clearly. Yet, while many things have been blasted to bits, certain old truths abide, and some new facts become visible—new mountain peaks for our guidance. In the Epistle to the Hebrews, written, I have always believed, by a woman, there is an arresting passage, which might be the collect for this day of destiny. It speaks of "the removing of those things that are shaken, as things that are made, that those things which cannot be shaken may remain." Many things which seemed to be solid enough, turned out to be merely stolid, and they are gone, while other things overlooked, or taken for granted, have become vastly important; and there are new factors, some as follows:

First, the recuperative power of humanity, its resilience after disaster, is astonishing; again and again whole nations have been laid waste, only to be rebuilt. Looking at pictures of Cologne, one sees only litter, rubbish, vast destruction, and it seems hopeless—little left standing but the Cathedral. Wide areas of the most thickly populated districts of London, too, are open spaces. The buildings were so old and rotten that the very vibrations of the blitz pulverized them; much of the debris has been brought to America as ballast and used in the making of roads in the State of New York. Other and more precious things have been badly damaged, but man will rebuild, in time, the wreck he has wrought.

Second, for the first time, by the mass production made possible by the magic of science, it is now possible to produce enough food to feed that whole race, so that no one need go hungry, except for his own indolence or the greed of his fellows. It would be difficult to overestimate the significance and importance of this item and its influence on history in days ahead, especially to one who knows anything of the past—how millions have gone to bed hungry and undernourished. The facts are not a credit to our race or our religion.

Third, today even the man in the street realizes, to a degree never before known, as a fact and not as a dream—if he has eyes to see and a mind to think—that the race is one family living in one world, and that the safety and hope of all depend upon the security, liberties and intelligent goodwill and co-operation of each nation, each race, each man. The type of mind most to be dreaded is the small-scale, stick-in-the-mud mind, which learns nothing and forgets nothing, and thinks that all change is tragedy. Today it is not enough to live and let live; we must live and help live, having discovered the togetherness of everything and everybody.

Fourth, by the same token, the spiritual life of the race is one, perhaps it is one thing—"the life of God in the soul of man," taking many forms and expressions. Exclusiveness must be excluded; China and India have something to tell us about the way and will of God. In short, to put it bluntly, if we are ever to have a religion of brotherhood on earth, we must first have a Brotherhood of Religion. So, and only so, can we hope for the spiritual life which alone can save us from defeat and disaster, and another slip backward into the bottomless pit.

Fifth, ages ago it was said that "justice is the life-blood of nations"; a worker must have industry, a soldier must have courage, a ruler must have wisdom, but everybody must have justice—else humanity rots, society goes to pieces. Justice in the end is our only security, and of one thing we may be sure in days ahead, unless there is more security—that is, more justice—for everybody, there will be less security for anybody. It is up to mankind, working together, to arrange its economic affairs so that the raw materials of the earth and its abundant fruits are justly administered and distributed, thus removing the chief cause of conflict.

Sixth, years ago I saw one of the last letters written by John Galsworthy, whom I so much admired—he whose heart was broken by the injustice of the world. Here are some of his words: "For the advance of civilization the solidarity of the English-speaking races is vital. Without it there is no bottom on which to build. . . . They have got to stand together, not in aggressive and jealous policies, but in defence and championship of the self-helpful, self-governing, 'live and let live' philosophy of life. . . . He that ever gives a thought to the life of man at large, to the waste and cruelty of existence, will remember that if American or Briton fail himself, or fail the other, there can but be for both, and for all other peoples, a swift and awful fall into an abyss. . . . We shall not fail— neither ourselves, nor each other. Our comradeship will endure."

Seventh, as early as 1835, Alexis de Tocqueville, a young nobleman of France, writing of *Democracy in America*, predicted, with clairvoyant vision, that the United States and Russia would one day lead the world. Today his prophecy has come true, with much else besides, including the advent of China as a great nation, which is a major fact of modern history. For that reason it is necessary, for our own peace and for the peace of the race, that Russia and our Republic come to a clearer understanding and a more intelligent co-operation; else there will be dangerous schism.

Eighth, to put it finally, the task of the future requires the eradication of the sceptic and cynical attitude toward an unprecedented social and moral order. Nothing but the very essence of the religious spirit, at its highest and best, can achieve this expectancy, an atmosphere of hope—faith, and yet again faith—in the possibility, nay, the inevitability, of immense and profound change. Only by such faith can the will to rivalry be overcome by the will to fellowship, a spiritual pressure coming out of the heart of the people; an energized religion, a will to creation. Such, in swift survey, is the human scene as this record closes—never have I had so much hope for my country and my race.

THINGS TO COME

Faith is for youth; trust is for old age. No one can see, even in outline, the shape of things to come. History has been stepped-up incredibly and is now exceeding the speed limit. Still, it is my belief, in spite of old rancors, new envies, and the chaos of the hour, that we are entering the greatest era in the story of man, destined to see changes such as man has never seen. From the Stone Age to the Atomic Age man has "stumbled forward," as Carlyle said; he has never sat down and deliberately planned his advance, as he is now trying to do. Today, for the first time—due to the tragedy of global war and the apocalyptic power of the Atomic Bomb, its threats and prophecies—those who have eyes to see realize that the race must learn to live together, or together be destroyed. Perhaps, if man masters the means of living, he will find time to think of the meaning of life. The age upon which we are entering will be greater than the Revival of Learning, when Europe climbed out of the shadow of the Dark Ages, with a Greek New Testament in her hand; greater than the spacious days of Queen Elizabeth and the splendor of Shakespeare. It will be greater, even, than the age of Washington in America, when "a new nation" was brought forth in a new world, and "government of the people, by the people, for the people" was established for the first time among men. Only, in the new age this spirit and principle shall be the possession of all men, regardless of race, color or creed—and man everywhere shall be free to look from the lap of earth into the face of God, unafraid.

It can be done; it is inevitable. The morning of the world is young, and man is only a step or two on his march to the City of God. Man must not be judged by his past; he exists to surpass himself. Already he has found new powers and dominions to which we can set no limit, and today he is peeping on tip-toe through a keyhole into regions unguessed and uncharted. As he has discovered new potencies in nature, new elements, new distances, so in the realm of spiritual reality he will unlock new depths and order his life by a diviner law. Soon or late he will live in a frontierless and unfortified world, ruled by moral intelligence, scientific skill and practical good will. The Christian era lies ahead of us!

Some of the new age, if only its beginning, I shall see with my earthly eyes; new explorations not only into the basic forces of the universe, but into human relationships—new feats of social engineering, unimaginable victories over diseases of the body and of the spirit; perhaps over hatred, intolerance, and exclusiveness. Slowly—so slowly—the Church is moving away from the sectarianism which I denied from the first, and have fought all my life, toward "the Coming Great Church," in whose fellowship man will walk in the way of truth, and "hold the faith in unity of spirit, in the bond of peace, and in righteousness of life," as the Prayer Book bids us pray and live. These things, and more than I can even dream, I shall not live to behold; but "though my body be destroyed, yet shall I see God, whom I shall see for myself, and not as a stranger"; I shall see the outworking of His holy will for my race, for my country—aye, for my tiny life, fragile, fleeting, wistful, but unafraid and undefeated—if not here, then with other and clearer eyes out yonder with the dwellers in the City on the Hill.

"Another Finis, another slice of life which old Time has devoured," Thackeray wrote in a pensive mood; only I do not repeat his words in any such mood of white melancholy. "I may have to write the word once or twice, perhaps, and then the end of Ends. A few chapters more, and then the last, and behold Finis coming to an end—and the Infinite Beginning."

Bibliography

THIS LIST does not include articles in magazines, such as *The Atlantic Monthly,* The *Forum, The Century, Religion in Life,* or contributions or introductions to books, or estimates of my work by various writers. Also, the number of addresses printed in pamphlet form is incomplete. The items are arranged topically, not chronologically.

JOURNALS EDITED

THE IDEALIST, 1903
THE MIDDLE-WEST MAGAZINE, 1906
THE BUILDER, 1914-16
THE MASTER MASON, 1924-26

BOOKS EDITED

THE TORCH SERIES, 6 vols.
BEST SERMONS, 1924-27
MY IDEA OF GOD, A SYMPOSIUM
IF I HAD BUT ONE SERMON TO PREPARE

BIOGRAPHIES

DAVID SWING, POET-PREACHER
LINCOLN AND HERNDON
WESLEY AND WOOLMAN

PREACHING

SOME LIVING MASTERS OF THE PULPIT
THE NEW PREACHING
   English Edition also
PREACHING IN LONDON, DIARY
   English Edition also
PREACHING IN NEW YORK, DIARY

SERMONS

DIXON DAILY SUN, 1903-9
CEDAR RAPIDS REPUBLICAN, 1910-16
CHRISTIAN COMMONWEALTH, LONDON, 1916-19
CHRISTIAN WORLD PULPIT, LONDON, 1908-1920
AN AMBASSADOR
THE SWORD OF THE SPIRIT. (England)
   American Edition also
TWO GREAT HYMNS. (England)
CITY TEMPLE TIDINGS, 1919. (London)
SERMONS AND LECTURES, 6 vols.
THE MERCY OF HELL
RELIGIOUS BASIS OF A BETTER WORLD ORDER
THE TRUTH AND THE LIFE
GOD AND THE GOLDEN RULE
THINGS I KNOW IN RELIGION
THE ANGEL IN THE SOUL
THE AMBASSADOR, 6 vols.
WHERE ARE WE IN RELIGION?

MASONIC

THE BUILDERS, A STORY AND STUDY OF MASONRY
   English, Dutch, Spanish, Swedish, Syrian Editions
THE RELIGION OF MASONRY
   English, Dutch and Spanish Editions
THE MEN'S HOUSE
SHORT TALKS ON MASONRY
MODERN MASONRY
THE GREAT LIGHT IN MASONRY
BROTHERS AND BUILDERS. (England)
LITTLE MASONIC LIBRARY (Edited). 20 vols.
BRITISH FREEMASONRY, DIARY

ESSAYS

LIVING EVERY DAY
THE STUFF OF LIFE
LIVING UP TO LIFE
LIVE, LOVE AND LEARN

DEVOTIONAL

THE ETERNAL CHRIST
HIS CROSS AND OURS
  National Lenten Book for the Episcopal Church, 1941
WHAT HAVE THE SAINTS TO TEACH US?
ALTAR STAIRS, A BOOK OF PRAYERS
  "A little book that softly talks with God"

ADDRESSES

ALBERT PIKE, IOWA CONSISTORY NO. 2
THE MISSION OF MASONRY, Grand Lodge of Iowa
ABRAHAM LINCOLN, Iowa Historical Society
ABRAHAM LINCOLN, Union League, Philadelphia
MEMORIES OF A LINCOLN STUDENT, Union League, Philadelphia
THE SPIRITUAL LIFE OF LINCOLN, Lincoln Society U. S. Springfield, Ill.
THE WINTER OF LIBERTY, Sons of the Revolution, Philadelphia.
THE WILL TO FELLOWSHIP, Pearson Lecture, Boston
IMMORTALITY, National Universalist Church
WE HERE HIGHLY RESOLVE, Gettysburg, 75th Anniversary of the Battle
THE FUTURE IN AMERICA, Washington Association of New Jersey

Index

Bowie, Dr. Russell, 295
Boyd, W. R., 113-114, 142, 295
Brewer, Luther, 111-112, 115, 136
Bright, John, 171
Broadus, John A., 55, 56
Broadway, New York, on, 211-212
Broadway Tabernacle, 142, 211
Brock, Norman, 261
Brooke, Stopford, 58
Brooks, Phillips, 56, 93, 243, 263, 343, 346-347
Brotherhood of man, on, 72-73, 85, 100, 134, 157-159, 160, 214-215, 266, 298, 366, 371-374
Brown, Dr. Arthur, 234
Brown, John, 114, 116, 219
Browning, Robert, 57, 254
Bryan, Dodd, 261
Bryan, William J., 70, 256
Bryce, Lord, 193-194
Builder, The (journal of the Masonic Lodge), 133-135, 136
Bunyan, John, 123, 138, 184, 286
Burford Inn, England, 140
Burkhalter, Dr. Edward, 112-113, 125-126, 136, 142
Burlingame, George, 273
Burns, Robert, 141, 351
Burroughs, John, 130
Burt, Struthers, 238
Burton, William, 18, 28
Butler, Samuel, 353

Cadman, Dr. S. Parkes, 205, 226, 234, 285
Caldwell, Erskine, 291
Calvary Church, of Philadelphia, 258
Campbell, R. J., 136, 138, 140, 152
Carlin, George A., 296
Carlyle, Thomas, 51, 218, 321, 373
Carnegie, Andrew, 59-60
Carnegie Music Hall, Pittsburgh, 295
Carpenter, George, 111
Carpet-bag regime, 23
Cartwright, Peter, 119
Cathedral of St. John the Divine, of New York, 295
Catholic Church, on the, 33, 47, 343-344
Cats, on, 35
Cave, Dr. R. C., 81-84, 92
Cavendish Street Chapel, of Manchester, England, 170-171
Cecil, Lord Robert, 195
Cedar Rapids Republican, 112, 113, 129
Central Baptist Church, of England, 275

Central Church, of Chicago, 84, 106-107, 127, 129
Chamberlain, Joseph, 60, 171
Channing, William Ellery, 65, 94
Charing Cross Hospital, of London, 287
Charnwood, Lord, 193-194, 276
Charter of the United Nations, 197, 362
Chester Cathedral, of England, 279-280
Chesterton, G. K., 166, 169, 196
Childhood, on
  neuroses deriving from, 327-328
  remembering, 12-14
Children of Joseph Fort Newton, 101-102, 108, 130-131, 250, 253, 255, 278
China, on, 371, 372
Choate, Joseph, 368
Christ Church, of Philadelphia, 234
Christ Church Cathedral, of St. Louis, 263
Christening of children, on, 103-104
Christian Commonwealth, 136, 153
Christian World Pulpit, of London, 112
Church, on the
  sectarianism, 18, 31-34, 80-81, 85, 157-159, 196, 203, 222, 236, 251, 256-257, 374
  social obligations of, 195-196
  universality of, 80-81, 85, 125, 157-159, 222, 232, 235, 251
Churches—See:
  Albanian Greek Orthodox Church, of Phila.
  Arlington Church, of Boston
  Broadway Tabernacle, of New York
  Calvary Church, of Phila.
  Cathedral of St. John the Divine, of New York
  Cavendish St. Chapel, of Birmingham, Eng.
  Central Baptist Church, of England
  Central Church, of Chicago
  Chester Cathedral, of England
  Christ Church, of Phila.
  Church of St. Luke, of Phila.
  Church of St. Luke and the Epiphany, of Phila.
  Church of the Ascension, of New York
  Church of the Christian Unity, of Rockford, Ill.
  Church of the Divine Paternity, of New York
  Church of the Epiphany, of Phila.
  Church of the Holy Apostles, of Phila.

INDEX
381

Churches—See (Cont.):
Church of the Holy Sepulchre, of
London
Church of the Holy Trinity, of
Phila.
Church of the Messiah, of New York
Church of the World, of Kansas City
City Road Chapel, of England
City Temple, of London
Cologne Cathedral
Everyday Church, of Boston
Fifth Avenue Presbyterian Church,
of New York
First Baptist Church, of Paris, Texas
First Christian Church, of Louisville
First Christian Church, of Paris,
Texas
First Church, of Phila.
First Congregational Church, of De-
troit
First Methodist Church, of Dixon,
Ill.
First Presbyterian Church, of Cedar
Rapids, Iowa
First Presbyterian Church, of Phila.
Fourth Presbyterian Church, of
Louisville
French Church, of New York
Grace Church, of New York
Holy Trinity Church, of Brighton,
England
Holy Trinity Church, of Phila.
King's Chapel, of Boston
Lincoln, Abraham, Center, of Chi-
cago
Little Brick Church, of Cedar
Rapids, Iowa
Liverpool Cathedral
Madison Avenue Presbyterian
Church, of New York
Memorial Church of St. Paul, of
Phila.
Milan Cathedral
Monkgate Methodist Church, of
England
New Old South Church, of Boston
Non-Sectarian Church, of St. Louis
North Church, of Boston
Old St. Paul's Church, of Phila.
Park Street Church, of Boston
Peni-El Temple, of New York
People's Church, of Chicago
People's Church, of Dixon, Ill.
People's Church, of St. Paul, Minn.
Rose Hill Church, of Whiteside
Co., Texas
St. Andrew's Church, of London
St. James' Church, of Phila.
St. Luke's Episcopal Church, of
Dixon, Ill.

Churches—See (Cont.):
St. Mark's Anglican Church, of
England
St. Martin's Church, of Birming-
ham, Eng.
St. Martin in the Fields, of England
St. Paul's Cathedral, of London
St. Paul's Church, of Chester, Pa.
St. Paul's Church, of Overbrook,
Phila.
St. Paul's Church, of Richmond, Va.
St. Stephen's Church, of Phila.
San Marco Cathedral, of Venice
Second Church, of Boston
Tremont Temple, of Boston
Trinity Church, of Boston
Trinity Church, of New York
United Churches, of Montclair, N. J.
Washington Cathedral, of Washing-
ton, D. C.
Welsh Baptist Church
West London Synagogue
Westminster Abbey
Winchester Cathedral, England
Woodward Avenue Church, of De-
troit
Church of St. Luke, of Phila., 15
Church of St. Luke and the Epiphany,
of Phila., 15, 231, 258-270, 294
Church of the Ascension, of New
York, 295
Church of the Christian Unity, of
Rockford, Ill., 84
Church of the Divine Paternity, of
New York, 184, 199, 204-231
Church of the Epiphany, of Phila.,
15
Church of the Holy Apostles, of Phila.,
257-258
Church of the Holy Sepulchre, of
London, 157
Church of the Holy Trinity, of Phila.,
258, 343
Church of the Messiah, of New York,
216
Church of the World, of Kansas City,
85
Churchill, Winston, 176, 194, 278, 291
City Road Chapel, of England, 275,
286
City Temple, of London, 56, 62, 127,
136-200, 218, 223, 250-251, 272, 275,
287, 350
Civil War, on the American, 22-23, 135
Clark, Elmer T., 305
Clarke, Sir George, 60
Clarke, James Freeman, 72
Clay, Henry, 14, 17, 115
Clemens, Samuel, 89-90, 357
Clifford, Dr. John, 160, 174, 199